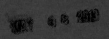

PATISSERIE

First published in the United States of America in 2013
by Rizzoli International Publications, Inc.
300 Park Avenue South
New York, NY 10010
www.rizzoliusa.com

2013 2014 2015 2016 / 10 9 8 7 6 5 4 3 2 1

Distributed in the U.S. trade by Random House, New York

Printed in China

Senior editor: Christopher Steighner
Translator: Carmella Abramowitz Moreau
Project editor: Jane Sigal
Typesetters: Nancy Sylbert, Carol Liebowitz
Assistant designer: Kayleigh Jankowski
Proofreaders: Leda Scheintaub, Liana Krissoff
Indexer: Kathy Barber
Researcher: Beth Green
Photographers: Alain Gelberger, Carmen Barea
Food and prop stylists: Catherine Bouillot, Stéphanie Champalle

ISBN: 978-0-8478-3962-9

Library of Congress Control Number: 2012940385

PATISSERIE

CHRISTOPHE FELDER

MASTERING THE FUNDAMENTALS
OF FRENCH PASTRY

3,200 STEP-BY-STEP PHOTOS

RIZZOLI
NEW YORK

Christophe Felder was already a pastry wizard at age 23 when he was appointed head pastry chef at the elite Hôtel de Crillon in Paris. Today, he creates new desserts, particularly for the refined Japanese palate, writes numerous books, works as a corporate consultant, trains professionals, and teaches at his cooking schools.

This pastry chef, chocolatier, and ice cream and candy maker was born into a family of Alsatian bakers in the town of Schirmeck, in eastern France. The aromas of butter, spices, chocolate, and caramel that filled his home, the tastes and colors of seasonal fruit that went into the pastries, and his experience working at his father's side: these helped shape Felder's respect for what a top baker can do with the best-quality ingredients and set him on the path to perfect his own skills. Now his passion is sharing the expertise he has gained.

Precise technique, common sense, and playfulness are all elements of Felder's pastry making. His guiding principles are to surprise and satisfy. One signature dessert, the Tennisia, is an edible tennis ball of passion fruit cream and apricot-lemon compote encased in a lemony white chocolate sphere. His confections, such as Baccarat, flavored with crème de cassis, vanilla, and verbena, and Bisous-Bisous, a poppy cream, grapefruit, strawberry, and saffron cream pastry, are prepared in restaurants around the world.

After leaving the family bakery, Felder followed the course of a traditional journeyman pastry chef. In 1981, he apprenticed for two years at the Strasbourg *pâtisserie* Litzer-Vogel, then at Bourguignon in Metz, and at Oberweis in Luxembourg in 1985.

In 1986, he moved to Paris, where he was in charge of decorations and special-occasion cakes at the famed gourmet emporium Fauchon. From 1987 to 1989 he adapted his craft to the restaurant kitchen, working for Michelin three-star chef Guy Savoy. Then as *chef pâtissier* at the prestigious Crillon hotel until 2004, he was the youngest pastry chef at a luxury hotel of this category. His creations helped reinvent the plated dessert in a restaurant setting. Right through his years at the Crillon, he trained and encouraged the budding talents on his team; today they head pastry kitchens at Paris palace hotels or have founded their own companies.

In 2002, Felder began a new career as culinary consultant for Henri Charpentier, a Japanese company with more than fifty pastry shops and tearooms. Since then, he has split his time between consulting work, creating pastries in Paris and Strasbourg, and teaching in France, Japan, the USA, Belgium, Spain, Brazil, Germany, Mexico, the Netherlands, Italy, and Uruguay.

In 2004, he founded the Christophe Felder Desserts Attitudes company. In 2005, with two friends, he bought the Kléber Hôtel and the EtC Hôtel, in Strasbourg, and Le Gouverneur Hôtel, in Obernai, all designed with a pastry chef's eye for detail. In 2009, Felder opened the Studio Christophe Felder in Strasbourg, a pastry school for home cooks. In Paris, he gives weekly classes at the Jardin d'Acclimatation.

Felder has received numerous awards over the course of his career. In 2004, he was granted the Chevalier des Arts et des Lettres. In 1989, he won the gold medal (with distinction) at the Foire Européenne de Strasbourg and, in 1991, the trophy for Best Paris Pastry Chef. In 2000, he earned the Marianne d'Or, a national prize for excellence. The same year the national daily *Le Monde* named him one of Five Rising Star Chefs. In 2003, he received the National Academy of Ice Cream Making Award in Paris. In 2005, his cookbook *Mes 100 Recettes de Gâteaux* was selected from six hundred works as the best pastry book, and in 2006, at the gastronomic festival of Angoulême, his pioneering *Leçons de Pâtisserie*, an anthology of step-by-step recipes, won the prize for innovation. In 2010, he was made a Chevalier de Mérite National in recognition of his accomplishments.

Felder has written many books on pastry making for the home baker—some translated into several languages. Since 1999, he has published more than twenty titles, including *Les Clafoutis de Christophe*, *Les Gratins de Christophe* (published in English as *Gratins: Golden-Crusted Sweet and Savory Dishes*), *Le Chocolat de Christophe*, *Mes 100 Recettes de Gâteaux*, *Glaces et Desserts Glacés*, *Les Meilleurs Macarons*, *Les Meilleurs Spéculoos*, and of course, *Leçons de Pâtisserie*, in nine volumes.

In 2005, I launched the cookbook collection *Leçons de Pâtisserie* (*Lessons in Pastry*) with a volume of holiday recipes, *Les Gâteaux de l'Avent*, followed by eight other titles. *Patisserie* is a compilation of the complete series.

My idea was to demystify the intricacies of professional pastry making for the home baker without oversimplifying the techniques. I came up with a format for presenting the recipes that is as close to the way I teach them at my cooking schools as possible. In thousands of photos, you can see, for instance, the process of folding an airy meringue into a dense mixture without deflating the egg whites and what exactly the texture of choux pastry should be like when just enough beaten egg is added.

In 2006, the series was awarded the prize for innovation at the Gastronomades d'Angoulême, a gastronomic festival that showcases local specialties as well as contemporary cuisine and provides an opportunity for the general public to meet cooking professionals. The step-by-step concept was a source of inspiration to many; magazines have been using it ever since, proof of how appropriate it is to the subject.

Pastry making differs from savory cooking in the precision it requires. Basic skills need to be put into practice from the start; weights, measures, and times must be followed scrupulously. It's like being back at school and learning the building blocks of any subject; creativity only comes later. There's no room for cheating: you can't skip a few teaspoons here or add a few handfuls there. You have to follow the recipe.

If I've made baking sound like a procession of daunting science experiments, don't be discouraged. In this comprehensive book, the recipes are broken down into their basic components. Step-by-step instructions give you the confidence to follow even advanced techniques, and I have provided the maximum amount of information for each recipe.

Still, I've remained faithful to the art of pastry making. What you'll find here are the recipes professionals use. I have removed none of the essentials; not an ingredient, not a tip is missing. I have not simplified the procedures either; rather, I have clarified and amplified the methods and terms, and eliminated professional jargon. Adapting these recipes for the home baker means explaining rather than popularizing. So here you have the complete recipes for all the classics plus new creations, and they are sure to come out perfectly, if you just follow the steps.

The pleasure of a fine pastry lingers forever.

—Christophe Felder

SLES ETE PAT LET PA

ET
LES
TARTES

Making Pastry

The pastry and tart recipes in this book mainly call for all-purpose flour. It is easy to work with and you will quickly get good results with it.

Use granulated sugar unless another kind of sugar is called for.

Most of the pastry recipes here yield about 1 lb. (500 g) of dough. If a recipe does not require this entire amount, simply flatten the remaining dough into a disk, cover it with plastic wrap, and freeze for another use. To get the best results after freezing, thaw the dough overnight in the refrigerator.

Puff pastry may seem complicated to prepare, but in reality all you need is the time to follow the recipe properly. Homemade puff pastry is far superior to anything you can buy. While you're at it, double the quantities, because puff pastry dough freezes well when carefully wrapped. (Wrap each 1 lb./500 g of dough tightly in plastic, wax paper, or parchment paper, and then place in a freezer bag.)

Don't skimp on the chilling time. A rest in the refrigerator relaxes any gluten that would toughen during baking and lets the dough fully absorb the water.

Both stand mixer and hand methods are given, and either can be used.

Average dough weight required per pan size

7 in. (16 cm): 4 to 5 oz. (120 to 140 g)

8 in. (20 cm): 6 to 7 oz. (180 to 200 g)

9 in. (24 cm): 8 to 9 oz. (240 to 260 g)

11 in. (28 cm): 9½ to 11 oz. (280 to 320 g)

How to Use the Main Types of Pastry

	Basic Characteristics	Primary Use	Other Uses	Ideal Baking Temperature	Oven Position
Pâte Brisée *Short Pastry*	Quick and simple. Easy to work with after resting (chilling).	Tarts with juicy fruits but no creamy filling.	Quiches.	400 to 425° F (200 to 220° C).	Bottom third of the oven.
Pâte Brisée Fondante *Soft Short Pastry*	Keeps its shape well when baked, even in a relatively high-sided pan. More crumbly than short pastry.	Tarts with a liquid filling.	Cheese tart, custard flan.	400 to 425° F (200 to 220° C).	Bottom third of the oven.
Pâte Sucrée *Sweet Pastry*	Pleasant taste, easy to prepare. Fairly dry.	Classic dessert tarts (chocolate, lemon).	Butter cookies, almond-cream tartlets.	325 to 350° F (160 to 180° C).	Center.
Pâte Sablée *Crumbly Sweet Pastry*	Crumbly, melting texture. Rich in butter but light in texture.	Tarts filled after baking.	Shortbread, cake bases.	350 to 400° F (180 to 200° C).	Center.
Sablé Breton *Shortbread Pastry*	Just roll out, transfer to the pan, and that's it!	Tarts filled with fruit after baking.	Shortbread cookies.	325 to 350° F (160 to 180° C).	Center.
Feuilletage Minute *Quick Puff Pastry*	Quick and easy.	Plain pastry cream Napoleons, traditional galettes.	Savory cheese snacks.	400° F (200° C).	Center.
Feuilletage Inversé *Inside-Out Puff Pastry*	Fairly complicated, but worth the effort!	Tarts, Napoleons, and galettes des rois (almond-cream puff pastries).	Savory snacks, apple turnovers.	325 to 350° F (160 to 180° C).	Center, on a parchment paper–lined baking sheet.
Feuilletage Chocolat *Chocolate Puff Pastry*	Unique color and taste.	Orange pastry cream Napoleons, traditional galettes.	Fruit tarts (pear, orange).	325 to 350° F (160 to 180° C).	Center, on a parchment paper–lined baking sheet.

Pâte Brisée
Short Pastry

Tarte aux Quetsches
Plum Tart

Short Pastry

Place the butter, flour, salt, and sugar in a large bowl and beat with a wooden spoon or the paddle attachment of a stand mixer until the mixture forms fine crumbs (1).

Beat in the water (2).

Stop as soon as the dough is smooth (3).

Flatten the dough into a disk and cover with plastic wrap (4). Chill for at least 2 hours.

Preheat the oven to 400° F (200° C). Butter the tart pan.

On a lightly floured work surface, roll out the dough about ⅛ inch (3 mm) thick.

Drape the dough over the rolling pin and transfer it to the tart pan. Trim the overhang so it is flush with the rim of the pan.

Prick the base of the tart shell with a fork (5).

Filling

Spread the breadcrumbs in the tart shell (6). This protects the shell from the moisture of the plums and helps keep it crisp.

Cut the plums in half and pit them.

Make a small lengthwise incision in one end of each plum half (7) and arrange the plums in the tart shell (8).

Bake the tart for 35 to 40 minutes, until the crust is golden and the fruit is tender.

Mix the sugar with the cinnamon and sprinkle it on the tart.

Let cool slightly and serve warm.

Serves 6 to 8
Level: Basic/Easy
Prep: 20 min.
Chill: at least 2 hr.
Bake: 35 to 40 min.

Special equipment
A 9-inch (24 cm) tart pan
with a removable bottom

Short Pastry

1 stick (4 oz., 125 g) butter, diced
2 cups (9 oz., 250 g) all-purpose flour
1 tsp. salt
3½ tbsp. (1½ oz., 40 g) sugar
½ cup (125 ml) cold water

Filling

½ cup (2 oz., 50 g) fine dry breadcrumbs
1 lb. (500 g) Italian prune plums or other plums
2 tbsp. (¾ oz., 25 g) sugar
½ tsp. ground cinnamon

1 Combine the butter, flour, salt, and sugar.

2 Beat in the water.

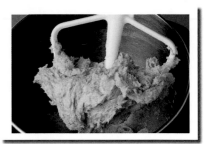

3 Mix just until the dough is smooth.

4 Cover with plastic wrap.

5 Prick the tart shell with a fork.

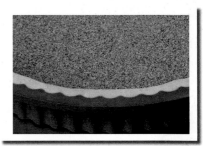

6 Spread breadcrumbs in the tart shell.

7 Make an incision in the pitted plums.

8 Arrange the plums in the tart shell. Sprinkle with cinnamon sugar when baked.

Pâte Sablée
Crumbly Sweet Pastry

Tarte à l'Orange
Orange Cream Tart

Crumbly Sweet Pastry

Sift the flour into a large bowl (1) and add the butter and sugar (2).

Using your fingertips, rub the butter into the dry ingredients (3).

Continue rubbing until the mixture forms fine yellow crumbs (4).

Add the egg yolk (5) and knead until the dough is smooth and forms a ball.

Flatten the dough into a disk and cover with plastic wrap. Chill for at least 2 hours.

Orange Cream

Bring the orange juice and zest to a boil in a heavy saucepan over medium heat.

Beat the sugar with the whole eggs, egg yolks, and cornstarch in a medium bowl until the sugar dissolves.

Remove the pan from the heat and gradually whisk in the egg mixture.

Return the pan to the heat and cook the orange cream, whisking constantly, until it thickens (6). Let boil for 10 seconds.

Serves 6 to 8
Level: Basic/Easy
Prep: 40 min.
Chill: at least 2 hr.
Bake: 15 to 20 min.

Special equipment
A 9-inch (24 cm) tart pan with a removable bottom

Crumbly Sweet Pastry

2 cups (9 oz., 250 g) all-purpose flour
1 stick plus 1 tbsp. (5 oz., 140 g) butter, diced
½ cup (3½ oz., 100 g) sugar
1 egg yolk

Orange Cream

1 cup (230 ml) orange juice, preferably freshly squeezed
Finely grated zest of 2 oranges
⅓ cup (2½ oz., 75 g) sugar
3 whole eggs
2 egg yolks
2½ tbsp. (1 oz., 25 g) cornstarch
1½ sticks (6 oz., 185 g) butter, diced

Finish

¼ cup (2 oz., 50 g) light brown sugar

1 Sift the flour into a bowl.

2 Add the diced butter and sugar.

3 Using your fingertips, rub in the butter.

4 Continue rubbing until uniform yellow crumbs form.

5 Knead in the egg yolk.

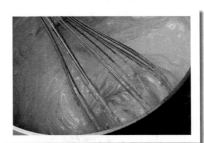

6 Cook the orange cream over medium heat.

continued

Remove the pan from the heat and whisk in the butter (7).

Whisk until the orange cream is smooth and shiny (8).

Scrape the cream into a shallow bowl, press a piece of plastic wrap directly on the surface, and chill completely.

Preheat the oven to 350° F (180°C). Butter the tart pan.

On a lightly floured work surface, roll out the dough about ⅛ inch (3 mm) thick.

Drape the dough over the rolling pin and transfer it to the tart pan. Trim the overhang so it is flush with the rim of the pan. Prick the base of the tart shell with a fork.

Bake for 15 to 20 minutes, until golden. Remove from the oven and let cool, then remove the tart shell from the pan.

Finish

Lightly whisk the orange cream. Spread it in the tart shell and smooth with a thin spatula.

Place in the freezer for 5 minutes.

Sprinkle the top evenly with the brown sugar (9).

Using a caramelizing iron, lightly brown the surface of the tart (10). Alternatively, use a kitchen torch or broil the tart on the top shelf of the oven.

7 Remove the pan from the heat and whisk the diced butter into the cooked cream.

8 Whisk the cream until smooth.

9 Sprinkle the cooled tart with light brown sugar.

10 Melt the sugar on the surface with a caramelizing iron or kitchen torch.

Pâte Brisée Fondante
Soft Short Pastry

Tarte aux Fruits Rouges-Pistache
Berry and Pistachio Tart

Soft Short Pastry

Place the butter in the bowl of a stand mixer and beat it at low speed with the paddle attachment until softened (1).

Make sure the milk is warm so that it combines well and add to the bowl along with the egg yolk. Beat until smooth (2).

Add the fleur de sel and sugar (3) and beat until smooth (4).

Sift the flour and beat it into the butter mixture (5).

Continue beating at low speed until the dough is smooth (6 and 7).

Flatten the dough into a disk and cover with plastic wrap. Chill for at least 2 hours.

Filling

Break the eggs into the bowl of a stand mixer. Add the ground almonds, sugar, cream, pistachios, butter, kirsch, and flour. Beat at medium speed until the batter is smooth, about 2 minutes. Chill.

Preheat the oven to 350° F (180° C). Butter the tart pan.

On a lightly floured work surface, roll out the dough about ⅛ inch (3 mm) thick.

Drape the dough over the rolling pin and transfer it to the tart pan. Trim the overhang so it is flush with the rim of the pan. Prick the base of the tart shell with a small knife (8).

Spread the berries in the shell and pour in the filling (9).

Bake for 40 minutes, or until the filling is set.

Let the tart cool completely in the pan before removing it. Sift the confectioners' sugar over the top before serving.

Serves 6 to 8
Level: Basic/Easy
Prep: 30 min.
Chill: at least 2 hr.
Bake: 40 min.

Special equipment
A 9-inch (24 cm) tart pan with a removable bottom

Soft Short Pastry

1½ sticks (6 oz., 185 g) butter, softened
1½ tbsp. (25 ml) warm milk
1 egg yolk
1 tsp. fleur de sel
1 tsp. sugar
2 cups (9 oz., 250 g) all-purpose flour

Filling

3 eggs
¼ cup (1 oz., 25 g) ground almonds
½ cup (3½ oz., 100 g) sugar
⅔ cup (150 ml) heavy cream
1 oz. (30 g) unsalted pistachios, skinned
2 tbsp. (25 g) butter, melted
½ tbsp. kirsch
½ tbsp. all-purpose flour
7 oz. (200 g) assorted berries
¼ cup (1 oz., 30 g) confectioners' sugar

1 Beat the butter with the paddle attachment at low speed.

2 Beat in the warm milk and egg yolk.

3 Add the fleur de sel and sugar.

4 Continue to beat until smooth.

5 Beat in the sifted flour.

6 The dough must be smooth.

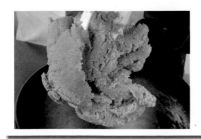

7 This is the texture of the dough when it is ready.

8 Line the tart pan with the dough and make incisions in the base.

9 Spread the berries in the shell and pour in the filling.

Pâte à Crumble
Crumble Pastry

Crumble Raisins-Poires
Grape and Pear Crumble

Preheat the oven to 350° F (180° C).

Crumble Pastry
Place the flour, brown and granulated sugars, butter, ground almonds, cinnamon, and salt on a work surface (1).
Squeeze the ingredients together with your hands (2), then knead when they begin to come together.
The butter gradually combines with the dry ingredients (3, 4, and 5).

Using your fingertips, crumble the dough into small clumps (6).

Filling
Peel the pears and squeeze some of the lemon juice on them to discourage browning (7).
Cut the pears in half and remove the cores. Cut each half lengthwise into 3 slices and squeeze more lemon juice on them.
Combine the sugar, cinnamon, and coriander in a large bowl.
Toss the pear slices in the spiced sugar (8).

Combine the pears and grapes in the ramekins and sprinkle with crumble pastry (9).
Bake for about 20 minutes, until the tops are golden.
Serve warm.

Serves 6
Level: Basic/Easy
Prep: 20 min.
Bake: 20 min.

Special equipment
6 ramekins or other individual
baking dishes

Crumble Pastry

1 cup plus 2 tbsp. (5 oz., 150 g)
  all-purpose flour
⅓ cup (2½ oz., 75 g) light brown
  sugar
⅓ cup (2½ oz., 75 g) granulated
  sugar
1¼ sticks (5 oz., 150 g) butter, diced
1¾ cups (5 oz., 150 g) ground
  almonds
1 tsp. ground cinnamon
2 pinches salt

Filling

3 firm, ripe pears
1 lemon, halved
⅓ cup (2 oz., 60 g) sugar
½ tsp. ground cinnamon
½ tsp. ground coriander
1 bunch Muscat grapes, stems
  removed

1 Place all the pastry ingredients on the work surface.

2 Begin squeezing them together.

3 Knead with both hands to incorporate the butter into the dry ingredients.

4 Continue to knead.

5 The butter softens and combines with the dry ingredients.

6 Crumble the dough with your fingertips.

7 Peel the pears and moisten with lemon juice.

8 Roll the pears in the sugar mixture.

9 Fill ramekins with the fruit and sprinkle the pastry on top.

Pâte à Beignet
Fritter Batter

- -

Beignets de Fraise
Strawberry Fritters

Fritter Batter

Sift the flour into a bowl (1).

Separate 2 of the eggs, adding the whites to a medium bowl and the yolks to the flour.

Add the salt and remaining 1 whole egg to the flour (2).

Whisk the ingredients until smooth (3).

Gradually whisk in the milk (4) until the batter is smooth and fluid (5).

Makes about 2½ dozen
small fritters
Level: Basic/Easy
Prep: 20 min.
Cook: 20 min.

Special equipment
30 wooden skewers
A deep-fry thermometer

Fritter Batter

¾ cup plus 2 tbsp. (3 oz., 100 g)
  all-purpose flour
3 eggs
1 pinch salt
½ cup (100 ml) milk
1 tbsp. (20 g) sugar

Fritters

4 cups (1 liter) grapeseed oil, or other
  neutral oil
30 large strawberries
½ cup (3½ oz., 100 g) sugar
1 tsp. ground cinnamon

1 Sift the flour into a bowl.

2 Add the egg yolks, whole egg, and salt.

3 Whisk until a thick batter forms.

4 Gradually pour in the milk, whisking constantly.

5 The batter should be fluid and smooth.

continued

Whip the egg whites, gradually adding the sugar, until they hold a soft peak (6).

Gently fold the egg whites into the batter using a flexible spatula (7).

The batter should be smooth and light (8).

Fritters

Heat the oil to 350° F (180° C) in a large saucepan or a deep fryer.

Meanwhile, hull the strawberries. Stab each with a wooden skewer, keeping the strawberry at the end of the skewer so you can safely immerse it in the hot oil.

Combine the sugar and cinnamon in a shallow bowl.

Dip the strawberries, one by one, in the batter (9).

Carefully add them to the hot oil and cook until golden. Work with no more than 2 strawberries at a time to keep the oil at a constant temperature.

Drain the fritters on paper towels and coat in the cinnamon sugar (10).

Discard the skewers, let the fritters cool slightly, and serve.

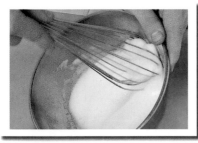

6 Whip the egg whites until they hold soft peaks, gradually adding the sugar.

7 Gently fold the egg whites into the batter with a flexible spatula.

8 The batter should be smooth, liquid, and light.

9 Dip the skewered strawberries in the batter to coat.

10 Carefully add the strawberries, 2 at a time, to the hot oil, then coat in the cinnamon sugar.

Sablé Breton
Shortbread Pastry

- -

Tarte Tatin Pomme-Rhubarbe
Apple-Rhubarb Upside Down Tart

Shortbread Pastry

Whisk the egg yolks with the sugar in a large bowl (1) until pale and thick (2).

Add the butter (3) and beat with a wooden spoon until smooth (4).

Sift the flour with the salt and baking powder into the bowl (5) and beat until smooth (6).

Flatten the dough into a disk and cover with plastic wrap (7). Chill for at least 2 hours.

Caramelized Apples

Preheat the oven to 350° F (180° C). Line a baking sheet with parchment paper.

Combine the sugar and water in a small saucepan. Cook over medium heat, stirring with a wooden spoon, until the sugar dissolves.

Let the syrup simmer, without stirring, until it turns light amber. Watch carefully as it cooks, and immediately remove the pan from the heat.

Pour the caramel evenly onto the parchment paper and let cool.

Meanwhile, peel, quarter, and core the apples.

Spread the apples in a layer in an ovenproof nonstick skillet. Break the caramel into pieces and arrange them on top of the apples.

Add the butter and orange juice.

Cover the skillet tightly with foil and bake for about 20 minutes, until the apples are tender and one side is coated in caramel. Leave the oven on.

Serves 6 to 8
Level: Basic/Intermediate
Prep: 45 min.
Chill: at least 2 hr.
Cook: 40 min.

Special equipment
A 9-inch (24 cm) pastry ring or a tart pan with a removable bottom

Shortbread Pastry

3 egg yolks
⅔ cup (4½ oz., 130 g) sugar
1¼ sticks (5 oz., 150 g) butter, softened
1⅔ cups (7 oz., 200 g) all-purpose flour
1 pinch salt
2½ tsp. (11 g) baking powder

Caramelized Apples

½ cup (3½ oz., 100 g) sugar
3 tbsp. water
4 Honeycrisp or other baking apples
1 tbsp. butter
Juice of ½ orange

Rhubarb Compote

¼ cup (2 oz., 50 g) sugar
2 tbsp. water
7 oz. (200 g) rhubarb, peeled and thinly sliced
3 oz. (80 g) white chocolate
2 tangerines, peeled and cut in between the membranes into segments
Apricot preserves, for brushing

1 Whisk the egg yolks with the sugar.

2 The mixture should be pale and creamy.

3 Add the softened butter.

4 Beat with a wooden spoon until smooth.

5 Sift the flour with the salt and baking powder into the bowl.

6 Beat with a wooden spoon until smooth.

7 Press the dough into a disk and cover with plastic wrap.

continued

Rhubarb Compote

Combine the sugar, water, and rhubarb in a medium saucepan. Cook over medium heat, stirring occasionally, until very soft, about 5 minutes.
Transfer to a bowl and chill.

Remove the dough from the refrigerator (8). Butter the pastry ring.
On a lightly floured sheet of parchment paper, roll out the dough about ⅛ inch (4 to 5 mm) thick (9).
Stamp out the crust with the pastry ring. Leave on the ring and remove the excess dough (10). Transfer the crust on the paper to a baking sheet.
Bake for 15 to 20 minutes, until golden. Remove from the oven and let cool, then remove the pastry ring.

Meanwhile, finely chop the white chocolate. In a bowl set over a saucepan filled with 1 inch (2.5 cm) of barely simmering water, or in 30-second bursts in a microwave oven, melt the chocolate. Stir until smooth.
Brush a thin layer of melted chocolate on the base of the crust (11). This protects it from the moisture of the fruit.
Spread the rhubarb over the chocolate (12).
Arrange the apples, caramel side up, around the tart. Top with the tangerine segments.
Melt the apricot preserves over medium heat, stirring occasionally. Lightly brush it on the tart.
Serve immediately.

8 This is what the dough looks like after 2 hours' chilling.

9 On a sheet of lightly floured parchment paper, roll out the dough.

10 Stamp out the crust and remove the excess dough.

11 Brush the cooled tart shell with a thin layer of melted white chocolate.

12 Spread the rhubarb compote on the crust.

Pâte à Linzer
Linzer Pastry

Mon Linzer
My Linzertorte

Linzer Pastry

Sift the flour with the baking powder, cocoa powder, and cinnamon into a large bowl (1).

Add the sugar, butter, almonds, and salt (2).

Using your hands (3), rub the butter into the dry ingredients (4).

Continue rubbing until the mixture forms fine crumbs (5).

Add the eggs and lemon zest (6).

Beat with a wooden spoon until smooth (7).

Flatten the dough into a disk and cover with plastic wrap (8).

Chill for at least 2 hours.

Raspberry Jam

Combine the raspberries and sugar in a saucepan and cook over medium heat, stirring constantly.

When the mixture begins to boil, add the redcurrant jelly and lemon juice.

Bring to a boil and cook, stirring, for 2 minutes.

Scrape the jam into a bowl and let cool completely.

Plum Jam

Cut the plums in half and remove the pits.

Combine the plums and sugar in a medium saucepan and cook over medium heat, stirring constantly, until very soft.

Puree the plums, using an immersion blender or a food processor, until smooth.

Scrape into a bowl and let cool completely.

Serves 8; makes 2 7-inch
(18 cm) tortes
Level: Basic/Easy
Prep: 40 min.
Chill: at least 2 hr.
Cook: 15 to 20 min.

Special equipment
2 7-inch (18 cm) pastry rings
or tart pans with a removable
bottom

Linzer Pastry

2 cups (9 oz., 250 g) all-purpose
flour
1¼ tsp. (5½ g) baking powder
1½ tbsp. (10 g) unsweetened cocoa
powder
1 pinch ground cinnamon
⅔ cup (4½ oz., 125 g) sugar
1 stick (4 oz., 125 g) butter, diced
½ cup (2½ oz., 65 g) chopped
almonds
1 pinch salt
2 eggs
Finely grated zest of 1 lemon

Raspberry Jam

10 oz. (250 g) raspberries
¾ cup (5 oz., 150 g) sugar
⅓ cup (3½ oz., 100 g) redcurrant
jelly
2 tsp. (10 ml) lemon juice

Plum Jam

¾ lb. (350 g) plums
1¼ cups (9 oz., 250 g) sugar

1 Sift the flour with the baking powder, cocoa powder, and cinnamon into a bowl.

2 Add the sugar, butter, almonds, and pinch of salt.

3 Squeeze the ingredients together with your hands.

4 Rub the butter into the dry ingredients with your fingertips.

5 The texture should be sandy.

6 Add the eggs and lemon zest.

7 Beat with a wooden spoon.

8 Cover with plastic wrap.

continued

Preheat the oven to 350° F (180° C). Butter the pastry rings.

On a lightly floured sheet of parchment paper, roll out the dough about ⅛ inch (3 mm) thick.

Stamp out 2 crusts with the pastry rings (9).

Leave on the rings and reserve the excess dough. Transfer the crusts on the paper to a baking sheet.

Dip your finger in water and lightly moisten the rim of each crust (10).

Using some of the reserved dough, roll out 2 ropes about 22 inches (55 cm) long and the height of the pastry ring.

Carefully fit them around the moistened edges of the crusts (11).

Prick the base of the crusts with a fork (12).

Using an offset spatula, spread 1 crust with the raspberry jam and the other with the plum jam (13).

Roll out the remaining dough to slightly less than ⅛ inch (2 mm) thick and cut it into strips ¾ inch (2 cm) wide.

Make a lattice pattern with the strips for decoration (14). Alternate the direction of the dough strips as you lay them across the torte, arranging one lengthwise, then one crosswise, and so on.

Bake for 15 to 20 minutes; the crust does not brown much. Remove from the oven and let cool, then remove the pastry ring.

9 On a lightly floured sheet of parchment paper, roll out the dough and stamp out 2 crusts.

10 Moisten the edge of the crust with your finger.

11 Place a rope of dough around the edge of each crust.

12 Prick the base with a fork.

13 Spread each crust with one of the fruit jams.

14 Use the remaining dough to make strips for a lattice pattern.

Pâte Sucrée
Sweet Pastry

Tarte Crème de Citron
Lemon Curd Tart

Sweet Pastry

Place the butter in a medium bowl and sift in the confectioners' sugar (1).

Split the vanilla bean lengthwise and scrape out the seeds. Add the vanilla seeds, ground almonds, and salt to the bowl (2).

Beat the ingredients with a wooden spoon (3) until smooth (4).

Break the egg into the bowl and beat it in (5).

Sift the flour into the bowl (6) and beat just until the flour is absorbed into the dough (7).

Flatten the dough into a disk and cover with plastic wrap. Chill for at least 2 hours.

Candied Lemon Slices

Cut the lemon into very thin slices, slightly less than ⅛ inch (2 mm) thick.

Bring the sugar and water to a boil in a medium saucepan over medium heat. Add the lemon slices and cook until the peel is almost translucent, about 10 minutes.

Let cool in the syrup.

Preheat the oven to 350° F (180° C). Butter the pastry ring. Line a baking sheet with parchment paper.

On a lightly floured work surface, roll out the dough slightly less than ⅛ inch (2 mm) thick.

Drape the dough over the rolling pin and transfer it to the pastry ring. Trim the overhang so it is flush with the rim of the ring.

Transfer to the prepared baking sheet. Prick the base of the tart shell with a fork (8).

Bake for 15 to 20 minutes, until golden. Let cool completely.

Serves 6 to 8
Level: Basic/Intermediate
Prep: 40 min.
Chill: at least 3 hr.
Cook: 25 to 30 min.

Special equipment
A 9-inch (24 cm) pastry ring or a tart pan with a removable bottom

Sweet Pastry

1 stick (4 oz., 120 g) butter, softened
⅔ cup (3 oz., 80 g) confectioners' sugar
1 vanilla bean, 1 tbsp. vanilla sugar, or 1 tsp. vanilla extract
3 tbsp. (1 oz., 25 g) ground almonds
1 pinch salt
1 egg
1⅔ cups (7 oz., 200 g) all-purpose flour

Candied Lemon Slices

1 lemon
½ cup (3½ oz., 100 g) sugar
¾ cup (200 ml) water
⅓ cup (3½ oz., 100 g) apricot preserves
⅓ cup (3½ oz., 100 g) quince jelly

Lemon Curd

2 lemons
½ cup (120 ml) lemon juice
⅔ cup (4 oz., 120 g) sugar
3 eggs
1½ sticks (6 oz., 175 g) butter, diced

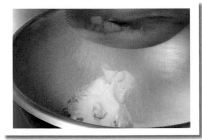

1 Sift the confectioners' sugar into the softened butter.

2 Add the vanilla seeds, ground almonds, and salt.

3 Beat with a wooden spoon.

4 This is the texture at this stage.

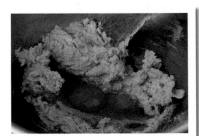

5 Beat in the egg.

6 Sift the flour into the mixture.

7 Beat the dough just until the flour is absorbed.

8 Roll out the dough slightly less than ⅛ inch (2 mm) thick, line the pastry ring with it, and prick the base of the tart shell with a fork.

continued

Lemon Curd

Using a vegetable peeler, remove the colored zest from the lemons in strips, leaving the white pith.

Combine the lemon zest, lemon juice, sugar, and eggs in a small saucepan (9). Heat over medium heat, whisking constantly.

Bring the mixture to a simmer, whisking (10).

Place the butter in a medium bowl. Remove the pan from the heat and strain the mixture into the butter (11).

Process with an immersion blender until smooth, about 2 minutes (12). Or use a whisk.

Let the lemon curd cool slightly, then spread it in the prepared tart shell (13).

Chill the tart for at least 1 hour.

Drain the candied lemon slices on paper towels and arrange them on the tart.

Combine the apricot preserves and quince jelly in a small saucepan and melt over medium heat, stirring occasionally.

Lightly brush the melted jelly over the top.

Chill until served.

9 Combine the lemon zest, lemon juice, sugar, and eggs in a small saucepan.

10 Whisk over medium heat until it starts to simmer.

11 Strain the mixture into the diced butter.

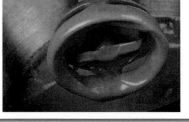

12 Process the curd with an immersion blender until smooth, about 2 minutes.

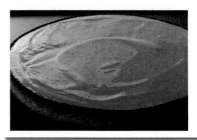

13 Spread the lemon curd in the tart shell.

Pâte Sucrée Cannelle
Sweet Cinnamon Pastry

Tarte Fromage Blanc Sucré
Fromage Blanc Cheesecake

Sweet Cinnamon Pastry

Place the butter in a medium bowl and sift in the confectioners' sugar (1).

Add the ground almonds, salt, and orange zest (2).

Beat with a flexible spatula until smooth (3).

Break the egg into the mixture and stir it in gently (4).

Add the flour and cinnamon (5). Beat until smooth (6 and 7).

Flatten the dough into a disk and cover with plastic wrap (8). Chill for at least 2 hours.

Serves 6 to 8
Level: Basic/Easy
Prep: 35 min.
Chill: at least 2 hr.
Cook: 25 min.

Special equipment
A 9-inch (24 cm) springform pan
Pie weights, dried beans, or rice

Sweet Cinnamon Pastry

1 stick (4 oz., 120 g) butter, softened
⅔ cup (3 oz., 80 g) confectioners' sugar
¼ cup (1 oz. 30 g) ground almonds
1 pinch salt
Finely grated zest of 1 orange
1 egg
1⅔ cups (7 oz., 200 g) all-purpose flour, sifted
1 tsp. ground cinnamon

Filling

8 oz. (250 g) fromage blanc (see *Notes*), ricotta cheese, or Greek-style yogurt
1¼ cups (300 ml) milk
1 pinch salt
⅓ cup (1½ oz., 50 g) cornstarch mixed with 1 tsp. vanilla extract
½ cup (4 oz., 125 g) egg whites (about 4)
⅓ cup (2¼ oz., 65 g) sugar

Egg Glaze

2 egg yolks

1 Sift the confectioners' sugar into the softened butter.

2 Stir in the ground almonds, salt, and grated orange zest.

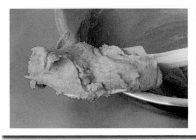

3 Beat until smooth with a flexible spatula.

4 Stir in the egg.

5 Add the flour and cinnamon.

6 Beat until smooth.

7 This is the texture you are looking for.

8 Cover with plastic wrap and chill for at least 2 hours.

continued

Preheat the oven to 350° F (180° C). Butter the springform pan.

On a lightly floured work surface, roll out the dough about ⅛ inch (3 mm) thick.

Drape the dough over the rolling pin and transfer it to the springform pan. Trim the overhang so it is flush with the rim of the pan. Prick the base of the tart shell with a fork.

Line the tart shell with parchment paper and fill with the pie weights (9).

Bake for 15 to 20 minutes, until lightly browned.

Remove the pie weights and parchment paper and let cool completely.

Increase the oven temperature to 425° F (210° C).

Filling

Heat the fromage blanc, milk, and salt in a saucepan over medium heat, whisking until smooth.

Place the cornstarch and vanilla in a bowl and whisk in a little of the hot fromage blanc mixture to dilute it.

When the fromage blanc mixture begins to simmer, whisk in the cornstarch mixture (10).

Cook over medium heat, whisking, until the mixture thickens, about 1 minute, then remove the pan from the heat.

Whip the egg whites, gradually adding the sugar, until they hold firm peaks (11).

Whisk the egg whites, one-third at a time, into the fromage blanc mixture (12).

Egg Glaze

Lightly beat the egg yolks in a cup with a fork.

Spread the filling in the tart shell.

Lightly brush with the egg glaze (13).

Bake on the top shelf of the oven for 3 to 5 minutes, just until the top of the cheesecake is lightly browned; remove from the oven so the filling does not cook again.

Let cool. Remove the sides of the pan and serve.

Notes: Fromage blanc is a tangy fresh cheese often served with fruit, a coulis (fruit sauce), or sugar for dessert.

Please note that the finished recipe contains raw egg.

9 Line the tart shell with parchment paper and fill it with pie weights, dried beans, or rice.

10 Bring the fromage blanc and milk to a boil. Whisk in the cornstarch mixture and cook over medium heat until thickened.

11 Whip the egg whites with the sugar until firm.

12 Whisk the beaten egg whites into the fromage blanc.

13 Spread the mixture in the tart shell and lightly brush the top of the cheesecake with egg glaze.

Pâte à Savarin
Baba Pastry

Savarin Marie-Galante
Cream-Filled Babas

Baba Pastry

Crumble the yeast into a medium bowl and whisk in the milk (1).

Add 2 tbsp. of the flour and whisk until smooth and elastic (2).

Cover this starter with the remaining flour (see *Notes*). Let rise until the starter is doubled in volume under the flour, about 30 minutes (3).

Add 2 of the eggs to the starter (4) and beat with a wooden spoon until the dough is smooth and fairly firm (5).

Add the remaining egg (6) and beat until the dough is soft but elastic, 2 to 3 minutes (7).

Add the butter (8).

Beat the dough well until smooth, 2 to 3 minutes (9).

Add the sugar and salt (10) and beat for 1 minute.

Cover the bowl with a clean kitchen towel and let the dough rise in a warm place for 30 minutes (11).

Butter the baba molds.

Spoon the dough into a pastry bag fitted with a plain tip and pipe it into the baba molds, filling them two-thirds full. Use a pair of scissors to cut the dough (12). Or use a spoon to fill the molds.

Dip the back of a spoon into flour and use it to smooth the dough. This helps the babas rise straight while baking.

Let the babas rise in their molds until they double in volume, about 30 minutes.

Preheat the oven to 350° F (180° C).

Transfer the babas to a baking sheet and bake for 20 minutes, until golden brown.

Turn them out onto a wire rack and let cool for 5 minutes.

Makes 1 dozen babas
Level: Basic/Intermediate
Prep: 40 min.
Rise: 1 hr. 30 min.
Cook: 30 min.

Special equipment
12 baba molds

Baba Pastry

½ cake (.3 oz.,10 g) fresh yeast
¼ cup (50 ml) milk
1¾ cups (8 oz., 225 g) all-purpose
   flour
3 eggs
3 tbsp. (50 g) butter, softened
1½ tbsp. (¾ oz., 20 g) sugar
1 tsp. (5 g) salt

Pastry Cream

1 cup (250 ml) milk
½ vanilla bean, split lengthwise,
   seeds scraped
⅓ cup (2 oz., 60 g) sugar

3 egg yolks
2½ tbsp. (1 oz., 25 g) cornstarch
2 tbsp. (25 g) butter, diced

Syrup

4 cups (1 liter) water
2⅔ cups (1 lb. 2 oz., 500 g) sugar
1½ oranges
1½ lemons
1 vanilla bean, split lengthwise,
   seeds scraped
2 sticks cinnamon
2 pods star anise

Finish

Apricot preserves, for brushing
Sliced seasonal fruit, for
   garnishing (optional)

1 Dilute the yeast with the milk.

2 This is the texture of the starter when the flour is added.

3 The starter should double in volume under the flour.

4 Add 2 of the eggs.

5 Beat with a wooden spoon until the dough is fairly firm.

6 Beat in the remaining egg.

7 Continue beating the dough with the wooden spoon for 2 to 3 minutes.

8 Add the softened butter.

continued

Pastry Cream

Bring the milk, vanilla seeds, and half the sugar to a boil in a small saucepan.

Whisk the egg yolks with the cornstarch and remaining sugar in a small bowl.

Whisk the egg yolk mixture into the milk (13).

Cook over medium heat until the pastry cream is smooth and thick, about 1 minute (14).

Remove the pan from the heat and beat in the butter (15).

Scrape the pastry cream into a shallow bowl, press a piece of plastic wrap directly on the surface, and chill completely.

Syrup

Bring the water and sugar to a boil in a large saucepan.

Using a vegetable peeler, remove the colored zest from the oranges and lemons in strips, leaving the white pith.

Add the citrus zest, vanilla bean, seeds, cinnamon, and star anise to the syrup.

Remove the pan from the heat and let infuse until lukewarm (it should be the same temperature as your finger), about 10 minutes (16).

Transfer the syrup to a large shallow baking dish. Add the babas and let soak, turning them often (17).

Transfer them to a rack set over a baking sheet to drain for 10 minutes.

Finish

Melt the apricot preserves in a small saucepan over medium heat, stirring occasionally. Lightly brush the preserves on the babas.

Lightly whisk the pastry cream and, using a spoon or pastry bag, spread a dollop on top of each baba.

Garnish with the fruit, if desired.

Notes: In Alsace, in eastern France, bakers often cover the starter with flour instead of plastic wrap before letting it rise. The flour is later beaten into the starter to make the dough.

It is best to bake the babas a day or two before soaking them to help keep them from falling apart in the syrup.

9 Beat again for 2 to 3 minutes.

10 Mix in the sugar and salt.

11 Cover with a clean kitchen towel and let rise for 30 minutes.

12 Butter the molds and pipe in the dough, snipping it when each mold is two-thirds full.

13 Whisk the egg mixture into the boiling milk.

14 Cook the pastry cream over medium heat until it thickens.

15 Remove the pan from the heat and beat in the butter.

16 Bring the water and sugar to a boil and add the citrus zest, vanilla, and spices. Remove from the heat and let infuse.

17 Transfer the lukewarm syrup to a shallow baking dish, add the babas, and let soak.

Pâte Sucrée Chocolat
Chocolate Sweet Pastry

Tarte Mousse Chocolat
Chocolate Mousse Tart

Sweet Chocolate Pastry

Sift the confectioners' sugar into the bowl of a stand mixer. Add the ground almonds, butter, salt, and vanilla sugar (1).

Beat the ingredients at low speed with the paddle attachment (2) until the mixture is smooth (3). Or use a wooden spoon.

Add the egg and beat (4) until smooth (5).

Sift the flour with the cocoa powder into the bowl (6) and beat in until smooth (7).

Flatten the dough into a disk and cover it with plastic wrap (8). Chill for at least 2 hours.

Serves 6 to 8
Level: Basic/Easy
Prep: 40 min.
Chill: at least 2 hr.
Bake: 20 to 25 min.

Special equipment
A 7-inch (18 cm) square ring
or a 9-inch (24 cm) round
pastry ring

¾ cup (3 oz., 95 g) confectioners'
    sugar
¼ cup (1 oz., 30 g) ground
    almonds
1¼ sticks (5 oz., 150 g) butter,
    softened
1 pinch salt
1 tbsp. vanilla sugar or 1 tsp.
    vanilla extract
1 egg, at room temperature
1¾ cups (8 oz., 225 g) all-
    purpose flour
2 tbsp. (15 g) unsweetened cocoa
    powder

10 oz. (290 g) bittersweet
    chocolate (65% cocoa)
1¾ sticks (7 oz., 200 g) butter
2 whole eggs
2 egg yolks
⅓ cup (2 oz., 60 g) sugar

1 Sift the confectioners' sugar into the bowl of a stand mixer and add the ground almonds, butter, salt, and vanilla sugar.

2 Beat at low speed with the paddle attachment.

3 The mixture should be quite smooth.

4 Beat in the egg.

5 Continue beating until the egg is absorbed.

6 Sift the flour with cocoa powder into the bowl.

7 Beat until the dough is smooth.

8 Flatten the dough into a disk and cover with plastic wrap.

continued

Preheat the oven to 350° F (170° C). Line a baking sheet with parchment paper.

Butter the pastry ring and place it on the prepared baking sheet.

On a lightly floured work surface, roll out the dough slightly less than ⅛ inch (2 mm) thick.

Drape the dough over the rolling pin and transfer it to the pastry ring. Trim the overhang so it is flush with the rim of the ring. Prick the base of the tart shell with a fork.

Bake for 15 to 20 minutes, until a light crust forms on top. Let cool.

Increase the oven temperature to 375° F (190° C).

Filling

Finely chop the chocolate. In a bowl set over a saucepan filled with 1 inch (2.5 cm) of barely simmering water, or in 30-second bursts in a microwave oven, melt the chocolate with the butter. Stir until smooth.

Break the whole eggs into a medium bowl and add the egg yolks. Add the sugar and whisk until the mixture is pale and thick, about 5 minutes (9).

Fold in the chocolate with a flexible spatula until smooth (10, 11, and 12).

Slightly mound the filling in the tart shell and smooth the top with a spatula (13 and 14).

Bake for about 5 minutes, watching carefully so it doesn't burn.

Let cool completely before serving.

9 Whisk the whole eggs with the egg yolks and sugar until the mixture is pale and thick.

10 Gradually add the melted chocolate mixture.

11 Gently fold in the chocolate.

12 Continue folding until the mixture is smooth.

13 Spread the filling in the cooled tart shell.

14 The shell should be very full.

Pâte à Choux
Choux Pastry

Tarte Chouquettes
Choux Puff Tartlets

Choux Pastry
Preheat the oven to 350° F (180° C). Lightly butter
a baking sheet.

Combine the water, milk, sugar, salt, and butter in a
medium saucepan.

Bring to a simmer over medium heat (1). When the
butter melts, remove the pan from the heat. Beat in the flour with a wooden
spoon (2).

Continue beating until the dough pulls away from the pan to form a ball (3).

Return the pan to medium heat and beat for 30 seconds to dry out the dough (4).

Transfer the dough to a bowl to stop the cooking.

Break 4 of the eggs into the bowl, one by one, beating with a wooden spoon
after each addition until smooth (5).

Lightly beat the remaining egg. Beat as much as needed into the bowl to make
a dough that is very shiny and just falls from the spoon (6).

Egg Glaze
Lightly beat the egg in a cup with a fork.

Spoon the dough into the pastry bag fitted with the plain tip. On the prepared
baking sheet, pipe the dough into 1-inch (2.5 cm) rounds, spacing 1 inch
(2.5 cm) apart (7). There should be at least 35. Or use a spoon to make balls.

Lightly brush with the egg glaze (8).

Bake for 20 minutes, or until the choux are puffed and browned.

Transfer the choux to a rack to cool. Leave the oven on.

Serves 8
Level: Basic/Intermediate
Prep: 40 min.
Chill: 45 min.
Bake: 40 to 45 min.

Special equipment
A pastry bag
A ⅓-inch (8 mm) plain tip
A 4-inch (10 cm) cookie cutter
8 3-inch (8 cm) pastry rings
or tart pans with a
removable bottom
A ⅓-inch (8 mm) star tip

Choux Pastry

½ cup (125 ml) water
½ cup (125 ml) milk
1 tsp. sugar
1 tsp. salt
1 stick (4 oz., 115 g) butter, diced
1 cup plus 1 tbsp. (5 oz., 140 g)
all-purpose flour
5 eggs

Egg Glaze

1 egg

Pastry Cream

1 cup (250 ml) milk
1 vanilla bean, split lengthwise,
seeds scraped

⅓ cup (2 oz., 60 g) sugar
3 egg yolks
2½ tbsp. (1 oz., 25 g) cornstarch
2 tbsp. (25 g) butter, diced

Finish

1 recipe Sweet Cinnamon Pastry
(page 42)
3½ oz. (100 g) bittersweet
chocolate
Apricot preserves, for dipping
2 oz. (50 g) pearl sugar
⅔ cup (150 ml) heavy cream
1 tbsp. confectioners' sugar

1 Bring the water, milk, sugar, salt, and butter to a simmer.

2 When the butter melts, remove from the heat and quickly beat in the flour.

3 Beat until the dough is smooth.

4 Return the pan to the heat, beating to dry it out.

5 Transfer the dough to a bowl and beat in the eggs, one by one, to adjust the consistency.

6 This shows the consistency of the dough. It should be very shiny and just fall from the spoon.

7 Pipe small choux puffs, spacing 1 inch (2.5 cm) apart.

8 Lightly brush the puffs with egg glaze.

9 Bring the milk to a boil with the vanilla seeds and half the sugar. Whisk in the egg yolk–cornstarch mixture, and remaining sugar.

continued

Pastry Cream

Bring the milk, vanilla seeds, and half the sugar to a boil in a medium saucepan.

Whisk the egg yolks with the cornstarch and remaining sugar in a small bowl just until the sugar dissolves (9).

Whisk the egg yolk mixture into the milk.

Cook the pastry cream over medium heat, whisking, until thick and smooth, about 1 minute (10).

Remove the pan from the heat and stir in the butter (11).

Scrape the pastry cream into a bowl, press a piece of plastic wrap directly on the surface, and chill completely, at least 1 hour.

Finish

On a lightly floured work surface, roll out the Sweet Cinnamon Pastry slightly less than ⅛ inch (2 mm) thick. Using the cookie cutter, stamp out 8 rounds of dough.

Butter the pastry rings or tart pans and lightly butter a baking sheet if using pastry rings.

Transfer the dough rounds to the rings. Trim the overhang so it is flush with the rim of the ring.

Prick the base of the tart shells (12). Bake for 15 to 20 minutes, until golden. Remove the tart shells from the rings. Let cool.

Finely chop the chocolate. In a medium bowl set over a saucepan filled with 1 inch (2.5 cm) of barely simmering water, or in 30-second bursts in a microwave oven, melt the chocolate. Stir until smooth.

Whisk the pastry cream. Spoon or pipe it into the tartlet shells (13).

Spoon more of the pastry cream into the pastry bag fitted with the plain tip. Pipe the cream into the choux puffs through a small hole in the base (14).

Melt the apricot preserves in a small pan over medium heat, stirring occasionally.

Dip the tops of the choux puffs in the preserves (15), then in the pearl sugar (16).

In a large cold bowl, whip the cream, gradually adding the confectioners' sugar, until it holds a firm peak.

Spoon the whipped cream into the pastry bag fitted with the star tip.

Arrange 3 choux puffs on each tartlet and decorate with the whipped cream. Top with a fourth choux puff. Drizzle the melted chocolate over the tartlets.

Notes: Do not use convection heat; the conventional setting is better for choux pastry. It is important not to open the oven door or the choux puffs will deflate.

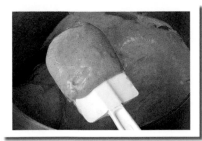

10 Stir the pastry cream constantly over medium heat until it simmers. The texture should be thick and smooth.

11 Remove from the heat and stir in the diced butter.

12 Line the tartlet rings and trim the overhang. Prick the shells with a fork.

13 Whisk the pastry cream and spread in the cooled tart shells.

14 Fill the choux puffs with pastry cream through a hole in the base.

15 Dip the tops of the choux puffs in the preserves.

16 Dip in the pearl sugar.

Pâte à Étirer
Strudel Pastry

Tourte Landaise
Apple Strudel Tart

Strudel Pastry

Sift the flour into a bowl (1).

Add the egg, water, salt, and 1 tbsp. oil (2).

Begin mixing the ingredients with one hand (3) and then knead well until the dough is smooth (4) and it no longer sticks to your fingers (5). Alternatively, use a stand mixer fitted with the dough hook attachment.

Continue kneading with both hands (6).

Remove the dough from the bowl and shape it into a smooth ball (7).

Place it in a deep clean bowl, add the remaining oil (8), and let the dough stand for about 7 minutes. This prevents the dough from drying out while it chills and makes it easier to work with later.

Discard the oil.

Cover the bowl with plastic wrap. Chill the dough for at least 2 hours.

Thirty minutes before stretching the dough, remove it from the refrigerator and bring to room temperature.

Filling

Peel and core the apples.

Slice them lengthwise about ⅛ inch (2 to 3 mm) thick and transfer to a large bowl. Add the liqueur and the 3½ tbsp. (1½ oz., 40 g) granulated sugar and toss to mix.

Serves 10 to 12;
makes 2 9-inch (24 cm) tarts
Level: Basic/Advanced
Prep: 45 min.
Chill: at least 2 hr.
Bake: 30 min.

Special equipment
A large white sheet or apron
2 9-inch (24 cm) tart pans with
a removable bottom
A pastry wheel

2¾ cups (12½ oz., 350 g) all-
  purpose flour
1 egg
⅔ cup (150 ml) cold water
1 pinch salt
1⅔ cups (400 ml) plus 1 tbsp.
  grapeseed oil

6 large Golden Delicious or other
  baking apples
2 tbsp. (30 ml) liqueur, such as
  Grand Marnier, amber rum, or
  whisky
1¼ cups (9 oz., 250 g) plus 3½
  tbsp. (1½ oz., 40 g) granulated
  sugar
1 stick (4 oz., 125 g) butter
½ cup (2¾ oz., 75 g)
  confectioners' sugar

1 Sift the flour into a bowl.

2 Add the egg, cold water, salt, and 1 tbsp. oil.

3 Begin kneading with one hand or use a stand mixer.

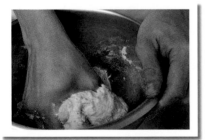

4 Knead well until the dough is smooth.

5 It should not stick to your fingers.

6 At this stage, work it a little with both hands.

7 Shape it into the roundest, smoothest possible ball.

8 Place it in a deep bowl and add the remaining oil. Leave for 7 minutes. Discard the oil, cover the bowl with plastic wrap, and chill for at least 2 hours, then bring to room temperature for 30 minutes. Make the filling.

continued

Spread the sheet on a large work surface and dust it with flour.

Place the dough on a lightly floured cutting board.

Flatten the dough with your palms until the surface is very smooth (9).

This makes it easier to stretch.

Cut the dough in half (10). Cover one half with plastic wrap and reserve.

Transfer the remaining dough to the prepared sheet. Pull and stretch the dough, starting in the center and working outward, until it is as thin and even as possible (11), about 48 by 30 inches (1.20 m by 80 cm). Don't worry if the dough tears; it will not be visible at the end.

Melt the butter (see *Notes*) and brush it evenly over the dough (12).

Lightly sprinkle it with some of the remaining granulated sugar (13).

Using the pastry wheel, slice it into 10-inch (25 cm) squares (14).

Stack 8 dough squares in one tart pan, leaving some overhang (15).

Fill the tart shell with half the apples (16).

Fold the dough over to enclose the apples (17).

Drape the remaining squares over the top and tuck them in.

Sift the confectioners' sugar over the top (18).

Repeat with the reserved dough and remaining filling.

Preheat the oven to 350° F (180° C).

Bake the tarts for about 30 minutes, until the pastry is crisp and lightly browned.

Notes: This pastry is very similar to brick and phyllo pastry, which you usually buy readymade. But homemade is far better, even though it requires practice and skill.

It's an extra step, but it's helpful to clarify the butter—that is, remove the milk solids—so the butter does not burn when the tart is baked. Clarified butter is easy to prepare if you start with at least 8 oz. (250 g). It can be refrigerated for up to 1 month, so you can make more than you need and have some on hand for another use. If the clarified butter has solidified, melt it before using.

To clarify butter: In a small saucepan, melt the butter over medium heat. Remove the pan from the heat and skim off the foam. Pour the remaining butter into a bowl, leaving the whitish milk solids at the bottom; discard the milk solids.

9 Place the dough on a cutting board and flatten it with your palms.

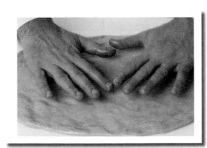

10 Continue flattening until the surface of the dough is perfectly smooth. Cut it in half.

11 Transfer one half to the floured sheet. Pull and stretch, making sure to work from all sides until the dough is very thin.

12 Brush the dough with melted butter.

13 Lightly sprinkle the dough with granulated sugar.

14 Using the pastry wheel, cut out 10 squares.

15 Stack 8 squares in the tart pan, leaving some overhang.

16 Fill the dish with apple slices.

17 Fold the dough over the apples. Drape the remaining squares on top.

18 Sift the confectioners' sugar over the top.

Feuilletage Minute
Quick Puff Pastry

Feuilleté Mandarine
Tangerine Napoleons

Quick Puff Pastry
Place the flour, butter, sugar, and salt in a medium bowl (1).
Squeeze the ingredients with your hand (2) until the flour combines with the butter (3).
The texture should be like a crumble (4).
Add the water (5).
Knead the ingredients, and the dough will gradually come together (6).
Cup your hand like a hook and continue kneading the dough (7 and 8).
The dough is ready when smooth (9).
Cover the dough with plastic wrap and chill for 30 minutes.

Pastry Cream
Bring the milk, vanilla seeds, and half the sugar to a boil in a small saucepan.
Whisk the egg yolks with the cornstarch, flour, and remaining sugar in a small bowl until the sugar dissolves and the mixture is smooth.
Gradually whisk the hot milk into the egg yolk mixture.
Return the pastry cream to the saucepan and cook over medium heat until thick and smooth, about 1 minute.
Remove the pan from the heat and whisk in the butter.
Scrape the pastry cream into a shallow bowl, press a piece of plastic wrap directly on the surface, and chill completely.

Serves 6
Level: Basic/Easy
Prep: 40 min.
Chill: 30 min.
Cook: 15 min.

Quick Puff Pastry

1⅔ cups (7 oz., 200 g) all-purpose flour
2 sticks (8½ oz., 240 g) butter, diced
¼ cup (2 oz., 50 g) sugar
2 tsp. salt
⅓ cup plus 1 tbsp. (90 ml) cold water

Pastry Cream

1 cup (250 ml) milk
½ vanilla bean, split lengthwise, seeds scraped

¼ cup (2 oz., 50 g) sugar
2 egg yolks
2 tbsp. (20 g) cornstarch
1 tsp. all-purpose flour
1 tbsp. (20 g) butter, diced

Finish

⅓ cup (2 oz., 50 g) confectioners' sugar
6 large tangerines

1 Place the flour, diced butter, sugar, and salt in a bowl.

2 Squeeze the ingredients with your hand.

3 Continue squeezing until the butter has absorbed the flour.

4 It should resemble a coarse crumble.

5 Pour in the water.

6 Continue kneading.

7 Work the dough well.

8 Cup your hand like a hook to get the best results.

9 The ingredients should come together to form a smooth dough.

continued

Preheat the oven to 350° F (180° C).

On a lightly floured work surface, roll out the dough into a rectangle about ⅛ inch (3 to 4 mm) thick (10). Trim to 16 by 12 inches (40 by 30 cm).

Drape the dough over the rolling pin and transfer it to a baking sheet. Prick it with a fork (11).

Cover the dough with parchment paper. Set a wire rack or second baking sheet large enough to cover it on top to keep the dough from rising as it bakes (12). (You want the pastry as flat as possible for this recipe.)

Bake for about 15 minutes, until golden brown.

Remove from the oven. Increase the oven temperature to 425° F (220° C).

Remove the parchment paper and the rack from the pastry and let cool slightly on the baking sheet.

Finish

Sift the confectioners' sugar over the pastry (13) and return it to the oven for 2 to 3 minutes, until caramelized. Let cool completely.

Peel the tangerines using a sharp knife and remove all the white pith. Cut between the membranes to release the segments. Cut each segment lengthwise in half.

Using a serrated knife, cut the pastry lengthwise into 2½-inch (6 cm) wide strips. Cut the strips crosswise into 3½-inch (9 cm) rectangles.

Cut each rectangle on the diagonal into triangles (14).

Just before serving, whisk the pastry cream until smooth. Spoon the pastry cream into a pastry bag fitted with a large plain tip and pipe a strip of pastry cream in the center of half the triangles (15). Or use a spoon.

Arrange the tangerine half-segments around it (16). If necessary, glue the tangerines in place with more pastry cream.

Top with the remaining puff pastry triangles and serve as soon as possible.

10 On a lightly floured work surface, roll out the dough into rectangle ⅛ inch (3 to 4 mm) thick. Trim the dough to 16 by 12 inches (40 by 30 cm).

11 Prick the dough all over with a fork.

12 Cover the dough with parchment paper and place a rack over it.

13 Sift confectioners' sugar over the baked puff pastry. Return it to the oven to caramelize.

14 Cut the pastry into triangles.

15 Pipe a strip of pastry cream in the center of half the triangles.

16 Surround the cream with tangerine segments and top with the remaining pastry triangles.

Kouign Amann
Sugary Breton Puff Pastries

Melt the 2 tsp. (10 g) butter in a small bowl; let cool.

Sift the flour into the bowl of a stand mixer (1).

Add the salt, then the yeast, keeping them separate (2).

Pour in the water and melted butter (3) and beat at low speed with the dough hook attachment until the dough is smooth and fairly firm, 2 to 3 minutes (4). Or use a wooden spoon.

Flatten the dough into a square, cover with plastic wrap, and chill for at least 1 hour.

On a lightly floured work surface, roll out the dough into a rectangle 12 by 8 inches (30 by 20 cm).

Dust the remaining 2 sticks (8 oz., 225 g) butter with flour. Using the rolling pin, flatten the butter into a rectangle 6 by 4 inches (15 by 10 cm).

Arrange the dough with a short side facing you. Place the butter in the center of the dough (5).

Fold the top and bottom dough edges over it to enclose the butter (6).

Rotate the dough clockwise 90° (a quarter-turn) so that an open edge is facing you. Roll it out into a rectangle 24 inches (60 cm) long and fold it in thirds, like a letter (7). This procedure is called a "turn."

Rotate the dough another quarter-turn (8) so that the open edge is facing you.

Makes about 1 dozen
individual pastries
Level: Advanced
Prep: 45 min.
Chill: at least 2 hr.
Rise: 30 to 40 min.
Bake: 20 to 25 min.

Special equipment
15 3-inch (8 cm) pastry rings

2 sticks (8 oz., 225 g) plus 2 tsp.
(10 g) butter
2¼ cups (9½ oz., 275 g) all-purpose
flour
1 tsp. salt
¼ cake (.15 oz., 5 g) fresh yeast
⅔ cup (165 ml) cold water
1½ cups (10 oz., 300 g) sugar

1 Sift the flour into the bowl of a stand mixer.

2 Add the salt and yeast, keeping them separate.

3 Beat in the water and melted butter with the dough hook.

4 The dough should be smooth and slightly elastic.

5 Roll out the dough into a rectangle and place the butter rectangle in the center.

6 Fold the dough over to enclose the butter.

7 Roll the dough out 24 inches (60 cm) long and fold it in thirds, like a letter.

8 Rotate the dough 90° (a quarter-turn).

continued

Roll out the dough again into a rectangle 24 inches (60 cm) long (9) and fold it in thirds (10).

Cover the dough with plastic wrap and chill for 1 hour.

Lightly sprinkle the work surface with sugar. Turn the dough so an open side is facing you and sprinkle with sugar. Roll out the dough into a rectangle again, using only the sugar, no flour.

Generously sprinkle the dough with sugar (11) and lightly press into the dough with the rolling pin (12).

Fold the dough in thirds (13) as before and sprinkle with sugar.

Rotate it a quarter-turn, roll it out into a rectangle, and sprinkle with sugar.

Fold the dough in thirds and sprinkle again with sugar. (14).

Roll out the dough into a square about ⅛ inch (4 mm) thick. Cut out 4-inch (10 cm) squares (15).

Mound the remaining ¼ cup (2 oz., 50 g) sugar on the work surface.

Place a square of dough on the sugar and fold each corner into the center (16, 17, 18, and 19).

9 Roll out the dough again 24 inches (60 cm) long.

10 Fold it in thirds.

11 Rotate the dough a quarter-turn so the open side is facing you and sprinkle with sugar.

12 Roll out again and sprinkle with sugar, lightly pressing it in with the rolling pin.

13 Fold in thirds again.

14 Rotate a quarter-turn, roll out, and fold in thirds, sprinkling with sugar at each step.

15 Roll out ⅛ inch (4 mm) thick. Cut into 4-inch (10 cm) squares.

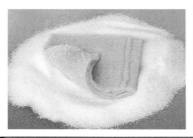

16 Mound the remaining sugar on a work surface and place the dough square on top. Fold the first corner toward the center.

17 Fold in the second corner.

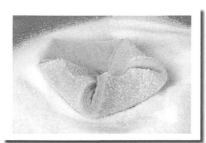

18 Fold in the third corner.

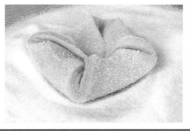

19 Fold in the fourth corner.

continued

Again, fold each corner into the center, but this time, the dough should be round (20, 21, and 22).

Line a baking sheet with parchment paper. Butter the pastry rings and set on the prepared baking sheet. Transfer the kouign amann to a pastry ring (23).
Repeat with the remaining dough squares. Place the baking sheet in a warm room, cover with plastic wrap, and let the pastries rise slightly for 30 to 40 minutes.

Preheat the oven to 350° F (180° C). Transfer the baking sheet to the center rack of the oven or even one of the higher racks, because the pastries tend to brown quickly on the bottom. Bake for 20 to 25 minutes, until golden. Let cool for a few minutes in the pastry rings, then transfer the pastries to a rack to cool completely.

Notes: Kouign Amman (pronounced kween-a-mun) takes its name from the Breton words for cake (kouign) and butter (amman).
Kouign Amann can be prepared as one large pastry.
It is best not to make this dough too far ahead of time, as the sugar melts in the refrigerator.

20 Last, fold in the angles made by the folds.

21 Continue to fold them, pressing down hard in the center.

22 This is the final shape: round.

23 Place each kouign amann in a buttered pastry ring. Let rise and bake.

Gâteau Basque
Buttery Basque Cake

Basque Pastry

Place the butter, sugar, and ground almonds in a medium bowl (1).

Beat the ingredients with a flexible spatula (2) and mix in the lemon zest (3).

Beat in the egg yolk and ½ egg until smooth (4).

Add the flour and salt (5) and beat until smooth (6).

Flatten the dough into a disk and cover with plastic wrap. Chill for at least 2 hours.

Filling

Bring the milk to a boil in a small saucepan over medium heat.

Whisk the egg yolks with the sugar and flour in a medium bowl until the sugar dissolves.

Gradually whisk the egg yolk mixture into the hot milk (7).

Continue cooking, whisking constantly, until the pastry cream thickens.

Pour in the rum (8) and simmer, whisking constantly, for 1 minute (9).

Remove the pan from the heat, press a piece of plastic wrap directly on the surface of the pastry cream, and let stand at room temperature.

Serves 6 to 8
Level: Easy
Prep: 40 min.
Chill: at least 2 hr.
Cook: 30 min.

Special equipment
A 9-inch (24 cm) pastry ring
or a tart pan with a
removable bottom

1½ sticks (6 oz., 175 g) butter, softened
⅔ cup (4½ oz., 125 g) sugar
1 cup (3 oz., 85 g) ground almonds
Finely grated zest of ½ lemon
1 egg yolk
½ egg (1 oz., 25 g) (see Notes)
1¾ cups (8 oz., 225 g) all-purpose flour
1 pinch salt

Filling

1 cup (250 ml) milk
3 egg yolks
¼ cup (1½ oz., 45 g) sugar
2 tbsp. (20 g) all-purpose flour, sifted
2 tbsp. (30 ml) dark rum
⅔ cup (5 oz., 150 g) cherry preserves

Egg Glaze

1 egg
1 pinch salt

1 Place the butter, sugar, and ground almonds in a bowl.

2 Beat with a flexible spatula.

3 Mix in the grated lemon zest.

4 Beat in the egg yolk and ½ egg.

5 Add the flour and salt.

6 Beat until the dough is smooth.

7 Bring the milk to a boil, add the egg yolk mixture, and whisk until thickened.

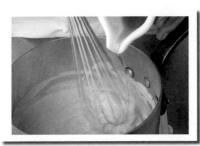

8 Whisk in the rum.

continued

Basic Pastry and Tarts   73

Preheat the oven to 350° F (180° C). Butter the pastry ring.

Cut the dough in half. Cover one half with plastic wrap and reserve.

Lightly knead the remaining dough to soften (10).

On a lightly floured sheet of parchment paper, roll out the dough about ⅛ inch (4 mm) thick (11).

Stamp out the crust with the pastry ring (12).

Leave on the ring and reserve the excess dough (13).

Transfer the crust on the paper to a baking sheet.

Dip your finger in water and lightly moisten the edge of the crust.

Roll the reserved excess dough into a rope about 1 inch (2.5 cm) in diameter (14).

Carefully fit it around the moistened edge of the crust (15).

Prick the base of the crust with a fork (16).

Spoon the pastry cream into a pastry bag fitted with a large plain tip and pipe the pastry cream around the edge (17). Or use a spoon.

Beat the cherry preserves to loosen them. Spread in the center.

Lightly brush the top of the rope with water (18). It should look like the photo (19).

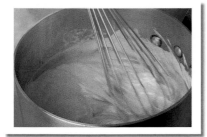

9 Simmer the pastry cream, whisking constantly, for 1 minute.

10 Cut the dough in half. Lightly knead one half to soften it.

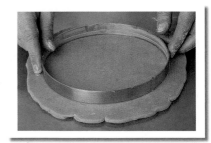

11 Flatten it into a disk and roll out ⅛ inch (4 mm) thick.

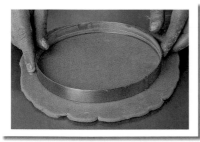

12 Butter the pastry ring and cut out a disk.

13 Remove the excess dough.

14 Use the extra to shape an even rope of dough.

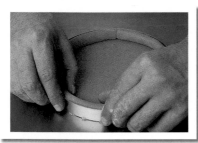

15 Carefully fit the rope against the edge of the crust.

16 Prick the base with a fork.

17 Pipe or spoon the pastry cream around the edge.

18 Fill with cherry preserves. Lightly brush the top of the dough rope with water.

19 Here is the bottom half of the cake on a baking sheet.

continued

On a lightly floured work surface, roll out the reserved dough into a disk ⅛ inch (4 mm) thick.

Drape the dough over the rolling pin and transfer it to the pastry ring (20).

Trim the overhang so it is flush with the rim of the ring (21).

Remove the excess dough (22).

Egg Glaze
Lightly beat the egg and salt in a cup with a fork.

Brush the top of the cake with the egg glaze (23).

Using the tines of a fork, score the top of the cake in a decorative manner (24).

Bake for about 30 minutes, until golden.

Let cool for a few minutes before removing the pastry ring.

Notes: Gâteau Basque is in the Basic Pastry and Tarts chapter because it is more like a double-crusted shortbread tart than a cake.

This version of the classic contains both of the two traditional fillings: rum pastry cream and cherry preserves. You can use just one, if you prefer.

To measure one-half egg, break an egg into a cup and lightly beat it. Measure the beaten egg in tablespoons and use half the amount.

20 Drape the second rolled-out dough round over the rolling pin and transfer it to the pastry ring.

21 Use the rolling pin to trim the edge.

22 Remove the excess dough.

23 Lightly brush the cake with the egg glaze.

24 Decorate the top with the tines of a fork.

Feuilletage Chocolat
Chocolate Puff Pastry

Mille-Feuille Chocolat
Chocolate Napoleon

Chocolate Puff Pastry

Melt the 6 tbsp. (3 oz., 85 g) butter in a small saucepan; let cool.

Sift the flour with the cocoa powder into the bowl of a stand mixer (1).

Pour in the water, melted butter, and fleur de sel (2).

Beat at low speed with the dough hook attachment (3) until the dough is smooth and fairly firm, 2 to 3 minutes (4).

Flatten this dough (*détrempe*) into a square, cover with plastic wrap, and chill for at least 2 hours.

On a lightly floured work surface, roll out the dough into a square about ½ inch (1 cm) thick.

Dust the remaining 3 sticks (12 oz., 335 g) butter with flour. Using the rolling pin, flatten the butter into a square. Arrange it in the center of the dough like a diamond (5).

Fold the dough around the butter like an envelope (6).

Run the rolling pin over the edges to smooth the surface (7).

Roll out the dough into a rectangle about ⅓ inch (8 to 9 mm) thick (8).

Fold the dough in thirds, like a letter (9).

Cover the dough with plastic wrap and chill for at least 10 minutes.

Serves 10
Level: Basic/Advanced
Prep: 1 hr.
Chill: at least 6 hr.
Cook: 25 to 30 min.

Chocolate Puff Pastry

- 3 sticks (12 oz., 335 g) plus 6 tbsp. (3 oz., 85 g) butter
- 4 cups (1 lb. ½ oz., 500 g) all-purpose flour
- ½ cup (2 oz., 60 g) unsweetened cocoa powder
- 1 cup plus 1 tbsp. (265 ml) cold water
- 1 tbsp. (10 g) fleur de sel

Sugar Glaze

- ⅓ cup (2 oz., 50 g) confectioners' sugar

Chocolate–Coriander Cream

- 2 cups (500 ml) heavy cream
- 1 tbsp. crushed coriander seeds
- 5 oz. (140 g) bittersweet chocolate (60% cocoa)

Chocolate Ganache

- ⅓ cup (80 ml) heavy cream
- 1 tsp. sugar
- 3 oz. (80 g) bittersweet chocolate (60% cocoa)
- 2 tsp. (10 g) butter

1 Sift the flour with the cocoa.

2 Add the water, melted butter, and fleur de sel to the bowl.

3 Gently beat the ingredients until they are thoroughly combined.

4 This is the texture you are looking for.

5 Roll out the dough into a square about ½ inch (1 cm) thick. Flatten the butter into a square and place in the center of the dough.

6 Fold the dough around the butter like an envelope.

7 Run the rolling pin over the edges to smooth the surface.

8 Roll out the dough into a rectangle about ⅓ inch (8 to 9 mm) thick.

9 Fold the dough in thirds, like a letter.

continued

On a lightly floured work surface, arrange the dough so that an open edge is facing you (10).

Apply pressure with the rolling pin at the top and the bottom of the dough so that the layers remain straight (11).

Roll out the dough into a rectangle about ⅓ inch (8 to 9 mm) thick (12).

Fold the dough in thirds, like a letter (13).

Rotating the dough 90° clockwise (a quarter-turn) so that an open edge is facing you, rolling it out into a rectangle, and folding it in thirds is called a "turn."

Cover the dough with plastic wrap and chill for at least 2 hours, preferably overnight.

Give the dough 2 more turns. Cover with plastic wrap and chill for at least 2 hours.

Give the dough another quarter-turn and repeat the last rolling and folding.

Cut the dough in half. Cover one half with plastic wrap and reserve for another use. Roll out the remaining dough into a sheet 16 by 12 inches (40 by 30 cm) (14).

At this stage, it is important to work evenly. Roll out the dough lengthwise without attempting to reach the desired length immediately. Then roll it out crosswise. Alternate the rolling until the desired dimensions are reached. If the dough seems slightly elastic while you are working, let it rest for a few minutes on the work surface before continuing.

Drape the dough over the rolling pin and transfer it to a baking sheet. Prick the dough with a fork.

Let the dough rest at room temperature or in the refrigerator.

Preheat the oven to 350° F (180° C).

Cover the dough with parchment paper. Set a wire rack or second baking sheet large enough to cover it on top to keep the dough from rising as it bakes. (You want the pastry as flat as possible for this recipe.)

Bake for 25 minutes, or until fairly dark.

Remove from the oven. Increase the oven temperature to 425° F (220° C).

Remove the parchment paper and the rack from the pastry and let cool slightly on the baking sheet.

Using a serrated knife, cut the pastry crosswise into 3 equal strips (15).

Sugar Glaze
Sift the confectioners' sugar over the pastry (16) and return it to the oven for 2 to 3 minutes, until caramelized. Let cool completely.

10 Turn the dough so that an open edge is facing you.

11 Press down at the top and bottom to make sure the folds are aligned.

12 Roll out again.

13 Fold into thirds, wrap, and chill. Repeat the procedure 2 more times, rotating the dough 90° (a quarter-turn) so that an open edge is facing you, rolling, and folding. Chill.

14 Rotate, roll, and fold the dough, then roll out again to make a rectangle, 16 by 12 inches (40 by 30 cm).

15 Let the baked pastry cool and cut crosswise into 3 equal strips.

16 Sprinkle with confectioners' sugar and caramelize.

17 Bring half the cream to a boil.

18 Add the crushed coriander seeds and let infuse.

continued

Chocolate-Coriander Cream

Bring half the cream to a boil in a medium saucepan over medium heat (17).
Add the coriander seeds (18), remove the pan from the heat, and let infuse for about 10 minutes.

Finely chop the chocolate and place it in a medium bowl. Bring the coriander cream to a boil and strain it, whisking, into the chocolate in two or three additions (19 and 20).
Gradually whisk in the remaining cream until smooth (21).
Chill for 30 minutes to 1 hour.

Fill a large bowl with ice water. Place the bowl of chocolate cream in the ice water. Whip the cream until it holds a soft peak (22).
Spoon the chocolate cream into a pastry bag fitted with a medium plain tip and pipe lines of cream lengthwise on one puff pastry strip (23). Or spread the cream with a thin spatula.
Place a second pastry strip on the cream (24) and pipe with cream (25).
Top with the last pastry strip (26). Chill for 30 minutes before serving.

Chocolate Ganache

Bring the cream to a boil with the sugar in a small saucepan. Finely chop the chocolate and add to a small bowl with the butter. Pour the hot cream into the chocolate, and whisk until smooth. Spread the ganache on the top of the Napoleon.

Notes: Use the least possible amount of flour when rolling out the dough. Too much will affect both the taste and texture.

For puff pastry it's important to work on a cold surface. For this reason pastry chefs like to use marble. You can chill your work surface with a bag of ice.

You can halve the Chocolate Puff Pastry recipe, but it is more practical to make a large quantity. Keep the unused dough well covered with plastic wrap in the freezer. Thaw it in the refrigerator.

The Napoleon can be refrigerated for up to 2 days.

19 Reheat the coriander cream and strain it, in two or three additions, into the chocolate.

20 Gently whisk the chocolate with the cream until smooth.

21 Gradually whisk in the cold cream.

22 Place the bowl of chocolate cream in ice water. Whip just until it holds soft peaks.

23 Pipe lines of cream on one layer of puff pastry.

24 Top the cream with a second pastry strip.

25 Pipe another layer of cream.

26 Cover with the third layer of pastry, chill, and spread the chocolate ganache on top.

Feuilletage Inversé
Inside-Out Puff Pastry

Tarte Bucolique
Almond-Cream Fruit Tart

Inside-Out Puff Pastry

Melt 1 stick (4 oz., 115 g) of the butter in a small saucepan; let cool.

Pour the water and white vinegar into a large bowl, add the fleur de sel (1), and stir to dissolve.

Sift in 2¾ cups (12½ oz., 350 g) of the flour and add the melted butter (2).

Cup your hand like a hook and knead the dough (3) until smooth and fairly firm (4).

Flatten this dough (*détrempe*) into a rectangle, cover with plastic wrap, and chill for at least 2 hours.

Dice the remaining 3 sticks plus 2 tbsp. (13 oz., 375 g) butter and place in a large bowl. Add the remaining 1 cup plus 2 tbsp. (5 oz., 150 g) flour (5).

Rub the ingredients with your fingertips until the butter is incorporated into the flour (6), then knead until smooth (7).

Flatten the dough into a rectangle (8), cover with plastic wrap, and chill for at least 2 hours.

Serves 8 to 10
Level: Basic/Advanced
Prep: 1 hr.
Chill: at least 6 hr.
Cook: 25 to 35 min.

A 10-inch (24 cm) tart pan
with a removable bottom or
a pastry ring

Inside-Out Puff Pastry

4 sticks plus 2 tbsp. (1 lb. 2 oz., 500 g) butter
⅔ cup (150 ml) cold water
1 tbsp. white vinegar
2 tbsp. (½ oz., 18 g) fleur de sel
4 cups (1 lb. 2 oz., 500 g) all-purpose flour
¼ cup (2 oz., 50 g) sugar

Almond Cream

7 tbsp. (3½ oz., 100 g) butter, softened
½ cup (3½ oz., 100 g) sugar
2 eggs
1 cup (3½ oz., 100 g) ground almonds
½ cup (4 oz., 130 g) pastry cream (optional, page 46)

Fruit Filling

3 Honeycrisp or other baking apples
2 firm ripe peaches
7 oz. (200 g) raspberries

1 Dissolve the fleur de sel in the water and vinegar.

2 Sift in some of the flour, then add the melted butter.

3 Cup your fingers like a hook and knead.

4 Continue kneading until the dough *(détrempe)* is smooth.

5 Add more flour to the diced butter.

6 Rub the ingredients with your fingertips to incorporate the butter into the flour.

7 Knead until the dough is smooth.

8 Flatten into a rectangle.

continued

On a lightly floured work surface, roll out the *détrempe* into a rectangle about ½ inch (1 cm) thick.

Roll out the remaining buttery dough into a rectangle twice the size of the *détrempe*.

Arrange the buttery dough with a short side facing you. Place the *détrempe* in the center of the dough (9).

Fold the bottom (10) and top dough edges over it to enclose the *détrempe* (11).

Rotate the dough 90° clockwise (a quarter-turn) so that an open edge is facing you. Roll it out into a rectangle about ⅓ inch (8 to 9 mm) thick (12).

Fold the bottom third of the dough so it covers two-thirds of the dough (13).

Fold the top third so that it meets the edge of the first fold (14).

Fold the entire dough in half to make a "double turn" (15 and 16).

Cover with plastic wrap and chill for at least 2 hours (17).

9 Roll out the *détrempe* into a rectangle. Roll out the buttery dough into a rectangle twice the size of the *détrempe*. Place the *détrempe* in the center of the buttery dough.

10 Fold the bottom edge over the *détrempe*.

11 Fold the top edge over to enclose the *détrempe*.

12 Rotate the dough 90° (a quarter-turn) so that an open edge is facing you. Roll out ⅓ inch (8 to 9 mm) thick.

13 Fold the bottom third of the dough so it covers two-thirds of the dough.

14 Fold the top third downward to meet the fold.

15 Fold the entire dough in half. This makes a double fold.

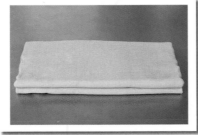

16 This is what it looks like after the double fold.

17 Cover with plastic wrap and chill.

continued

Arrange the dough with an open side facing you and roll it out again ⅓ inch (8 mm) thick (18).

Repeat steps 12 to 17 to repeat the double folding. Chill for at least 2 hours.

Almond Cream

Beat the butter with a wooden spoon in a medium bowl until smooth.

Add the sugar (19) and beat until creamy (20).

Beat in the eggs (21).

Add the ground almonds (22) and stir until smooth (23).

Fold in the pastry cream, if desired (24), until the filling is smooth.

Arrange the dough with an open side facing you, and roll it out again ⅓ inch (8 mm) thick.

Fold it in thirds, like a letter, to make a "simple fold" (25).

Cut the dough in half. Cover one half with plastic wrap and reserve for another use.

Sprinkle the work surface with sugar and roll out the remaining dough about ⅛ inch (2 to 3 mm) thick (26).

Sprinkle the dough with sugar (27) and lightly press it in with the rolling pin.

18 Arrange the dough with an open side facing you and roll out again ⅓ inch (8 mm) thick. Repeat steps 12 to 17. Chill.

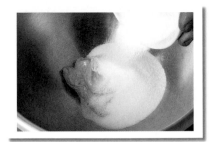

19 Cream the butter with the sugar.

20 The mixture should be very soft and fluffy.

21 Beat in the eggs.

22 Stir in the ground almonds.

23 Stir with a wooden spoon until smooth.

24 Fold in the pastry cream, if desired.

25 Arrange the dough with an open side facing you and roll out ⅓ inch (8 mm) thick. Fold it in thirds, like letter.

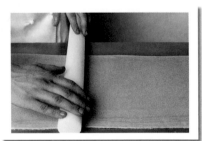

26 Roll out the dough slightly less than ⅛ inch (2 to 3 mm) thick.

27 Sprinkle the work surface and the dough with sugar and press it in with the rolling pin.

continued

Preheat the oven to 350° F (180° C). Butter the tart pan.

Drape the dough over the rolling pin and transfer it to the tart pan, pressing the dough in around the edges (28).

Trim the overhang so it is flush with the rim of the pan (29 and 30). Prick the base of the tart shell with a fork.

Lightly press the edge of the dough up the side of the pan with your fingertips to make a raised border (31) and pinch to decorate (32).

Fruit Filling

Peel, quarter, and core the apples. Quarter the peaches.

Spread a thin layer of the almond cream in the tart shell. Arrange the apples, peaches, and raspberries on top (33).

Bake for 25 to 35 minutes, until the fruit is tender and the cream is set.

Notes: In traditional puff pastry, the flour-and-water détrempe is wrapped around a buttery core. In Inside-Out Puff Pastry, it's the reverse.

These amounts make 2 lb. 10 oz. (1.2 kg) of Inside-Out Puff Pastry. You can halve the recipe, but it is more practical to make a large quantity. Keep the unused dough well covered with plastic wrap in the freezer. Thaw it in the refrigerator.

The almond cream can be covered with plastic wrap and chilled for up to 2 days.

28 Line the tart pan, pressing the dough in around the edges.

29 Trim the overhang so it is flush with the rim of the pan.

30 Remove the excess dough.

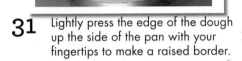

31 Lightly press the edge of the dough up the side of the pan with your fingertips to make a raised border.

32 Pinch the border to decorate.

33 Prick the base, spread a thin layer of cream in the shell, and arrange the fruit on top.

THE
CRE

Making French Creams, Custards, and Puddings

Blanching Sugar

Granulated sugar needs to be dissolved unless it's used as a crunchy coating. If it is not melted in a hot liquid, a recipe will call for it to be whisked, for example into egg yolks, just until it dissolves. Using a whisk or electric mixer, whip the mixture until the grains can no longer be seen. Recipes with this step usually require no further whipping because the sugar is generally cooked or otherwise processed at a later stage.

Folding

Whipping egg whites and heavy cream results in delightfully light mixtures. So the last thing you want to do is burst all those bubbles. Recipes generally call for folding "gently," the idea being to keep as much airiness as possible. If there is a large quantity of a whipped ingredient to fold in, it is easier to work in batches. Holding a flexible spatula in one hand, rotate the bowl slowly with the other as you stir some of the whipped cream or egg whites from the center outwards, making sure not to press the mixture against the sides of the bowl, which squashes those little bubbles. Continue until the mixture is smooth and repeat for the next batch.

Whipping Cream

For best results, chill both the heavy cream and the bowl well before you begin. Whip at medium speed to incorporate tiny air bubbles. If you're using a whisk or hand-held mixer, rotate it around the bowl (the way a stand mixer works). The cream begins to increase in volume. Some recipes call for cream that is doubled in volume; others, for a firm peak, depending on the consistency of what it will be combined with. Be careful not to overbeat; you may end up with something approaching the consistency of butter, and there's no going back.

Whipping Egg Whites

When whipping egg whites, first make sure your bowl is perfectly clean and grease-free. Separate the eggs, adding the whites and yolks to separate bowls. If any egg yolk escapes into the whites, fish it out. Begin whipping at medium speed to incorporate the air in fine bubbles. This creates a more stable structure than if you whip at high speed. Egg whites should be whipped until they hold a soft peak (a little tip will bend over slightly) or until they hold a firm peak (the tip will stand straight up), as for dacquoise (for instance, Mixed Fruit–White Chocolate Dacquoise, page 296). It is important to stop whipping egg whites before they become grainy. French meringue (page 544) and Italian meringue (page 538), both of which contain considerable quantities of sugar, should be whipped until dense, firm, and shiny.

The French Touch

Coulis

While a coulis—basically a sauce—may be sweet or savory, here it refers to pureed cooked or raw fruit, usually strained to make a finer texture. It can be sweetened or unsweetened depending on the fruit's ripeness or natural sugar content. A tart coulis can offset a mild cream in an interesting way. Making a coulis allows you to play with contrasting or complementary tastes and textures.

Verrines

Many of the individual creams and custards served in cups in this chapter are known as verrines (small glasses) in France. These desserts are not cooked in their serving dishes, so you do not need heatproof or ovenproof molds. The containers can be shot glasses, mismatched glasses, espresso or other coffee cups. Verrines allow you to offer a range of easy-to-eat creamy desserts at buffets. They are convenient for layering and contrasting textures. The different colors are especially attractive when visible through glass containers.

French Ingredients

Brick Pastry

Thin, crisp brick (or brik) pastry sheets are a specialty of North Africa used for both sweet and savory dishes. Brick is slightly sturdier than phyllo pastry, so if you use phyllo as a substitute, double the layers. Because it is crunchy when cooked, it provides an interesting textural contrast to soft desserts, such as Passion Fruit–Banana Creams (page 156).

Gelatin

Pastry chefs like to use gelatin in transparent sheets to lightly set desserts, such as Bavarian creams and marshmallows, because it yields a smoother texture than the powdered variety. You can substitute powdered gelatin. For 2 gelatin sheets (4 g), using a small saucepan, sprinkle 1½ tsp. of powdered gelatin over ¼ cup of the liquid in the recipe and let stand until softened, about 5 minutes. Place over low heat and cook, stirring often, until the gelatin dissolves. Let cool before proceeding with the recipe.

Vanilla Sugar

Vanilla sugar is a staple in French kitchens. It is available at specialty food shops and online, but is very easy to make. Split a vanilla bean lengthwise in half and place it in a jar with 1 to 2 cups of sugar. Seal and let stand for at least one week. You can also recycle a vanilla bean that has already been used to flavor pastry cream; just wash it and dry it well.

For 1 tbsp. of vanilla sugar, you can substitute the seeds of 1 vanilla bean or 1 tsp. vanilla extract plus 1 tbsp. regular sugar.

Meringues Chantilly
Meringue Pastries with Chantilly Cream

French Meringue

Combine the egg whites and a little of the granulated sugar in a clean, dry bowl and whisk until frothy (1). Or whip in a stand mixer fitted with the whisk attachment.

Gradually add the remaining granulated sugar, whisking constantly (2).

Continue whisking until the egg whites are smooth, glossy (3), and hold a firm peak (4).

Sift the ¾ cup (3½ oz., 100 g) confectioners' sugar into the meringue (5) and gently fold it in with a flexible spatula (6).

Preheat the oven to 300° F (150° C). Line a baking sheet with parchment paper.

Spoon the meringue into the pastry bag fitted with the plain tip and pipe 4-inch-long (10 cm) strips of meringue (7).

Sift the remaining ⅓ cup (2 oz., 50 g) confectioners' sugar over the meringues (8).

Bake for 8 minutes. Reduce the oven temperature to 200° F (90° C) and bake for about 2 hours, until the meringues are completely dry inside.

Let cool completely on the baking sheet.

Serves 6
Level: Basic/Easy
Prep: 20 min.
Bake: 2 hr. 10 min.

Special equipment
A pastry bag
A medium plain tip
A medium star tip

3 egg whites
½ cup (3½ oz., 100 g) granulated sugar
¾ cup (3½ oz., 100 g) plus ⅓ cup (2 oz., 50 g) confectioners' sugar

1 cup (250 ml) heavy cream
¼ cup (2 oz., 50 g) sugar
1 tsp. kirsch
1 tsp. vanilla extract

1 Combine the egg whites and a little of the granulated sugar in a clean, dry bowl and whisk until frothy.

2 Gradually add the remaining granulated sugar, whisking constantly.

3 The meringue should be smooth and glossy.

4 This is the texture you are looking for.

5 Sift the confectioners' sugar into the meringue.

6 Gently fold it in with a flexible spatula.

7 Pipe strips of meringue on a parchment-lined baking sheet.

8 Sift more confectioners' sugar over the meringues.

continued

Chantilly Cream

Fill a large bowl with ice water.

Pour the cream into a medium bowl and place in the ice water (9).

Whip the cream until it holds a soft peak (10).

Add the sugar (11), kirsch (12), and vanilla extract (13), whisking constantly. Stop when the cream holds firmly to the whisk.

Stick flat sides of the meringues together, two by two, using some of the Chantilly cream as glue (14).

Spoon the remaining Chantilly cream into the pastry bag fitted with the star tip and pipe rosettes on each meringue (15).

Note: This pastry should be eaten the day it is prepared.

9 Pour the cream into a medium bowl and place in ice water.

10 Whip the cream until it holds a soft peak.

11 Whisk in the sugar.

12 Whisk in the kirsch.

13 Add the vanilla extract and whisk until the cream holds a firm peak.

14 Stick pairs of meringues together, using the Chantilly cream as glue.

15 Pipe rosettes on top.

Crème Caramel
Caramelized Vanilla Custards

Caramel

Fill a medium bowl with cold water.

Add half the sugar to a small heavy saucepan (1).

Melt it over medium heat, stirring with a wooden spoon (2).

Add the remaining sugar (3) and cook, stirring, until the color turns light amber and the mixture is smooth (4).

Remove the pan from the heat. The caramel will be very hot and will continue to cook. Let it stand until the color darkens. The best way to judge the color is to let the caramel run off the spoon (5).

Dip the saucepan in the cold water to stop the cooking (6).

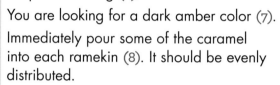

You are looking for a dark amber color (7).

Immediately pour some of the caramel into each ramekin (8). It should be evenly distributed.

Let the caramel cool completely.

Serves 8 Level: Easy Prep: 20 min. Cook: 1 hr. Special equipment 8 ramekins or custard cups	**Caramel** 1¼ cups (9 oz., 250 g) sugar **Vanilla Custard** 6 whole eggs 4 egg yolks 1 cup (7 oz., 200 g) sugar 1½ vanilla beans, split lengthwise, seeds scraped, or 1½ tsp. vanilla extract 4 cups (1 liter) milk

1 Pour half the sugar into a heavy saucepan.

2 Melt the sugar over medium heat, stirring with a wooden spoon.

3 Add the remaining sugar.

4 Cook, stirring, until light amber.

5 Remove the pan from the heat; the caramel will continue to cook.

6 When it is a medium amber color, dip the saucepan in a bowl of cold water.

7 This is the color and texture you are looking for.

8 Immediately divide the caramel among the ramekins.

9 Break the whole eggs into a bowl and add the yolks.

continued

Preheat the oven to 325° F (160° C). Line a large roasting pan with parchment paper.

Vanilla Custard

Break the whole eggs into a medium bowl and add the egg yolks (9).

Lightly whisk the eggs to mix (10). Whisk in the sugar just until it dissolves (11). Be careful not to whisk too hard; the mixture should not be foamy or lose its yellow color (12).

Add the vanilla seeds to the egg mixture and process with an immersion blender until smooth (13). Or use a whisk.

Gradually pour in the milk (14), while processing with the immersion blender.

Strain the mixture through a fine sieve (15) to remove any bits of egg.

Ladle the custard mixture into the ramekins (16).

Place the ramekins in the prepared roasting pan. Pour in enough water to reach ½ inch (1 cm) up the sides of the ramekins.

Bake for 1 hour, or until the custard is set.

Remove the ramekins from the roasting pan and let cool.

Run a thin knife around the custards (17).

Invert a plate on each ramekin and, holding the plate and ramekin together, carefully turn out the custard onto the plate; the caramel sauce will run out.

Remove the ramekin (18) and enjoy!

10 Lightly whisk the eggs to mix.

11 Pour in the sugar.

12 Whisk lightly, just until the sugar dissolves.

13 Add the vanilla seeds and process with an immersion blender.

14 Gradually pour in the milk, continuing to process.

15 Strain the custard.

16 Ladle the custard over the hardened caramel.

17 Run a small knife around each ramekin.

18 Turn the custard out onto a plate and remove the ramekin.

Flan à l'Alsacienne
Vanilla Flan with Apples

Pastry Cream

Pour the milk into a medium saucepan and add half the sugar (1).

Bring to a boil over medium heat.

Combine the flour, cornstarch mixture, eggs, and remaining sugar in a medium bowl (2). Whisk until smooth (3).

Whisk the hot milk into the egg-flour mixture (4).

Return the pastry cream to the saucepan (5) and cook over medium heat, whisking constantly, until it comes to a boil and thickens (6 and 7).

Remove the pan from the heat, press a piece of plastic wrap directly on the surface, and let stand at room temperature.

Serves 4
Level: Basic/Easy
Prep: 20 min.
Cook: 10 min.

Special equipment
4 individual baking dishes

Pastry Cream

2 cups (500 ml) milk
⅔ cup (4 oz., 120 g) sugar
1 tsp. all-purpose flour
¼ cup (1½ oz., 40 g) cornstarch
   mixed with 1 tbsp. vanilla extract
2 eggs

Filling

2 Honeycrisp or other baking
   apples
1 tbsp. (20 g) butter
2 tbsp. (¾ oz., 20 g) candied
   orange peel (page 452)
1 tbsp. (20 ml) orange liqueur

1 Heat the milk and half the sugar over medium heat.

2 Combine the remaining sugar with the egg-flour mixture in a bowl.

3 Whisk until smooth.

4 Whisk the boiling milk into the egg-flour mixture.

5 Return the pastry cream to the saucepan.

6 Cook over medium heat, whisking constantly.

7 As soon as the pastry cream begins to boil and thickens, remove from the heat.

continued

Filling

Peel, quarter, and core the apples. Cut each apple into 8 slices (8).

Melt the butter in a medium skillet over medium heat.

Add the apples and candied orange peel (9).

Cook, stirring occasionally, until coated with butter.

Cover (10) and cook until the apples are lightly browned and tender, about 5 minutes.

Add the orange liqueur, tilt the skillet, and carefully ignite (11).

When the flames subside, remove the skillet from the heat.

Preheat the broiler.

Divide the apples and candied orange peel among the baking dishes (12).

Spoon the pastry cream into a pastry bag fitted with a medium plain tip and pipe it on the fruit, filling the dishes (13). Or use a flexible spatula.

Broil on the top rack of the oven for 3 to 5 minutes, until the surface is lightly browned in spots.

Let cool slightly before serving.

8 Cut each peeled, cored apple into 8 slices.

9 Cook the apples with the butter and candied orange peel.

10 Cover and cook over medium heat for 5 minutes.

11 Pour in the orange liqueur and flambé it.

12 Divide the apples among the baking dishes.

13 Cover with pastry cream.

Crème Brûlée Vanille au Zeste de Citron Vert

Lime-Vanilla Crème Brûlée

Split the vanilla beans lengthwise. Scrape out the seeds with a paring knife (1).

Bring the milk and vanilla beans and seeds to a boil in a small saucepan over medium heat (2).

Remove the pan from the heat and let infuse for 10 minutes. Remove the vanilla beans.

Serves 4
Level: Easy
Prep: 20 min.
Bake: 1 hr. 15 min.

Special equipment
4 individual gratin dishes

2½ vanilla beans
1 cup (250 ml) milk
5 eggs
⅓ cup (2½ oz., 70 g) granulated
  sugar
1 cup (250 ml) heavy cream
½ lime
½ cup (3½ oz., 100 g) light brown
  sugar

1 Split the vanilla beans lengthwise and scrape out the seeds with a paring knife.

2 Bring the milk and vanilla seeds and beans to a boil in a small saucepan over medium heat. Remove from the heat and let infuse.

3 Separate the eggs and place the yolks in a bowl.

4 Whisk the sugar into the egg yolks.

5 Whisk just until the sugar dissolves. The mixture should not become pale.

continued

Separate the egg whites from the yolks (3), adding each to separate bowls. Reserve the egg whites for another use.

Whisk the granulated sugar into the egg yolks (4) just until the sugar dissolves (5).

Preheat the oven to 200° F (100° C).

Add the cream to the egg yolk–sugar mixture (6), whisking until smooth (7).

Whisk the cooled milk into the egg yolk–sugar mixture (8) until smooth (9).

Using a citrus zester, remove the colored zest from the lime in fine julienne strips, leaving the white pith. Or use a vegetable peeler and cut the zest into julienne strips with a knife.

Divide the zest among the gratin dishes.

Ladle the custard into the dishes (10).

Bake for about 1 hour 15 minutes, depending on the size of the ramekins, just until the custard is slightly wobbly. Let cool completely.

Sift half of the brown sugar in an even layer over the custards (11).

Using a kitchen torch, caramelize the sugar (12). Or broil the custards on the top shelf of the oven.

Sprinkle the crème brûlées with the remaining brown sugar (13) and caramelize again (14).

Serve immediately.

6 Pour the cream into the egg yolks.

7 Whisk until the mixture is smooth.

8 Add the cooled milk.

9 Whisk until smooth.

10 Divide the lime zest among the gratin dishes and ladle in the custard.

11 Sift brown sugar evenly over the cooked custards.

12 Caramelize the sugar with a kitchen torch.

13 Sift another layer of brown sugar over the top.

14 Caramelize again and serve immediately.

Poires Caramelisées à la Crème Chiboust au Citron

Lemon Chiboust Cream with Caramelized Pears

Caramelized Pears

Peel (1), quarter, and core the pears (2).

Cook the sugar in a medium skillet over medium heat, stirring with a wooden spoon, until it melts and turns a light amber color (3).

Add the pears to the skillet.

Cook them until coated with caramel on one side, 1 to 2 minutes (4), then turn (5) and cook until tender and caramelized on all sides. Remove from the heat.

Lemon Chiboust Cream

Soak the gelatin sheets in cold water until softened, 5 to 10 minutes. Squeeze dry.

Bring the cream, water, and lemon zest to a boil in a small saucepan over medium heat (6).

Separate the egg whites and yolks, adding each to separate bowls.

Add the 2 tbsp. (¾ oz., 25 g) sugar to the egg yolks (7), then the cornstarch (8).

Whisk just until the sugar dissolves (9).

Serves 6
Level: Basic/Intermediate
Prep: 25 min.
Cook: 10 min.
Chill: at least 30 min.

2 firm, ripe pears
2½ tbsp. (1 oz., 30 g) sugar

3 gelatin sheets (6 g)
½ cup (120 ml) heavy cream
2 tbsp. water
Finely grated zest of 2 lemons
4 eggs
2 tbsp. (¾ oz., 25 g) plus ⅓ cup
 (2 oz., 60 g) sugar
1 tbsp. (⅓ oz., 10 g) cornstarch

⅓ cup (2½ oz., 70 g) sugar

1 Peel the pears with a knife or vegetable peeler.

2 Quarter them and remove the cores.

3 Melt the sugar in a skillet and cook until it caramelizes.

4 Add the pears and cook until caramelized on one side, 1 to 2 minutes.

5 Turn the quarters so they cook and color evenly. Remove when tender.

6 Bring the cream, water, and lemon zest to a boil over medium heat.

7 Combine the egg yolks and 2 tbsp. (¾ oz., 25 g) sugar in a bowl.

8 Add the cornstarch.

9 Whisk just until the sugar dissolves.

continued

Whisk half the lemon cream into the egg yolks until smooth (10).

Return the lemon custard to the saucepan (11) and cook over medium heat, whisking constantly, just until it thickens (12).

Remove the pan from the heat and whisk in the softened gelatin until dissolved (13).

Whip the egg whites, gradually adding the remaining sugar (14), until they hold firm peaks.

Add one-third of the egg whites to the lemon custard (15) and whisk until smooth (16) to lighten the mixture (17).

Gently fold in the remaining egg whites with a flexible spatula (18).

Spoon the Chiboust cream into a pastry bag fitted with a large plain tip and pipe mounds into glasses or small bowls. Or spoon the cream into the glasses.

Divide the pears among the glasses.

Top with more cream (19).

Chill until the cream is set, at least 30 minutes.

Caramel

Just before serving, pour the sugar into a small heavy saucepan. Melt it over medium heat, stirring with a wooden spoon. Cook until the color turns medium amber.

Immediately drizzle the caramel over the Chiboust cream and serve.

Note: This dessert can be prepared in the morning to serve for dinner (make the caramel just before serving).

10 Whisk half of the lemon cream into the egg yolks.

11 Return the lemon custard to the saucepan.

12 Cook over medium heat, whisking, until thickened.

13 Remove from the heat and whisk in the softened gelatin until dissolved.

14 Whip the egg whites, gradually adding the remaining sugar, until they hold a firm peak.

15 Whisk one-third of the egg whites into the lemon custard.

16 Whisk until smooth.

17 This will lighten the custard and make it easier to combine with the remaining egg whites.

18 Gently fold in the remaining egg whites with a flexible spatula.

19 Fill the glasses, layering cream, then pears, and finishing with more cream.

Verrine au Lait d'Amande
Almond Cream–Rhubarb Cups

Rhubarb Compote

Soak the gelatin sheets in cold water until softened, 5 to 10 minutes. Squeeze dry.

Split the vanilla bean lengthwise and scrape out the seeds.

Place the rhubarb in a medium heavy saucepan and add the sugar (1).

Add the strawberries, cloves, and vanilla bean and seeds (2).

Squeeze the lemon juice through a sieve over the fruit (3).

Cook the fruit over medium heat, stirring with a wooden spoon, until very soft, about 5 minutes (4).

Add the softened gelatin (5) and stir into the fruit until dissolved.

Remove the cloves and vanilla bean. Transfer the rhubarb to a bowl and chill.

Serves 8
Level: Easy
Prep: 20 min.
Cook: 10 min.
Chill: at least 2 hr.

2 gelatin sheets (4 g)
1 vanilla bean
1 lb. (500 g) rhubarb, peeled and thinly sliced
¼ cup plus 2 tbsp. (3 oz., 80 g) sugar
3½ oz. (100 g) strawberries, quartered
2 whole cloves
1 lemon, halved

2½ gelatin sheets (5 g)
½ cup (100 ml) milk
⅔ cup (150 ml) almond milk
1 cup (250 g) heavy cream

1 Place the rhubarb in a heavy saucepan and add the sugar.

2 Add the strawberries, cloves, and vanilla bean and seeds.

3 Squeeze in the lemon juice through a sieve.

4 Cook over medium heat, stirring with a wooden spoon.

5 Stir in the softened gelatin until dissolved.

continued

Creams, Custards, and Puddings   119

Almond Cream

Soak the gelatin sheets in cold water until softened, 5 to 10 minutes. Squeeze dry.

Bring the milk to a boil in a small saucepan over medium heat (6).

Whisk the softened gelatin into the hot milk until dissolved (7).

Remove the pan from the heat and whisk in the almond milk (8).

Let the mixture cool slightly until it reaches body temperature (the same temperature as your finger).

Whip the cream until it holds a soft peak.

Whisk the almond milk mixture into the whipped cream (9).

Whisk until smooth (10).

Spoon the rhubarb compote into glasses or small bowls, filling them halfway (11).

Top with the almond cream (12).

Chill until set, at least 2 hours.

Note: If you like, brew sweetened green tea with mint and drizzle 2 or 3 tsp. into each glass.

6 Bring the milk to a boil over medium heat.

7 Whisk the softened gelatin into the hot milk.

8 Remove the pan from the heat and whisk in the almond milk.

9 Whisk the almond mixture into the whipped cream.

10 Whisk until smooth.

11 Fill the glasses halfway with the rhubarb compote.

12 Top with the almond cream.

Verrine Chocolat Blanc
White Chocolate Bavarian Cups

Bavarian Cream

Soak the gelatin sheet in cold water until softened, 5 to 10 minutes. Squeeze dry.

Finely chop the white chocolate and place it in a bowl.

Bring the milk to a boil in a medium saucepan over medium heat. Remove the pan from the heat and whisk in the egg yolk (1 and 2).

Return the saucepan to low heat and cook, stirring with a wooden spoon, until the custard thickens slightly (3).

It is ready when it coats a spoon; if you draw a finger across the back of the spoon, it should leave a clear trail (4).

Remove the pan from the heat and stir in the softened gelatin until dissolved (5).

Serves 4
Level: Basic/Intermediate
Prep: 20 min.
Chill: at least 2 hr.

1 gelatin sheet (2 g)
4 oz. (125 g) white chocolate
   (see *Note*)
½ cup (125 ml) milk
1 egg yolk
¾ cup (200 ml) heavy cream

Finish

8 oz. (250 g) raspberries
2 pink grapefruits

1 Bring the milk to a boil and whisk in the egg yolk.

2 Whisk until smooth.

3 Cook the cream over low heat, stirring with a wooden spoon, until slightly thickened.

4 If you draw a finger across the back of the spoon, it should leave a clear trail.

5 Remove the pan from the heat and stir in the softened gelatin.

continued

Pour the hot custard into the white chocolate (6).
Let the chocolate melt for 5 minutes (7) and then stir until smooth (8).

Whip the cream until it holds a firm peak. It should be smooth and shiny (9).
If the chocolate mixture has begun to set by this time, heat it very gently to melt; let cool. Scrape the whipped cream into the chocolate mixture (10) and fold it in with a flexible spatula (11).

Finish
Divide the raspberries among parfait glasses or small bowls (12).
Ladle or spoon the Bavarian cream into the glasses (13).
Gently tap each glass in your hand to settle the cream and chill until set, at least 2 hours.

Peel the grapefruits using a sharp knife and remove all the white pith. Cut between the membranes to release the segments. Drain the segments on paper towels.
Just before serving, add the grapefruit to the glasses.

Note: White chocolate is very sweet, so no additional sugar is needed.

6 Pour the hot cream into the chopped white chocolate.

7 Let the white chocolate melt for 5 minutes. Do not stir.

8 Stir with a wooden spoon until smooth.

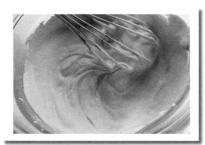

9 Whip the cream until it holds a firm peak.

10 Scrape the whipped cream into the white chocolate custard.

11 Gently fold in the cream with a flexible spatula.

12 Divide the raspberries among the glasses.

13 Pour the Bavarian cream over the raspberries.

Panacotta Vanille-Passion
Vanilla–Passion Fruit Panna Cotta

Measure and prep your ingredients and arrange them on the counter (1).

Panna Cotta
Soak the gelatin sheets in cold water until softened, 5 to 10 minutes.

Split the vanilla bean lengthwise and scrape out the seeds (2).

Bring the cream, vanilla bean and seeds, and sugar to a boil in a medium saucepan over medium heat (3).

Drain the gelatin and squeeze dry (4).

Remove the pan from the heat, add the softened gelatin, and whisk until dissolved (5).

Strain the panna cotta into a serving dish (6). Chill until set, about 3 hours.

Passion Fruit Caramel
Split the vanilla bean lengthwise and scrape out the seeds.

Combine the sugar and vanilla bean and seeds in a small heavy saucepan (7).

Cook over medium heat, stirring with a wooden spoon, until the sugar melts and turns a medium amber color (8).

Reduce the heat to low and carefully stir in the passion fruit juice to stop the cooking. Stir in the water (9).

Cook for 2 minutes, then strain into a heatproof bowl (10).

Let the caramel cool completely, drizzle it over the panna cotta, and serve.

Serves 4
Level: Easy
Prep: 20 min.
Chill: at least 3 hr.

Panna Cotta

2½ gelatin sheets (5 g)
1 vanilla bean
2 cups (500 g) heavy cream
⅓ cup (2½ oz., 75 g) sugar

Passion Fruit Caramel

½ vanilla bean
¼ cup (2 oz., 50 g) sugar
¼ cup (50 ml) passion fruit juice
¼ cup (50 ml) still mineral water

1 Have all your ingredients and utensils ready to go before cooking.

2 Split the vanilla bean lengthwise and scrape out the seeds.

3 Bring the cream, vanilla bean and seeds, and sugar to a boil.

4 Drain the softened gelatin sheets and squeeze dry.

5 Whisk the gelatin into the hot cream.

6 Strain the panna cotta into a serving dish.

7 Combine the sugar and vanilla bean and seeds in a heavy saucepan.

8 Cook the sugar over medium heat until it turns a medium amber color.

9 Reduce the heat to low and gradually pour in the passion fruit juice, then the water.

10 Strain the caramel and let cool.

Crème de Semoule Parfum d'Agrumes

Citrus Semolina Parfait

Measure and prep your ingredients and arrange them on the counter (1).

Serves 4 to 6 Prep: 15 min. Cook: 15 min. Chill: at least 2 hr.	Citrus Semolina Parfait 1 lemon 1 orange 1 vanilla bean 1 cup (250 ml) milk 1 tbsp. (½ oz., 15 g) sugar 1 tbsp. (15 g) butter ¼ cup (2 oz., 50 g) fine semolina ⅓ cup (80 ml) heavy cream	Apricot Compote ½ vanilla bean 5 oz. (150 g) pitted apricots ¼ cup (2 oz., 50 g) sugar

1 Have all your ingredients ready to go before cooking.

2 Grate the lemon zest.

3 Grate the orange zest.

4 Split the vanilla bean lengthwise and scrape out the seeds.

5 Pour the milk and sugar into a medium heavy saucepan.

continued

Citrus Semolina Parfait

Finely grate the lemon zest (2) and orange zest (3).

Split the vanilla bean lengthwise and scrape out the seeds (4).

Pour the milk into a heavy saucepan and add the sugar (5).

Add the butter (6), lemon and orange zest, and vanilla seeds and bring to a boil (7).

Gradually sprinkle in the semolina (8), stirring with a wooden spoon, until the semolina has absorbed most of the liquid and is soft (you will need to taste it) (9).

Remove from the heat and chill slightly.

Whip the cream until it holds a firm peak.

Scrape it into the semolina (10) and gently fold in until smooth (11).

Transfer to small bowls and chill until set, at least 2 hours.

Apricot Compote

Split the vanilla bean lengthwise and scrape out the seeds.

Place the apricots, sugar, and vanilla bean and seeds in a medium saucepan.

Cook over medium heat until the fruit softens, about 5 minutes (12).

Remove the vanilla bean. Transfer to a serving dish and let cool.

Serve the semolina parfait with the warm apricot compote.

6 Add the butter.

7 Add the citrus zest and vanilla bean seeds and bring to a boil.

8 Sprinkle in the semolina, stirring.

9 This is what the cooked semolina looks like.

10 Scrape in the whipped cream.

11 Gently fold the whipped cream into the semolina.

12 Cook the apricots with the sugar and vanilla bean and seeds over medium heat until softened, about 5 minutes.

Crème Diplomate
Orange Brioche Pudding

Using a serrated knife, slice the brioche about ¾ inch (1.5 cm) thick (1).
Dice the brioche slices (2).

Break the whole eggs into a large bowl and add the egg yolks. Whisk in
1½ cups (10 oz., 300 g) of the sugar (3).
Whisk in the orange liqueur (4).
Gradually whisk in the milk (5).

Serves 6 to 8
Level: Easy
Prep: 15 min.
Cook: 1 hr.

Special equipment
6 to 8 ramekins or other
individual baking dishes

8 oz. (240 g) brioche loaf
4 whole eggs
4 egg yolks
2 cups (13½ oz., 400 g) sugar
2 tsp. (10 ml) orange liqueur
4 cups (1 liter) milk
3 tbsp. (40 g) butter
2 oz. (50 g) candied orange peel
(page 452)

1 Cut the brioche into fairly thick slices with a serrated knife.

2 Cut the slices into dice.

3 Whisk the sugar with the whole eggs and egg yolks.

4 Whisk in the orange liqueur.

5 Gradually whisk in the milk.

continued

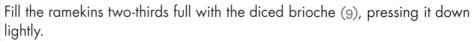

Preheat the oven to 350° F (180° C).

Melt the butter in a small saucepan or in the microwave oven.

Lightly brush the ramekins with the butter (6).

Add the remaining ½ cup (3½ oz., 100 g) sugar to the ramekins (7).

Turn to coat the bottom and sides (8). Tap out the excess.

Fill the ramekins two-thirds full with the diced brioche (9), pressing it down lightly.

Finely dice the candied orange peel (10) and divide among the ramekins (11).

Ladle the orange cream into the molds (12).

The brioche will absorb the liquid like a sponge. Add a little more orange cream to make sure the brioche is well soaked (13).

Place the ramekins in a roasting pan and pour in enough water to reach ½ inch (1 cm) up the sides (14).

Bake for about 1 hour. Insert a knife in the center and lightly press; if any liquid rises to the surface, continue baking. Let cool before serving.

6 Lightly brush the ramekins with melted butter.

7 Coat the ramekins with sugar.

8 This is what the inside of the ramekins should look like.

9 Fill the ramekins with the brioche dice two-thirds full.

10 Finely dice the candied orange peel.

11 Divide the orange peel among the ramekins.

12 Ladle the orange cream into the ramekins.

13 Let the brioche absorb the orange cream.

14 Place the molds in a roasting pan and pour in enough water to reach ½ inch (1 cm) up the sides.

Petits Pots de Crème
Little Custard Pots

Preheat the oven to 200° F (90° C).

Tea Custard

Bring the milk and cream to a boil in a medium saucepan over medium heat (1).

Whisk the egg yolks with the sugar in a medium bowl just until the sugar dissolves (2).

Remove the pan from the heat and add the tea (3). Whisk, and let infuse until cool, about 10 minutes (4).

Pour the cream into the egg-sugar mixture (5) and whisk until smooth (6).

Strain out the tealeaves (7 and 8).

Ladle the custard into the cups.

Serves 8
Level: Easy
Prep: 15 min.
Cook: 1 hr. 30 min.

Special equipment
8 custard cups or ramekins
(see *Note*)

Custard

1 cup (250 ml) milk
1 cup (250 ml) heavy cream
5 egg yolks
¼ cup plus 2 tbsp. (3 oz., 85 g) sugar

Flavorings

Tea: 2 tbsp. black tealeaves
Vanilla: 2 vanilla beans, split lengthwise, seeds scraped
Coffee: 2 tbsp. (20 g) ground coffee plus ½ tsp. (2 g) instant coffee

1 Bring the milk and cream to a boil over medium heat.

2 Whisk the egg yolks with the sugar.

3 Add the tea to the hot milk and cream.

4 Whisk and let infuse for 10 minutes.

5 Pour the flavored cream into the eggs.

6 Whisk until smooth.

7 Strain out the tealeaves.

8 This is what the tea custard should look like.

continued

Vanilla Custard

Bring the milk, cream, and vanilla beans and seeds to a boil in a medium saucepan over medium heat (9).

Remove the pan from the heat and let infuse until cool, about 10 minutes.

Whisk the egg yolks with the sugar in a medium bowl (10) just until the sugar dissolves.

Strain the cream into the egg-sugar mixture and whisk until smooth (11).

Ladle the custard into the cups (12 and 13).

Coffee Custard

Bring the milk and cream to a boil in a medium saucepan over medium heat.

Remove the pan from the heat, add the ground coffee and instant coffee, and let infuse until cool, about 10 minutes.

Whisk the egg yolks with the sugar in a medium bowl just until the sugar dissolves.

Strain the cream into the egg-sugar mixture and whisk until smooth.

Ladle the custard into the cups.

Finish

Transfer the custard cups to a baking sheet and bake for 1 hour 30 minutes, until set.

Let cool and serve.

Note: The traditional individual lidded porcelain custard cups used to make pots de crème are especially charming, but any small deep baking dishes can be used.

9 Bring the milk, cream, and vanilla beans and seeds to a boil.

10 Whisk the egg yolks with the sugar.

11 Whisk the flavored cream into the eggs.

12 Fill the custard cups.

13 This is what they should look like before baking.

Verrine Cappuccino
Cappuccino Custard Cups

Cappuccino Custard

Combine the milk, cream, and coffee in a small saucepan (1).

Bring to a boil, whisking, over medium heat (2).

Whisk the sugar with the egg yolks in a medium bowl just until the sugar dissolves (3).

Strain the coffee cream into the egg yolks, whisking (4).

Return the custard to the saucepan and cook over low heat, stirring with a wooden spoon, until the custard thickens slightly (180°F, 82°C) (5).

It is ready when it coats a spoon; if you draw a finger across the back of the spoon, it should leave a clear trail.

Finely chop the milk chocolate and place in a bowl. Pour in half the custard, stirring with a wooden spoon (6).

Pour in the remaining custard (7) and stir until smooth (8).

Pour the custard into glasses or custard cups (9) and chill until set, at least 3 hours.

Finish

Just before serving, peel the blood orange, removing all the white pith.

Slice the orange crosswise ⅛ inch (4 mm) thick.

Whip the cream until it holds a soft peak. Gently fold in the confectioners' sugar.

Spoon the whipped cream into the cappuccino cups and garnish with a slice of blood orange. Serve immediately.

Serves 6
Level: Easy
Prep: 15 min.
Chill: at least 3 hr.

⅔ cup (150 ml) milk
⅔ cup (150 ml) heavy cream
1 tbsp. ground coffee
2½ tbsp. (1 oz., 30 g) sugar
3 egg yolks
6 oz. (180 g) milk chocolate

1 blood orange
½ cup (100 ml) heavy cream
2 tbsp. (15 g) confectioners' sugar

1 Pour the milk and cream into a saucepan and stir in the ground coffee.

2 Whisk the mixture over medium heat.

3 Whisk the sugar with the egg yolks.

4 Strain the coffee cream into the egg yolks.

5 Cook over low heat, stirring with a wooden spoon, until the custard thickens slightly.

6 Pour some of the custard over the finely chopped chocolate and stir until smooth.

7 Add the remaining custard.

8 Stir until smooth.

9 Pour the cappuccino custard into glasses or cups.

Crème de Fromage Blanc
Fromage Blanc Creams with Fig Preserves

Measure and prep your ingredients and arrange them on the counter (1).

Fromage Blanc Cream
Soak the gelatin sheets in cold water until softened, 5 to 10 minutes.
Squeeze dry.
Place the egg yolks in a medium bowl (2) and add the sugar (3).
Whisk well (4) until the mixture becomes pale and foamy (5).
Place the gelatin in a bowl and melt in the microwave oven for a few seconds.
Add the lemon juice.
Whisk the lemon gelatin into the egg yolks (6).

Serves 6
Level: Easy
Prep: 20 min.
Freeze: at least 2 hr.

Special equipment
6 individual dome-shaped molds
or individual cups or ramekins

Fromage Blanc Cream

3 gelatin sheets (6 g)
2 egg yolks
½ cup (3 ½ oz., 100 g) sugar
1 tbsp. (15 ml) lemon juice
8 oz. (250 g) fromage blanc, ricotta
   cheese, or Greek-style yogurt
Finely grated zest of 1 lemon
1 ¼ cups (300 ml) heavy cream

Fig Preserves

⅔ cup (7 oz., 200 g) fig preserves
1 tbsp. water

1 Have all your ingredients and utensils ready to go before cooking.

2 Separate the eggs and put the yolks in a bowl.

3 Add the sugar to the yolks.

4 Whisk well.

5 The mixture should be pale and foamy.

6 Melt the gelatin and combine it with the lemon juice. Whisk into the yolk mixture.

continued

Whisk the fromage blanc into the lemon mixture (7).

Add the lemon zest (8).

Whip the cream until it holds a soft peak. Add the whipped cream to the fromage blanc mixture (9) and gently fold it in with a flexible spatula (10).

Ladle the fromage blanc cream into the molds (11).

Freeze until set, at least 2 hours.

Fig Preserves

Combine the fig preserves and water in a small saucepan and melt over low heat, stirring.

Just before serving, insert a paring knife into the base of each cream (12), remove it from the mold, and dip the rounded side into the melted preserves (13).

Let the excess preserves drip back into the pan (14).

Transfer the creams to plates and serve.

7 Whisk the fromage blanc into the lemon mixture.

8 Finely grate the lemon zest into the fromage blanc mixture.

9 Add the whipped cream to the fromage blanc.

10 Gently fold it in with a flexible spatula.

11 Ladle the cream into the molds.

12 Insert a knife into the base of each dome to prize it out of the mold.

13 Dip each cream into the melted fig preserves.

14 Let the excess preserves drip back into the pan.

Crème de Cheesecake
Creamy Cheesecake Cups

Preheat the oven to 350° F (170° C). Line a baking sheet with parchment paper.

Crumble Pastry
Place the butter, sugar, and flour on a work surface.

Squeeze the ingredients together with your hands (1), then knead when they begin to come together.

Using your fingertips, crumble the dough into small clumps (2).

Spread them on the prepared baking sheet (3) and bake for about 10 minutes, until golden. Let cool completely. Leave the oven on.

Cheesecake Cream
Warm the butter in a medium saucepan over very low heat (4) for a few seconds. Whisk just until it is very soft (5)—do not let it melt—and immediately remove the pan from the heat.

Whisk in the sugar and eggs (6).

Add the cream cheese (7) and whisk well (8).

The cream should be perfectly smooth (9).

Reserve about ⅓ cup (100 g) of the cream. Divide the remaining cream among the ovenproof bowls (10), filling them two-thirds full.

Transfer to a baking sheet and bake for 15 minutes.

Remove from the oven and fill the hollows that form with the reserved cream.

Bake for 5 minutes.

Let cool at room temperature. Do not chill.

Finish
Arrange some of the crumble pastry around each bowl. Drizzle 2 tbsp. of the strawberry puree in the center.

Serves 4
Level: Intermediate
Prep: 20 min.
Cook: 30 min.

Special equipment
4 individual ovenproof bowls,
ramekins, or cups

3 tbsp. (50 g) butter, diced
¼ cup (2 oz., 50 g) sugar
⅔ cup (2½ oz., 75 g) all-purpose flour

1 stick (4 oz., 125 g) butter, diced
¾ cup (4½ oz., 135 g) sugar
3 eggs
8 oz. (250 g) cream cheese

10 strawberries, pureed and strained

1 Squeeze the butter, sugar, and flour together with your hands.

2 Using your fingertips, crumble the dough into small clumps.

3 Spread the crumbs on a parchment paper–lined baking sheet.

4 Warm the butter over very low heat, whisking.

5 As soon as the butter softens, remove from the heat.

6 Whisk in the sugar and eggs.

7 Add the cream cheese.

8 Whisk it in well.

9 The texture should be completely smooth.

10 Divide the mixture among the bowls.

Verrine de Yaourt
Almond-Orange Yogurt Cups

Yogurt Cream

Soak the gelatin sheets in cold water until softened, 5 to 10 minutes. Squeeze dry.

Finely grate the orange zest. Cut the oranges in half and squeeze the juice (1).

Finely dice the almond paste and place in a small saucepan. Add the orange juice and zest (2).

Whisk in the confectioners' sugar (3).

Cook over low heat, whisking, until smooth.

Add the softened gelatin and whisk until dissolved (4).

Add the yogurt (5) and whisk until smooth (6). Remove the saucepan from the heat and let cool to lukewarm (see *Notes*).

Whip the cream until it holds a firm peak (7).

Gently fold the yogurt mixture into the whipped cream using a flexible spatula (8 and 9).

When the two mixtures are blended (there are no streaks), pour the yogurt cream into jars or cups (10).

Chill until set, at least 2 hours.

Garnish

Just before serving, peel the oranges, removing all the white pith. Cut between the membranes to release the segments. Drain them on paper towels. Add the orange segments and zest to the yogurt cups.

Notes: To speed up the cooling process before adding the whipped cream, place the saucepan in a bowl of ice water and whisk the yogurt mixture just until lukewarm. Do not refrigerate or the gelatin will begin to set.

The yogurt mixture should feel just slightly warmer than your fingertip; any warmer will deflate the whipped cream.

Yogurt Cream

Serves 4
Level: Easy
Prep: 20 min.
Chill: at least 2 hr.

3 gelatin sheets (6 g)
2 oranges
2 oz. (50 g) almond paste
¼ cup plus 2 tbsp. (2 oz., 60 g) confectioners' sugar
⅔ cup (180 ml) plain yogurt
½ cup (120 ml) heavy cream

Garnish

2 oranges
Finely julienned orange zest

1 Grate the orange zest and squeeze the juice.

2 Combine the diced almond paste, orange juice, and zest in a small saucepan.

3 Whisk in the confectioners' sugar.

4 Cook over low heat, whisking, until the almond paste melts. Whisk in the softened gelatin.

5 Whisk in the yogurt.

6 Continue to whisk until the mixture is smooth.

7 Whip the cream until it holds a firm peak.

8 Fold the whipped cream into the lukewarm yogurt mixture with a flexible spatula.

9 Work gently so as not to deflate the whipped cream.

10 Pour the mixture into jars or cups.

Tiramisu aux Fraises
Strawberry Tiramisu

Strawberry Coulis

Cut the strawberries in half and place in a food processor. Add the water, confectioners' sugar, and lemon juice. Puree until smooth.

Strain the coulis into a large shallow baking dish and chill.

Mascarpone Cream

Separate the egg whites from the yolks, adding each to separate bowls (1).

Add half the sugar to the egg yolks (2).

Whisk until pale and foamy (3).

Add the mascarpone (4) and whisk until smooth (5).

Whip the egg whites, gradually adding the remaining sugar (6), until they hold a soft peak (7).

Add one-third of the egg whites to the mascarpone cream (8) and whisk until smooth to lighten the mixture.

Gently fold in the remaining egg whites with a flexible spatula (9) until smooth (10).

Serves 5
Level: Easy
Prep: 20 min
Chill: at least 2 hr.

7 oz. (200 g) strawberries, hulled
2 tbsp. cold water
1 tbsp. confectioners' sugar
Juice of ½ lemon

3 eggs
½ cup (3½ oz., 100 g) sugar
1½ cups plus 2 tbsp. (375 ml)
    mascarpone

10 ladyfingers
14 oz. (400 g) strawberries, hulled

¼ cup plus 2 tbsp. (2½ oz., 80 g)
    sugar
A few drops red food coloring

1 Separate the eggs.

2 Whisk the egg yolks with half the sugar.

3 Whisk well until foamy and pale.

4 Add the mascarpone.

5 Whisk in the mascarpone until smooth.

6 Whip the egg whites, gradually adding the sugar.

7 Continue whisking until they hold a soft peak.

8 Whisk some of the beaten egg whites into the mascarpone mixture.

9 Gently fold in the remaining egg whites.

10 This is what the mascarpone cream should look like.

continued

Creams, Custards, and Puddings   151

Finish

Spread the ladyfingers in the strawberry coulis and let soak, turning them once, for 5 minutes (11).

Cut them crosswise in half (12).

Cut the strawberries lengthwise in half and arrange them, cut side out and tips up, against the sides of the glasses (13).

Spoon the mascarpone cream into a pastry bag fitted with a plain tip and pipe the cream into the glasses (14). Or use a spoon.

Top with a soaked half ladyfinger and add another layer of cream (15).

Top with another soaked ladyfinger (16) and drizzle with strawberry coulis (17).

Cut the remaining strawberries into small dice and scatter them on top. Divide the remaining cream among the glasses (18) and smooth with a thin spatula (19).

Chill the tiramisus for at least 2 hours.

Whisk the sugar with the food coloring until smooth. Sprinkle the tops of the tiramisu with the colored sugar.

Note: Please note that the finished recipe contains raw egg.

11 Soak the ladyfingers in the strawberry coulis, turning once, for 5 minutes.

12 Cut the ladyfingers crosswise in half.

13 Arrange the strawberry halves around the sides of the glasses.

14 Add a dollop of mascarpone cream.

15 Place a ladyfinger half on top and cover with another layer of cream.

16 Add another ladyfinger half.

17 Drizzle strawberry coulis over the top.

18 Fill with a layer of cream.

19 Smooth with a thin spatula.

Verrine d'Abricot
Creamy Apricot-Almond Cups

Apricot Cream

Soak the gelatin sheets in cold water until softened, 5 to 10 minutes.

Place the apricots and sugar in a medium bowl (1).

Puree the fruit with the sugar using an immersion blender until smooth (2). Or use a standard blender or food processor.

Combine the almonds with the syrup and water in a medium saucepan and process with an immersion blender until slightly grainy.

Warm the almond mixture over low heat.

Remove the gelatin from the water and squeeze dry (3).

Add to the almond mixture and stir until dissolved. Remove from the heat and let cool.

Stir the almond mixture into the pureed apricots with a flexible spatula (4).

Whip the cream until it holds a soft peak.

Gently fold the whipped cream into the apricot mixture with a flexible spatula until smooth (5 and 6).

Ladle the apricot cream into parfait glasses (7) and chill until set, at least 2 hours.

Finish

Melt the sugar in a small saucepan, stirring with a wooden spoon, over medium heat. Cook until the color turns light amber. Carefully add the butter; this will stop the cooking.

Add the apricot halves and stir until coated with the caramel.

Remove the pan from the heat and let the apricots cool slightly.

Arrange in the apricot-almond cups. Sprinkle with the chopped almonds and serve.

	Apricot-Almond Cream	Finish
Serves 6 Level: Easy Prep: 15 min. Chill: at least 2 hr.	2 gelatin sheets (4 g) 10 oz. (300 g) halved, pitted apricots ⅔ cup (4½ oz., 125 g) sugar ⅓ cup (2 oz., 60 g) blanched almonds 1½ tbsp. (25 g) almond syrup 2 tbsp. still mineral water 1¼ cups (300 ml) heavy cream	1 tbsp. sugar 1 tbsp. (15 g) butter 5 apricots, halved and pitted A few blanched almonds, coarsely chopped, for garnishing

1 Combine the apricots and sugar.

2 Puree them until smooth.

3 Heat the almonds-syrup-water mixture over low heat and stir in the softened gelatin.

4 Stir the almond mixture into the apricot puree.

5 Add the whipped cream.

6 Gently fold in with a flexible spatula.

7 Fill 6 glasses with the apricot-almond cream.

Crème Passion-Banane
Passion Fruit-Banana Creams

Measure and prep your ingredients and arrange them on the counter (1).

Passion Fruit Cream

Pour the juice into a medium saucepan and add the banana. Puree with an immersion blender (2). Or use a standard blender or food processor.

Whisk in the eggs (3) and sugar.

Cook over medium heat, whisking constantly (4), until it registers 200° F (90° C) on an instant-read thermometer and begins to simmer. Immediately remove the pan from the heat.

Whisk in the butter (5).

Process with an immersion blender until the mixture is smooth and shiny, about 1 minute (6). Or use a whisk.

Pour the passion fruit cream into Asian porcelain soupspoons or cups (7).

Transfer to a baking sheet and chill until set, at least 1 hour.

Serves 4
Level: Intermediate
Prep: 20 min.
Cook: 10 min.
Chill: at least 1 hr.

Passion Fruit Cream

½ cup (125 ml) passion fruit juice
½ cup (5½ oz., 160 g) mashed
 banana
5 eggs
¼ cup plus 2 tbsp. (3 oz., 90 g)
 sugar
1 stick (4 oz., 120 g) butter, diced

Spice Ruffle

½ tsp. ground cinnamon
½ tsp. ground allspice
2 sheets brick pastry or 4 sheets
 thawed phyllo pastry
3 tbsp. (40 g) butter, melted
1 tbsp. (⅓ oz., 10 g) confectioners'
 sugar

Finish

Confectioners' sugar, for sifting
½ banana, thinly sliced

1 Have all your ingredients and utensils ready to go before cooking.

2 Process the juice with the banana and cook over medium heat.

3 Whisk in the eggs and sugar.

4 Whisk constantly just until the cream simmers; remove from the heat.

5 Whisk in the diced butter.

6 Process with an immersion blender until smooth and silky, about 1 minute.

7 Pour the cream into Asian porcelain soupspoons.

continued

Spice Ruffle

Preheat the oven to 400° F (200° C).

Combine the cinnamon with the allspice.

Remove the paper between the sheets of brick pastry and stack the sheets. Or cover the phyllo sheets with a damp kitchen towel and work with one sheet at a time.

Brush the top sheet with butter (8). Sift confectioners' sugar, then the spices over the top (9 and 10) and transfer to a baking sheet.

Continue with the remaining pastry sheets, stacking them on the baking sheet. Bake for 7 to 8 minutes, until golden brown, and let cool.

Line another baking sheet with parchment paper.

Cut the pastry into irregularly shaped strips (11) using a knife or pastry wheel.

Transfer to the prepared baking sheet.

Finish

Just before serving, arrange the spice ruffle on the creams.

Sift confectioners' sugar over the tops and garnish with banana slices.

8 Butter the sheets of pastry.

9 Sift confectioners' sugar over the top.

10 Sift cinnamon and allspice over the top.

11 Cut out irregular strips of baked pastry.

Verrine de Fruits Rouges
Berry Mousse Cups

Berry Mousse

Puree the berries with the sugar in a deep bowl using an immersion blender (1). Or use a standard blender or food processor.

Strain the puree into a medium bowl, pressing on the solids (2). There should be about ¾ cup (7 oz., 200 g) of coulis.

Whisk one-quarter of the cream into the coulis (3).

Whip the remaining cream until it holds a firm peak. Gently fold it into the coulis with a flexible spatula (4) until smooth (5).

Spoon the berry mousse into a pastry bag fitted with a plain tip and pipe it into cups (6). Or use a spoon.

Chill for 1 hour.

Berry Topping

Measure and prep your ingredients and arrange them on the counter (7).

Quarter the strawberries. Combine the sugar and redcurrants in a medium bowl (8).

Place the strawberries in a fine sieve (9) and use the back of a ladle or soupspoon to crush them over the redcurrants. Toss the redcurrants with the strawberry juice (10).

Add the topping to the berry cups and serve.

Serves 4
Level: Easy
Prep: 15 min.
Chill: 1 hr.

Berry Mousse

8 oz. (250 g) assorted red berries
⅓ cup (2 oz., 60 g) sugar
1⅔ cups (400 ml) heavy cream

Berry Topping

3½ oz. (100 g) strawberries, hulled
2½ tsp. (⅓ oz., 10 g) sugar
1½ oz. (40 g) redcurrants, stems
  removed

1 Blend the berries with the sugar.

2 Strain the puree, pressing on the solids to extract the juice.

3 Add some cream to the coulis.

4 Whip the remaining cream and gently fold it in with a flexible spatula.

5 Continue until perfectly smooth.

6 Fill the cups.

7 Have all your ingredients and utensils ready to go.

8 Add the sugar to the redcurrants.

9 Place the strawberry quarters in a fine sieve.

10 Crush them through the sieve using a small ladle or soupspoon to make the topping.

Crème de Marron
Chestnut Cream Cups

Chestnut Cream

Scrape the chestnut cream into a medium bowl and chill.

Scrape the chestnut puree into another bowl and beat with a flexible spatula to soften (1).

Add the chestnut cream and rum to the puree (2) and beat well (3).

Press this mixture through a fine sieve into another bowl (4) to give it a more delicate texture.

Coffee Chantilly Cream

Whip the cream with the sugar until it holds a firm peak (5).

Place the instant coffee in a small bowl and add half the espresso (6).

Stir to dissolve the instant coffee; reserve.

Serves 6
Level: Easy
Prep: 20 min.
Chill: at least 1 hr.

Chestnut Cream

3 ½ oz (100 g) chestnut cream
(see *Notes*)
3 ½ oz (100 g) chestnut puree
(see *Notes*)
1 tbsp. dark rum

Coffee Chantilly Cream

¾ cup (200 ml) heavy cream
1 tbsp. sugar
1 tsp. instant coffee
¼ cup plus 2 tbsp. (100 ml) very
strong espresso, cold

1 Soften the chestnut puree with a flexible spatula.

2 Stir in the chestnut cream and rum.

3 Beat well.

4 Press the mixture through a sieve to make it more delicate.

5 Whip the cream with the sugar until it holds a firm peak.

6 Combine half the espresso with the instant coffee.

continued

Add the remaining espresso to the whipped cream (7) and whisk until smooth (8).

Spoon the chestnut cream into a piping bag fitted with a star tip and pipe into demitasse cups (9). Or use a spoon.

Add about 1 tsp. of the reserved instant coffee–espresso to each cup (10).

Add the Chantilly cream to the cups (11) and smooth the tops with an offset or thin spatula so the surface is perfectly flat (12).

Chill the cups for at least 1 hour before serving.

Notes: Purée de marrons *contains pureed chestnuts and water.*

Crème de marrons, *also known as chestnut spread, is made of chestnuts, sugar, and vanilla, and may also contain glucose and glacéed chestnuts.*

As a garnish, add 1 tbsp. of briar rose preserves to each cup.

7 Pour half the espresso into the whipped cream.

8 This makes espresso Chantilly cream.

9 Pipe or spoon mounds of chestnut cream into each cup ¾ inch (1.5 cm) deep.

10 Add 1 tsp. instant coffee–espresso to each cup.

11 Fill with espresso Chantilly cream.

12 Smooth the surface.

Verrine Chocolat-Framboise
Chocolate-Raspberry Custard Cups

Fill a large bowl with ice water.

Whisk the sugar with the egg yolks in a medium bowl just until the sugar dissolves (1).

Finely chop the chocolate and puree the raspberries (2).

Bring the milk and cream to a boil in a small saucepan over medium heat.

Whisk the milk-cream mixture into the egg yolks and sugar (3).

Return the custard to the saucepan (4).

Cook over low heat, stirring with a wooden spoon, just until the custard registers 180° F (82° C) on an instant-read thermometer (5) and thickens slightly.

It is ready when it coats a spoon; if you draw a finger across the back of the spoon, it should leave a clear trail.

Immediately transfer the pan to the ice water to stop the cooking (6).

Serves 6
Level: Easy
Prep: 20 min.
Chill: at least 2 hr.

¼ cup plus 2 tbsp. (3 oz., 80 g) sugar
4 egg yolks
7 oz. (200 g) bittersweet chocolate
   (60 to 70% cocoa)
10 oz. (300 g) raspberries
⅔ cup (150 ml) milk
5 tbsp. (100 ml) heavy cream

1 Whisk the sugar with the egg yolks just until the sugar dissolves.

2 Finely chop the chocolate and puree the raspberries.

3 Whisk the milk-cream mixture into the egg yolks.

4 Return the custard to the saucepan.

5 Heat until it thickens slightly (180° F, 82° C).

6 Place the saucepan in ice water to stop the cooking.

continued

Pour the custard into the chopped chocolate (7) and stir with a wooden spoon (8) until smooth and shiny (9).

Stir in the raspberry puree (10).

Process the custard with an immersion blender until smooth (11). Or use a whisk.

Strain out the raspberry seeds (12). This makes an extremely smooth custard.

Ladle the chocolate-raspberry custard into cups (13) and chill until set, at least 2 hours.

Note: Garnish the custards with halved raspberries and chocolate shavings, if you like.

7 Pour the custard into the chopped chocolate.

8 Stir gently.

9 This is the texture you are looking for: smooth and shiny.

10 Stir the raspberry puree into the chocolate cream.

11 Process with an immersion blender for extra smoothness.

12 Strain out the raspberry seeds.

13 Fill the cups.

Crème Chocolat Noir
Bittersweet Chocolate Custards

Finely chop the chocolate and place in a medium bowl.

Whisk the sugar with the egg yolks in a medium bowl (1) just until the sugar dissolves (2).

Bring the milk and cream to a boil in a medium saucepan over medium heat (3).

Whisk the hot milk into the egg yolks (4).

Return the custard to the saucepan (5). Cook over low heat, stirring with a wooden spoon, just until the custard registers 180° F (82° C) on an instant-read thermometer (6) and thickens slightly.

It is ready when it coats a spoon; if you draw a finger across the back of the spoon, it should leave a clear trail.

Remove the pan from the heat and pour one-third of the custard into the chopped chocolate (7). Stir gently with a wooden spoon (8).

Serves 4
Level: Easy
Prep: 20 min
Chill: at least 2 hr.

4 oz. (120 g) bittersweet chocolate
(70% cocoa)
2½ tbsp. (1 oz., 30 g) sugar
3 egg yolks
⅔ cup (150 ml) milk
⅔ cup (150 ml) heavy cream

1 Combine the sugar and egg yolks.

2 Whisk just until the sugar dissolves.

3 Bring the milk and cream to a boil over medium heat.

4 Whisk the hot milk into the egg-sugar mixture.

5 Return the custard to the saucepan.

6 Cook the custard over low heat, stirring with a wooden spoon, just until it registers 180° F (82° C) and lightly coats the back of a spoon.

7 Pour one-third of the custard into the chopped chocolate.

8 Stir gently with a wooden spoon.

continued

Continue stirring until smooth (9).

Add one-third more custard (10) and stir it in (11).

Add the remaining custard (12 and 13) to the chocolate and stir until the mixture is smooth and shiny (14).

For extra smoothness, process briefly with an immersion blender (15).

Use a small ladle to fill custard cups or ramekins (16).

Chill until set, at least 2 hours.

Note: Garnish the custards with curls of white chocolate, if you like.

9 Continue stirring until smooth.

10 Pour in another third of the custard.

11 Stir until blended.

12 Add the last third of the custard.

13 Make sure you have scraped all the custard into the chocolate.

14 Stir until perfectly smooth.

15 For extra smoothness, process briefly with an immersion blender.

16 Fill the cups.

Verrine 4 Chocolats
Layered Chocolate-Pistachio Cups

Finely chop the three types of chocolate and place in separate bowls (1).
Place the pistachio paste in a fourth bowl.

Whip 2 cups (500 ml) of the cream until it holds a soft peak and chill.

Bring the milk and remaining cream to a boil in a medium saucepan over medium heat.
Whisk the sugar with the egg yolks in a medium bowl just until the sugar dissolves.
Whisk a little of the hot milk into the egg yolks until smooth.
Return the custard to the saucepan and cook over low heat, stirring with a wooden spoon, just until the custard thickens slightly (2).

It is ready when it coats a spoon; if you draw a finger across the back of the spoon, it should leave a clear trail. Remove the pan from the heat.

Soak the gelatin sheets in cold water until softened, 5 to 10 minutes. Squeeze dry.
Add 1 gelatin sheet to the white chocolate.
Add the remaining gelatin to the pistachio paste (3).

Add one-quarter (3⅓ oz.; 95 g) of the custard to the bittersweet chocolate (4).
Repeat with the milk chocolate (5), white chocolate (6), and pistachio paste (7).

Serves 6
Level: Intermediate
Prep: 30 min.
Chill: at least 2 hr.

Special equipment
A digital scale
A small whisk

3¼ oz. (90 g) bittersweet chocolate
   (60 to 70% cocoa)
3¼ oz. (90 g) milk chocolate
3¼ oz. (90 g) white chocolate
1½ oz. (40 g) pistachio paste
   (see *Notes*)
2¼ cups (550 ml) heavy cream
1 cup (250 ml) milk
2½ tbsp. (1 oz., 30 g) sugar
3 egg yolks
2 gelatin sheets (4 g)

1 Finely chop the 3 types of chocolate.

2 Prepare a custard with the cream, milk, sugar, and egg yolks.

3 Add 1 softened gelatin sheet to the pistachio paste and the other to the white chocolate.

4 Pour one-quarter of the custard (3⅓ oz.; 95 g) into the bittersweet chocolate.

5 Pour one-quarter into the milk chocolate.

6 Pour one-quarter into the white chocolate.

7 Add the remaining custard to the pistachio paste.

continued

Using a small whisk, gently mix each of the four mixtures (8) until smooth (9), cleaning and drying the whisk between mixtures.

Add one-quarter (4½ oz., 125 g) of the whipped cream to the pistachio mixture (10).

Repeat with the three other mixtures (11).

Fold in the whipped cream with a flexible spatula (12, 13, 14, 15, and 16), cleaning and drying the spatula between mixtures.

Divide the bittersweet chocolate Bavarian cream among cups or glasses. Lightly rap the cup on the palm of your hand to settle the cream (17). You may need to chill the cups to be sure one cream doesn't blend with the next.

Repeat with the white chocolate, milk chocolate, and pistachio Bavarian creams.

Chill the cups for at least 2 hours before serving.

Notes: For homemade pistachio paste, chop 7 oz. (200 g) unsalted, shelled pistachios in a food processor. Add 5 tbsp. almond syrup and process until a thick paste forms, 5 to 10 minutes.

Work in a room that is not too cold so that the Bavarian creams do not set too fast.

8 Mix the bittersweet chocolate with a small whisk.

9 Whisk the remaining three creams until smooth.

10 Add one-quarter of the whipped cream to the pistachio cream.

11 Add one-quarter to each of the other three creams.

12 Gently fold the cream into the bittersweet chocolate with a flexible spatula.

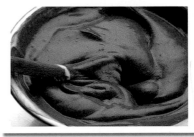

13 The mixture must be perfectly smooth.

14 Repeat the folding with the milk chocolate cream.

15 Repeat with white chocolate cream.

16 Repeat with the pistachio cream.

17 Fill the cups, rapping them lightly against the palm of your hand to even out each layer.

CO
RA
TION

Tempering Chocolate

Pastry chefs use couverture chocolate, richer in cocoa butter than ordinary chocolate, for their creations. The higher cocoa butter content means that it melts easily. You can find couverture at specialty stores or online at valrhona.com.

To be sure that your chocolate is glossy and has a distinctive snap, it must be tempered. Follow these instructions to make exquisite decorations.

First, finely chop the chocolate so it melts evenly. Place it in a bowl set over a saucepan filled with 1 inch (2.5 cm) of barely simmering water, making sure that the bottom of the bowl does not touch the water in the pan. (The heat would scorch the chocolate.) Alternatively, use a double boiler. Let the chocolate melt, stirring from time to time, until it is completely smooth and reaches the appropriate temperature using a chocolate or instant-read thermometer.

Bittersweet chocolate must register 131° F (55° C).
Milk chocolate must register 122° F (50° C).
White chocolate must register 113° F (45° C).

Pour three-quarters of the melted chocolate on a marble slab or other cold, perfectly dry surface (moisture is the enemy of tempered chocolate). Keep the remaining chocolate warm.

Working with a thin spatula, keep spreading and turning the chocolate to cool it to the correct temperature. Check with a thermometer.

Bittersweet chocolate must register 82 to 84° F (28 to 29° C).
Milk chocolate must register 81 to 82° F (27 to 28° C).
White chocolate must register 79 to 81° F (26 to 27° C).

Scrape the stirred chocolate into a slightly warmed bowl. Gradually stir in the remaining warm chocolate just until the proper temperature is reached. Check the temperature constantly.

Bittersweet chocolate must register 88 to 90° F (31 to 32° C).
Milk chocolate must register 84 to 86° F (29 to 30° C).
White chocolate must register 84 to 86° F (29 to 30° C).

When the correct temperature is reached, stop adding the warm chocolate.

If necessary at any stage, reheat the chocolate, preferably in a brief burst in the microwave oven.

For more details, see the tempering curves on page 363.

Cooking Sugar

Here is some advice on cooking sugar for caramel and sugar decorations.

Techniques

Gently stir the sugar and water, and always begin cooking on medium heat.

Remember to keep the sides of the saucepan clean: wash them with a heatproof pastry brush dipped in water.

When the desired result is reached, immediately dip the bottom of the saucepan in cold water to stop the cooking. But do not leave the pan for long or the sugar will thicken too quickly.

Cooked sugar is very hot and can give you a serious burn. Make sure children are well out of harm's way.

It's a good idea to wear clean kitchen gloves turned inside out to protect your hands; use these gloves only to make sugar decorations.

There are two methods to test the stage reached in the caramelization process:

Use a thermometer for an accurate result.

Scoop out a little cooked sugar and drop it into a bowl of very cold water. Remove the sugar and touch it with your fingertips. Interpret the result using the following table.

NAME	TEMPERATURE	TOUCH TEST AFTER REMOVAL FROM COLD WATER	USE
Syrup	212° F (100° C)	Coats the spoon	Basic syrup
Small thread stage	223° F (106° C)	Pulls into threads between fingers	Pâtes de fruit (Fruit pastes)
Soft ball stage	239 to 241° F (115 to 116° C)	Forms soft ball when rolled	Jams and jellies
Firm ball stage	248 to 255° F (120 to 124° C)	Forms firm ball when rolled	Italian meringue
Hard ball stage	257 to 262° F (125 to 128° C)	Forms hard ball that holds it shape	Marshmallows
Soft crack stage	266 to 284° F (130 to 140° C)	Threads bend before breaking	Candies
Hard crack stage	293 to 311° F (145 to 155° C)	Forms brittle threads that break when bent	Poured, pulled, spun, bubble sugar, etc.
Light caramel	311 to 320° F (155 to 160° C)	Light brown	Caramel coating for fruit, fritters, etc.
Caramel	329 to 347° F (165 to 175° C)	Dark brown	Crème caramel or flavoring

When sugar is cooked to the desired stage, be careful not to let it cook any further. It heats up very quickly and above 356° F (180° C), it smokes, blackens, and is too dark to use.

Storing sugar decorations

To keep sugar decorations for a few days, store them in an airtight container, preferably polystyrene. It is essential to minimize moisture—sugar's main enemy—as much as possible.

Place a moisture-absorbing agent at the bottom of the container (salt works well) and cover it with a sheet of parchment paper.

Ingredients

For decorative pieces, use granulated sugar or, even better, sugar cubes, because they contain the purest ingredients. Do not use confectioners' sugar.

If possible, use still mineral or filtered water. But tap water also works.

Equipment

Saucepan
You will need a medium saucepan, preferably copper, alternatively stainless steel, with a heavy bottom so that the sugar does not cook too quickly.

If you use a copper pan, clean the inside with table salt dissolved in white vinegar. Rub both the inside and the outside for an especially shiny pan. Rinse well under cold running water and dry with a clean kitchen towel.

Thermometer
Use a candy thermometer with a range of 170 to 400° F (80 to 200° C). Do not use a chocolate thermometer; the typical range is more limited (from about 50 to 250° F, 10 to 120° C) and it would soon be damaged. You can also use an instant-read thermometer.

Silicone baking mats
These baking mats are easy to find and make working with cooked sugar much easier.

Pastry brush
Use a perfectly clean heatproof pastry brush dipped in cold, clear water to clean the sides of the saucepan while the sugar cooks. This prevents sugar from crystallizing on the sides of the pan. Crystallized sugar gives caramelized sugar a grainy texture.

Almond Paste

There are two types of almond paste.

Cooked almond paste

This is the most common. It is a very pale color, the result of grinding blanched almonds and combining them with confectioners' sugar and sugar cooked to 243° F (117° C).

This type is available in varying proportions of almonds and sugar. Try to use almond paste with 33% (or even 22%) almonds for decorative pieces. It holds better than paste with 50% almonds, which is better for eating.

Almond paste is available with the following percentages of ground almonds: 22%, 33%, 50%, and 60%.

Read the label on the package before you start using it!

Raw almond paste

Raw almond paste is yellow to light brown, and is generally very soft. It is made with ground blanched almonds, granulated sugar, and confectioners' sugar. The percentage of almonds is indicated on the package.

Raw almond paste is generally used to make cakes.

Chips de Fraises
Strawberry Chips

Preheat the oven to 175° F (80° C). Line a baking sheet with a silicone baking mat or parchment paper.

Combine the confectioners' sugar and egg white in a small bowl (1).
Whisk until smooth (2). The texture should be pourable, but not runny. If necessary, add a little confectioners' sugar or egg white.

Hull the strawberries. Slice them lengthwise slightly less than ⅛ inch (2 to 3 mm) thick (3).
Arrange the most attractive slices on the prepared baking sheet (4).
Reserve the rest for another use.
Stir the rose water into the confectioners' sugar–egg white mixture, if desired (5).
Brush each strawberry slice with this mixture (6).

Bake for about 1 hour 30 minutes. Carefully remove the chips from the baking sheet to cool or they might break. They are very brittle once they have cooled.
Transfer to an airtight container.

Notes: Serve these chips to end a meal or use to decorate strawberry ice cream or Fraisier (page 284).
The crispness of the chips depends on the variety of strawberry and the thickness of the slices.

Makes about 2 dozen
Level: Easy
Prep: 15 min.
Cook: 1 hr. 30 min.

1½ tbsp. (¾ oz., 20 g) confectioners' sugar
1 egg white
6 large strawberries
A few drops rose water (optional)

1 Combine the confectioners' sugar with the egg white.

2 Whisk the mixture until smooth.

3 Hull the strawberries and slice them slightly less than ⅛ inch (2 to 3 mm) thick.

4 Arrange the most attractive slices on a lined baking sheet.

5 Add a few drops of rose water to the egg white mixture.

6 Brush the strawberry slices evenly with the mixture.

Chips de Pomme Verte
Granny Smith Chips

Preheat the oven to 175° F (80° C). Line a baking sheet with a silicone baking mat or parchment paper.

Cut off a rounded slice on the side of each apple (1).

Slice the apples vertically slightly less than ⅛ inch (2 to 3 mm) thick (2). Or use a mandoline.

Squeeze the lemon juice into a small bowl, add each apple slice (3), and turn to coat (4).

Arrange the slices on the prepared baking sheet (5).

Sift the confectioners' sugar over the apples (6).

Let the sugar dissolve (7).

Bake for about 1 hour 30 minutes. Carefully remove the chips to cool or they might break. They are very brittle once they have cooled.

Transfer to an airtight container.

Notes: Granny Smiths are best for making apple chips, as their sweet and tangy taste intensifies when dried.

These chips melt in your mouth, and there's nothing quite like them to end a meal.

Use the chips to decorate a holiday table; they make an unusual edible treat.

Try the chips with cheese or with green apple sorbet and a shot of Calvados or other apple brandy.

Makes about 1½ dozen
Level: Easy
Prep: 10 min.
Cook: about 1 hr. 30 min.

2 Granny Smith apples (see *Notes*), as similar in size as possible
1 lemon, halved
¾ cup (3½ oz., 100 g) confectioners' sugar

1 Slice off the rounded sides of each apple.

2 Slice ⅛ inch (2 to 3 mm) thick.

3 Dip them in lemon juice.

4 Turn to coat.

5 Arrange on a lined baking sheet.

6 Sift with confectioners' sugar.

7 Let the sugar dissolve.

Roses Cristallisées
Candied Rose Petals

Line a baking sheet with parchment paper.

Cut off the rose stem (1).

Hold the base of the rose in one hand and the petals in the other (2) so you can separate the petals cleanly (3).

Spread the petals flat on the prepared baking sheet. Discard any that are blemished or too small (4).

Place the egg white in a small bowl and the sanding sugar in a medium bowl. Dip the pastry brush in the egg white, wiping any excess on the rim of the bowl (5).

Carefully brush both sides of each petal (6).

For the most attractive result, brush the egg white in as thin a layer as possible.

Add the petals to the sanding sugar, cup side up, a few at a time (7).

Sprinkle with sugar to coat (8).

Tap each petal gently on your fingers to remove any excess sugar (9).

Repeat with all the petals, arranging them as you work on the prepared baking sheet (10).

Let dry out overnight in a warm room.

When the petals are dry, they will be very brittle. They can be stored for 1 month in an airtight container.

Notes: The rose can be any color. Pink is especially attractive.

Use candied rose petals to decorate Mother's Day and Valentine's Day cakes or to add old-fashioned charm to a cup of berry ice cream or custard.

Drizzle rose syrup over them to serve after a meal for a delicate treat.

Please note that the finished recipe contains raw egg.

Makes about 1½ dozen
Level: Easy
Prep: 15 min.
Dry: overnight, preferably

1 unsprayed rose (see *Notes*)
1 egg white
1 cup (7 oz., 200 g) sanding sugar

1 Cut off the stem of the rose.

2 Pinch the base with one hand and carefully remove the receptacle (inner core) of the flower.

3 The petals will separate.

4 Arrange the most attractive petals on a lined baking sheet.

5 Break the egg white into a small bowl and dip in the pastry brush. Wipe off any excess.

6 Brush a thin layer of egg white on both sides of each petal.

7 Place a few petals in a bowl of sanding sugar.

8 Sprinkle the petals cup side up to create an even sugar coating.

9 Lightly tap the petals on your fingers to shake off any excess sugar.

10 Arrange the petals on a baking sheet and let dry out overnight.

Copeaux de Chocolat Noir
Bittersweet Chocolate Cigarettes

Melt the chocolate and temper it according to the instructions on page 182. This is the ideal texture of tempered chocolate (1).

Make sure your work surface is clean and perfectly dry.

Pour a little of the tempered chocolate in a strip on the work surface (2).

Thinly spread it in a band using the offset spatula (3) until smooth and even (4).

Let the chocolate harden until set but still pliable.

The photo shows the difference between tempered chocolate and hardened chocolate (5).

Holding a chef's knife at a 45° angle, shave the chocolate off the work surface into tight cylinders (6).

If the chocolate hardens too much, warm it by lightly rubbing the surface with the palms of your hands. (7).

Continue making the cigarettes (8).

Transfer to a plate and let firm up completely, a few minutes, or arrange them directly on the cake to be decorated.

Notes: Start with a small quantity of chocolate until you get used to shaving it. And don't forget that practice makes perfect!

It's a good idea to close the kitchen window so that the chocolate doesn't set too quickly.

These cigarettes are extremely attractive on a chocolate cake.

You can also make them with milk chocolate; check the appropriate temperature for tempering on page 182.

Decorates 1 8-inch (20 cm) cake
Level: Easy
Prep: 20 min.

Special equipment
An offset spatula

10 oz. (300 g) bittersweet chocolate
(at least 55% cocoa)

1 This is what tempered chocolate looks like.

2 Pour out a little in a strip on the work surface.

3 Thinly spread it in a band with an offset spatula.

4 Make sure it is even and smooth.

5 This is the difference between tempered chocolate and hardened chocolate.

6 Hold the knife at a 45° angle and scrape the chocolate into cigarette shapes.

7 If the chocolate hardens too quickly, warm it a little with your hands.

8 Continue to cut the cigarettes. Let harden completely before using.

Feuilles en Chocolat
Chocolate Leaves

Melt the chocolate and temper it according to the instructions on page 182.
Line a baking sheet with parchment paper.

Paint the shiny side of longer leaves with the tempered chocolate (1 and 2).
If you want curved shapes, drape the leaves over a rolling pin (3).
If you have holly leaves, paint them on the back (4) for a neater result.
Be careful not to brush too thick or thin a coating of chocolate on the leaf (5),
which would detract from their natural look.

Arrange the leaves on the prepared baking sheet and chill until set, about 1 hour.
If the chocolate has not been correctly tempered, you will have to keep the
leaves in the refrigerator until using them.

If the chocolate has been properly
tempered, peel off the leaves from the
chocolate. Bend the chocolate leaf
slightly (6). This is what they should look
like (7).

Sift the cocoa powder generously over the
dessert or cake to be decorated (8).
Spread the cocoa powder evenly over the
top with a pastry brush to fill any gaps or
uneven spots (9).
Arrange the chocolate leaves on top (10).

*Note: A simple decorating technique is to
sift confectioners' sugar lightly over the top
of a dessert. Then embellish with chocolate
leaves.*

Makes about 1½ dozen
Level: Intermediate
Prep: 20 min.
Chill: 1 hr.

About 20 fresh, unblemished leaves, such as holly, bay, or other leaves with pronounced veining

7 oz. (200 g) bittersweet chocolate (50 to 60% cocoa)

Unsweetened cocoa powder, for sifting

1 Paint the leaves with the tempered chocolate.

2 Make sure the chocolate isn't too thin or too thick.

3 Drape longer leaves on a rolling pin to give them a slight curve.

4 Paint holly leaves on the back.

5 This is what they should look like. Let harden on parchment paper.

6 Carefully peel off the real leaves and slightly bend the chocolate leaf.

7 This is what the long leaves should look like.

8 Sift cocoa powder over a chocolate cake.

9 Spread the cocoa powder to hide any imperfections.

10 Decorate with the chocolate leaves.

Sapin et Feuille de Houx en Chocolat

Chocolate Christmas Trees and Holly Leaves

Melt the chocolate and temper it according to the instructions on page 182 (1).

Place a disposable pastry bag or a sturdy plastic bag, pointy side down, in a tall container, such as a glass measuring cup.

Fold the top over the rim as much as possible to keep the bag stable, and pour in the chocolate (2).

Gently twist the top of the bag, concentrating the chocolate in the bottom, and close with a clothes peg or bag clip (3) so the chocolate does not ooze up.

Line a baking sheet with parchment paper. Snip off a small tip from the pastry bag with scissors (4); the chocolate will start flowing.

Chocolate Christmas Trees

Pipe fine lines on the parchment paper, starting with a point at the top and making increasingly wide strokes (5). Keep the pressure on the bag even as you work and do your best to move steadily.

Pipe about 20 trees (6).

Chocolate Holly Leaves

Pipe pear shapes with a sharp tip (7).

When you have piped out 3 leaves, use a toothpick to draw out the prickly sides (8). Do not make more than three at a time or the chocolate will harden before you have a chance to draw the details.

Make as many leaves as you need (9).

Chill the decorations until hardened, about 1 hour, before using.

Makes about 3 dozen
Level: Intermediate
Prep: 20 min.
Chill: 1 hr.

10 oz. (300 g) bittersweet chocolate
  (at least 55% cocoa)

1 Temper the chocolate.

2 Fit the pastry bag over the rim of a tall container and pour in the chocolate.

3 Twist the top and close with a clothes peg or bag clip.

4 Snip off the very tip of the pastry bag.

5 Pipe the Christmas trees, starting with a point at the top and then making wide lines, working as smoothly as possible.

6 Pipe as many trees as you need.

7 For the holly leaves, pipe pear shapes with a sharp tip.

8 Pipe 3 holly leaves and draw out the sharp edges with a toothpick.

9 Continue making three at a time, working as delicately as possible.

Chocolat sur Plaque
Chocolate Bands

Preheat the oven to 250° F (120° C).

Chocolate Bands
Finely chop the chocolate. In a bowl set over a saucepan filled with 1 inch (2.5 cm) of barely simmering water, or in 30-second bursts in a microwave oven, melt the chocolate. Stir until smooth.

Place 2 baking sheets in the oven until fairly hot to the touch (113° F, 45° C). Remove 1 baking sheet from the oven and turn it upside down on a work surface.

Pour a small quantity of the melted chocolate on the baking sheet (1).

Spread it out with a pastry brush (2) as evenly as possible less than ⅛ inch (2 mm) thick. Reserve any excess (3).

This is what it should look like (4).

You can rap the sheet on the work surface to even out the layer of chocolate.

Chill until set, at least 1 hour. Repeat with the second warm baking sheet.

Chocolate Glaze
Bring the cream and sugar to a boil in a small saucepan over medium heat.

Finely chop the chocolate and place in a bowl.

Pour half of the hot cream into the chocolate. Let the chocolate melt slightly.

Stir with a wooden spoon until smooth.

Add the remaining cream and stir until smooth.

Stir in the butter until the chocolate is smooth and shiny. Let cool slightly.

Pour the melted chocolate on the cake to be decorated (5) and spread it over the top with the offset spatula (6).

Let the glaze set before decorating it.

Decorates 1 8-inch (20 cm) cake
Level: Intermediate
Prep: 30 min.
Chill: at least 1 hr.

Special equipment
An offset spatula
A triangular spatula

10 oz. (300 g) bittersweet chocolate
(at least 55% cocoa)

¼ cup plus 2 tbsp. (100 g) heavy
cream
1 tsp. sugar
3 oz. (85 g) bittersweet chocolate
(60 to 70% cocoa)
1 tbsp. (15 g) butter, finely diced

1 Melt the chocolate and let cool slightly. Pour a small quantity onto a warmed baking sheet (113° F, 45° C).

2 Thinly spread the chocolate with a pastry brush.

3 Remove any excess chocolate; the layer should be slightly less than ⅛ inch (2 mm) thick.

4 Lightly rap the baking sheet to smooth the surface.

5 When the glaze has cooled, pour it on the cake.

6 Spread the glaze with an offset spatula and let harden.

continued

Place the hardened chocolate sheet in a warm place until pliable.

If necessary, warm it up with the palms of your hands, but be careful not to apply any pressure (7).

Using the triangular spatula, scrape up a band of chocolate about 2 inches (5 cm) wide from the baking sheet, catching it with your hand (8).

Then guide it with a skewer or chopstick (9).

Scrape with the triangle (10) and simultaneously curl with the skewer (11).

This is the piece to use in the center of the cake (12).

Place it on the glazed cake (13).

Continue scraping bands off the baking sheet and arrange them around the first band (14) until the cake is completely covered (15).

Let harden in a cool or cold room and serve.

Notes: This decoration is by no means easy to get right on the first try, but it's worth practicing because the effect on a simple chocolate cake is spectacular.

Use a similar technique to make ruffles. Scrape off a band of chocolate just as you would for a plain band and lightly press the chocolate in the opposite direction with your finger to make a fan.

7  Bring the chocolate on the baking sheet to room temperature.

8  Using the triangular spatula, scrape a chocolate band off the work surface and catch it with the other hand.

9  Continue to curl the chocolate band with a skewer or chopstick.

10  Try to move the spatula and skewer at the same speed.

11  This will produce even bands of chocolate about 2 inches (5 cm) wide.

12  This is what the central chocolate band should look like.

13  Place it in the center of the glazed cake.

14  Arrange more bands around the central piece as you make them.

15  Cover the cake completely.

Spaghettis de Chocolat
Chocolate Spaghetti

Place 2 baking sheets in the freezer for at least 30 minutes before starting the recipe. Place a plate in the refrigerator.

Finely chop the chocolate. In a bowl set over a saucepan filled with 1 inch (2.5 cm) of barely simmering water, melt the chocolate. Check that it does not exceed 104° F (40° C) on an instant-read thermometer. Stir until smooth and the chocolate feels slightly cool to your finger (86° F, 30° C).

Place a disposable pastry bag or a sturdy plastic bag, pointy side down, in a tall container.

Fold the top over the rim as much as possible to keep the bag stable, and pour in the chocolate.

Gently twist the top of the bag, concentrating the chocolate in the bottom, and close with a bag clip.

Working quickly, place one baking sheet upside down on the work surface.

Snip off a very small tip from the pastry bag with scissors; the chocolate will start flowing.

Small Nests

Pipe a continuous strand, working back and forth across the length of the baking sheet (1 and 2). Keep the pressure even on the bag.

Let the chocolate harden just until pliable, a few seconds. Immediately pinch together the ends and slide a spatula under one end to loosen from the baking sheet (3).

Lift the strands from one end and twirl them into a nest (4).

Transfer to the chilled plate to harden completely, about 10 minutes.

Repeat to make as many nests as you need. If the baking sheet begins to warm up, use the second one.

Large Nests

Increase the space a little between the threads, and double the number (5).

Let harden just until pliable and you can push the threads together (6).

Pinch together the ends (7) and twirl then into a nest (8 and 9).

Let harden on a chilled plate, about 10 minutes, and then remove carefully.

Makes 4 small nests
Level: Advanced
Freeze: 30 min.
Prep: 20 min.

10 oz. (300 g) white chocolate

1 Pipe a continuous strand of chocolate, working back and forth across the cold baking sheet.

2 Make about 10 zigzags each way.

3 Wait a few moments, then push the ends together.

4 Twirl the strands into a nest.

5 To make larger nests, pipe more chocolate strands across the cold sheet.

6 Let harden until pliable and push the ends together.

7 Pinch the ends together.

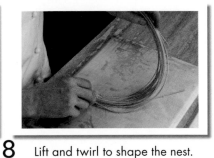

8 Lift and twirl to shape the nest.

9 Still working on the cold sheet, press both ends together to consolidate the nest.

Souris en Pâte d'Amandes
Almond Paste Mice

There are no precise measurements for modeling these mice. Make them different sizes to resemble a little family.

Knead one-third of the almond paste with enough of the cocoa powder to make a dark brown color. If it is too dry, add a drop of water.

Knead the white almond paste (1) until it is smooth and pliable (2).

Dust the almond paste and work surface with potato starch (3).

Roll the almond paste into an even log (4).

Roll out the brown almond paste into a smaller log (5).

Cut off the end of the white log, and then cut off a thick slice (6).

Makes a mice family of 4
Level: Easy
Prep: 20 min.

10 oz. (300 g) white almond paste
Unsweetened cocoa powder,
   for coloring
Potato starch, for dusting

1 Knead the white almond paste.

2 Knead until smooth and pliable.

3 Dust the almond paste and work surface with potato starch.

4 Roll two-thirds of the white almond paste into an even log.

5 Roll the brown almond paste into a smaller log.

6 Cut off the end, then cut off a thick slice.

continued

Roll the slice into a ball and pinch one side into a tip (7).

This is the body of one mouse (8).

Cut off 2 equal pieces of brown almond paste, roll each into a ball, and pinch slightly to make ears (9).

Press them into the body near the tip, slightly flattening them at the base (10).

Shape another small piece of brown almond paste into a ball and roll it between the palms of your hands to make a tail (11).

Attach it to the back of the body, giving it a realistic curve (12).

Use the end of a chopstick to lightly press below each ear to make spaces for the eyes (13).

Shape 2 very small balls of brown almond paste to make the eyes.

Note: Children can make these mice too—under adult supervision, of course!

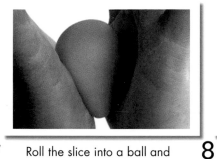

7 Roll the slice into a ball and then pinch one end to make a tip.

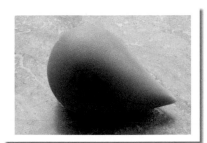

8 This is the body of one mouse.

9 Shape 2 small pieces of brown almond paste to make ears.

10 Lightly press them in above the nose.

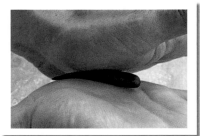

11 Roll the tail out of a small piece of brown almond paste.

12 Place it to curl over the back.

13 Using the end of a chopstick, make small indentations for the eyes.

Kong-Kong en Pâte d'Amandes
Almond Paste Gorilla

Knead two-thirds of the almond paste with enough of the cocoa powder to make a dark brown color. If it is too dry, add a drop of water.

Dust the work surface with potato starch.

Roll the brown almond paste into a ball (1). Cut off one-third (2).

Shape the remaining two-thirds into a smooth ball and pinch (3) and roll it into a pear shape (4).

Roll a small piece of the white almond paste and flatten it (5).

Place this disk on the rounded part of the pear shape (6).

Use the end of a chopstick to make a belly button in the white disk (7).

Makes 1 baby gorilla
Level: Easy
Prep: 20 min.

3½ oz. (100 g) white almond paste
Unsweetened cocoa powder, for coloring
Potato starch, for dusting

1 Roll the brown almond paste into a large ball.

2 Cut off one-third.

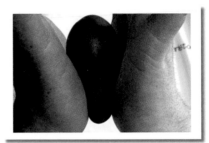

3 Use the larger part of the ball to form an elongated pear shape.

4 This is the shape you should have.

5 Roll a small white ball and flatten it between your hands.

6 Place it on the rounded part of the pear.

7 Press in lightly to shape the belly button.

continued

Cut the pear shape lengthwise in half, stopping just where it thickens (8) to make two arms (9).

Sit the gorilla up and mold the arms to the sides (10).

Using some of the remaining brown almond paste, make a small ball. Make a smaller white ball and stick it to the brown ball (11).

Lightly press together and place this head on the body (12). Use the end of the chopstick to make a mouth in the white ball.

To make ears, roll two small brown balls and indent them with the chopstick (13).

Attach the ears to the head, pinching them in at the base (14).

Roll a small brown ball for the nose and make indentations in the head for the eyes (15).

Finish the arms and legs: If you wish, change the position of the arms (16).

Shape the legs out of brown almond paste. Make smaller brown balls for the paws. Roll 6 very small white balls for the claws.

To make the eyes, roll 2 small white balls and 2 even smaller brown balls. Carefully insert the brown balls into small indentations on the white balls, and fit them into the head.

Notes: This animal is a little more complicated to make than the mouse, but it is certainly impressive.

If your first attempt is not quite what you're looking for, just try again!

8 Cut the long part of the pear almost in half.

9 This makes the arms.

10 Sit the gorilla on its base and mold the arms to its sides.

11 To make the head, shape a brown ball and then a slightly smaller white one.

12 Place the head on the top of the body and make an indentation for the mouth using the chopstick.

13 To make the ears, shape 2 small brown balls and hollow them out a little with the chopstick.

14 To attach the ears, pinch lightly at the base.

15 Make indentations for the eyes and stick a small brown nose on the mouth.

16 Arrange the arms as you wish. Make the legs with 2 more balls. Don't forget the eyes and the claws.

Plaquette Anniversaire
Happy Birthday Plaques

Almond paste can be sticky, so dust your work surface with potato starch (1).
Knead the almond paste until smooth and pliable. If it is too dry, add a drop of water.

Roll out the almond paste slightly less than ⅛ inch (2 to 3 mm) thick (2). If you prefer, roll it out on a sheet of parchment paper.
Cut out a leaf shape (3 and 4) and remove the excess almond paste (5).
Cut out other shapes if you like (6).

Decorates 1 8-inch (20 cm) cake
Level: Intermediate
Prep: 15 min.

Potato starch or confectioners' sugar, for dusting
3½ oz. (100 g) white almond paste
1 tbsp. Nutella or other chocolate-hazelnut spread

1 Dust the work surface with potato starch.

2 Knead the almond paste until soft and pliable and roll it out slightly less than ⅛ inch (2 to 3 mm) thick.

3 Cut out the shapes of your choice (here, a leaf).

4 Cut quickly to keep a neat shape.

5 Remove the excess almond paste.

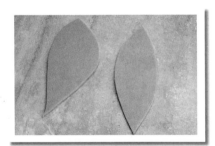

6 Make different shapes.

7 Cut a right-angled triangle from halfway along the bottom to halfway along the left-hand side. Fold the triangle from the point, bringing one side over the other. Flatten out the triangle, leaving a crease.

continued

Lesson 52

Parchment Paper Cone

Cut a rectangle of parchment paper. Turn it so a long side is facing you. Cut a right-angled triangle from halfway along the bottom to halfway along the left-hand side.

Fold the triangle from the point, bringing one side over the other (7).

Flatten out the triangle, leaving a crease where the paper was folded. Tightly roll the paper into a cone (8) using the crease as a guideline, and hold it with one hand.

Use the other hand to roll the small cone along the rest of the paper (9), holding the tip firmly so that it does not unroll (10).

There will be a point of paper sticking out over the top of the cone (11).

Tuck this point into the cone (12), and staple or tape it (13) so the cone does not unroll.

Scoop up the Nutella with the tip of a knife and place it in the cone, as close to the tip as possible (14).

Fold the top of the cone over once (15) and then fold it over again to the other side (16).

Snip off the tip off with scissors. Cut this very small so that just a thin line of the hazelnut spread will come out when you pipe.

Pipe the inscription on the almond paste leaves, keeping the pressure on the paper cone even as you work and do your best to write steadily (17 and 18).

Notes: Practice writing on a sheet of parchment paper until you get the hang of it before you start on the almond paste. It is a good idea to have a model in front of you, so write out your message by hand before piping it out in chocolate.

When you master the technique, you will be able to write directly on a cake or write in white using royal icing (page 262).

8 Tightly roll the smaller part of the paper into a cone, holding the tip firmly.

9 Roll the larger part of the paper over the cone, increasing its size.

10 Here is a tightly rolled cone.

11 There will be a point of paper sticking out.

12 Tuck it into the cone.

13 Staple or tape the cone together.

14 Drop in the chocolate-hazelnut spread into the cone from the tip of a knife.

15 Fold over the top of the cone.

16 Make another fold in the opposite direction so that it is on the other side of the visible line of paper.

17 Snip off the tip. Apply just enough pressure for an even stream of "ink" to flow out.

18 Write the message (here, *Joyeux Anniversaire*, Happy Birthday).

Décor "Smoking"
Formal Evening Attire

Chocolate Glaze

Bring the cream and sugar to a boil in a small saucepan over medium heat.

Finely chop the chocolate and place in a bowl.

Pour half of the hot cream into the chocolate. Let the chocolate melt slightly. Stir with a wooden spoon until smooth.

Add the remaining cream and stir until smooth.

Add the butter and stir until the chocolate is smooth and shiny. Let cool slightly.

Invert the cake to be decorated on a wire rack (1).

Place the rack on a baking sheet to catch any drips (2).

The photo shows what the glaze looks like when it is ready to use (3). It should be just slightly warm to the touch.

Pour the glaze over the cake (4) and cover it completely (5).

Use the offset spatula to smooth the surface and wipe off any excess glaze (6).

Lightly rap the rack on the baking sheet to even out the glaze (7).

Let set, preferably in a cool room. Or place it in the refrigerator, but remove it as soon as it hardens.

Decorates 1 10-inch (25) cake
Level: Intermediate
Prep: 30 min.

Special equipment
An offset spatula

Chocolate Glaze

1 ¼ cups (300 ml) heavy cream
1 tbsp. sugar
9 oz. (250 g) bittersweet
 chocolate (60 to 70% cocoa)
3 tbsp. (50 g) butter, diced

Bow Tie and Shirt

5 oz. (150 g) white almond paste
A few drops red food coloring
Unsweetened cocoa powder,
 for coloring
Potato starch, for dusting

1 Invert the cake to be decorated on a wire rack.

2 Set the rack over a baking sheet or a sheet of wax paper.

3 This is what the glaze looks like when it is ready to use.

4 Pour the glaze over the cake.

5 Cover it completely.

6 Smooth it with an offset spatula and remove any excess.

7 Lightly rap the rack to even out the glaze.

8 Roll out the red almond paste slightly less than ⅛ inch (2 to 3 mm) thick.

continued

Bow Tie and Shirt

Knead the almond paste until smooth and pliable. If it is too dry, add a drop of water.

Cut off about three-quarters of the almond paste and knead in a few drops of red food coloring.

Knead half of the remaining white almond paste with enough of the cocoa powder to make a dark brown color.

Dust the work surface with potato starch and roll out the red almond paste (8) slightly less than ⅛ inch (2 to 3 mm) thick.

Cut out a triangle (9 and 10) almost as long as the cake.

Fold over the two upper corners to create shirt lapels (11).

Roll out the remaining white almond paste slightly less than ⅛ inch (2 to 3 mm) thick (12) and trim it into a small rectangle (13), just long enough to make the bow tie.

Pinch in the center of the long side (14) to shape it.

Cut a very small white strip from the excess to make a knot and wrap it around the pinched-in center of the bow tie (15 and 16).

Roll the brown almond paste into 3 brown balls for buttons (17).

If you have set the bow tie in place to see the effect, remove it before transferring the shirt to the cake (18).

Place the bow tie at the collar (19), and the decoration is in place!

Notes: You can bake your favorite chocolate cake in the size recommended.

This decoration is excellent for Father's Day.

It would also be perfect on a white cake, for New Year's, for instance, when you could add festive almond paste streamers in different colors.

9 Cut out a triangle.

10 It should be almost as long as the cake.

11 Fold the top corners to shape shirt lapels.

12 Roll out the small piece of white almond paste.

13 Cut out a narrow rectangle.

14 Pinch it with two fingers in the center of the length.

15 Cut out a small strip to wrap around the bow tie.

16 This is what the bow tie should look like.

17 Roll 3 small brown buttons and position them on the shirt.

18 Remove the bow tie to transfer the shirt easily to the cake.

19 Position the bow tie at the collar.

Masquage
Almond Paste Masking

Buttercream

Break the eggs into a bowl and lightly whisk them to mix.

Set the bowl over a saucepan filled with 1 inch (2.5 cm) of barely simmering water, add the sugar, and whisk until the sugar dissolves.

Remove the bowl from the heat and beat with a hand-held mixer at high speed until lukewarm and fluffy, about 5 minutes. Beat in the butter until the buttercream is shiny and smooth, about 2 minutes. Reserve at room temperature.

Place the cake to be decorated on a flat disk, plate, plastic, or cardboard—anything you can manipulate easily.

Dollop a little buttercream on the cake (1) and spread it in an even layer over the top with a thin spatula (2).

Lift up the disk and spread more buttercream around the sides, turning the cake (3).

Completely cover the cake with buttercream (4), then set the cake on the work surface and smooth the top and sides (5). The buttercream should be perfectly even. Remove any excess.

Chill the cake.

Almost Paste Masking

Knead the almond paste until smooth and pliable. If it is very dry, add a drop of water.

Dust the work surface with potato starch (6).

Roll out the almond paste into a round slightly less than ⅛ inch (2 to 3 mm) thick and large enough to cover the top and sides of the cake (7).

Drape the almond paste over the rolling pin (8) and position it over the cake.

Decorates 1 8-inch (20 cm) cake
Level: Easy
Prep: 25 min.
Chill: 20 min.

Buttercream

2 eggs
¾ cup (5 oz., 150 g) sugar
2 sticks (8 oz., 250 g) butter, diced and softened

Almond Paste Masking

8 oz. (250 g) white almond paste
Potato starch, for dusting

1 Dollop a little buttercream on top of the cake.

2 Spread it out with a thin spatula; it should be perfectly smooth and even.

3 Hold the cake up with one hand and cover the sides, adding buttercream with a thin spatula as you work.

4 Continue until the sides are covered.

5 Smooth the top again, making sure the angles are neat. Remove any excess from the sides.

6 Knead the almond paste. Dust the work surface with potato starch.

7 Roll out the almond paste.

8 It should be slightly larger than the total surface of the cake, and slightly less than ⅛ inch (2 to 3 mm) thick. Drape it over the rolling pin.

continued

Gently unroll the almond paste over the cake (9), without pulling (10).

Smooth the top with your fingertips to remove any air pockets (11).

Shape the almond paste to the sides of the cake (12 and 13).

Carefully trim the excess and adjust it so that all the edges are clean and sharp (14 and 15).

If any of the corners tear, just pinch the hole together with your fingers (16).

Use a small piece of cardboard to help trim the edges and round off the corners (17). Slide it gently, applying very light pressure, and the almond paste will smooth itself out.

Gather the excess almond paste into a ball.

Dust the work surface again with potato starch and roll the almond paste into a long thin rope (18).

Gently press it around the base of the cake (19) without leaving fingerprints.

Tie the ends together in a pretty knot (20).

Chill the cake for 20 minutes to set the buttercream and serve.

Notes: This is a simplified recipe for buttercream, but it is excellent.

A heart shape is relatively tricky to mask; it is easier to cover a round cake as a starting point.

Decorate your cake with almond paste roses, candied rose petals, write "Mother" on the top using a parchment paper cone (pages 224, 190, and 212), and you will have the perfect Mother's Day cake.

9 Position it over the cake.

10 Unroll it little by little.

11 Smooth out any air pockets with your fingertips.

12 Shape the almond paste to the sides of the cake.

13 Continue all round the cake.

14 Cut off the excess paste cleanly with a knife.

15 Work as neatly as possible.

16 Pinch the angles together so they are smooth.

17 Use a small piece of cardboard to smooth the sides of the cake.

18 Roll the remaining almond paste into a thin rope.

19 Gently press it around the base of the cake without leaving fingerprints.

20 If you can, tie a small, neat knot.

Roses en Pâte d'Amandes
Almond Paste Roses

Knead the almond paste until smooth and pliable. If it is too dry, add a drop of water.

Cut the paste in half.

Dust the work surface with potato starch.

Roll one half of the almond paste into a log slightly less than ½ inch (1 cm) in diameter, and cut it into 8 equal pieces (1).

Join 2 pieces to make a small cone shape (2) to use as the base of the rose.

Roll the remaining 6 pieces into balls and slightly flatten them on the work surface (3).

Flatten them with the heel of your hand, leaving about one-third of the edge slightly thicker than the rest (4).

Lightly roll a lightbulb over the thinner outer edges of the petals (5), making very small movements (don't touch the bulb itself). Or use a fingertip (6).

Makes 2 roses
Level: Intermediate
Prep: 20 min.

Special equipment
A lightbulb

5 oz. (150 g) white almond paste
Potato starch, for dusting

1 Roll out half the almond paste into a log and cut it into 8 equal pieces.

2 Press 2 pieces together to make a cone shape.

3 Roll the remaining 6 pieces into balls and slightly flatten them on the work surface. These will be the petals.

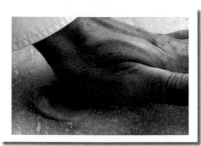

4 Then flatten them with the heel of your hand, leaving part of the rim thicker than the rest.

5 Use the lightbulb to thin the outer parts of the petal.

6 You can also use your fingertip.

continued

Lift the petals from the work surface with a small knife (7).

Wrap the first petal around the base of the rose (8), thicker edge down, taking care not to crush it. It should retain its petal shape.

Continue with the remaining petals, lightly pinching their outer edges (9) so that they look as real as possible.

Press them to the base, slightly overlapping (10).

Try to keep the shape as round as possible for an attractive result.

The photo shows what the finished rose looks like (11).

The next photo shows what a petal looks like before it is attached to the rose (12).

To finish the rose, trim the base with scissors (13).

Repeat with the remaining almond paste.

Notes: Try to make one or two roses just for practice; you will easily get the hang of it.

If the almond paste sticks to your fingers, dust them with potato starch.

It will be easier to place the petals correctly if you work with a photo of a rose.

If possible, work on a marble or granite work surface.

7 Remove each petal from the work surface with a small knife.

8 Press the first petal lightly around the cone.

9 Lightly pinch the outer edge of the other petals.

10 Place them one by one around the cone to imitate a rose.

11 This is what the rose will look like when all the petals are attached.

12 This is what a petal should look like before it is affixed to the cone.

13 Trim the base with scissors.

Nougatine
Almond Brittle

Preheat the oven to 350° F (170° C).

Spread the almonds on a baking sheet and bake for 5 to 7 minutes, until lightly toasted. Keep them warm.

Place the sugar in a medium heavy saucepan, preferably copper (1), and melt it over medium heat, stirring with a wooden spoon.

Cook the sugar, stirring, until it turns a light amber color (2).

Reduce the heat to low and add the lemon juice (3).

Cook the caramel until it turns a medium amber color. Check the color by letting some of the caramel drip off the spoon (4).

Add the warm almonds (5) and stir to coat them with the caramel (6).

Pour the mixture onto a silicone baking mat (7) or lightly oiled work surface.

Using the baking mat, shape the mixture into a ball. At this stage, it is extremely hot, so do not touch it (8). If you are using an oiled work surface, shape the mixture with silicone oven mitts or a wooden spoon.

Let the nougatine cool until it no longer spreads out on its own.

Roll it out with a heatproof rolling pin until very thin and smooth (9). Or cover it with a sheet of parchment paper and roll it out with a standard rolling pin.

Large Nougatine Cup
Place the sheet of nougatine in a heatproof bowl and immediately press in a slightly smaller bowl to shape it (10). Let cool completely before using.

Small Nougatine Cups
Have 8 heatproof cups ready to shape at the same time, because the nougatine hardens quickly. If it hardens too much, soften it in a 250° F (120° C) oven.

Makes 1 large nougatine cup or
4 small cups
Level: Intermediate
Prep: 20 min.
Cook: 10 min

1⅓ cups (4 oz., 100 g) sliced
blanched almonds
1¼ cups (9 oz., 250 g) sugar
5 drops lemon juice or 4½ tbsp.
(3½ oz., 100 g) glucose syrup

1 Stir the sugar in a heavy saucepan over medium heat.

2 Cook until the color turns a light amber.

3 Add the lemon juice or glucose syrup.

4 Let cook until the color turns a medium amber.

5 Add the toasted sliced almonds.

6 Stir to coat the almonds with the caramel.

7 Pour onto a silicone baking mat.

8 Use the baking mat to shape the hot almonds into a ball so you don't burn yourself.

9 Roll out using a heatproof rolling pin.

10 Use a 2 different-sized bowls to shape a large nougatine bowl.

Noisettes Caramélisées
Caramelized Hazelnuts

Preheat the oven to 350° F (170° C).

Spread the hazelnuts on a baking sheet and bake for about 10 minutes, until lightly toasted.

Prepare a steady base on your work surface. A small upside down bucket or a few dictionaries will be high enough.

Arrange the piece of polystyrene on the base so it sticks out on one side. Keep the polystyrene in place by weighing it down with a bag of sugar or flour.

Place a sheet of parchment paper underneath the polystyrene to catch the caramel as it drips.

Fill a bowl with cold water. Pour half the sugar into a medium heavy saucepan (1).

Melt it over medium heat, stirring with a wooden spoon (2).

Pour in the remaining sugar (3) and stir (4).

Reduce the heat to low and cook, stirring, until the sugar changes from a light amber liquidy paste (5) to a fluid, medium amber caramel (6).

Remove the pan from the heat and stop the cooking by dipping the bottom of the pan in the cold water. This ensures that the caramel does not continue to darken.

Pierce each of the hazelnuts with a toothpick, being careful not to crack any (7).

Dip the hazelnuts, one by one, in the caramel (8 and 9). Then insert the other end of the toothpick into the polystyrene to hang down (10).

The caramel will naturally drip from the hazelnuts, forming tips. If they are too long, trim them with scissors.

Let the caramel harden on the hazelnuts, then remove from the polystyrene.

Notes: Do not leave the saucepan in the ice water for long or the caramel will set.

Use these hazelnuts to decorate a cake or a chocolate mousse. They are quick, easy to make, and stylish.

Makes about 2½ dozen
Level: Easy
Prep: 20 min.
Cook: 10 min.

Special equipment
1 polystyrene rectangle, about
16 by 8 inches (40 by 20 cm)

3½ oz. (125 g) skinned hazelnuts
1 cup (7 oz., 200 g) sugar

1 Toast the hazelnuts and prepare a base, then pour half the sugar into a saucepan.

2 Stir with a wooden spoon until it melts.

3 Add the remaining sugar.

4 Continue to stir.

5 At this point the sugar is a light amber liquidy paste.

6 Cook the sugar to a fluid, medium amber caramel.

7 Gently insert the toothpicks into the hazelnuts, being careful not to crack them.

8 Dip the hazelnuts, one by one, in the caramel.

9 The caramel will have thickened by now.

10 Hang the hazelnuts from the polystyrene so the caramel drips, forming wispy tips.

Pièce de Décor
Decorative Sculpture

Combine the sugar and water in a medium heavy saucepan (1) and stir with a wooden spoon (2).

Bring to a boil over medium heat, washing down the crystals on the sides of the pan with a moistened pastry brush.

Add the honey. Attach the candy thermometer to the pan, making sure it does not touch the bottom (3).

Cook the sugar, watching carefully, until it registers 311° F (155° C), 10 to 15 minutes.

Makes 1 small decorative
sculpture
Level: Advanced
Prep: about 1 hour

Special equipment
An 8-inch (20 cm) pastry ring
A candy thermometer

2⅔ cups (1 lb. 2 oz., 500 g) granulated
sugar or sugar cubes
⅔ cup (150 ml) still mineral water
2 tbsp. mild honey, such as acacia
1 tbsp. grapeseed oil
Red food coloring
A few drops 95% alcohol or vodka

1 Pour the sugar and water into a heavy saucepan.

2 Stir over medium heat. Wash down the crystals on the sides on the pan with a moistened pastry brush.

3 When the sugar comes to a boil, add the honey and attach the candy thermometer so it does not touch the bottom of the saucepan.

4 Oil the inside of the pastry ring.

5 Crumple a sheet of foil.

6 Set the pastry ring over the smoothed-out foil.

continued

Base

Lightly oil the pastry ring (4).

Crumple a sheet of foil (5) and smooth it out.

Place the pastry ring on top (6).

Fill a bowl with cold water. Check the temperature of the sugar with the thermometer (7).

When the sugar is ready, remove the pan from the heat (8) and dip the bottom in the cold water until the sugar stops bubbling (9).

Starting at the center of the ring, gradually pour in about half of the cooked sugar, adding a few drops of the food coloring at the same time (10).

Fill the ring with a layer of sugar slightly less than ¼ inch (6 to 7 mm) thick (11).

Adding the food coloring to the sugar as it's poured creates a marbled effect (12).

Let the sugar cool completely.

Remove the pastry ring and carefully cut off the excess foil with scissors (13).

7 The temperature of the sugar should register 311° F (155° C).

8 Remove the saucepan from the heat.

9 Dip the saucepan in a bowl of cold water until the sugar stops bubbling.

10 Carefully pour about half the sugar into the ring, adding a few drops of food coloring as you pour.

11 Fill the ring with a layer of sugar slightly less than ¼ inch (6 to 7 mm) thick.

12 The food coloring will create a marbled effect.

13 When the sugar has cooled, carefully remove the pastry ring and cut off the excess foil.

continued

Bubble Sugar

Drizzle the alcohol on a sheet of parchment paper.

Return the remaining sugar to the heat and bring to a boil. Pour half of the sugar in a strip along the edge of the parchment paper nearest you (14).

Pick up the 2 corners of the parchment paper nearest you (15) and carefully lift them (16) to spread the sugar over the paper (17). It will form small bubbles.

Either leave the sugar flat or drape it over a rolling pin to curve it (18).

Let cool completely.

Sugar Flames

Reheat the remaining sugar gently over low heat and color it red. Let cook until slightly thickened.

Dip a thin spatula into the colored sugar (19) and spread it out on another sheet of parchment paper (20), making curved, flamelike shapes (21). Reserve a little sugar in the pan to use as glue for assembling the piece.

The photo shows what the flames should look like (22).

Let harden.

Assemble

Trim the base. Carefully prize the bubble sugar off the parchment paper. Break it into a few pieces. Use the sugar remaining in the saucepan to stick the bubble sugar and flames on the base. Be as imaginative as you like, but try to keep your sculpture light and airy.

Notes: This piece will brighten up a centerpiece and impress your guests.
You can also use bubble sugar and flames individually to decorate cakes.

14 Drizzle a few drops of alcohol over a sheet of parchment paper. Bring the remaining sugar to a boil and immediately pour half in a strip on the paper.

15 Take the 2 nearest corners of the paper.

16 Gently lift them up.

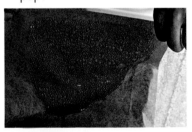

17 The sugar will spread and form bubbles.

18 If you wish, you can drape the hot bubble sugar over a rolling pin to curve it.

19 Color the remaining sugar and reheat it over low heat. Let thicken. Dip the tip of a thin spatula into it.

20 Spread it out over parchment paper.

21 Paint curved shapes with the thin spatula.

22 This is what the flames should look like.

Sucre Filé
Spun Sugar

Cover the floor below your work surface with newspaper. Arrange 2 wooden chopsticks on the work surface so they stick out over the floor, spacing them well apart. Keep them in place with books or a bag of flour.

Combine the sugar, water, and glucose in a heavy medium saucepan (1).
Bring to a boil over medium heat (2).

Attach the candy thermometer to the pan, making sure it does not touch the bottom.

Cook the sugar, watching carefully, until it registers 311° F (155° C), 10 to 15 minutes (3).

Occasionally wash down the crystals on the sides of the pan with a moistened pastry brush (4).

The photo shows what the cooked sugar should look like (5).

If you don't have a candy thermometer, dip a spoon in the boiling sugar, then immediately plunge it into ice water (6). When you remove it from the water, it should harden quickly to a brittle texture.

Fill a bowl with cold water. When the sugar is ready, remove the pan from the heat and dip the bottom in the cold water. Remove, add the red food coloring, and stir with a chopstick (7).

Let stand until the sugar stops bubbling and thickens, about 1 minute.

Dip 2 forks, back to back, in the sugar, letting some of the sugar drip back into the pan (8).

Still holding the forks together, quickly move them back and forth over the 2 chopsticks (9), making fine threads. Repeat 2 or 3 times before shaping.

Carefully gather the spun sugar with your hands (10) and arrange over the cake.

Note: This decoration is best made shortly before the cake is served, because spun sugar softens with humidity. If you make it ahead of time, store it in an airtight container.

Decorates an 8-inch (20 cm) cake
Level: Intermediate
Prep: 20 min.

Special equipment
A candy thermometer

1½ cups (10½ oz., 300 g) sugar
½ cup (100 ml) still mineral water
2½ tbsp. (1¾ oz., 50 g) glucose syrup
A few drops food coloring, preferably red

1 Combine the sugar, water, and glucose in a heavy pan.

2 Stir gently over medium heat.

3 Boil until the temperature registers 300° F (150° C).

4 Wash down the crystals on the sides of the pan with a moistened pastry brush.

5 This is what the cooked sugar should look like.

6 Scoop out a little sugar and drop it in ice water. It should be brittle.

7 Stir in the food coloring with a chopstick.

8 Let the sugar rest until the bubbling stops. Dip 2 forks, back to back, in the sugar.

9 Move the forks back and forth over the 2 chopsticks.

10 Shape the spun sugar with your hands.

Fleurs en Caramel
Caramel Flowers

Combine the sugar and water in a medium heavy saucepan and stir with a wooden spoon.

Bring to a boil over medium heat, washing down the crystals on the sides of the pan with a moistened pastry brush.

Add the honey and cook, watching carefully, until the color turns light caramel (see table, page 183).

Fill a bowl with cold water. When the caramel is ready, remove the pan from the heat and dip the bottom in the cold water until the caramel stops bubbling.

Drop about 20 teaspoonfuls of caramel onto a sheet of parchment paper, shaping them into small disks (1).

Drop about 60 mounds of caramel on more sheets of parchment paper.

Reserve the remaining caramel.

Pull out each mound with a spoon (2) to make petals.

Make petals of different sizes (3).

Depending on the pressure you apply, you can make them thinner or thicker (4).

Let harden (5).

Attach the petals to the disks (6), dipping the edge of each petal in the reserved caramel to make them sticky. Or warm the petals with the flame of a lighter. Be careful not to burn yourself!

Attach 3 petals to each disk (7) and let harden.

It may be necessary to soften the reserved caramel while you are working. Gently reheat it over low heat, stirring constantly; do not let it boil.

Note: This is a very simple but dramatic decoration. It's perfect for learning how to work with sugar. Be very careful, though, because caramel is super hot.

Makes about 20
Level: Intermediate
Prep: 25 min.

1 ¼ cups (9 oz., 250 g) sugar
⅓ cup (75 ml) mineral water
2 ½ tbsp. mild honey, such as acacia,
    glucose syrup, or 10 drops lemon juice

1 Drop about 20 teaspoonfuls of caramel onto parchment paper and flatten into disks.

2 Drop more caramel on the paper and pull out with a spoon to make about 60 petals; reserve the remaining caramel.

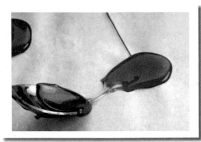

3 Shape each petal slightly differently.

4 Vary the pressure of the spoon for different shapes.

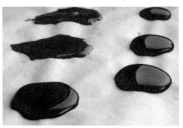

5 Let harden.

6 Dip each petal in the reserved caramel to make them sticky. Or warm an edge of each petal with the flame of a lighter.

7 Arrange 3 petals on each disk and let cool completely.

Fleurs en Dragées
Jordan Almond Flowers

Combine the sugar and water in a medium heavy saucepan and stir with a wooden spoon.

Bring to a boil over medium heat, washing down the crystals on the sides of the pan with a moistened pastry brush.

Add the honey and cook, watching carefully, until the color turns light caramel (see table, page 183).

Fill a bowl with cold water. When the caramel is ready, remove the pan from the heat and dip the bottom in the cold water until the caramel stops bubbling.

Drop small dots of caramel on a sheet of parchment paper (1)

Make as many dots as you want flowers (2). These are the bases of your flowers.

If you intend to use caramel for the centers of the flowers, make the appropriate number of smaller dots.

Let harden. Reserve the remaining caramel.

Dip the base of each almond in the reserved caramel (3).

Attach the almond to the hardened bases (4).

It may be necessary to soften the reserved caramel while you are working. Gently reheat it over low heat, stirring constantly; do not let it boil.

Attach at least 3 almonds for each flower, more for bigger flowers (5).

For the centers of the flowers, stick a smaller dot of caramel (6) or an almond of another color (7). Vary the shapes and sizes.

Let set completely.

Makes about 20	1 ¼ cups (9 oz., 250 g) sugar
Level: Easy	⅓ cup (75 ml) still mineral water
Prep: 25 min.	1 tbsp. mild honey, such as acacia, glucose syrup, or 4 drops lemon juice
	At least 60 Jordan almonds, more for larger flowers

1 Drop small dots of caramel from a spoon.

2 Make as many dots as you want flowers. If using caramel for the centers, drop out the appropriate number of smaller dots.

3 Dip the base of each almond in reserved caramel.

4 Attach it, at a slight angle, to the base.

5 Stick at least three almonds to each base.

6 Add a smaller dot to the center of each flower.

7 Or use almonds of a different color to make the centers.

Branche Caramel
Caramel Twigs

Fill a bowl with cold water. Pour half the sugar into a medium heavy saucepan. Melt it over medium heat, stirring with a wooden spoon. Stir in the remaining sugar. Reduce the heat to low and cook, stirring, until the sugar changes from a light amber liquidy paste to a fluid, medium amber caramel.

Remove the pan from the heat and stop the cooking by dipping the bottom of the pan in the cold water.

Stir in the food coloring (1). It should be the color shown in photo (2).

Makes 1 piece
Level: Easy
Prep: about 30 min.

Special equipment
A 7-inch (16 to 18 cm)
pastry ring

2 cups (14 oz., 400 g) sugar
A few drops red food coloring
2 small dry twigs, with very few leaves

1 Stir the red food coloring into the caramel.

2 This is the color you are looking for.

3 Place the twigs on the parchment paper.

4 Dip a spoon into the colored caramel.

5 Drizzle it carefully over the twigs.

6 Coat completely, turning them over carefully so you don't burn yourself.

continued

Place a twig on a sheet of parchment paper (3) and dip a spoon into the colored caramel (4). Drizzle the caramel over the branch (5), coating it completely (6).

Being very careful not to burn yourself with the hot caramel, turn the twig over and coat the other side.

Line a baking sheet with a silicone mat or parchment paper.

Set the pastry ring on the prepared baking sheet and pour in the remaining caramel (7); reserve a little for attaching the twigs later.

The surface must be perfectly smooth (8).

Let cool completely, about 10 minutes. This is your base.

Carefully remove the ring (9).

Gently reheat the reserved caramel over low heat, stirring constantly; do not let it boil (10).

Dip the bases of the twigs in the softened caramel (11) and arrange them on the base (12, 13, and 14).

Carefully transfer the decoration to a baking sheet or flat plate for transporting.

Note: Use this decoration for your table during the holidays, combined with other decorations, such as almond paste roses or chocolate leaves. And why not add a mouse?

7 Set the ring on the lined baking sheet and fill it with caramel, reserving a little in the pan.

8 The surface must be perfectly smooth. Let harden for about 10 minutes.

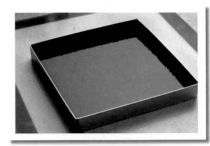

9 Carefully remove the ring.

10 Gently reheat the caramel in the saucepan and dip in the bases of the twigs.

11 Attach the twigs to the caramel square.

12 Attach one twig.

13 Then attach the other.

14 Touch up any bald spots with more caramel.

Rose en Sucre Tiré
Pulled Sugar Rose

Fill a bowl with cold water. Lay a silicone baking mat on your work surface.

Combine the sugar cubes and water in a medium heavy saucepan (1) and stir (2).

Bring to a boil over medium heat, washing down the crystals on the sides of the pan with a moistened pastry brush (3).

Make sure that the sugar cooking near the sides of the saucepan does not change color (4).

Add the lemon juice (5). This will make it easier to work the sugar later.

Attach the candy thermometer to the pan, making sure it does not touch the bottom.

Makes about 5 roses
Level: Advanced
Prep: 45 min.

Special equipment
Silicone baking mat
A candy thermometer with a
range up to 356° F (180° C)
A sugar lamp (see *Notes*)

1 lb. 2 oz. (500 g) sugar cubes
¾ cup (200 ml) still mineral water
½ tsp. lemon juice
Red food coloring

1 Combine the sugar cubes and water in a heavy saucepan.

2 Stir gently.

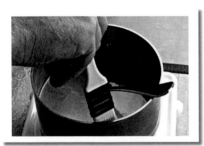

3 Wash down the crystals on the sides of the pan with a moistened pastry brush.

4 The sugar must not change color as it cooks.

5 When it boils, add the lemon juice.

6 Add as much food coloring as you need to make the roses.

7 Moisten the edges of the pan again if there are any sugar crystals.

8 Continue cooking to 300° F (148 to 150° C).

continued

Add enough of the food coloring so you have the color you want (6). Again, clean the sides of the pan with the pastry brush (7).

Check the temperature. It should not exceed 300° F (148 to 150° C) (8).

When the sugar is ready, remove the pan from the heat and dip the bottom in the cold water until the sugar stops bubbling.

Carefully pour the sugar on the center of the baking mat (9).

When the sugar begins to thicken, use the mat to fold in the edges of the sugar and gather the sugar together (10).

Fold it over (11) to make a ball (12).

The sugar will continue to spread; you must gather it together again once or twice before beginning to shape it.

Put on rubber gloves to continue working the sugar. Check the consistency (13): if it is fairly firm and no longer spreads, it is ready.

Pull it (14) and fold it over itself; it will become satiny (15). The color will lighten and it will become shiny.

Do not overwork it at this stage otherwise it will lose its shine, so stop pulling and folding as soon as it is uniformly shiny (16).

9 Pour the cooked sugar in the center of a silicone baking mat. Put on gloves to protect your hands.

10 Let the sugar thicken briefly and begin to fold in the edges.

11 Fold the baking mat over the sugar to help shape a ball.

12 Gather the sugar together into a ball.

13 Continue working it into a solid mass so that it does not spread. It must become firm.

14 When it is cool enough, begin stretching it.

15 Fold it over on itself so it becomes satiny.

16 This is what it looks like when it is smooth and shiny. Cut off a few small pieces and shape them into cones.

continued

Place the sugar under the sugar lamp switched to medium heat.

Cut off 2 small pieces and mold them into cone shapes to use as the base of the roses.

Stretch the sugar to one side (17) to make it thinner. Pull it into a round shape (18) and cut it with scissors (19) to form a petal shape. Fold it over lightly (20).

Wrap this folded petal around the cone to make the bud of the rose (21).

Repeat to make 3 or 4 more petals, depending on their size, to wrap around the bud (22).

Then make another petal but do not fold it; instead, curve it lightly (23) to give it a natural shape.

Make a few more petals (24). Let them harden and then stick them to the flower by melting them very lightly at their base with the flame of a lighter (25).

When the rose is the desired size (26), place it on a smooth, clean surface and let cool.

Keep the remaining sugar under the lamp so it can be easily manipulated.

Notes: Working with sugar is fairly complicated and takes practice, but the result is well worth it and will add another dimension to your cakes and pièces montées (classic cakes for celebrations, like weddings).

It's best to use sugar cubes, as they contain fewer impurities than confectioners' sugar or other forms of granulated sugar.

A sugar lamp is useful for keeping sugar at the right temperature to be worked. It is available at kitchen supply stores. A very powerful lightbulb will also do the trick.

Alternatively, place the cooked sugar in the microwave oven for a few seconds.

It will be easier to place the petals correctly if you work with a photo of a rose.

17 Place the sugar under a lamp at medium heat and stretch it to one side to make it thinner.

18 Pull it into a small round shape.

19 Cut it to shape a petal.

20 Fold it over lightly.

21 Wrap it around one of the cones.

22 Wrap 3 or 4 petals around the cone to make the bud.

23 Shape the outside petals without folding them; instead, give them a slight curve.

24 This is what the petals should look like. Let harden.

25 Soften the base slightly with the flame of a lighter.

26 Attach the petal to the flower. Add enough petals to make the desired size.

Pastillage
Pastillage

Soak the gelatin sheet in cold water until softened, 5 to 10 minutes. Squeeze dry.

Sift the confectioners' sugar into a bowl (1) with the potato starch (2).

Melt the softened gelatin in a small saucepan over very low heat (3). Or melt briefly in a bowl in the microwave oven.

Stir in the water and lemon juice (4) until smooth.

Stir the gelatin into the confectioners' sugar with a wooden spoon (5).

Beat well (6) until it forms a paste. Pour the paste onto your work surface.

Makes about 20 leaves
Level: Easy
Prep: 20 min.
Chill: about 1 hr.
Dry: Overnight

Special equipment
Shaped cookie cutters

1 gelatin sheet (2 g)
2 cups (9 oz., 250 g) confectioners'
  sugar
2½ tbsp. (1 oz., 25 g) potato starch
1 tbsp. plus 1 tsp. (20 ml) water
2 tsp. lemon juice
All-purpose flour, for shaping the leaves

1 Sift the confectioners' sugar.

2 Sift in the potato starch.

3 Heat the gelatin over very low heat in a saucepan.

4 Add the water and lemon juice.

5 When the mixture is smooth, stir it into the sifted ingredients.

6 Beat well until it forms a paste.

continued

Using the heel of your hand, scrape the paste on the work surface in a sliding motion (7) until it is smooth.

Flatten the paste into a square (8).

Cover it with plastic and chill until firm, about 1 hour (9).

Place the flour in a bowl.

Dust the work surface with potato starch (10) and cut off a piece of pastillage. Wrap up the remaining paste so it does not dry out.

Roll out the piece of pastillage (11) slightly less than ⅛ inch (2 to 3 mm) thick (12).

Cut it into leaf shapes (13), making quick cuts with a sharp paring knife.

Remove the excess pastillage (14) and press it into a ball. Cover immediately with plastic wrap.

Score the veins on the leaves with the back of a knife (15).

Place them on the flour in the bowl and using the flour as a soft support, curl the leaves slightly to give them a natural shape (16). Let dry overnight.

You can also cut out shapes with cookie cutters (17) and make openwork patterns, using pastry tips, for example (18).

Let dry overnight before using.

Notes: Pastillage has many uses. Make leaves, plaques for greetings, and shape it into fruit, using it like almond paste.

These leaves are very easy to make. Use them to decorate fruit tarts, fruit-filled cakes, and plated desserts. You can even use them for grand pièces montées (see page 212).

Store pastillage tightly wrapped in the refrigerator until you use it. It keeps well.

Heat it for just a few seconds in the microwave oven before using.

7 Scrape the paste on the work surface in a sliding motion with the heel of your hand.

8 Flatten it into a square and cover with plastic wrap.

9 Wrap it tightly before chilling.

10 Dust the work surface with potato starch.

11 Cut off the quantity you will need and roll it out.

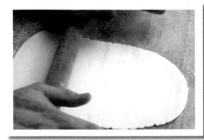

12 Roll it out slightly less than ⅛ inch (2 to 3 mm) thick.

13 Cut out leaf shapes.

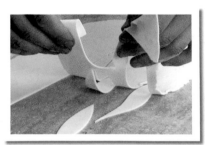

14 Remove the excess. Gather it into a ball and wrap it.

15 Using the back of a knife, score the veins of the leaves.

16 Place the leaves over the flour, applying a little pressure to give them a natural shape.

17 You can also cut out shapes with cookie cutters.

18 Make open work patterns with pastry tips.

Champignons Meringués
Meringue Mushrooms

Preheat the oven to 175° F (80° C). Line 2 baking sheets with parchment paper.

In a bowl set over a saucepan filled with 1 inch (2.5 cm) of barely simmering water, combine the egg whites and sugar (1). Begin whisking and whisk until the mixture turns white (2) and registers 113 to 122° F (45 to 50° C) on a candy thermometer (3).

Remove the bowl from the heat and continue beating with a hand-held mixer (4) until the meringue cools completely. It will now be fairly firm.

Spoon the meringue into a pastry big fitted with a plain medium tip. Pipe small, pointy balls on a prepared baking sheet (5).

The photo shows what the stems should look like (6). Bake for 15 minutes. Remove the stems from the oven and leave the oven on.

Makes about 30
Level: Easy
Prep: 25 min.
Bake: 1 hr. 25 min.

Special equipment:
A candy thermometer
A pastry bag
A medium plain tip

4 egg whites
1¼ cups (8½ oz., 240 g) sugar
Unsweetened cocoa powder, for sifting

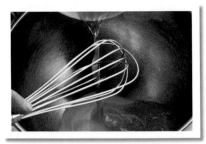

1 Combine the egg whites and sugar in a saucepan set over barely simmering water.

2 Whisk until the mixture turns white.

3 Continue until the meringue is fairly hot, 113 to 122° F (45 to 50° C).

4 Remove the bowl from the heat and beat with a hand-held mixer until completely cooled.

5 Spoon the meringue into a pastry bag with a plain tip and pipe balls with a pointed tip on a lined baking sheet.

6 This is what they should look like.

continued

Meanwhile, prepare the caps. Pipe small, flat balls on the second prepared baking sheet (7), lightly pressing with the tip.

Prepare as many caps as you have stems (8).

Sift cocoa powder over the caps and lightly blow on it (9).

Bake for 10 minutes. Remove the caps from the oven and leave the oven on.

Make a small hollow in the base of the caps with a small knife (10). Carefully place them over the stems, pressing lightly (11).

Finish assembling the remaining mushrooms (12) and bake for 1 hour, or until they are completely dried.

Notes: These meringues are much better than any you can buy in a store, so try making them. Prepare them in any size you like.

The meringues can be stored in an airtight container for a few days.

7 Pipe the caps, making fairly flat balls.

8 Prepare the same number of caps as stems.

9 Sift cocoa powder over the caps and blow gently so it is evenly distributed.

10 Make a little indentation in the base of the cap with a knife.

11 Insert the pointed tip of the stem.

12 Assemble all the mushrooms.

Présentoir en Glace Royale
Presentation Base in Royal Icing

Royal Icing

Sift the confectioners' sugar into a large bowl.

Add the egg whites (1) and beat with a wooden spoon (2) until the sugar dissolves (3).

Whip the mixture to a mayonnaise consistency and add the lemon juice (4).

Continue whipping until the icing is thick but pourable (5).

Place the piece of polystyrene on your work surface (6).

Makes 1 medium presentation base
Level: Intermediate
Prep: 25 min.
Dry: Overnight

Special equipment
A piece of polystyrene for holding a cake

4 cups (17½ oz., 500 g) confectioners' sugar
¼ cup plus 2 tbsp. (3½ oz., 100 g) egg whites (about 3½)
1 tsp. lemon juice

1 Sift the confectioners' sugar into a bowl and add the egg whites.

2 Begin beating the egg whites with a wooden spoon.

3 Continue until the confectioners' sugar has dissolved.

4 Whisk the mixture and add the lemon juice.

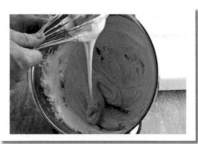

5 Whisk until the icing is thick but pourable.

6 Place the piece of polystyrene on your work surface.

continued

Cut the polystyrene into any shape you want with a knife heated over a flame.

Dollop a large quantity of icing on the base (7) and spread it out in a layer over the top with a thin spatula (8).

Lift up the base and spread more icing on the sides, turning the base and covering it completely (9).

Return the base to the work surface and smooth the top of the royal icing (10). It should be perfectly smooth.

If necessary, rap the base gently to remove any imperfections.

Hold the base up again and smooth the sides, turning the base (11).

The best way to smooth the icing is to pull the spatula toward you as you pull it down (12).

Remember that the layer of royal icing should be fairly thick so you can decorate it.

When the sides are smooth, make the decoration with a small thin spatula (13).

The photo shows a detail of the decoration (14).

Let the base dry out overnight at room temperature.

The royal icing will harden enough to hold a cake.

Notes: This is a classic support for wedding and other special-occasion cakes. You can make it square, round, or any other shape.

Use food coloring to tint the royal icing and vary the effect.

Add pastillage, rolled, broken sugar, and sugar flowers that you can attach with royal icing.

Please note that the finished recipe contains raw egg.

7 Dollop a large quantity of icing on the base.

8 Spread it out over the top.

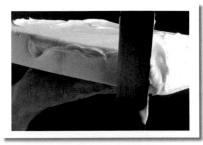

9 Lift up the base and spread more icing on the sides, turning the base and covering it completely.

10 Return the base to the work surface and use the large spatula to smooth the surface. Rap lightly to remove any imperfections.

11 Hold the base in one hand and smooth the sides, leaving enough to make the decorations.

12 The best way to do this is to draw the spatula toward you as you pull it down.

13 Use a small thin spatula to make the decorations on the sides.

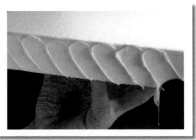

14 This is what the spatula stroke looks like.

L E

GATE

CLASS

Making Classic Cakes and Desserts

Getting Organized

Plan ahead. Many of these cakes include a *biscuit* (sponge cake) or dacquoise (nut meringue), which is best made a day in advance and stored in an airtight container or tightly covered in plastic wrap and kept in the refrigerator.

Making Syrups

You will make more syrup than you are likely to need, but you can brush the cake layers with as little or as much as you like. Just don't drench them!

Baking the Cake Layers

To bake *biscuit* (sponge cake), génoise, or dacquoise, use convection heat. For choux pastry, use conventional heat, because this is what best dries out the pastry.

Whatever type of heat, make sure the thermostat of your oven is accurate.

Many of the cake batters are piped with a pastry bag, which makes them especially light. If you spread them with a spatula, be careful not to overwork the batter or press down too hard.

The layers are all very thin and bake quickly. Follow the indications for baking times and other guides to testing for doneness.

Baking times are given for single layers. If you prefer, bake both layers at once. Position racks in the upper and lower thirds of the oven. If you are not using convection heat, switch the baking sheets between racks halfway through and increase times by a few minutes.

The cakes should remain soft and delicate; overcooking results in a rubbery texture.

Chilling the Cakes

Most of the cakes in this chapter should be kept in the refrigerator. The chilling time allows the slightly dry cake layers to absorb moisture from the filling and the flavors to blend. (Think about how a refrigerator cake works.) Remove the cakes about 10 minutes before serving. The exceptions are cakes or pastries prepared with choux or puff pastry, which are best assembled at the last minute to keep the pastry crispy.

Presentation and Decoration

A lovely presentation base will show off a cake you're making for a birthday or other special occasion. You'll find an example on page 262. Decorations to add to your cake can be found throughout the Decorations chapter (page 180).

Storing the Cakes

Most of the recipes in this chapter make large cakes. It is actually much easier to prepare an intricate cake for twenty people than for four to five. This is how pastry chefs usually work, cutting large elaborate cakes into individual servings for sale instead of baking medium-sized cakes for four or eight and selling them whole.

So if you make one of these cakes for more than the number of your guests, freeze half of it for another occasion. It will keep well and taste just as delicious if well covered in plastic wrap. The cakes can be frozen for three to four weeks without any problem.

This storing and freezing advice applies to all the cakes in this book, except for the Fraisier (page 284), because the strawberries in this cake become watery when thawed (unlike raspberries) and for those using choux pastry, such as the Éclairs (page 318) and Paris-Brest (page 314).

Baked choux pastry does not freeze well at all, nor does baked puff pastry. They are best assembled just before serving to keep them crisp.

The French Cake Layers

French layer cakes are not the dramatic high-risers of American diners. Traditionally, they are composed of thin foamy layers, cakes that are leavened by whipping eggs, whole or separated, or egg whites.

Biscuit (Sponge Cake)

To make *biscuit*, egg whites are whipped with sugar until firm, then egg yolks are added and sifted flour is gently folded in with a flexible spatula. Biscuit Moka (page 302) is made with sponge cake.

Biscuits à la Cuillère (Ladyfingers)
Ladyfingers are prepared with *biscuit* batter, but are usually piped into puffy fingers instead of sheets or disks and then dusted with confectioners' sugar to make them slightly crisp when baked. The classic use of ladyfingers is as a spongy lining for Bavarian cream–filled charlottes, in such recipes as Charlotte aux Poires (page 352).

Biscuit au Chocolat (Chocolate Sponge Cake)
To turn *biscuit* into *biscuit au chocolat*, unsweetened cocoa powder is sifted with the flour. Sometimes a little melted chocolate is added, as well as melted butter. If either melted chocolate or butter is added, the cake is slightly more difficult to prepare, because the melted ingredients tend to deflate the whipped egg whites, but the taste is superior. In this chapter Poire-Caramel (page 334), Chocolat-Framboise (page 340), and Marronnier (page 346) all use chocolate sponge cake.

Dacquoise

Dacquoise is baked nut meringue. It's made of egg whites whipped with granulated sugar, to which ground almonds, hazelnuts, or walnuts, and sometimes confectioners' sugar, are added. Variations are found in Framboisier (page 280), Succès Praliné (page 288), Dacquoise au Citron Vert (page 292), and Dacquoise aux Fruits (page 296).

Some recipes call for the addition of a little flour, but this makes the texture denser.

Génoise (Genovese Cake)

Génoise is similar to *biscuit*, but the eggs are whipped whole.

Joconde (Joconde Cake)

In this cake hybrid, eggs are whipped whole, then further lightened with whipped egg whites. In this chapter, it's used in Opéra (page 310).

The French Fillings

Buttercream

Buttercream, the silky filling often used in macarons, is one of the finest frostings in pastry making. It is prepared with Italian meringue—egg whites whipped with hot sugar syrup—and/or with egg yolks whipped with hot sugar syrup and beaten with creamed butter. Very fresh butter of the finest quality is essential. It should be whipped for a long time at various stages for the lightest texture and best flavor. Ultimately, the quality depends on the final mixing; it should be well beaten, at medium speed, to incorporate as much air as possible.

It is flavored just before using. Coffee, pistachio, and caramel are a few favorites.

Buttercream freezes very well. For best results, thaw it overnight in the refrigerator and then lightly heat the bowl of a stand mixer, for example by holding it over a gas burner for a few seconds. Place the buttercream in the bowl and whip well until it regains its original texture.

Chiboust Cream

This filling is pastry cream that has been lightened with delicate French meringue (egg whites whipped with sugar). It is often set with a little gelatin to help keep its volume.

Today, Chiboust cream is hard to find because it is complicated to prepare and does not keep long. But it is delicious and worth the effort.

The best expression of this old-fashioned cream is as the wavy topping on Saint-Honoré (page 322).

Mousseline Cream

Mousseline cream is made of buttercream blended with pastry cream plus a flavoring, such as praline, pistachio, vanilla, or rose water. It is used in Paris-Brest (page 314) and Fraisier (page 284), for example.

Pastry Cream

This is every pastry chef's basic cream preparation. The recipe here, which uses cornstarch and a good proportion of egg yolks, is foolproof and delicious.

Choose a heavy saucepan for making it, such as a stainless steel–lined copper pan, because pastry cream scorches easily in a thin pan.

Note that pastry cream cannot be frozen.

Equipment

Baking Pans

Chefs typically use cake rings (rectangular, round, and square), which have no bottoms. Baking sheets lined with parchment paper serve as the bottoms. Select stainless steel rings if possible. You can also bake with rubber rings, but they are not as practical as stainless steel and, in fact, pastry chefs do not use them when making these elaborate cakes.

It is possible to make your own ring using cardboard, too.

Classic French cakes are not high-rise affairs; they are discretely low. If you buy a stainless steel ring, it should be 1¾ inches (4 cm) high for all the cakes here assembled in rings, with the exception of the Opéra (page 310), which requires a ring 1¼ inches (3 cm) high. For the Opéra you can simply press a cardboard base into a 1¾ inch (4 cm) high ring.

Electric Mixers

A stand mixer is a very useful appliance, especially when making buttercream, which requires you to pour hot sugar syrup down the side of a bowl while whipping. But a hand-held electric mixer works perfectly well. And an old-fashioned large whisk and bowl—a spotless unlined copper bowl gives the most volume—can also be used for whipping eggs. If using a hand-held mixer or whisk, place a kitchen towel under your bowl for stability.

Offset Spatula

An offset spatula is far easier to handle than a standard spatula when smoothing batter that's below the rim of a cake ring.

Pastry Bag and Tips

You will need a pastry bag and tips of various sizes and shapes (plain or star-shaped).

Sieve

Use a fine sieve for sifting flour, confectioners' sugar, and unsweetened cocoa powder.

Thermometers

A candy thermometer is indispensable for measuring the temperature of cooked sugar to make, for instance, Italian meringue, a component in Buttercream (page 276).

Crème Pâtissière
Pastry Cream

Line a baking sheet with plastic wrap.

Split the vanilla bean lengthwise in half and scrape out the seeds.

Bring the milk and vanilla bean and seeds to a boil in a medium heavy saucepan over medium heat (1).

Remove from the heat and let infuse for 10 minutes.

Meanwhile, combine the sugar and cornstarch in a medium bowl. Add the egg yolks (2).

Whisk just until the sugar dissolves; do not let the mixture become pale (3).

Return the milk to the heat and bring to a boil. Whisk one-third of the milk into the egg yolk–cornstarch–sugar mixture (4 and 5).

Whisk in the remaining milk.

Return the mixture to the saucepan, straining it through a fine sieve, and cook over medium heat, whisking constantly (6).

As soon as the pastry cream begins to thicken, remove it from the heat (7).

Whisk in the butter until smooth.

Scrape the pastry cream onto the prepared baking sheet (8) and wrap it in the plastic, pressing out all the air (9). Chill completely.

Notes: It's important to use whole milk when preparing pastry cream.

This pastry cream is especially light because cornstarch is used to thicken it instead of the traditional flour.

Makes about 2½ cups (1 lb. 12 oz., 800 g)	1 vanilla bean
Level: Basic/Easy	2 cups (500 ml) milk (see *Notes*)
Prep and cook: 15 min.	⅔ cup (4¼ oz., 120 g) sugar
	3 tbsp. (1½ oz., 50 g) cornstarch
	6 egg yolks (4 oz., 120 g)
	3 tbsp. (1½ oz., 50 g) butter

1 Bring the milk to a boil with the split vanilla bean and seeds.

2 Whisk the sugar and cornstarch with the egg yolks until smooth.

3 Do not let the mixture become pale.

4 Gradually whisk the boiling milk into the egg yolk mixture.

5 Continue to whisk until smooth.

6 Return the mixture to the saucepan, straining it through a fine sieve, and cook over medium heat, whisking constantly.

7 When the cream thickens, remove the pan from the heat.

8 Scrape the pastry cream onto the lined baking sheet.

9 Wrap it carefully so that it does not form a skin on top.

Crème au Beurre
Buttercream

Italian Meringue

Combine ½ cup (3½ oz., 100 g) of the sugar and the water in a small heavy saucepan (1).

Cook over medium heat, stirring with a wooden spoon, until the sugar dissolves.

Bring to a boil, washing down any crystals on the sides of the pan with a moistened pastry brush.

Dip the candy thermometer in the syrup, making sure it does not touch the bottom.

Cook the sugar, watching carefully, until it registers 244° F (118° C) (2).

Meanwhile, place the egg whites in the bowl of the stand mixer fitted with the whisk attachment. Just before the sugar is ready, whip the egg whites with the remaining 2 tbsp. (1 oz., 25 g) sugar (3) at medium speed until they hold a soft peak.

Carefully pour the sugar syrup down the side of the bowl into the whites (4) and whip until the mixture cools to room temperature, about 10 minutes. Scrape the Italian meringue into a bowl (5).

Makes about 5 cups
(2 lb. 4 oz., 1 kg)
Level: Basic/Intermediate
Prep and cook: 20 min.

Special equipment
A candy thermometer
A stand mixer

Italian Meringue

½ cup plus 2 tbsp.
  (4½ oz., 125 g) sugar
3 tbsp. (40 g) water
⅓ cup (2½ oz., 70 g) egg whites
  (about 2½)

Egg Yolk Buttercream

5 egg yolks
1¼ cups (8½ oz., 240 g) sugar
¼ cup plus 2 tbsp. (100 ml) water
3 sticks (12½ oz., 360 g) butter,
  softened

1 Heat ½ cup (3½ oz., 100 g) of the sugar and the water over medium heat.

2 Cook, watching carefully, until the temperature registers 244° F (118° C).

3 Meanwhile, begin whipping the egg whites with 2 tbsp. (1 oz., 25 g) sugar at medium speed.

4 When the syrup has reached the right temperature, pour it down the side of the bowl.

5 Continue whipping until the mixture cools and transfer it to another bowl.

continued

Egg Yolk Buttercream

Whip the egg yolks in the stand mixer fitted with the whisk attachment at low speed (6).

Meanwhile, cook the sugar with the water in a medium heavy saucepan over medium heat until it registers 244° F (118° C) (7 and 8).

Carefully pour the syrup down the side of the bowl into the egg yolks (9) and beat at high speed until the mixture is thick and pale. At this stage, it forms a ribbon when it flows from the beater back into the bowl (10). Transfer it to another bowl.

Whip the butter in the mixer (11) until it is creamy and smooth (12).

Scrape the egg yolk mixture into the whipped butter. Beat at low speed until the texture is light. Beat in the Italian meringue (13) at very low speed (14, 15, and 16) until smooth.

Notes: Some buttercreams are prepared with only Italian meringue or egg yolks; this one contains both.

Buttercream can be covered with plastic wrap and left at cool room temperature for up to 4 hours.

Beat in the flavor of your choice, such as pistachio, coffee, praline, or a liqueur, just before using.

Buttercream can be frozen. Let it thaw overnight in the refrigerator. Whip it again at medium speed in the mixer until very light, about 10 minutes.

6 Whip the egg yolks at low speed.

7 Meanwhile, heat the sugar and water in a saucepan.

8 Cook until the syrup registers 244° F (118° C).

9 Pour the syrup down the side of the bowl into the egg yolks.

10 Whip at high speed until the mixture becomes pale and thick.

11 Now whip the butter in the mixer.

12 Beat until smooth and creamy.

13 Add the Italian meringue.

14 Beat in at very low speed.

15 Continue at low speed until the buttercream is light and fluffy.

16 This is what the buttercream should look like.

Framboisier
Raspberry-Nut Layer Cake with Pistachio Buttercream

Preheat the oven to 350° F (180° C). Line 2 baking sheets with parchment paper.

Almond-Hazelnut Dacquoise
Finely grind the ground almonds with the ground hazelnuts in a food processor.
Whip the egg whites with a little sugar (1) at medium speed until they hold a soft peak.
Add the remaining sugar and whip the egg whites until firm and glossy (2).
Gently fold in the ground nuts with a flexible spatula (3) until smooth (4).

Spoon the dacquoise batter into a pastry bag fitted with a ½ inch (1 cm) plain tip and pipe half into bands on each of the prepared baking sheets (5). Or spread in a layer with a thin spatula.

Bake 1 sheet at a time for 15 to 20 minutes, until lightly browned. Rotate the sheet halfway through baking.

Transfer the dacquoise to a rack and let cool.

Makes 1 16 by 12-inch
(40 by 30 cm) cake
Level: Intermediate
Prep: 1 hr.
Bake: 15 to 20 min. per
dacquoise layer
Chill: at least 1 hr.

Special equipment
A candy thermometer

2⅔ cups (8 oz., 230 g) ground almonds
¾ cup (2½ oz., 70 g) ground hazelnuts
1⅓ cups (10½ oz., 300 g) egg whites
   (about 10)
1½ cups (10 oz., 280 g) sugar

1 recipe Buttercream (page 276)
⅓ oz. (10 g) pistachio paste
   (see Notes, page 176)
14 oz. (400 g) raspberries

1 Whip the egg whites with a little sugar until they hold soft peaks.

2 Add the remaining sugar and whip until glossy.

3 Fold in the ground almonds and hazelnuts.

4 Use a flexible spatula, being careful not to deflate the mixture.

5 Pipe strips of the dacquoise onto baking sheets lined with parchment paper.

continued

Filling

Whip the Buttercream at medium speed until very light, about 10 minutes.

Add the pistachio paste and whip at low speed (6) until very smooth, about 1 minute.

Spoon two-thirds of the pistachio buttercream into the pastry bag and pipe in bands to cover one dacquoise (7). Or use a thin spatula.

Arrange the raspberries in parallel rows on the buttercream (8).

Pipe a thin layer of the remaining buttercream over the raspberries (9) and top with the second dacquoise (10), lightly pressing so it sticks to the buttercream (11).

Chill the cake until the buttercream sets, at least 1 hour.

Cut into slices with a fine serrated knife.

Note: Just before serving, decorate the cake with raspberries rolled in melted raspberry jam, if you like.

6 Beat the pistachio paste into the Buttercream.

7 Pipe two-thirds of the pistachio buttercream over one dacquoise.

8 Arrange the raspberries in parallel rows.

9 Pipe the remaining buttercream over the raspberries.

10 Top with the second dacquoise.

11 Lightly press the dacquoise so it sticks to the buttercream.

Fraisier

Strawberry Layer Cake with Mousseline Cream

Kirsch Syrup

Combine the sugar and water in a small saucepan and cook over medium heat, stirring, until the sugar dissolves. Remove from the heat, let cool, and stir in the kirsch.

Ladyfinger Sponge Cake

Preheat the oven to 350° F (180° C). Line 2 baking sheets with parchment paper.

Sift the flour.

Whip the egg whites at medium speed until they hold a soft peak (1).

Add the granulated sugar and whip until the egg whites are firm and glossy (2).

Add the egg yolks (3) and whip until smooth, about 5 seconds (4 and 5).

Gradually fold in the sifted flour (6) with a flexible spatula.

Spread half the cake batter on each of the prepared baking sheets and smooth with a thin spatula (7). Sift confectioners' sugar evenly over the tops (8).

Bake 1 sheet at a time for 10 to 12 minutes, until lightly browned. Rotate the sheet halfway through baking.

Transfer the cake to a rack and let cool.

Place the cake ring on one sponge cake. Cut off the excess (9). Repeat with the second sponge cake. Leave on the ring.

Makes 1 12 by 8-inch
(30 by 20 cm) cake
Level: Intermediate
Prep: 1 hr.
Bake: 10 to 12 min. per
sponge cake layer
Chill: at least 1 hr.

Special equipment
A candy thermometer
A 12 by 8-inch (30 by 20 cm)
cake ring

Kirsch Syrup

⅓ cup (2½ oz., 70 g) sugar
½ cup (120 ml) water
1 tbsp. plus 1 tsp. (20 ml) kirsch

Ladyfinger Sponge Cake

1 cup plus 2 tbsp. (5 oz., 150 g)
all-purpose flour
6 eggs, separated
¾ cup (5 oz., 150 g) granulated
sugar
⅓ cup (2 oz., 50 g) confectioners'
sugar

Mousseline Cream

½ recipe Buttercream
(page 276)

½ cup (5 oz., 150 g)
Pastry Cream (page 274)
1 tbsp. (20 g) pistachio paste
(optional, see *Notes*, page 176)

Strawberries

1 lb. (500 g) strawberries, hulled
2½ tbsp. (1 oz., 30 g) sugar

French Meringue

2 egg whites
⅓ cup (2 oz., 60 g) granulated sugar
⅓ cup (1½ oz., 40 g) confectioners'
sugar

Apricot Glaze

13 oz. (370 g) apricot preserves
2 tbsp. water

1 Whip the egg whites until they hold a soft peak.

2 Gradually add the granulated sugar and whip until firm.

3 Add the egg yolks.

4 Whip very briefly to incorporate them.

5 This is what the mixture should look like.

6 Gradually fold in the sifted flour with a flexible spatula.

7 Carefully spread the cake batter onto 2 lined baking sheets.

8 Dust the tops with confectioners' sugar.

9 Place the cake ring on one sponge cake and trim the edges.

continued

Mousseline Cream

Whip the Buttercream at medium speed until very light, about 10 minutes. Whisk the Pastry Cream until smooth. Add the Pastry Cream and pistachio paste, if desired, to the Buttercream and whip at low speed until smooth, about 1 minute.

Brush the sponge cake in the ring with kirsch syrup.

Strawberries

Spread two-thirds of the mousseline cream over the cake in the ring, then arrange the strawberries, tops against the sides of the ring (10).

Arrange the remaining strawberries in the center (11). Sprinkle the strawberries with the sugar (12).

Spread the remaining mousseline cream over the strawberries (13) and smooth it with a thin spatula (14).

Place the second sponge cake on the mousseline cream (15) and brush it with more syrup (16).

Chill until the cream sets, at least 1 hour.

French Meringue

Whip the egg whites with a little granulated sugar at medium speed until they hold a soft peak. Add the remaining granulated sugar and whip until firm and glossy.

Sift the confectioners' sugar into the meringue and gently fold in with a flexible spatula.

Spread the meringue over the top of the cake and smooth it with a thin spatula (17). Lightly and evenly brown the surface with a kitchen torch (18). Or broil it on the top shelf of the oven for 3 to 5 minutes, until lightly browned.

Apricot Glaze

Melt the apricot preserves with the water over medium heat, stirring occasionally. Strain through a fine sieve into a small bowl.

Pour the glaze over the meringue (19) and smooth it with a thin spatula (20 and 21).

Carefully remove the ring and slice the cake.

Notes: This cake can be refrigerated for up 2 days. It cannot be frozen, because the strawberries would get watery when thawed.

10 Spread two-thirds of the mousseline cream over the cake in the ring.

11 Arrange the strawberries, turning those at the edge to face outwards.

12 Sprinkle with sugar.

13 Spread the remaining cream over the strawberries.

14 Smooth it with a thin spatula.

15 Carefully place the second cake on top of the cream.

16 Brush it with the syrup.

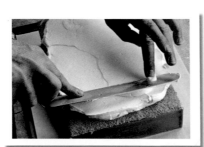

17 Spread the meringue over the top of the cake.

18 Lightly brown the surface with a kitchen torch.

19 Pour over the strained apricot preserves.

20 Smooth it carefully.

21 This is what the finished cake looks like.

Succès Praliné
Hazelnut-Praline Dacquoise

Hazelnut Praline

Preheat the oven to 350° F (170° C).

Spread the hazelnuts on a baking sheet and bake for about 10 minutes, until lightly toasted (1). Leave the oven on.

Cook the sugar and water in a small heavy saucepan over medium heat, stirring with a wooden spoon, until the temperature registers 244° F (118° C).

Stir in the toasted hazelnuts (2). The sugar will crystallize slightly. Continue cooking over low heat, stirring constantly, until the nuts are coated in caramel (3 and 4). Return to the baking sheet and let cool. Crush with a pestle or rolling pin (5).

Grind 2½ oz. (75 g) of the crushed hazelnut praline to a paste and reserve for the hazelnut-praline buttercream.

Almond-Hazelnut Dacquoise

Finely grind the ground almonds with the hazelnuts in a food processor (6).

Pour the ground nuts into a bowl.

Whip the egg whites with a little sugar at medium speed until they hold a soft peak (7).

Add the remaining sugar and whip the egg whites until firm and glossy (8).

Gently fold in the ground nuts with a flexible spatula (9) until smooth (10).

Makes 1 16 by 12-inch
(40 by 30 cm) cake
Level: Intermediate
Prep: 1 hr.
Bake: 15 to 20 min. per
dacquoise layer
Chill: at least 1 hr.

Special equipment
A candy thermometer
A 16 by 12-inch (40 by 30 cm)
cake ring

Hazelnut Praline

1¼ cups (5½ oz., 160 g) chopped
   hazelnuts
½ cup (3¼ oz., 90 g) sugar
2 tbsp. (30 ml) water

Almond-Hazelnut Dacquoise

2 cups (6 oz., 165 g) ground almonds
1¼ cups (5½ oz., 160 g) hazelnuts
1½ cups (11 oz., 320 g) egg whites
   (about 11)
1⅔ cups (11 oz., 315 g) sugar

Hazelnut-Praline Buttercream

¾ recipe Buttercream (page 276)
2½ oz. (75 g) hazelnut-praline paste
   (reserved from the hazelnut praline)

Finish

Confectioners' sugar, for sifting

1 This is what the toasted hazelnuts look like.

2 Cook the sugar and water over medium heat to 244° F (118° C) and stir in the hazelnuts.

3 Cook over low heat, stirring, for 5 minutes.

4 Stir until the hazelnuts are completely coated.

5 Coarsely crush the cooled hazelnuts.

6 Grind the ground almonds with the whole hazelnuts in a food processor.

7 Whip the egg whites with a little sugar.

8 Add the remaining sugar and whip until they are firm and glossy.

9 Add the ground nuts to the egg whites.

10 Gently fold in with a flexible spatula to incorporate them, being careful not to deflate the dacquoise.

continued

Line 2 baking sheets with parchment paper.

Spoon the dacquoise batter into a pastry bag fitted with a ½ inch (1 cm) plain tip and pipe half into bands on each of the prepared baking sheets (11). Or spread in a layer with a thin spatula.

Bake 1 sheet at a time for 15 to 20 minutes, until lightly browned. Rotate the sheet halfway through baking.

Transfer the dacquoise to a rack and let cool.

Hazelnut-Praline Buttercream

Whip the Buttercream at medium speed until very light, about 10 minutes.

Add the reserved hazelnut paste (12).

Whip at low speed until smooth, about 1 minute (13).

Place the cake ring on one dacquoise. Cut off the excess (14). Repeat with the second dacquoise. Leave on the ring.

Spread the buttercream over the dacquoise in the ring (15) and smooth it with a thin spatula (16). Sprinkle with the caramelized hazelnuts (17), reserving some for garnish.

Place the second dacquoise on top (18). Remove the ring.

Finish

Sift the top of the cake with confectioners' sugar (19) and spread evenly with a pastry brush (20). Sift again with confectioners' sugar (21).

Chill the cake until the buttercream sets, at least 1 hour. Cut into slices with a fine serrated knife. Sprinkle with the reserved caramelized hazelnuts before serving.

11 Pipe the dacquoise onto the lined baking sheets.

12 Gently stir the hazelnut paste into the Buttercream.

13 Beat at low speed until the mixture is completely smooth, without any streaks.

14 Trim the excess dacquoise from around the ring with a sharp knife.

15 Smooth the praline buttercream over the dacquoise in the ring with a spatula.

16 The surface should be even.

17 Sprinkle caramelized hazelnuts over the cream.

18 Place the second dacquoise on top.

19 Sift with confectioners' sugar.

20 Brush the confectioner's sugar to cover the dacquoise completely.

21 Sift more confectioners' sugar over to finish the cake.

Dacquoise au Citron Vert
Lime-Coconut Dacquoise with Raspberries

Rum Syrup

Combine the sugar and water in a small saucepan and cook over medium heat, stirring, until the sugar dissolves. Remove from the heat, let cool, and stir in the rum.

Coconut Dacquoise

Preheat the oven to 350° F (180° C). Line 2 baking sheets with parchment paper.

Finely grind the ground almonds with the hazelnuts in a food processor.

Pour the ground nuts into a bowl.

Whip the egg whites with a little sugar at medium speed until they hold a soft peak (1).

Add the remaining sugar and whip the egg whites until firm and glossy (2).

Gently fold in the ground nuts with a flexible spatula (3) until smooth (4).

Spoon the dacquoise batter into a pastry bag fitted with a ½ inch (1 cm) plain tip and pipe half into bands on each of the prepared baking sheets (5). Or spread in a layer with a thin spatula.

Sprinkle with the coconut. (6)

Bake 1 sheet at a time for 15 to 20 minutes, until nicely browned. Rotate the sheet halfway through baking.

Transfer the dacquoise to a rack and let cool.

Makes 1 16 by 12-inch
(40 by 30 cm) cake
Level: Intermediate
Prep: 1 hr.
Bake: 15 to 20 min. per
dacquoise layer
Freeze: at least 2 hr.

Special equipment
A 16 by 12-inch (40 by 30 cm)
cake ring

Rum Syrup

¼ cup (2 oz., 50 g) sugar
⅓ cup (70 ml) water
1 tsp. dark rum

Coconut Dacquoise

2⅔ cups (8 oz., 230 g) ground
    almonds
¾ cup (2½ oz., 70 g) hazelnuts
1⅓ cups (10½ oz., 300 g)
    egg whites (about 10)
1½ cups (10 oz., 280 g) sugar
1⅓ cups (3½ oz., 100 g)
    unsweetened shredded coconut

Lime Mousse

6 gelatin sheets (12 g)
1⅔ cups (400 ml) heavy cream
⅓ cup (70 ml) lemon juice
½ cup (3½ oz., 100 g) sugar
1 cup (250 ml) lime juice

Finish

14 oz. (400 g) raspberries

1 Begin whipping the egg whites with a little sugar at medium speed.

2 This is what the whites look like when they hold a firm peak.

3 Gently fold in the ground nuts with a flexible spatula.

4 Stir until the dacquoise is smooth but not deflated.

5 Pipe the dacquoise batter onto lined baking sheets.

6 Sprinkle evenly with the shredded coconut.

7 Melt the gelatin over low heat and stir in the lime juice.

continued

Lime Mousse

Soak the gelatin sheets in cold water until softened, 5 to 10 minutes.

Pour the cream into a large bowl and chill.

Combine the lemon juice and sugar in a small heavy saucepan over medium heat and stir with a wooden spoon until the sugar dissolves.

Squeeze the gelatin dry. Add the softened gelatin to the lemon syrup and stir over low heat just until dissolved. Add the lime juice (7) and remove from the heat. Whisk well and let cool at room temperature so the gelatin does not set.

Whip the chilled cream until it holds a soft peak.

Transfer one-third of the whipped cream to another large bowl and add the lime gelatin (8). Whip until the cream holds a firm peak (9).

Gently fold in the remaining whipped cream with a flexible spatula (10).

Finish

Place the cake ring on one dacquoise. Cut off the excess (11).

Repeat with the second dacquoise. Leave on the ring (12).

Brush the dacquoise in the ring with the rum syrup.

Pour three-quarters of the lime mousse into the ring (13).

Scatter the raspberries over the top (14), pour in the remaining mousse, and spread it with a thin spatula.

Brush the second dacquoise with rum syrup (15) and carefully place it in the ring on the mousse (16).

Freeze the cake until the mousse sets, at least 2 hours. Cut into slices with a fine serrated knife.

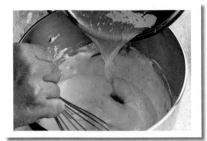

8 Whisk the lime gelatin into one-third of the whipped cream.

9 Whip until the whipped cream holds a firm peak.

10 Gently fold in the remaining whipped cream with a flexible spatula.

11 Trim the dacquoise around the edge of the cake ring.

12 This is the neat result you are looking for.

13 Pour three-quarters of the lime mousse over the dacquoise in the ring.

14 Scatter the raspberries over the mousse and fill with the remaining mousse.

15 Brush the second dacquoise with the rum syrup.

16 Place it carefully on the cream filling.

Dacquoise aux Fruits
Mixed Fruit–White Chocolate Dacquoise

Hazelnut Dacquoise

Preheat the oven to 350° F (180° C). Line 2 baking sheets with parchment paper.

Spread 1 cup (4½ oz., 130 g) of the hazelnuts in a pie pan and bake for about 10 minutes, until lightly toasted. Leave the oven on.

Let cool slightly and rub off the skins with a kitchen towel.

Coarsely chop the toasted hazelnuts in a food processor (1). Transfer to a large bowl.

Makes 1 16 by 12-inch
(40 by 30 cm) cake
Level: Intermediate
Prep: 1 hr.
Bake: 15 to 20 min. per
dacquoise layer
Freeze: at least 2 hr.

Special equipment
A 16 by 12-inch (40 by 30 cm)
cake ring

Hazelnut Dacquoise

2¼ cups (10 oz., 300 g) hazelnuts
1⅓ cups (6 oz., 175 g)
confectioners' sugar
1⅓ cups (10½ oz., 300 g)
egg whites (about 10)
¼ cup plus 2 tbsp. (3 oz., 80 g)
granulated sugar

White Chocolate Bavarian Cream

2 gelatin sheets (4 g)
9 oz. (250 g) white chocolate
2 egg yolks
1 vanilla bean
1 cup (250 ml) milk
3 tbsp. Cointreau or other orange
liqueur
1½ cups (380 ml) heavy cream

Mixed Fruit

5 oz. (150 g) canned pears, diced
5 oz. (150 g) diced pineapple
5 oz. (150 g) cherries, pitted and
halved
5 oz. (150 g) peaches, diced
14 oz. (400 g) raspberries

Glaze

1 small jar (8 oz., 250 g) quince
jelly

1 Coarsely chop the toasted hazelnuts in a food processor.

2 Grind the remaining hazelnuts with the confectioners' sugar.

3 Process to a fine powder.

4 Combine the two hazelnut preparations.

continued

Finely grind the remaining hazelnuts with the confectioners' sugar in the food processor (2 and 3).

Stir into the coarsely chopped hazelnuts (4).

Whip the egg whites with a little granulated sugar at medium speed until they hold a soft peak (5).

Add the remaining granulated sugar and whip until firm and glossy.

Gently fold in the hazelnut mixture with a flexible spatula (6) until smooth (7).

Spread half the dacquoise in a layer on each of the prepared baking sheets with a thin spatula (8).

Bake 1 sheet at a time for 15 to 20 minutes, until lightly browned. Rotate the sheet halfway through baking.

Transfer the dacquoise to a rack and let cool.

White Chocolate Bavarian Cream
Soak the gelatin sheets in cold water until softened, 5 to 10 minutes. Squeeze dry.

Break the white chocolate into pieces and place it in a bowl with the softened gelatin (9).

Place the egg yolks in a medium bowl.

Split the vanilla bean lengthwise in half and scrape out the seeds.

Bring the milk and vanilla bean and seeds to a boil in a medium saucepan over medium heat (10).

Remove the pan from the heat whisk the milk into the egg yolks (11).

Return this custard to the saucepan and cook over low heat, stirring with a wooden spoon. It is ready when it coats a spoon; if you draw a finger across the back of the spoon, it should leave a clear trail and register 180° F (82° C) on an instant-read thermometer (12).

Immediately pour the custard into the white chocolate (13). Let the chocolate melt for 5 minutes. Stir until smooth.

5 Whip the egg whites with a little granulated sugar.

6 Gently fold the hazelnut mixture into the meringue.

7 Be careful not to deflate the egg whites.

8 Spread the batter on the lined baking sheets.

9 Add the softened gelatin to the chopped white chocolate.

10 Bring the milk to a boil with the vanilla bean and seeds.

11 Whisk the hot milk into the egg yolks.

12 Cook the custard over low heat until a thermometer registers 180° F (82° C), or when the mixture coats the back of a spoon, and remove from the heat.

13 Pour into the white chocolate.

continued

Whisk in the Cointreau (14).

Whisk the cream in a large bowl until it holds a firm peak.

If the white chocolate has set, melt it, whisking, over a saucepan filled with 1 inch (2.5 cm) of barely simmering water.

Gently fold the white chocolate custard into the whipped cream (15) with a flexible spatula.

Place the cake ring on one dacquoise. Cut off the excess. Repeat with the second dacquoise. Remove the ring.

Mixed Fruit

Line a baking sheet with parchment paper. Place the cake ring on the prepared baking sheet. Spread the pears, pineapple, cherries, and peaches in the ring (16).

Scatter the raspberries over the top.

Pour two-thirds of the white chocolate Bavarian cream over the fruit (17) and smooth with a thin spatula (18).

Place one dacquoise on top (19) and pour the remaining cream over the top (20).

Smooth with a flexible spatula (21).

Lightly press the other dacquoise on the cream (22).

Freeze the cake until the Bavarian cream sets, at least 2 hours.

Invert a large platter over the ring and, holding the baking sheet and ring together, carefully turn out the cake onto the platter with the fruit layer on the top. Remove the baking sheet, paper, and ring.

Melt the quince jelly lightly over medium heat, stirring occasionally. Lightly brush it on the cake. Cut into slices using a fine serrated knife.

14 Stir in the Cointreau.

15 Incorporate the Bavarian cream into the whipped cream.

16 Spread the diced fruit and raspberries in the ring.

17 Pour two-thirds of the Bavarian cream over the fruit.

18 Smooth it with an offset spatula.

19 Carefully place one dacquoise on the cream.

20 Pour in the remaining cream.

21 Spread it out evenly with a flexible spatula or thin spatula.

22 Carefully top with the second dacquoise.

Biscuit Moka
Moka Cake

Rum Syrup
Combine the sugar and water in a small saucepan and cook over medium heat, stirring, until the sugar dissolves. Remove from the heat, let cool, and stir in the rum.

Toasted Almonds
Preheat the oven to 350° F (180° C).

Spread the almonds on a baking sheet and bake for about 10 minutes, until lightly toasted. Leave the oven on.

Sponge Cake
Line a baking sheet with parchment paper. Line the cake ring with a strip of parchment paper 3 inches (8 cm) wide. Place the cake ring on the prepared baking sheet.

Sift the flour with the cornstarch and baking powder (1).

Whip the egg whites at medium speed until they hold a soft peak.

Meanwhile, whisk the egg yolks with ¼ cup (1¾ oz.; 50 g) of the sugar (2).

Add the remaining sugar to the egg whites and whip until firm and glossy (3).

Continue to whisk the yolks and sugar until the mixture is pale and thick (4).

Add the egg whites to the yolk mixture (5).

Gently fold in with a flexible spatula (6).

Gradually fold in the dry ingredients (7) just until smooth.

Spread the cake batter in the prepared ring and smooth with the offset spatula (8 and 9).

Bake for at least 20 minutes, until lightly browned.

Remove the ring, transfer the cake to a rack, and let cool.

Makes 1 8-inch (20 cm)
round cake
Level: Advanced
Prep: 1 hr.
Bake: 30 min.
Chill: at least 1 hr.

Special equipment
An 8-inch (20 cm) round
cake ring
An offset spatula

Rum Syrup

⅓ cup (2½ oz., 70 g) sugar
½ cup (120 ml) water
1 tbsp. plus 1 tsp. (20 ml) dark rum

Toasted Almonds

1⅓ cups (3½ oz., 100 g) sliced
blanched almonds

Sponge Cake

1 cup (4 oz., 120 g) all-purpose
flour
3 tbsp. (1 oz., 30 g) cornstarch
1¼ tsp. (5 g) baking powder
5 eggs, separated
¾ cup (5 oz., 150 g) sugar

Moka Buttercream

½ recipe Buttercream (page 276)
1 tsp. instant coffee powder
dissolved in 3 tbsp. espresso or
strong coffee

1 Sift the flour with the cornstarch
and baking powder.

2 Whisk the egg yolks with
one-third of the sugar.

3 Begin beating the egg whites
with the remaining sugar.

4 The egg yolk mixture should be
pale and thick.

5 Add the whipped egg whites to
the egg yolk mixture.

6 Gently fold in with a flexible
spatula.

7 Gradually fold in the sifted
dry ingredients.

8 Fill the lined pastry ring with
the batter.

9 Smooth it out with an offset
spatula.

continued

Moka Buttercream

Whip the Buttercream at medium speed until very light, about 10 minutes.

Add the coffee (10) and whip at low speed until smooth, about 1 minute.

Cut the cake horizontally in half with a long serrated knife.

Brush the cut side of the bottom cake layer generously with rum syrup (11).

Dollop slightly less than half of the coffee buttercream on the bottom layer (12) and smooth with a thin spatula (13).

Position the second cake layer, cut side up, on top and brush with rum syrup (14).

Dollop more of the buttercream on top (15) and spread until smooth (16).

Cover the sides of the cake (17) with buttercream, reserving a little at room temperature for a final, thin top layer. Smooth the sides.

Chill the cake until the buttercream sets, at least 1 hour.

Spread the reserved buttercream over the top and smooth with a thin spatula (18).

Pull a serrated knife or icing comb across the top of the cake, zigzagging, to decorate (19).

Smooth the sides of the cake once more (20) and press on the sliced almonds with your hands. (21).

Note: Try different flavors for this sponge: coffee, vanilla, and chocolate are the most popular. It is a traditional cake for festive occasions in Alsace.

10 Whip the Buttercream with the coffee until smooth.

11 Brush the bottom cake layer with the rum syrup.

12 Spread the buttercream over the bottom layer.

13 Smooth it with a spatula.

14 Position the second cake layer, cut side up, on top and brush with rum syrup.

15 Spread buttercream over the top.

16 Smooth it with a spatula.

17 Spread the buttercream around the sides.

18 Add a final layer of buttercream on the top.

19 Pull a serrated knife across the top of the cake, zigzagging, to decorate.

20 Make sure the sides and angles of the cake are smooth.

21 Hold the cake up and press the sliced almonds around the sides with your hand.

Vacherin Glacé Alsacien
Meringue-Ice Cream Cake

French Meringue

Whip the egg whites with 2½ tbsp. (1 oz., 30 g) of the sugar at medium speed until frothy (1).

Gradually add ⅓ cup (2½ oz., 70 g) of the sugar and whip until the meringue is, glossy, white, and holds a firm peak (2).

Add the remaining ½ cup (3½ oz., 100 g) sugar and gently fold it in with a flexible spatula (3 and 4).

Preheat the oven to 300° F (150° C). Line a baking sheet with parchment paper. Using a plate or lid as a template, draw 2 7-inch (18 cm) circles on the paper, spacing them slightly apart, to use as guides.

Spoon the meringue into a pastry bag fitted with a ½ inch (1 cm) plain tip and pipe 2 disks on the prepared baking sheet, working in a spiral from the center out (5). Or use a thin spatula.

Bake for 8 minutes. Reduce the oven temperature to 200° F (90° C) and bake for about 2 hours, until the meringues are completely dry inside.

Let cool on the baking sheet.

Vacherin

Place the cake ring on one meringue. Remove the excess. Repeat with the second meringue (6 and 7). Leave on the ring.

Remove the vanilla ice cream and the sorbet from the freezer and let soften just enough to spread.

Spoon the vanilla ice cream into the ring (8) and smooth with the back of the spoon. You may need to freeze the dessert to be sure one layer doesn't melt into the next.

Spoon the sorbet into the ring (9).

Makes 1 8-inch (20 cm)
round cake
Level: Intermediate
Prep: 1 hr.
Bake: 2 hr.
Freeze: at least 1 hr.

Special equipment
A pastry bag fitted with a
Saint-Honoré tip (see *Notes*)
An 8-inch (20 cm) round cake
ring, 3 inches (8 cm) deep
A wide icing comb (optional)

French Meringue

3 egg whites
1 cup (7 oz., 200 g) sugar

Vacherin

1 pint (10 oz., 300 g) vanilla ice
cream
1 pint (10 oz., 300 g) raspberry or
strawberry sorbet

Chantilly Cream

1 cup (250 ml) heavy cream
¼ cup (2 oz., 50 g) sugar
2 tsp. (10 ml) kirsch
1 tsp. vanilla extract

1 Begin whipping the egg whites with a little sugar.

2 This is what the meringue should look like when whipped with half the sugar.

3 Add the remaining ½ cup (3½ oz., 100 g) sugar.

4 Fold it in with a flexible spatula.

5 Pipe 2 7-inch (18 cm) meringue disks.

6 Place the pastry ring over each meringue disk.

7 Trim the edges by gently pressing on the ring.

8 Cover one meringue disk with vanilla ice cream.

9 Spread a layer of raspberry sorbet on top.

continued

Smooth the sorbet with the spoon (10).

Carefully place the second meringue on the sorbet and lightly press it down (11), being careful not to break it.

Freeze until the vacherin sets, at least 30 minutes.

Chantilly Cream

Fill a large bowl with ice water.

Pour the cream into a medium bowl and place in the ice water. Whip the cream until it holds a soft peak. Add the sugar, kirsch, and vanilla and whip until the cream holds firmly to the whisk.

Gently heat the ring with a kitchen torch to release the cake (12). Or rub it with your hands.

Carefully remove the ring (13).

Dollop a little Chantilly cream on the cake (14) and spread it in an even layer over the top with a thin spatula.

Spread more Chantilly cream around the sides (15).

Smooth the top (16) and sides with a thin spatula. The Chantilly cream should be perfectly even. Remove any excess.

Freeze the cake until the Chantilly cream sets, at least 30 minutes.

Spread more Chantilly cream on the sides, smoothing it with the spatula (17).

For a decorative finish, pull the icing comb around the cake, if desired (18).

Spoon the remaining Chantilly cream into the pastry bag fitted with a Saint-Honoré tip and pipe waves over the top (19), starting from the edge and working towards the center (20).

Freeze the cake. Remove it 30 minutes before serving.

Notes: At any time during the assembly of the cake, you can freeze it briefly so it's easier to work with.

A Saint-Honoré pastry tip is a large plain one with a V-shaped slit.

Just before serving, you can garnish the cake with fresh fruit, such as raspberries or strawberries and orange slices or segments.

10 Smooth the sorbet with the back of a spoon.

11 Carefully press the second meringue disk on the sorbet.

12 Gently heat the metal with a kitchen torch.

13 Remove the ring.

14 Cover the top with Chantilly cream.

15 Smooth the Chantilly cream around the sides.

16 Carefully smooth the top.

17 Chill, then smooth another layer of Chantilly cream over the sides of the cake.

18 Decorate the sides with an icing comb, if you like.

19 Pipe waves of cream over the top.

20 Work from the edge towards the center.

Opéra
Glazed Chocolate and Coffee Layer Cake

Coffee Syrup
Combine the coffee, sugar, and instant coffee and stir with a wooden spoon until the sugar dissolves.

Joconde Cake
Preheat the oven to 400° F (200° C). Line 3 baking sheets with parchment paper.

Combine the whole eggs, egg yolks, ground almonds, and ¾ cup plus 2 tbsp. (6 oz., 175 g) of the sugar in the bowl of a stand mixer fitted with the whisk attachment (1).
Whip at high speed for 15 minutes (2).
Pour the batter into a large bowl (3).
Whip the egg whites at medium speed until they hold a soft peak.
Add the remaining sugar and whip until firm and glossy.
Add the whipped egg whites to the egg-almond mixture (4) and gently fold in with a flexible spatula (5).

Gradually sift in the flour and gently fold it in (6) just until smooth.

Spread one-third of the cake batter on each of the prepared baking sheets (7).
Bake 1 sheet at a time for 10 to 12 minutes, until lightly browned. Rotate the sheet halfway through baking.
Transfer the cake to a rack and let cool.

Chocolate Ganache
Finely chop the chocolate and place in a medium bowl.
Bring the milk and cream to a boil in a small saucepan and pour into the chocolate. Add the butter and whisk until smooth (8).

Coffee Buttercream
Whip the Buttercream at medium speed until very light, about 10 minutes.
Dissolve the instant coffee in the espresso. Add to the Buttercream and whip at low speed until smooth (9).

Makes 1 16 by 12-inch
(40 by 30 cm) cake
Level: Advanced
Prep: 1 hr.
Bake: 10 to 12 min. per
sponge cake layer
Chill: at least 1 hr.

Special equipment
3 baking sheets
A stand mixer
A 16 by 12-inch (40 by 30 cm)
cake ring
A 16 by 12-inch (40 by 30 cm)
homemade cardboard base,
½ inch (1 cm) high
An offset spatula

1 Combine the whole eggs, egg yolks, ground almonds, and sugar.

2 Beat at high speed for 15 minutes.

3 This is what the batter should look like.

4 Add the whipped egg whites.

5 Gently fold them into the batter with a flexible spatula.

6 Gradually fold in the sifted flour.

7 Spread one-third of the cake batter on each of 3 lined baking sheets.

8 Whisk the hot milk–cream mixture into the chopped chocolate and butter to make ganache.

9 Whip the Buttercream with the coffee mixture until very smooth and light.

continued

Place the cake ring on one sponge cake. Cut off the excess. Repeat with the remaining sponge cakes. Remove the ring.

Line a baking sheet with parchment paper. Place the cardboard base on the prepared baking sheet, line with parchment paper, and place the cake ring around it (10 and 11).

Place one sponge cake in the ring and brush with the coffee syrup (12).

Spread half of the coffee buttercream over the cake in the ring with the offset spatula (13).

Carefully place the second sponge cake on top and brush with coffee syrup.

Spread with a thin layer of ganache (14 and 15).

Place the third sponge cake on top (16). Brush with coffee syrup (17).

Spread the remaining buttercream over the top (18) and smooth with the spatula (19).

Chill until the fillings set, at least 1 hour.

Chocolate Glaze

Finely chop the chocolate and place in a medium bowl with the shortening and oil. Place over a saucepan filled with 1 inch (2.5 cm) of barely simmering water and let melt, stirring constantly with a flexible spatula, just until the chocolate reaches between 95 and 104° F (35 to 40° C). Remove the bowl from the heat.

Carefully remove the ring and cardboard base from the cake.

Pour the glaze over the top of the cake (20), smooth three or four times with the offset spatula (21), and chill until it sets.

Cut into slices using a thin knife. Dip the knife into very hot water and wipe it dry after each cut.

10 Place the base and ring over a lined baking sheet.

11 Line the base with parchment paper.

12 Brush one sponge cake with coffee syrup.

13 Spread half of the buttercream over the cake.

14 Place another sponge cake on top and spread with ganache.

15 Spread it evenly with an offset spatula.

16 Place the third sponge cake on top.

17 Brush it with the syrup.

18 Spread with the remaining buttercream.

19 Smooth it with an offset spatula.

20 Pour the glaze over the cake.

21 Smooth several times for a flawless finish.

Paris-Brest
Praline Buttercream Choux Pastry

Choux Pastry

Preheat the oven to 350° F (180° C).

Combine the water, sugar, salt, and butter in a medium saucepan (1).

Bring to a simmer over medium heat. When the butter melts, remove the pan from the heat. Whisk in all the flour at once (2).

Continue whisking until the dough pulls away from the pan to form a ball.

Return the pan to medium heat and beat for 30 seconds to dry out the dough (3).

Remove the pan from the heat and break in 2 of the eggs, one by one (4), whisking after each addition until smooth (5).

Lightly beat the remaining egg. Whisk in as much as needed to make a dough that is very shiny and just falls from the spoon.

Egg Glaze

Lightly beat the egg in a cup with a fork.

Lightly butter a baking sheet and dust it with flour (6). Mark circles on the sheet with the cookie cutter, spacing them slightly apart, to use as guides (7).

Spoon the dough into the pastry bag fitted with the plain tip and pipe the dough into 3-inch (7 cm) rings on the prepared baking sheet (8).

Lightly brush with the egg glaze.

Makes 20 individual pastries
Level: Intermediate
Prep: 40 min.
Cook: 40 min.
Chill: 2 hr.

Special equipment
A 3-inch (7 cm) cookie cutter
or pastry ring
A pastry bag
A ⅓-inch (8 mm) plain pastry tip
A ⅓-inch (8 mm) star pastry tip

Choux Pastry

½ cup (125 ml) water
½ tsp. sugar
¼ tsp. salt
4 tbsp. (55 g) butter, diced
½ cup plus 1 tbsp. (2½ oz., 70 g)
   all-purpose flour, sifted
3 medium eggs

Egg Glaze

1 egg

Garnish

1⅓ cups (3½ oz., 100g) sliced
   blanched almonds

Mousseline Cream

1¾ cups (400 g) Buttercream
   (page 276)
¾ cup plus 2 tbsp. (250 g)
   Pastry Cream (page 274)
5 oz. (150 g) hazelnut-praline
   paste (see Succès Praliné,
   page 288)

Finish

Confectioners' sugar, for sifting

1 Place the water, sugar, salt, and butter over medium heat.

2 As soon as the butter melts, remove from the heat and pour in the flour.

3 Whisk until smooth.

4 Whisk in the eggs, one by one.

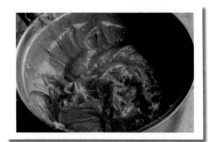

5 Whisk until the batter just falls from the spoon.

6 Butter a baking sheet and dust it with flour.

7 Make marks with a cookie cutter as guides to help with shaping the pastries.

8 Pipe rings of choux pastry.

continued

Garnish

Sprinkle the rings of dough with sliced almonds (9 and 10) and tilt and tap the baking sheet to remove the excess (11).

Bake for 25 minutes, or until puffed and lightly browned.
Transfer the rings to a rack and let cool.

Mousseline Cream

Whip the Buttercream at medium speed until very light, about 10 minutes.

Whisk the Pastry Cream until it is perfectly smooth. Add to the Buttercream and whip at low speed until smooth, about 1 minute (12).

Add the hazelnut-praline paste (13) and whip until smooth (14).

Finish

Cut the choux pastry rings horizontally in half using a long serrated knife (15).

Spoon the mousseline cream into the pastry bag fitted with a star tip and pipe the cream around the bottom halves (16). Carefully place the tops over the cream (17).

Lightly sift with confectioners' sugar (18).

Notes: Do not use a convection oven.

It is important not to open the oven door or the choux puffs will deflate.

The baked choux pastry can be stored in an airtight container for up to 3 days. They are best filled just before serving.

The mousseline cream can be prepared without Pastry Cream; the mixture will be slightly denser.

The Paris-Brest was created by a pastry chef in 1891 to honor the bicycle race of the same name, which crossed the town where he worked, just west of Paris. The shape, of course, represents a bicycle wheel.

9 Sprinkle the sliced almonds over the choux pastry rings.

10 The almonds will cover the baking sheet.

11 Tilt the baking sheet and tap off the excess almonds.

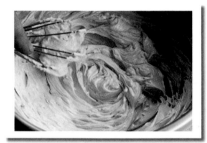

12 Whip the Pastry Cream well with the Buttercream.

13 Whip in the praline paste until smooth.

14 This is what the mousseline cream should look like.

15 Cut the pastries in half with a long serrated knife.

16 Pipe the mousseline cream around the bottom pastry halves.

17 Cover with the choux pastry tops.

18 Sift confectioners' sugar over the tops.

Éclairs
Vanilla and Coffee Éclairs

Éclairs

Preheat the oven to 350° F (180° C). Lightly butter a baking sheet and dust it with flour.

Combine the water, sugar, salt, and butter in a medium saucepan (1).

Bring to a simmer over medium heat. When the butter melts, remove the pan from the heat. Whisk in all the flour at once (2).

Continue whisking until the dough pulls away from the pan to form a ball.

Return the pan to medium heat and beat for 30 seconds to dry out the dough (3).

Remove the pan from the heat and break in 2 of the eggs, one by one (4), whisking after each addition until smooth (5).

Lightly beat the remaining egg. Whisk in as much as needed to make a dough that is very shiny and just falls from the spoon.

Egg Glaze

Lightly beat the egg in a cup with a fork.

Spoon the dough into the pastry bag and pipe into logs 4 to 5 inches (10 to 12 cm) long on the prepared baking sheet, spacing at least 1½ inches (3 to 4 cm) apart (6).

Lightly brush with the egg glaze.

Bake for 25 to 30 minutes, until puffed and golden brown (7).

Transfer the éclairs to a rack and let cool.

Vanilla and Coffee Pastry Creams

Whisk the Pastry Cream until it is perfectly smooth (8). Transfer half to a separate bowl. Dissolve the instant coffee in the espresso, add to one half of the Pastry Cream (9), and whisk until smooth.

Serves 6
Level: Intermediate
Prep: 45 min.
Bake: 25 to 30 min.

Special equipment
A pastry bag fitted with a
⅓-inch (8 mm) plain or star
pastry tip

Éclairs

½ cup (125 ml) water
½ tsp. sugar
¼ tsp. salt
4 tbsp. (2 oz., 55 g) butter
½ cup plus 1 tbsp. (2½ oz., 70 g)
    all-purpose flour
3 medium eggs

Egg Glaze

1 egg

Vanilla and Coffee Pastry Creams

1 recipe Pastry Cream (page 274)
¼ cup (15 g) instant coffee powder
3 tbsp. (40 ml) espresso, at room
    temperature

Vanilla and Coffee Glazes

8 oz. (250 g) white fondant icing
3½ tbsp. (50 ml) water
1 tsp. instant coffee diluted in
    3 tbsp. (40 ml) espresso

1 Heat the water, sugar, salt, and butter over medium heat.

2 Whisk in the flour. The dough should begin to dry out.

3 The flour should be completely absorbed.

4 Remove from the heat and whisk in the eggs, one by one.

5 Whisk constantly to work in the eggs.

6 Pipe log shapes 4 to 5 inches (10 to 12 cm) long.

7 This is how they should look after 20 minutes at 350° F (180° C).

8 Whisk the Pastry Cream to soften it.

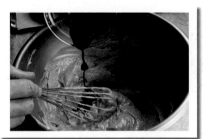

9 Flavor half the Pastry Cream with coffee, whisking it in well.

continued

Cut the éclairs horizontally almost in half with a serrated knife, and open like a book (10). Spoon the vanilla pastry cream into the pastry bag and pipe into half the éclairs (11). Use a clean pastry bag to fill the other half with coffee pastry cream (12).

Vanilla and Coffee Glazes

Melt the fondant icing in the water in a medium heavy saucepan over low heat, stirring with a wooden spoon, and cook until it registers 95° F (35°C) on an instant-read thermometer (13 and 14).

Remove from the heat and use the wooden spoon to glaze the tops of the vanilla éclairs (15 and 16).

Add the coffee mixture to the remaining fondant, mix well (17 and 18), and use to glaze the tops of the coffee éclairs (19, 20, and 21). Let set before serving.

Notes: Do not use a convection oven.
It is important not to open the oven door or the choux puffs will deflate.
You can add a teaspoon of eau-de-vie or brandy to the vanilla glaze, if you like.

10 Cut the éclairs horizontally almost in half and open like a book.

11 Fill half the éclairs with vanilla pastry cream.

12 Fill the other half with coffee pastry cream.

13 Melt the fondant over low heat, stirring with a wooden spoon.

14 Remove from the heat when it feels warm and the temperature reaches 95° F (35°C).

15 Coat the tops of the vanilla éclairs with vanilla glaze.

16 Make sure the glaze is even.

17 Add the coffee to the remaining fondant.

18 Mix in well until there are no streaks left.

19 Coat the tops of the coffee éclairs with coffee fondant.

20 Work carefully and neatly with a wooden spoon.

21 Wipe off any drips with a clean finger.

Saint-Honoré
Choux Puff Cake with Chiboust Cream

Puff Pastry Base

Line a baking sheet with parchment paper. On a lightly floured work surface, roll out the puff pastry ⅛ inch (3 mm) thick. Stamp out a disk with the pastry ring. Remove the excess dough. Drape the dough over the rolling pin and transfer to the prepared baking sheet. Chill.

Choux Pastry

Preheat the oven to 350° F (180° C). Lightly butter another baking sheet and dust it with flour.

Combine the water, sugar, salt, and butter in a medium saucepan (1).

Bring to a simmer over medium heat. When the butter melts, remove the pan from the heat. Whisk in all the flour at once (2).

Continue whisking until the dough pulls away from the pan to form a ball.

Return the pan to medium heat and beat for 30 seconds to dry out the dough (3).

Remove the pan from the heat and break in 2 of the eggs, one by one (4), whisking after each addition until smooth (5).

Lightly beat the remaining egg. Whisk in as much as needed to make a dough that is very shiny and just falls from the spoon.

Egg Glaze

Lightly beat the egg in a cup with a fork.

Spoon two-thirds of the dough into the pastry bag fitted with the plain tip. On the prepared baking sheet, pipe the dough into 1-inch (2.5 cm) rounds, spacing 1 inch (2.5 cm) apart (6). Or use a spoon to make balls.

Lightly brush with the egg glaze (7).

Bake for 20 to 25 minutes, until the choux are puffed and browned (8).

Transfer the choux to a rack and let cool. Leave the oven on.

Prick the disk of puff pastry with a fork (9).

Makes 1 9-inch (24 cm) cake
Level: Intermediate
Prep: 1 hr.
Cook: 40 to 50 min.

Special equipment
A 9-inch (24 cm) pastry ring
A pastry bag
A ⅓-inch (8 mm) plain pastry tip
A Saint Honoré tip (see *Notes*, page 308)

Puff Pastry Base

8 oz. (250 g) puff pastry dough (see Chocolate Puff Pastry, page 78, omitting the cocoa powder)

Choux Pastry

½ cup (125 ml) water
½ tsp. sugar
¼ tsp. salt
4 tbsp. (2 oz., 55 g) butter
½ cup plus 1 tbsp. (2½ oz., 70 g) all-purpose flour
3 medium eggs

Egg Glaze

1 egg

Chiboust Cream

2½ gelatin sheets (5 g)
6 eggs, separated
½ cup (3½ oz., 100 g) sugar
2½ tbsp. (1 oz., 25 g) cornstarch
1 vanilla bean
1 cup (250 ml) milk

Caramel

2 cups (14 oz., 400 g) sugar

1 Heat the water, sugar, salt, and butter over medium heat.

2 Pour in the flour.

3 Whisk until smooth.

4 Add the eggs, one by one, whisking constantly.

5 This is the soft consistency it should reach.

6 Pipe small rounds of dough.

7 Brush them with the egg glaze.

8 This is the golden color of baked choux pastry.

9 Prick the puff pastry base with a fork.

continued

Spoon the remaining dough into the pastry bag fitted with the plain tip and pipe 2 rings on the puff pastry disk: one around the edge and one in the center (10). Bake for 20 to 25 minutes, until puffed and browned.

Chiboust Cream

Soak the gelatin sheets in cold water until softened, 5 to 10 minutes.

Combine the egg yolks, half the sugar, and the cornstarch in a bowl and whisk (11) just until the sugar dissolves.

Split the vanilla bean lengthwise in half and scrape out the seeds.

Bring the milk and vanilla bean and seeds to a boil in a medium saucepan over medium heat. Remove the vanilla bean.

Whisk the hot milk into the egg yolk mixture (12).

Return the mixture to the saucepan and cook over medium heat, whisking constantly, just until this pastry cream thickens (13).

Remove the pan from the heat. Squeeze the gelatin dry and whisk into the hot pastry cream until dissolved (14).

Whip the egg whites with the remaining sugar at medium speed until they hold a soft peak, then whip at high speed until they hold a firm peak.

Add one-third of the egg whites to the pastry cream (15) and whisk until smooth to lighten the mixture.

Gently fold in the remaining egg whites with a flexible spatula (16 and 17).

Caramel

Fill a bowl with cold water. Pour half the sugar into a medium heavy saucepan. Melt it over medium heat, stirring with a wooden spoon. Pour in the remaining sugar and stir.

Reduce the heat to low and cook, stirring, until the sugar changes from a light amber liquid-y paste to a fluid, medium amber caramel.

Remove the pan from the heat and stop the cooking by dipping the bottom of the pan in the cold water.

Spoon some of the Chiboust cream into the pastry bag fitted with the plain tip. Pipe the cream into the choux puffs through a small hole in the bottom.

Dip the tops and bottoms of the choux pastries in the caramel, one by one, being careful not to burn your fingers (18).

Glue them around the edge of the puff pastry base so they are touching (19).

Spoon half of the Chiboust cream into the center of the cake (20).

Spoon the remaining Chiboust cream into the pastry bag fitted with the Saint-Honoré tip and pipe waves of the cream in the center (21).

10 Pipe 2 rings of choux pastry, one around the edge of the base, and the other in the center.

11 Whisk the egg yolks with half the sugar and the cornstarch.

12 Pour the hot milk over the yolk mixture, whisking.

13 Whisk well over medium heat.

14 Whisk in the softened gelatin.

15 Stir in one-third of the whipped egg whites.

16 Add the remaining egg whites.

17 Gently fold in until smooth with a flexible spatula.

18 Dip the bottom and top of each choux pastry in the caramel.

19 Glue them around the edge of the base.

20 Cover the center with half the Chiboust cream.

21 Pipe waves of the remaining Chiboust cream over the top using the special tip.

Mille-Feuille au Rhum
Rum Napoleons

Puff Pastry Layers

Preheat the oven to 350° F (180° C). Line 2 baking sheets with parchment paper.

On a lightly floured work surface, roll out the puff pastry ⅛ inch (3 mm) thick. Cut out 3 rectangles 12 by 5 inches (30 by 13 cm). Drape the dough over the rolling pin and transfer to the prepared baking sheets. Prick the dough with a fork.

Sprinkle the rectangles with sugar (1).

Cover the dough with parchment paper (2). Place a wire rack (3) or second baking sheet large enough to cover it on top to keep the dough from rising as it bakes. (You want the pastry as flat as possible for this recipe.)

Bake 1 sheet at a time for 20 to 25 minutes, until golden and lightly caramelized. Rotate the sheet halfway through baking.

Remove the parchment paper and the rack from the pastry and let cool slightly on the baking sheet.

Rum Pastry Cream

Whip the Pastry Cream at low speed until smooth.

Add the rum and whip just until smooth (4).

Serves 8
Level: Intermediate
Bake: 20 to 25 min.
Prep: 45 min.

14 oz. (400 g) puff pastry dough
  (see Chocolate Puff Pastry, page 78,
  omitting the cocoa powder)
¼ cup (2 oz., 50 g) sugar

1 recipe Pastry Cream (page 274)
2 tbsp. (30 ml) dark rum

10 oz. (300 g) white fondant icing
3½ tbsp. (50 ml) water
2 oz. (50 g) bittersweet chocolate

1 Sprinkle the puff pastry with sugar.

2 Cover with a sheet of parchment paper.

3 Place a rack or baking sheet on the covered pastry.

4 Gently whip the Pastry Cream with the rum.

continued

Spoon the rum pastry cream into a pastry bag fitted with a ⅓-inch (8 mm) plain tip and pipe bands lengthwise to cover one pastry rectangle (5). Or use a thin spatula.

Place a second pastry rectangle on top and pipe more bands of pastry cream (6). Top with the third rectangle (7). Let stand at room temperature.

Chocolate Glaze

Melt the fondant icing in the water over low heat, stirring with a wooden spoon, and cook until it registers 95° F (35°C) on an instant-read thermometer. Remove from the heat and pour on top of the napoleon (8).

Smooth the glaze with a thin spatula (9).

Finely chop the chocolate. Place in a small bowl set over a saucepan filled with 1 inch (2.5 cm) of barely simmering water, making sure that the bottom of the bowl does not touch the water. Let the chocolate melt. Remove the bowl from the heat and stir until smooth.

Scrape the melted chocolate into a parchment paper cone (see page 212), and pipe lines of chocolate crosswise on the glaze (10). Pull the tip of a small knife up and down the length of the napoleon to make the traditional herringbone pattern (11 and 12).

Let stand at room temperature until the glaze sets, about 15 minutes.

Cut the napoleon crosswise into slices with a fine serrated knife.

Notes: Readymade all-butter puff pastry dough can replace the homemade.
You can add a few drops of food coloring to the fondant icing.
The baked puff pastry can be stored in an airtight container for up to 3 days. Assemble the napoleon just before serving.

5 Pipe bands of rum pastry cream on the first layer.

6 Pipe more bands on the second layer.

7 Place the third layer of puff pastry on the cream.

8 Pour the glaze on top.

9 Spread it evenly with a thin spatula.

10 Pipe lines of melted chocolate with a parchment paper cone.

11 Drag a small knife perpendicular to the lines to make a herringbone pattern.

12 This is the completed pastry.

Tiramisu à l'Amaretto
Amaretto Tiramisu

Amaretto-Coffee Syrup
Combine the espresso, sugar, and Amaretto and stir until the sugar dissolves.

Coffee Sponge Cake
Preheat the oven to 350° F (180° C). Line 2 baking sheets with parchment paper.

Whip the egg whites at medium speed until they hold a soft peak (1).

Add the sugar and whip the egg whites until firm and glossy.

Add the egg yolks (2) and whip until smooth, about 5 seconds.

Add the instant coffee dissolved in the espresso (3) and whip at low speed until smooth.

Gradually sift the flour into the mixture (4) and gently fold in (5 and 6) with a flexible spatula.

Spread half the cake batter on each of the prepared baking sheets and smooth with a thin spatula (7).

Bake 1 sheet at a time for 10 to 12 minutes, until lightly browned. Rotate the sheet halfway through baking.

Transfer the cake to a rack and let cool.

Mascarpone Mousse
Pour the cream into a large bowl and chill.

Combine the sugar and water in a small heavy saucepan over medium heat and stir with a wooden spoon until the sugar dissolves.

Bring to a boil, washing down any crystals on the sides of the pan with a moistened pastry brush.

Dip the candy thermometer in the syrup, making sure it does not touch the bottom.

Cook the sugar, watching carefully, until it registers 239° F (115° C) (8).

Makes 1 16 by 12-inch
(40 by 30 cm) cake
Level: Easy
Prep: 1 hr.
Bake: 10 to 12 min. per sponge
cake layer
Freeze: at least 1 hr.

Special equipment
A candy thermometer
A stand mixer
A 16 by 12-inch (40 by 30 cm)
pastry ring

Amaretto-Coffee Syrup

⅔ cup (150 ml) lukewarm espresso
⅓ cup (2½ oz., 70 g) superfine
sugar
3 tbsp. (40 ml) Amaretto liqueur

Coffee Sponge Cake

6 eggs, separated
¾ cup plus 2 tbsp. (6½ oz., 180 g)
sugar
¾ cup (2 oz., 50 g) instant coffee
powder dissolved in 3 tbsp.
espresso
1 cup plus 2 tbsp. (5 oz., 150 g)
all-purpose flour

Mascarpone Mousse

1 ¾ cups (450 ml) heavy cream
½ cup plus 2 tbsp. (4 oz., 120 g)
sugar
3½ tbsp. (50 ml) water
4 egg yolks
3 gelatin sheets (6 g)
10 oz. (300 g) mascarpone

Finish

½ cup (2 oz., 50 g) unsweetened
cocoa powder

1 Begin beating the egg whites. Gradually add the sugar.

2 Pour the egg yolks into the beaten egg whites.

3 Gently beat in the coffee.

4 Sift in the flour.

5 Gently fold it in.

6 This is what the batter should look like.

7 Spread half the batter on each of the lined baking sheets.

8 Heat the sugar and water over medium heat to 239° F (115° C).

continued

Meanwhile, beat the egg yolks in the stand mixer fitted with the whisk attachment at low speed.

When the syrup is ready, carefully pour it down the side of the bowl into the yolks and beat at high speed until the mixture cools to room temperature (9), about 10 minutes.

Whip the chilled cream until it holds a firm peak.

Soak the gelatin sheets in cold water until softened, 5 to 10 minutes.

Whisk the mascarpone in a large bowl until smooth.

Gradually add the egg yolk mixture (10) and beat in with a flexible spatula until smooth (11).

Squeeze the gelatin dry, place it in a bowl, and melt in the microwave oven for a few seconds.

Stir a little of the mascarpone into the melted gelatin until smooth, then stir this mixture into the remaining mascarpone.

Beat one-third of the whipped cream into the mascarpone to lighten it (12).

Gently fold in the remaining whipped cream (13).

Place the cake ring on one sponge cake. Cut off the excess (14).

Repeat with the second sponge cake. Leave on the ring.

Brush the cake in the ring with coffee syrup (15). Spread half of the mascarpone mousse on top (16) and smooth with an offset spatula (17).

Place the second sponge cake on the mascarpone mousse (18) and brush it with syrup (19). Spread the remaining mousse over the top and smooth it (20) with a thin spatula.

Freeze the tiramisu until it sets, at least 1 hour.

To decorate, place a rack over the tiramisu and sift with the cocoa powder; remove the rack.

Remove the ring. Cut into slices with a fine serrated knife.

9 Pour the syrup down the side of the bowl into the egg yolks. Beat at high speed until cooled.

10 Pour a little of the egg yolk mixture into the beaten mascarpone.

11 Stir in well.

12 Add the whipped cream.

13 Gently fold in with a flexible spatula.

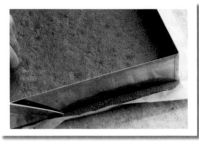

14 Place the ring on a sponge cake and trim the edges.

15 Brush the cake in the ring with coffee syrup.

16 Pour half the mascarpone mousse on the cake.

17 Smooth it with an offset spatula.

18 Place the second sponge cake on the mascarpone mousse.

19 Brush it with coffee syrup.

20 Carefully spread the remaining mascarpone mousse over the top.

Poire-Caramel
Pear-Caramel Chocolate Cake

Vanilla Syrup
Combine the water, sugar, and vanilla extract and stir with a wooden spoon until the sugar dissolves.

Chocolate Sponge Cake
Preheat the oven to 350° F (180° C). Line 2 baking sheets with parchment paper.
Sift the flour with the cocoa powder (1).
Whip the egg whites at medium speed until they hold a soft peak.
Add the sugar (2) and whip the egg whites until firm and glossy.
Add the egg yolks (3) and whip until smooth, about 5 seconds (4).
Gradually add the sifted dry ingredients (5) and gently fold in with a flexible spatula (6).

Makes 1 16 by 12-inch
(40 by 30 cm) cake
Level: Advanced
Prep: 1 hr.
Bake: 10 to 12 min. per sponge
cake layer
Freeze: at least 1 hr.

Special equipment
A 16 by 12-inch (40 by 30 cm)
cake ring

Vanilla Syrup

⅓ cup (70 ml) water
¼ cup (2 oz., 50 g) superfine sugar
½ tsp. vanilla extract

Chocolate Sponge Cake

1 cup plus 2 tbsp. (5 oz., 150 g)
all-purpose flour
3½ tbsp. (1 oz., 25 g) unsweetened
cocoa powder
1 cup (8½ oz., 240 g) egg whites
(about 8)
¾ cup plus 2 tbsp. (6½ oz., 180 g)
sugar
4 oz. (120 g) egg yolks (about 6)

Caramelized Pears

1 vanilla bean
¼ cup (2 oz., 50 g) sugar
1 lb. 5 oz. (600 g) peeled, diced
pears

Caramel Sauce

⅓ cup (2 oz., 60 g) sugar
⅔ cup (150 ml) heavy cream
2 tbsp. (1 oz., 30 g) butter

Caramel Mousse

2¼ cups (550 ml) heavy cream
6 gelatin sheets (12 g)
4 oz. (120 g) egg yolks (about 6)
1 cup plus 2 tbsp. (8 oz., 220 g)
sugar
⅓ cup (75 ml) water
1 cup plus 2 tbsp. (270 ml) milk

Finish

¾ cup (5 oz., 150 g) sugar
1 tsp. butter

1 Sift the flour with the cocoa powder.

2 Whip the egg whites with the sugar until they hold a firm peak.

3 Add the egg yolks.

4 Whip the mixture just until smooth.

5 Gradually add the sifted dry ingredients.

6 Gently fold them in with a flexible spatula.

continued

Spoon the cake batter into a pastry bag fitted with a ½ inch (1 cm) plain tip and pipe half into bands on each of the prepared baking sheets (7 and 8). Or spread in a layer with a thin spatula.

Bake 1 sheet at a time for 10 to 12 minutes, until just firm to the touch; the color will lighten slightly. Rotate the sheet halfway through baking.

Transfer the cake to a rack and let cool.

Caramelized Pears

Split the vanilla bean lengthwise in half and scrape out the seeds.

Cook the sugar in a medium skillet over medium heat, stirring with a wooden spoon, until it melts and turns a light amber color (9).

Add the pears and vanilla bean and seeds (10) and cook, stirring occasionally, until tender and caramelized on all sides, about 5 minutes (11). Remove from the heat. Remove the vanilla bean.

Caramel Sauce

Pour the sugar into a small heavy saucepan. Melt it over medium heat, stirring with a wooden spoon. Reduce the heat to low and cook, stirring, until the sugar changes from a light amber liquid-y paste to a fluid, medium amber caramel.

Meanwhile, slightly warm the cream in a microwave oven or in a small pan for just a few seconds; this will make it easier to combine with the caramel than if it were cold.

Carefully pour the cream into the caramel in three batches, stirring with a wooden spoon after each addition until smooth.

Add the butter and cook over medium heat until the caramel sauce is creamy and smooth, about 10 seconds. Remove from the heat.

Caramel Mousse

Pour the cream into a large bowl and chill.

Soak the gelatin sheets in cold water until softened, 5 to 10 minutes.

Combine the egg yolks and 2 tbsp. (1 oz., 25 g) of the sugar in a medium bowl and whisk just until the sugar dissolves (12).

Cook the remaining sugar in a small heavy saucepan over medium heat (13), stirring with a wooden spoon, until it melts and turns a medium amber color (14).

Continue cooking until it turns a dark amber color. Watch carefully; at this point just 5 seconds too long on the heat and it will burn. When plumes of smoke rise, carefully stir in the water (15). This will reduce the temperature, so slightly reheat the caramel. Remove from the heat.

Bring the milk to a boil in a small medium saucepan. Whisk it into the egg yolks (16) and return this custard to the saucepan (17). Pour in the watered-down caramel (18).

7 Pipe the sponge cake batter into bands on lined baking sheets.

8 Pipe half the batter on each baking sheet.

9 Cook the sugar for the pears to a light amber color over medium heat.

10 Add the diced pears and vanilla bean and seeds.

11 Cook, stirring, until tender, about 5 minutes.

12 Whisk the egg yolks with the sugar, without letting the mixture become pale.

13 Melt the sugar over medium heat.

14 Make a dark caramel. Keep an eye on it while it cooks.

15 Carefully stir the water into the caramel.

16 Whisk the hot milk into the egg yolks.

17 Return the mixture to the heat.

18 Whisk in the caramel.

continued

Cook over low heat, stirring with a wooden spoon, just until the custard registers 180° F (82° C) on an instant-read thermometer (19) and thickens slightly.

It is ready when it coats a spoon; if you draw a finger across the back of the spoon, it should leave a clear trail. Remove the pan from the heat.

Squeeze the gelatin dry (20) and stir it into the caramel custard with a wooden spoon (21) until dissolved. Let the mixture cool, but be careful that it does not set. If it does, reheat it very slightly.

Whip the cream until it holds a firm peak.

Beat one-third of the whipped cream into the caramel custard to lighten it.

Gently fold the caramel custard into the remaining whipped cream (22) with a flexible spatula until smooth (23).

Place the cake ring on one sponge cake. Cut off the excess. Repeat with the second sponge cake. Leave on the ring.

Brush the cake in the ring with vanilla syrup (24).

Spread the diced pears in the ring (25) and pour the caramel sauce over them.

Spread half of the caramel mousse on top (26).

Carefully place the second sponge cake on the mousse (27) and brush it with syrup.

Pour the remaining mousse over the top (28) and smooth it with a thin spatula (29).

Freeze until the mousse is set, at least 1 hour.

Finish

Line a baking sheet with parchment paper.

Cook the sugar in a small heavy saucepan over medium heat, stirring with a wooden spoon, until it melts and turns a dark amber color. Watch carefully; at this point just 5 seconds too long on the heat and it will burn. When the first plumes of smoke rise, carefully stir in the butter.

Pour the caramel in a thin layer on the prepared baking sheet and spread evenly with a thin spatula. Let cool, then finely crush with a rolling pin.

Sprinkle the crushed caramel over the top of the cake. Cut into slices with a fine serrated knife.

Note: You can reserve some of the caramelized pears and scatter them over the cake just before serving, if you like.

19 Cook the custard until the temperature registers 180° F (82° C), then remove from the heat.

20 Add the softened, drained gelatin.

21 Stir with a wooden spoon until the gelatin dissolves.

22 Pour the caramel custard into the whipped cream.

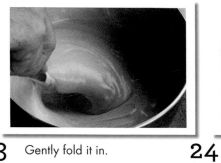

23 Gently fold it in.

24 Brush the sponge cake in the ring with the vanilla syrup.

25 Spread the pears in an even layer.

26 Cover the pears with half the caramel mousse.

27 Place the second sponge cake on the mousse.

28 Pour the remaining caramel mousse over the top.

29 Spread it evenly with a thin spatula.

Chocolat-Framboise
Glazed Raspberry–Chocolate Cake

Raspberry Syrup
Combine the raspberries, water, lemon juice, and sugar and stir with a wooden spoon until the sugar dissolves.

Chocolate Sponge Cake
Preheat the oven to 350° F (180° C). Line 2 baking sheets with parchment paper.

Sift the flour with the cocoa powder (1).

Whip the egg whites at medium speed until they hold a soft peak.

Add the sugar and whip the egg whites until firm and glossy (2).

Add the egg yolks (3) and whip until smooth, about 5 seconds (4).

Gradually add the sifted dry ingredients (5) and gently fold in with a flexible spatula (6).

Spoon the cake batter into a pastry bag fitted with a ½ inch (1 cm) plain tip and pipe half into bands on each of the prepared baking sheets (7 and 8). Or spread in a layer with a thin spatula.

Bake 1 sheet at a time for 10 to 12 minutes, until just firm to the touch; the color will lighten slightly. Rotate the sheet halfway through baking.

Transfer the cake to a rack and let cool.

Makes 1 16 by 12-inch
(40 by 30 cm) cake
Level: Intermediate
Prep: 1 hr.
Bake: 10 to 12 min. per sponge
cake layer
Freeze: at least 2 hr.

Special equipment
A candy thermometer
A stand mixer
A 16 by 12-inch (40 by 30 cm)
cake ring
An offset spatula

Raspberry Syrup

3½ oz. (100 g) raspberries, pureed
3½ tbsp. (50 ml) water
1 tbsp. lemon juice
¼ cup (2 oz., 50 g) superfine sugar

Chocolate Sponge Cake

1 cup plus 2 tbsp. (5 oz., 150 g)
all-purpose flour
3 tbsp. (¾ oz., 20 g) unsweetened
cocoa powder
1 cup (8½ oz., 240 g) egg whites
(about 8)
¾ cup plus 2 tbsp. (6½ oz., 180 g)
sugar
4 oz. (120 g) egg yolks (about 6)

Raspberry Compote

8 oz. (250 g) raspberries
13 oz. (370 g) raspberry
preserves

Chocolate Mousse

2 cups (500 ml) heavy cream
½ cup (3 oz., 90 g) sugar
3½ tbsp. (50 ml) water
4 egg yolks
1 whole egg
8 oz. (220 g) bittersweet
chocolate (70% cocoa)

Finish

3½ oz. (100 g) bittersweet
chocolate
⅓ cup (2 oz., 50 g) confectioners'
sugar

1 Sift the flour with the cocoa powder.

2 Whip the egg whites, gradually adding the sugar, until firm.

3 Add the egg yolks.

4 Whip until smooth.

5 Gradually pour in the sifted dry ingredients.

6 Fold them in with a flexible spatula.

7 Pipe bands of cake batter on lined baking sheets.

8 Make 2 even layers.

continued

Raspberry Compote
Combine the raspberries and preserves in a medium a saucepan. Cook over medium heat, stirring until thickened; the mixture should be thick when cooled. Remove from the heat.

Chocolate Mousse
Pour the cream into a large bowl and chill.

Combine the sugar and water in a small heavy saucepan over medium heat and stir with a wooden spoon until the sugar dissolves.

Bring to a boil, washing down any crystals on the sides of the pan with a moistened pastry brush.

Dip the candy thermometer in the syrup, making sure it does not touch the bottom.

Cook the sugar, watching carefully, until it registers 244° F (118° C) (9).

Meanwhile, beat the eggs yolks with the whole egg in the stand mixer fitted with the whisk attachment at low speed (10).

When the sugar syrup is ready, carefully pour it down the side of the bowl into the yolks and beat at high speed until the mixture cools to room temperature, about 10 minutes.

Finely chop the chocolate. Place it in a medium bowl set over a saucepan filled with 1 inch (2.5 cm) of barely simmering water and let melt, stirring constantly with a flexible spatula, just until it reaches 113° F (45° C) (11). Remove the bowl from the heat.

Whip the chilled cream until it holds a firm peak.

Scrape the chocolate into the egg mixture (12) and stir with a flexible spatula until smooth (13).

Beat one-third of the whipped cream into the mousse to lighten it (14).

Gently fold in the remaining whipped cream (15) until smooth (16).

9 Cook the sugar and water together to 244° F (118° C°).

10 Beat the eggs.

11 Melt the chocolate over a hot water bath until it reaches 113° F (45° C).

12 Scrape the chocolate into the egg mixture.

13 Stir it until smooth with a flexible spatula.

14 Pour in the whipped cream.

15 Fold it in with a flexible spatula.

16 This is what the chocolate mousse should look like.

continued

Finish

Finely chop the chocolate. Place it in a medium bowl set over a saucepan filled with 1 inch (2.5 cm) of barely simmering water and let melt. Remove the bowl from the heat. Stir with a flexible spatula until smooth.

Spread the melted chocolate over one sponge cake (17) and let it set.

Sift the confectioners' sugar over the chocolate (18).

Place the ring on the cake and cut off the excess. Repeat with the second cake. Leave on the ring.

Brush the cake in the ring with raspberry syrup (19).

Spread half the chocolate mousse in the ring (20) and smooth it with an offset spatula (21). Place the second sponge cake on the mousse (22) and brush it with raspberry syrup (23).

Spread the remaining mousse on top (24) and smooth it with an offset spatula (25).

Freeze until the mousse sets, at least 2 hours. Just before serving, gently reheat the raspberry compote. Remove the ring from the cake and spread the compote over the top. Smooth with a thin spatula (26).

Cut into slices with a fine serrated knife.

17 Spread the melted chocolate over one sponge cake.

18 Dust with confectioners' sugar.

19 Brush the sugar-dusted cake with half the raspberry syrup.

20 Spread half the mousse over the cake.

21 Smooth it with an offset spatula.

22 Place the second cake on the mousse.

23 Brush it with the remaining syrup.

24 Spread with the remaining mousse.

25 Smooth it with the offset spatula.

26 Cover the top of the cake with the raspberry compote.

Marronnier
Chocolate-Chestnut Layer Cake

Vanilla-Rum Syrup

Combine the sugar and water in a small saucepan and cook over medium heat, stirring, until the sugar dissolves. Remove from the heat, let cool, and stir in the rum and vanilla.

Chocolate Sponge Cake

Preheat the oven to 350° F (180° C). Line 2 baking sheets with parchment paper.

Whip the egg whites at medium speed until they hold a soft peak.

Add the sugar (1) and whip the egg whites until firm and glossy (2).

Add the egg yolks (3) and whip until smooth, about 5 seconds.

Gradually sift in the dry ingredients (4) and gently fold in with a flexible spatula (5) until smooth (6).

Spread half the cake batter on each of the prepared baking sheets and smooth with a thin spatula (7).

Bake 1 sheet at a time for 10 to 12 minutes, until just firm to the touch; the color will lighten slightly. Rotate the sheet halfway through baking.

Transfer the cake to a rack and let cool.

Makes 1 16 by 12-inch
(40 by 30 cm) cake
Level: Advanced
Prep: 1 hr.
Bake: 10 to 12 min per sponge
cake layer
Freeze: at least 1 hr.

Special equipment
A stand mixer
A candy thermometer
A 16 by 12-inch (40 by 30 cm)
cake ring
An offset spatula

¼ cup (2 oz., 50 g) sugar
⅓ cup (70 ml) water
1 tsp. dark rum
½ tsp. vanilla extract

1 cup (8½ oz., 240 g) egg whites
(about 8)
¾ cup plus 2 tbsp. (6½ oz., 180 g)
sugar
4 oz. (120 g) egg yolks (about 6)
1 cup plus 2 tbsp. (5 oz., 150 g)
all-purpose flour
3 tbsp. (20 g) unsweetened cocoa
powder

2¼ cups (550 ml) heavy cream
6 egg yolks
⅓ cup (2½ oz., 70 g) sugar
⅓ cup plus 1 tbsp. (90 ml) water
6 gelatin sheets (12 g)
1 lb. (500 g) chestnut cream or
spread (see Note)
2 tbsp. (30 ml) dark rum

7 oz. (200 g) chestnut cream or
spread
Bittersweet chocolate, for shaving

1 Gradually pour the sugar into the egg whites as they are whipped.

2 They should be very firm.

3 Incorporate the egg yolks into the beaten whites.

4 Sift in the flour with the cocoa powder.

5 Fold in the dry ingredients carefully.

6 This is what the batter should look like.

7 Spread it out on 2 lined baking sheets.

continued

Chestnut Mousse

Pour the cream into a large bowl and chill.

Beat the egg yolks in the stand mixer fitted with the whisk attachment at low speed (8).

Meanwhile, combine the sugar and 3½ tbsp. (50 ml) of the water in a small heavy saucepan over medium heat and stir with a wooden spoon until the sugar dissolves.

Bring to a boil, washing down any crystals on the sides of the pan with a moistened pastry brush.

Dip the candy thermometer in the syrup, making sure it does not touch the bottom.

Cook the sugar, watching carefully, until it registers 239° F (115° C) (9).

When the syrup is ready, carefully pour it down the side of the bowl into the yolks and beat at high speed until the mixture cools to room temperature, about 10 minutes (10).

Whip the chilled cream until it holds a firm peak.

Soak the gelatin sheets in cold water until softened, 5 to 10 minutes.

Combine the chestnut cream and the remaining water in a large bowl and beat with a wooden spoon until smooth.

Heat the rum in a small saucepan over low heat. Squeeze the gelatin dry. Add the rum to the gelatin (11) and whisk until it dissolves.

Add the rum gelatin to the chestnut cream (12) and beat in with a flexible spatula until smooth (13).

Gradually add the egg yolk mixture (14) and stir with a flexible spatula (15) until smooth.

Beat one-third of the whipped cream into the chestnut mousse to lighten it.

Add the remaining whipped cream (16) and gently fold in (17) until smooth (18).

8 Begin beating the egg yolks at low speed.

9 Cook the sugar and water to 239° F (115° C).

10 Carefully pour the hot syrup into the egg yolks. Beat until the texture is thick and foamy.

11 Pour the lukewarm rum over the drained gelatin sheets.

12 Add the rum gelatin to the chestnut cream.

13 Beat in well with a spatula.

14 Pour in the beaten yolks.

15 Fold in with a spatula.

16 Pour in the whipped cream.

17 Gently fold it in.

18 Mix just until just smooth.

continued

Finish

Place the cake ring on one sponge cake. Remove the excess (19).

Repeat with the second sponge cake. Leave on the ring.

Brush the cake in the ring with the vanilla-rum syrup (20).

Spread the chestnut cream over the top (21).

Pour half the chestnut mousse over the chestnut cream (22) and spread with the offset spatula. Place the second cake on the mousse (23) and brush it with syrup.

Spread the remaining mousse over the top (24) and smooth it with the offset spatula (25).

Freeze until the mousse is firm, at least 1 hour.

Shave the chocolate with a serrated knife or vegetable peeler. Sprinkle it generously over the top of the cake. Cut into slices with a fine serrated knife.

Note: Crème de marrons, *also known as chestnut spread, is made of chestnuts, sugar, and vanilla, and may also contain glucose and glacéed chestnuts.*

19 Trim the excess cake from around the edge of the ring.

20 Brush the cake in the ring with vanilla-rum syrup.

21 Spread the chestnut cream evenly over the top.

22 Spread with half the chestnut mousse and smooth it with an offset spatula.

23 Carefully place the second sponge cake on the mousse.

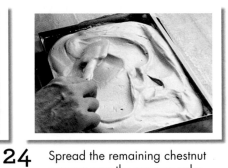

24 Spread the remaining chestnut mousse over the sponge cake.

25 Smooth it well.

Charlotte aux Poires
Pear Charlotte

Pear Syrup

Combine the sugar and water in a small saucepan and cook over medium heat, stirring, until the sugar dissolves. Remove from the heat, let cool, and stir in the vanilla and brandy.

Ladyfingers

Preheat the oven to 400° F (200° C). Line 2 baking sheets with parchment paper.

Sift the flour.

Whip the egg whites at medium speed until they hold a soft peak (1).

Gradually add the granulated sugar and whip the egg whites until firm and glossy (2).

Add the egg yolks (3) and whip until smooth, about 5 seconds (4 and 5).

Gradually fold in the sifted flour (6) with a flexible spatula.

Spoon the cake batter into the pastry bag and pipe 15 5-inch (12 cm) ladyfingers on 1 of the prepared baking sheets (7).

Using a plate or lid as a template, draw 2 5-inch (12 cm) circles on the paper of the second baking sheet, spacing them slightly apart, to use as guides.

Pipe 2 disks on the prepared baking sheet, working in a spiral from the center out.

Sift confectioners' sugar evenly over the tops (8).

Bake 1 sheet at a time for 8 to 10 minutes, until lightly browned. Rotate the sheet halfway through baking.

Transfer the disks and ladyfingers to a rack and let cool.

Serves 8
Level: Intermediate
Prep: 1 hr.
Bake: 8 to 10 min. per sheet
of ladyfingers
Chill: at least 2 hr.

Special equipment
A pastry bag fitted with a
½-inch (1 cm) tip
A 6-cup (1.5 l) charlotte mold or
soufflé dish

Pear Syrup

¼ cup (2 oz., 50 g) sugar
⅓ cup (70 ml) water
½ tsp. vanilla extract
1 tbsp. plus 1 tsp. pear brandy

Ladyfingers

1 cup (4 oz., 120 g) all-purpose flour
4 eggs, separated
⅔ cup (4 oz., 120 g) granulated
sugar
⅓ cup (2 oz., 50 g) confectioners'
sugar

Pear Bavarian Cream

1 cup plus 2 tbsp. (270 ml) heavy
cream
½ vanilla bean
⅔ cup (150 ml) milk
5 oz. (150 g) firm, ripe pears
5 gelatin sheets (10 g)
4 egg yolks
½ cup (3 oz., 90 g) sugar
1 tbsp. (15 ml) pear brandy

Pear Filling

10 oz. (300 g) peeled, diced pears

Finish

1 firm, ripe pear
1 lemon, halved
Quince jelly (optional)

1 Begin whisking the egg whites.

2 Gradually add the granulated sugar.

3 Pour in the egg yolks.

4 Whisk for a few more seconds.

5 This is what the mixture should look like.

6 Fold in the sifted flour.

7 Pipe the ladyfingers and 2 disks.

8 Sift confectioners' sugar over the tops.

continued

Pear Bavarian Cream

Pour the cream into a large bowl and chill.

Split the vanilla bean lengthwise in half and scrape out the seeds.

Bring the milk and vanilla bean and seeds to a boil in a medium saucepan over medium heat.

Remove the pan from the heat and let infuse for 10 minutes (9); remove the vanilla bean.

Peel and finely dice the pears.

Soak the gelatin sheets in cold water until softened, 5 to 10 minutes.

Mix the egg yolks with the sugar until the sugar dissolves (10).

Reheat the milk to boiling and whisk into the egg yolks (11).

Return this custard to the saucepan (12) and cook over low heat, stirring with a wooden spoon, until it thickens slightly.

It is ready when it coats a spoon; if you draw a finger across the back of the spoon, it should leave a clear trail and register 180° F (82° C) on an instant-read thermometer.

Remove the pan from the heat.

Squeeze the gelatin dry and whisk into the warm custard until dissolved (13).

Whisk in the brandy (14) and the diced pears (15).

Puree the mixture with an immersion blender or standard blender (16).

Whip the chilled cream until it holds a firm peak.

Beat one-third of the whipped cream into the pear mixture to lighten it (17).

Add the remaining whipped cream and gently fold in until smooth (18).

Fill a large bowl with ice water. Place the Bavarian cream in the ice water and let cool completely, stirring often.

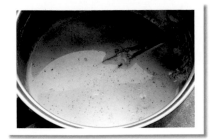

9 Let the vanilla bean infuse in the hot milk.

10 Combine the egg yolks and sugar.

11 Whisk the hot milk into the egg yolks.

12 Return to the saucepan.

13 Incorporate the softened, drained gelatin.

14 Stir in the pear brandy.

15 Add the diced pears.

16 Blend until smooth.

17 Carefully incorporate the whipped cream.

18 Use a small whisk to combine.

continued

Pear Filling

Lightly brush the ladyfingers with the pear syrup (19). Stand them upright, rounded sides out, around the edge of the mold, packing them tightly (20).

Pour in one-third of the Bavarian cream (21) and add one-third of the diced pears (22).

Brush one sponge cake disk generously with syrup (23).

Trim the disk, if needed, to fit inside the mold. Press it on the diced pears in the mold (24 and 25).

Pour one-third of the Bavarian cream into the mold (26) and scatter the remaining diced pears on top (27).

Pour in the remaining Bavarian cream to fill the mold (28).

Brush the second sponge cake disk lightly with pear syrup and trim it to fit just inside the ladyfingers (29).

Press it into the mold (30).

Chill the charlotte until the Bavarian cream sets, at least 2 hours.

Trim the ladyfingers flush with the rim of the mold.

Just before serving, quickly dip the mold into a bowl of very hot water and run a knife around the charlotte to loosen it. Invert a serving dish over the mold, and holding the mold and dish together, carefully turn out the charlotte onto the dish.

Finish

Thinly slice the pear lengthwise. Squeeze a little lemon juice over the slices and arrange several on the top of the charlotte.

If you like, melt the quince jelly with a little water over medium heat, stirring occasionally. Lightly brush the pear slices with quince jelly so they gleam.

Cut the charlotte into wedges with a fine serrated knife.

19 Brush the ladyfingers with the syrup.

20 Pack them tightly in the charlotte mold.

21 Pour one-third of the Bavarian cream into the mold.

22 Cover with diced pears.

23 Brush a sponge cake disk with syrup.

24 Place it on the diced pears.

25 Press in the disk.

26 Pour in more Bavarian cream.

27 Distribute the remaining diced pears evenly.

28 Pour in the remaining Bavarian cream to fill the mold.

29 Position the second sponge cake dish inside the ladyfingers.

30 Press it so that it is flush with the rim of the mold.

LES CHOCOLATS

ET PETITES BOUCHEES

Tempering Chocolate

Pastry chefs use couverture chocolate, richer in cocoa butter than ordinary chocolate, for their creations. The higher cocoa butter content means that it melts easily. You can find couverture at specialty stores or online at valrhona.com.

To be sure that your chocolate is glossy and has a distinctive snap, it should be tempered. Tempering takes a little practice to master. Recipes that require tempering are generally intermediate or advanced level.

Follow these instructions to make exquisite chocolates.

First, break or chop the chocolate into pieces. Place the chocolate in a bowl set over a saucepan with 1 inch (2.5 cm) of barely simmering water, making sure that the bottom of the bowl does not touch the water in the pan. (The heat would scorch the chocolate.) Alternatively, use a double boiler. Let the chocolate melt until it reaches the appropriate temperature using a chocolate or instant-read thermometer. Remove the bowl from the heat and stir until it is completely smooth.

Bittersweet chocolate should register 131° F (55° C).
Milk chocolate should register 122° F (50° C).
White chocolate should register 113° F (45° C).

Pour three-quarters of the melted chocolate on a marble slab or other cold, perfectly dry surface (moisture is the enemy of tempered chocolate). Keep the remaining chocolate warm.

Working with a thin spatula, keep spreading and turning the chocolate to cool it to the correct temperature. Check with a thermometer.

Bittersweet chocolate should register 82 to 84° F (28 to 29° C).
Milk chocolate should register 81 to 82° F (27 to 28° C).
White chocolate should register 79 to 81° F (26 to 27° C).

Scrape the stirred chocolate into a slightly warmed bowl. Gradually stir in the remaining warm chocolate just until the proper temperature is reached. Check the temperature constantly.

Bittersweet chocolate should register 88 to 90° F (31 to 32° C).
Milk chocolate should register 84 to 86° F (29 to 30° C).
White chocolate should register 84 to 86° F (29 to 30° C).

When the correct temperature is reached, stop adding the warm chocolate.

If necessary at any stage, reheat the chocolate, preferably in a brief burst in the microwave oven.

Bittersweet Chocolate Tempering Curve

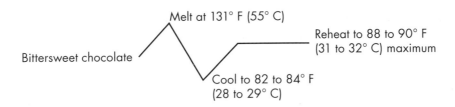

Typical composition of bittersweet chocolate: 55% cocoa and 45% sugar plus vanilla and soy lecithin.

Milk Chocolate Tempering Curve

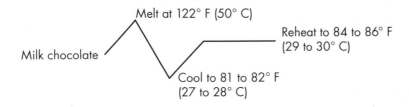

White Chocolate Tempering Curve

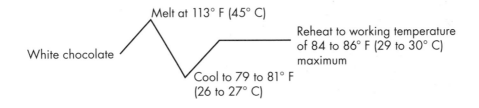

Ganache

A ganache is a combination of chocolate and a hot liquid (generally cream), a flavoring, and sometimes butter. Ganache is used on its own, for individual chocolates, as a filling for truffles, and in tarts and cakes. Methods of making this emulsion vary with the ingredients and involve melting chocolate by pouring a hot liquid over chopped chocolate, either in several additions or at once.

Amande Chocolat
Chocolate-Coated Almonds

Preheat the oven to 350° F (180° C).

Measure and prep your ingredients and arrange them on the counter (1).

Combine the almonds and cane syrup in a medium bowl (2 and 3).
Spread the almonds on a baking sheet and bake for 10 to 15 minutes, until lightly toasted (4).
Let cool completely.

Finely chop the chocolate. Place in a medium bowl set over a saucepan filled with 1 inch (2.5 cm) of barely simmering water, making sure that the bottom of the bowl does not touch the water. Let the chocolate melt. Remove the bowl from the heat and stir until smooth.

Fill a large baking pan or bowl with ice cubes and cover it with plastic wrap so that no cold water splashes.

Transfer the toasted almonds to a medium bowl and place it on the ice cubes.

Pour one-third of the chocolate into the almonds (5) and stir well with a wooden spoon (6), moving the bowl between the ice and a work surface. Make sure to incorporate any chocolate on the bottom of the bowl. The almonds will stick together initially but then separate.

Gradually stir in the remaining chocolate, alternating between the ice and work surface so the chocolate does not set too quickly.

This procedure helps ensure that the almonds are evenly coated (7, 8, and 9).

Makes about 1¼ cups
Level: Easy
Prep: 25 min.
Cook: 15 min.

1¼ cups (7 oz., 200 g) blanched almonds
2 tbsp. cane syrup or light corn syrup (see *Note*)
7 oz. (200 g) milk chocolate
2 pinches salt
¾ cup (3½ oz., 100 g) confectioners' sugar
3½ tbsp. (1 oz., 25 g) unsweetened cocoa powder

1 Have all your ingredients and utensils ready to go before cooking.

2 Pour the cane syrup over the almonds.

3 Use your hands to coat the almonds well.

4 This is what the toasted, coated almonds look like.

5 Place the bowl of caramelized almonds in a baking pan of ice cubes and pour in some of the melted chocolate.

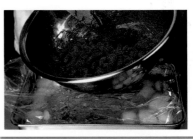

6 Stir well with a wooden spoon, incorporating any chocolate on the bottom of the bowl.

7 The almonds should be coated with chocolate.

8 Gradually stir in the remaining chocolate.

9 Continue to work, moving the bowl between the ice and a work surface.

continued

When all the chocolate has been added and the almonds are well coated, stir in the salt (10).

Sift the confectioners' sugar with the cocoa powder into a shallow baking pan (11) and whisk to combine (12). Add the coated almonds (13). You can stir them with a wooden spoon (14), but the best way to give them their final coating is to toss them (15) to avoid damaging the chocolate.

Store in an airtight container and serve with coffee.

Note: You can also use homemade sugar syrup. Bring ⅓ cup (2 oz., 60 g) sugar and 3½ tbsp. (50 ml) water to a boil in a small saucepan over medium heat and cook, stirring with a wooden spoon, until the sugar dissolves.

10 Mix in 2 pinches of salt.

11 Sift the confectioners' sugar with the cocoa powder.

12 Whisk the dry ingredients together.

13 Add the coated almonds.

14 Stir with a wooden spoon to coat them in the sweetened cocoa powder.

15 You can also toss them in a large bowl.

Mousse au Chocolat
Chocolate Mousse

Measure and prep your ingredients and arrange them on the counter (1).

Bring the cream to a boil in a small saucepan over medium heat.
Meanwhile, finely chop the chocolate and place it in a medium bowl (2).
Pour the hot cream over the chopped chocolate (3). Let it melt slightly, then whisk (4).
The cream and chocolate will combine to make a smooth, shiny ganache (5).

Add a pinch of salt to the egg whites and whip them until they hold a soft peak.
Gradually add the sugar (6) and whip until they hold a firm peak. Be careful not to over-beat them or they will become grainy.

Whisk the egg yolks into the ganache (7).
Scrape the chocolate mixture into the beaten egg whites. Gently fold in with a flexible spatula (8).
The mousse should be smooth (9), and no ganache should remain on the bottom of the bowl.

Spoon the chocolate mousse into a pastry bag and pipe the mousse into small glasses (10). Or spoon the mousse into small bowls.
Chill for at least 1 hour before serving.

Notes: You can drizzle caramel sauce (see page 336) over the individual chocolate mousses. Or for an unusual garnish, scatter a few crushed coriander seeds on the top.
Please note that the finished recipe contains raw egg.

Serves 12
Level: Easy
Prep: 15 min.
Chill: at least 1 hr.

⅓ cup plus 1 tbsp. (100 g) heavy cream
8 oz. (250 g) bittersweet chocolate (60 to 70% cocoa)
1 pinch salt
6 egg whites
3½ tbsp. (1½ oz., 40 g) sugar
2 egg yolks

1 Have all your ingredients and utensils ready to go before cooking.

2 Bring the cream to a boil and finely chop the chocolate.

3 Pour the boiling cream over the chocolate and let it melt.

4 Whisk to make a ganache.

5 The ganache should be smooth and shiny.

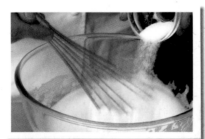

6 Begin whipping the whites. Gradually add the sugar.

7 Stir the egg yolks into the ganache.

8 Gently fold the chocolate into the whipped egg whites with a flexible spatula.

9 The mousse should be perfectly smooth.

10 Fill the small glasses with the mousse.

Carré Florentin
Florentine Squares

Preheat the oven to 350° F (180° C). Line a baking sheet with parchment paper.

Combine the honey, butter, sugar, and citrus zest in a small saucepan (1).

Cook over medium heat, stirring occasionally with a wooden spoon, until the sugar dissolves (2).

Bring to a boil, then immediately remove the pan from the heat and stir in the almonds (3), citrus peel, and peanuts (4) with a wooden spoon.

Spread the mixture in an even layer on the prepared baking sheet (5).

Bake for about 15 minutes, until lightly browned (6).

Sprinkle this praline with the fleur de sel and slide the parchment paper onto a cutting board (7).

Let cool slightly until firm enough to cut, then slice into 2-inch (5 cm) squares (8).

If the Florentine sheet becomes too brittle to cut, reheat it slightly in the oven.

Let cool completely.

Melt the chocolate and temper it according to the instructions on page 362.

Place a cooling rack over a sheet of wax or parchment paper. Transfer the florentines to the rack. Dip a spatula or wooden spoon in the tempered chocolate and drizzle stripes over the cookies (9).

Let the chocolate set completely before serving.

Makes about 3 dozen 2-inch
(5 cm) cookies
Level: Intermediate
Prep: 20 min.
Bake: 15 min.

3 tbsp. (2 oz., 60 g) mild honey
4 tbsp. (2 oz., 60 g) butter
⅓ cup (2 oz., 60 g) sugar
Grated zest of ½ orange
Grated zest of ½ lemon
⅔ cup (2 oz., 60 g) sliced almonds
2 tbsp. (20 g) diced candied lemon
    peel (see page 452)
2 tbsp. (20 g) diced candied orange
    peel (see page 452)
⅓ cup (1½ oz., 40 g) salted peanuts,
    coarsely chopped
1 pinch fleur de sel
3½ oz. (100 g) bittersweet chocolate
    (60 to 70 % cocoa)

1 Pour the honey, butter, and sugar into a saucepan and grate in the orange and lemon zest.

2 Cook over medium heat, stirring, to dissolve the sugar.

3 Bring to a boil, then remove from the heat and stir in the sliced almonds.

4 Stir in the diced orange and lemon peel and peanuts.

5 Spread the mixture in an even layer on a lined baking sheet.

6 This is the light golden color when baked.

7 Sprinkle with a pinch of fleur de sel. Slide onto a cutting board.

8 Cut out 2-inch (5 cm) squares.

9 Drizzle tempered chocolate stripes over the top with a spatula.

Mendiants Pistaches
Pistachio-Chocolate Bonbons

Preheat the oven to 350° F (180° C). Line a baking sheet with parchment paper.

Combine the pistachios and egg white in a small bowl (1) and add the sugar (2).
Mix with your fingertips until the texture is sandy (3).
Spread the sugar-coated pistachios on the prepared baking sheet and bake for 5 to 8 minutes, until dry (4 and 5).
Let cool completely.

Melt the chocolate and temper it according to the instructions on page 362.

Cover a work surface with plastic wrap, smoothing it so there are no wrinkles.

Using a spoon, make small ovals of chocolate (6).

Arrange 4 pistachios on each chocolate oval (7), pressing lightly.

Let set for 2 to 3 hours before serving.

Makes about 2½ dozen
Level: Easy
Prep: 20 min.
Bake: 5 to 8 min.
Set: 2 to 3 hr.

⅔ cup (2½ oz., 70 g) unsalted pistachios
1 tsp. egg white
3 tbsp. (1¼ oz., 35 g) sugar
5 oz. (150 g) bittersweet chocolate (60 to 70% cocoa)

1 Combine the pistachios with the egg white.

2 Add the sugar.

3 Working with your fingertips, coat the pistachios with the sugar.

4 Spread the pistachios on the lined baking sheet.

5 Bake the pistachios until completely dry and sandy on the outside.

6 Smooth a sheet of plastic wrap on a work surface. Make small ovals of tempered chocolate with a spoon.

7 Place 4 pistachios on each chocolate oval, pressing lightly.

Rose des Sables
Apricot-Corn Flake Chocolate Bars

Finely dice the dried apricots (1).

Line the baking pan with plastic wrap, leaving a generous overhang (2).

Melt the chocolate and temper it according to the instructions on page 362.

Combine the two types of corn flakes in a large bowl. Add the brown sugar and diced apricots.

Stir in the tempered chocolate and butter with a wooden spoon (3), being careful not to crush the corn flakes (4), until the corn flakes are coated with the chocolate (5).

Pour the mixture into the prepared baking pan (6).

Smooth with a wooden spoon and cover with plastic wrap (7).

Flatten the mixture by rolling a can over it (8).

Let set in a cool room for 20 minutes.

Chill for 5 minutes, then carefully turn it out onto a work surface.

Cut it into 1 by 1½-inch (3 by 4 cm) bars with a serrated knife (9).

Cut foil into rectangles and wrap the bar cookies (10). They will be easier to eat if wrapped.

Note: You can make these cookies with other types of cereals, like puffed rice. Or vary the dried fruits, and try milk or white chocolate instead of bittersweet.

Makes about 4 dozen
1 by 1½-inch (3 by 4 cm) bars
Level: Intermediate
Prep: 20 min.
Chill: 25 min.

Special equipment
A 10 by 8-inch (25 by 20 cm)
baking pan

⅓ cup (3 oz., 80 g) dried apricots
3½ oz. (100 g) bittersweet chocolate
  (60 to 70% cocoa)
3½ cups (3½ oz., 100 g)
  unsweetened corn flakes
1 cup (2 oz., 50 g) sweetened corn
  flakes
2 tbsp. (1 oz., 25 g) light brown
  sugar
1 tbsp. butter, melted and cooled

1 Dice the dried apricots.

2 Line the baking pan with plastic wrap, leaving an overhang so you can easily remove the mixture when it has set.

3 Combine the two sorts of corn flakes, the sugar, and dried apricots. Add the tempered chocolate and melted butter.

4 Gently stir with a wooden spoon.

5 The corn flakes should be completely coated in chocolate.

6 Pour the mixture into the lined baking pan.

7 Smooth with a spatula and cover with plastic wrap.

8 Roll a small can over the surface to flatten the mixture.

9 Turn out of the mold, remove the plastic wrap, and cut into bars with a serrated knife.

10 Wrap the bar cookies in rectangles of foil.

Ganache Rhum-Raisins
Rum-Raisin Ganache Squares

Measure and prep your ingredients and arrange them on the counter (1).

Heat the rum in a small saucepan and pour it over the raisins (2). Let soak until plump, at least 1 hour.

Finely chop the milk chocolate and place in a medium bowl. Bring the cream to a boil in a small pan over medium heat.
Gradually pour it over the chocolate (3), stirring after each addition, until the ganache is smooth (4).

Drain the raisins, reserving the rum. Coarsely chop them (5) and stir into the ganache (6).
Add the rum and stir well.
Line the baking pan with plastic wrap, leaving a generous overhang, and pour in the ganache (7). Chill until firm, at least 1 hour.

Makes about 4 dozen 1-inch
(2.5 cm) chocolates
Level: Easy
Prep: 20 min.
Soak: at least 1 hr.
Chill: at least 1 hr.

Special equipment
An 8-inch (20 cm) square
baking pan

¼ cup (60 ml) dark rum
½ cup (3 oz., 80 g) golden raisins
14 oz. (400 g) milk chocolate
½ cup (120 g) heavy cream
3½ oz. (100 g) bittersweet chocolate
  (60 to 70% cocoa)
2 tbsp. unsweetened cocoa powder

1 Have all your ingredients and utensils ready to go before cooking.

2 Warm the rum and pour it over the raisins.

3 Gradually pour the hot cream over the chopped milk chocolate.

4 Stir gently with a wooden spoon after each addition.

5 Coarsely chop the drained raisins.

6 Stir the chopped raisins and rum into the ganache.

7 Pour the ganache into a shallow baking pan lined with plastic wrap.

continued

Chocolate Desserts and Candies   377

Finely chop the bittersweet chocolate. Place it in a small bowl set over a saucepan filled with 1 inch (2.5 cm) of barely simmering water and let melt. Remove the bowl from the heat. Stir with a flexible spatula until smooth.

Transfer the ganache on the plastic wrap to a work surface. Pour 3 tbsp. of the melted bittersweet chocolate over the ganache (8) and spread it evenly with a thin spatula (9).

Let set slightly, about 2 minutes. Brush with cocoa powder (10).

Carefully turn the ganache over and repeat coating the other side (11).

Let the chocolate set slightly. Cut the ganache into 1-inch (2.5 cm) squares (12) or into the shape of your choice.

Notes: You can flambé the raisins with rum and add a pinch of cinnamon to the ganache.

Unless you can keep these chocolates in a cool room, store them in an airtight container in the refrigerator.

Lesson 91

8 Transfer the ganache to a work surface and pour over the melted chocolate.

9 Spread it smoothly with a thin spatula.

10 Brush a thin layer of cocoa powder over the top.

11 Spread a thin layer of melted chocolate over the other side and brush with cocoa powder.

12 Cut the ganache into the desired shapes.

Ganache Earl Grey

Earl Grey Ganache Squares

Measure and prep your ingredients and arrange them on the counter (1).

Bring the cream to a boil in a small saucepan over medium heat.
Remove the pan from the heat, add the tea, and let infuse for 5 minutes (2).

Meanwhile, finely chop the milk chocolate and place it in a medium bowl.

Strain the cream through a fine sieve into the chopped chocolate (3).

Let the chocolate melt slightly and then stir with a wooden spoon (4) until smooth.

Add the butter and stir until smooth (5).

Line the baking pan with plastic wrap, leaving a generous overhang, and pour in the ganache (6).

Chill until firm, at least 1 hour.

Makes about 4 dozen 1-inch
(2.5 cm) chocolates
Level: Easy
Prep: 30 min.
Chill: at least 1 hr.

Special equipment
An 8-inch (20 cm) square
baking pan

⅔ cup (150 g) heavy cream
1 tbsp. Earl Grey tealeaves
14 oz. (400 g) milk chocolate
4 tbsp. (2 oz., 60 g) butter, diced
3½ oz. (100 g) bittersweet chocolate
2 tbsp. unsweetened cocoa powder

1 Have all your ingredients and utensils ready to go before cooking.

2 Bring the cream to a boil and infuse the tea in it for 5 minutes.

3 Strain the flavored cream over the chopped chocolate.

4 Stir with a wooden spoon.

5 When the cream and chocolate are combined, stir in the diced butter.

6 Pour the ganache into a lined baking pan.

continued

Finely chop the bittersweet chocolate. Place it in a small bowl set over a saucepan filled with 1 inch (2.5 cm) of barely simmering water and let melt. Remove the bowl from the heat. Stir with a flexible spatula until smooth.

Transfer the ganache on the plastic wrap to a work surface. Pour half of the melted bittersweet chocolate over the ganache (7) and spread it evenly with a thin spatula (8).

Let set slightly, about 2 minutes. Sift cocoa powder over the top (9).

Carefully turn the ganache over and repeat coating the other side (10).

Spread the melted chocolate so it is even (11).

Let the chocolate set slightly. Cut the ganache into 1-inch (2.5 cm) squares (12) or into the shape of your choice.

Note: Unless you can keep these chocolates in a cool room, store them in an airtight container in the refrigerator.

7 Pour half of the melted chocolate over the top of the hardened ganache.

8 Smooth the melted chocolate with a metal spatula.

9 Let the chocolate set slightly and dust with cocoa powder.

10 Turn the ganache over and cover with melted chocolate.

11 Make sure the chocolate coating is even.

12 Cut into the desired shape.

Sucettes Chocolat à l'Anis
Aniseed-Chocolate Lollipops

Measure and prep your ingredients and arrange them on the counter (1).

Fill a medium bowl with ice water.

Pour the honey into a medium heavy saucepan (2) and bring to a boil (3). Add the sugar (4) and cook, stirring with a wooden spoon, until the sugar dissolves.

Return to a boil and cook for about 4 minutes. To check if the caramel is ready, scoop out a little with a spoon and drop it into the ice water (5). When you remove it, it should be very brittle (6).

Makes 8
Level: Easy
Prep: 20 min.
Cook: 4 min.

⅓ cup (4 oz., 120 g) mild honey, such as acacia
½ cup plus 2 tbsp. (4 oz., 120 g) sugar
8 drops lemon juice
2 oz. (50 g) bittersweet chocolate (60 to 70% cocoa), finely chopped
1 tbsp. (15 g) butter
4 licorice sticks, split lengthwise in half, or 8 lollipop sticks
A few pinches whole aniseed

1 Have all your ingredients and utensils ready to go before cooking.

2 Pour the honey into a heavy saucepan.

3 Bring it to a boil.

4 Add the sugar to the boiling honey and stir until dissolved.

5 Test the caramel: drop a teaspoon into a bowl of ice water.

6 The caramel should be brittle.

continued

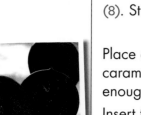

Immediately remove the pan from the heat and dip the bottom in the ice water until the bubbling stops. Stir in the lemon juice (7), the chocolate, and the butter (8). Stir with a wooden spoon until smooth (9).

Place a sheet of parchment paper on a work surface. Drop 8 tbsp. of chocolate caramel on the paper to make 8 mounds (10), spacing them well apart; leave enough room to insert a stick in each one.

Insert the sticks (11) and sprinkle with aniseed (12 and 13).

Let cool completely before removing them from the parchment paper (14).

Note: If you want to make a larger quantity of lollipops, wrap them individually in cellophane to store them.

7 Add 8 drops of lemon juice to the caramel.

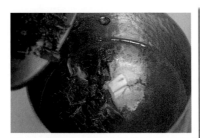

8 Add the chopped chocolate and butter.

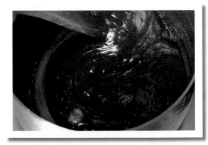

9 Stir until smooth.

10 Drop spoonfuls of caramel on the prepared baking sheet.

11 Press the licorice or lollipop sticks into the chocolate caramel.

12 Sprinkle with aniseed.

13 Make sure the sticks are properly inserted.

14 Remove from the baking sheet when cool.

Marzipan Citron
Lemon Marzipan Balls

Measure and prep your ingredients and arrange them on the counter (1).

Knead the almond paste until it is smooth and pliable. If it is too dry, add a drop of water. Cut into small pieces (2).

Split the vanilla bean lengthwise in half and scrape out the seeds.
Finely grate the lemon zest (3) and squeeze the juice.

Place the almond paste in a medium bowl and add the vanilla seeds, grated zest, and 2 tbsp. (30 ml) of lemon juice (4).

Beat with a wooden spoon or knead with your hands until smooth.

Lightly sift confectioners' sugar on a work surface (5).

Roll the almond paste into a long, even log (6) ¾ inch (2 cm) thick.

Makes about 4 dozen candies
Level: Easy
Prep: 25 min.
Freeze: at least 2 hr.

10 oz. (300 g) white almond paste (50% almonds, if possible)
1 vanilla bean
1 lemon
¾ cup (3½ oz., 100 g) confectioners' sugar
5 oz. (150 g) white chocolate

1 Have all your ingredients and utensils ready to go before cooking.

2 Cut the softened almond paste into small pieces.

3 Finely grate the lemon zest.

4 Beat the pieces of almond paste with the vanilla seeds and lemon zest and juice.

5 Place the smooth almond paste on a work surface dusted with confectioners' sugar.

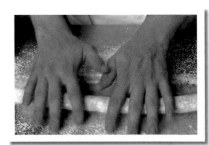

6 Roll it into a log ¾ inch (2 cm) thick.

continued

Cut the almond paste into ½-inch (1.5 cm) pieces (7).

Roll each piece between your palms into balls (8 and 9).

Place them on a dish and freeze until firm, about 2 hours.

Finely chop the white chocolate. Place it in a bowl set over a saucepan filled with 1 inch (2.5 cm) of barely simmering water and let melt. Remove the bowl from the heat. Stir until smooth.

Be careful not to overheat white chocolate, because it contains milk powder, which makes it more delicate than bittersweet chocolate.

Sift the remaining confectioners' sugar into a shallow baking pan.

Spread a little white chocolate on the palm of one hand (10).

Roll each almond paste ball between your palms to coat it lightly in white chocolate (11).

Toss them in the sifted confectioners' sugar to coat (12).

Place them in a sieve and gently roll them around to remove the excess confectioners' sugar (13).

Transfer to a baking sheet and freeze until firm, about 10 minutes. Serve with lemon tea.

7 Cut the log into ½-inch (1.5 cm) pieces.

8 Roll each piece between your palms into a ball.

9 This is the size they should be.

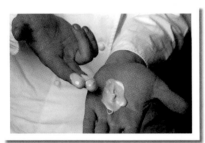

10 Spread a little white chocolate on the palm of one hand.

11 Roll the frozen almond paste balls to coat them in melted chocolate.

12 Roll them in the confectioners' sugar to coat.

13 Place them in a fine sieve to remove the excess confectioners' sugar.

Truffes au Café
Coffee Truffles

Measure and prep your ingredients and arrange them on the counter (1).

Coffee Truffles

Wrap the coffee beans in a kitchen towel and crush them with a rolling pin (2).

Bring the cream, water, and sugar to a boil in a medium saucepan over medium heat.

Remove the pan from the heat, add the crushed coffee (3), and let infuse for 5 minutes (4).

Finely chop the chocolate and place in a medium bowl. Strain the coffee cream into the chocolate (5) in two batches, whisking after each addition (6 and 7).

Makes about 4 dozen 1-inch
(2.5 cm) chocolates
Level: Easy
Prep: 20 min.
Infuse: 5 min.
Freeze: 2 hr. 30 min.

Special equipment
An 8-inch (20 cm) square
baking pan

Coffee Truffles

2 oz. (60 g) coffee beans
1 cup (250 ml) heavy cream
¼ cup (60 ml) water
3½ tbsp. (1½ oz., 40 g) sugar
10 oz. (300 g) bittersweet chocolate
(70% cocoa)
3 tbsp. (1½ oz., 40 g) butter, diced

Chocolate Coating

7 oz. (200 g) bittersweet chocolate
(60 to 70% cocoa)
1¾ cups (7 oz., 200 g) unsweetened
cocoa powder

1 Have all your ingredients and utensils ready to go before cooking.

2 Wrap the coffee beans in a kitchen towel and coarsely crush them with a rolling pin.

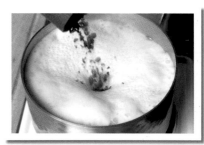

3 Bring the cream, water, and sugar to a boil and add the crushed coffee beans.

4 Let infuse for 5 minutes.

5 Strain half of the coffee cream into the chopped chocolate.

6 Whisk gently until smooth.

7 Whisk in the remaining coffee cream.

continued

Let the chocolate melt for 5 minutes, then stir with a whisk or wooden spoon until smooth (8).

Whisk in the butter until smooth (9).

Line the baking pan with plastic wrap, leaving a generous overhang. Pour in the ganache (10).

Press the overhang directly on the surface of the ganache (11) and freeze until firm, at least 2 hours.

Cut the ganache into ½ by 1-inch (1 cm by 2.5 cm) rectangles (12). Freeze until firm, about 30 minutes.

Chocolate Coating

Finely chop the chocolate. Place it in a medium bowl set over a saucepan filled with 1 inch (2.5 cm) of barely simmering water and let melt. Remove the bowl from the heat. Stir until smooth.

Sift the cocoa powder into a shallow baking pan.

Spread a little melted chocolate on the palm of one hand (13).

Roll each truffle gently between your palms to coat it lightly in melted chocolate (14).

Toss them in the cocoa powder to coat (15).

Place them in a sieve and shake to remove the excess cocoa powder.

8 Whisk until smooth.

9 Incorporate the butter.

10 Pour the ganache into a lined pan.

11 Cover with plastic wrap to prevent a skin from forming.

12 Cut the ganache into rectangles.

13 Spread melted bittersweet chocolate on the palm of one hand.

14 Roll a ganache rectangle between your palms.

15 Toss the rectangles in cocoa powder to coat them lightly.

Caramel au Chocolat
Chocolate Caramels

Measure and prep your ingredients and arrange them on the counter (1).
Line the baking pan with plastic wrap, leaving a generous overhang.

Finely chop the chocolate.

Combine the cream and chocolate in a medium heavy saucepan over low heat.

Add the honey (2) and sugar (3). Cook, stirring occasionally with a wooden spoon (4) until melted and smooth (5).

Bring to a boil over medium heat (6) and cook for about 10 minutes.

Makes about 4 dozen 1-inch
(2.5 cm) candies
Level: Easy
Prep: 30 min.
Cook: about 10 min.
Set: 2 hr.

Special equipment
An 8-inch (20 cm) square
baking pan
Food-safe cellophane,
for wrapping the candies

9 oz. (250 g) bittersweet chocolate
(50 to 60% cocoa)
1½ cups (400 ml) heavy cream
¼ cup plus 2 tbsp. (4 oz., 120 g)
mild honey, such as acacia
2 cups (14 oz., 400 g) sugar
2 pinches fleur de sel

1 Have all your ingredients
and utensils ready to go
before cooking.

2 Pour the cream and chocolate
into a saucepan over low heat
and add the honey.

3 Pour in the sugar.

4 Stir with a wooden spoon.

5 Cook over medium heat until
the mixture is smooth.

6 Bring to a boil and cook for
10 minutes.

continued

Fill a small bowl with ice water.

Remove the pan from the heat, scoop out a little caramel with a spoon, and drop it into the ice water (7 and 8).

You should be able to shape a small, fairly soft ball between your fingers (9).

Stir in the fleur de sel (10) and pour it into the prepared dish (11).

Cover with plastic wrap and let cool completely (12), about 2 hours.

Carefully invert the caramel onto a cutting board (13) and remove the plastic.

Cut it into 1-inch (2.5 cm) squares or rectangles (14 and 15).

Wrap the caramels in 4-inch (10 cm) squares of cellophane.

7  Test a little caramel in a small bowl of ice water.

8  Remove from the water and touch it.

9  You should be able to roll a small ball between your fingers. It should be fairly thick but soft.

10  Stir the fleur de sel into the caramel.

11  Pour the caramel into a lined pan.

12  Let cool completely at room temperature.

13  To turn out of the mold, pull up the edges of the plastic wrap.

14  Place the caramel on a chopping board and cut with a well-sharpened knife.

15  Cut out the shape of your choice.

Ganache Menthe Fraîche
Mint Ganache Bonbons

Measure and prep your ingredients and arrange them on the counter.

Mint Ganache

Bring the cream to a boil in a saucepan. Remove from the heat and snip in the mint leaves. Let infuse for 5 minutes (1).

Finely chop the chocolate and place in a medium bowl. Strain the mint cream into the chocolate (2).

Let the chocolate melt for 2 minutes, then stir with a flexible spatula until smooth (3).

Stir in the butter (4).

Line a baking sheet with parchment paper.

Spoon the ganache into a pastry bag fitted with a small tip and pipe small mounds of ganache on the paper, spacing well apart (5 and 6). Or use a spoon.

Carefully cover the mounds of ganache with plastic wrap (7). Lightly press each one with the bottom of a glass to flatten (8).

Let stand until set, at least 1 hour.

Candied Mint Leaves

Line a baking sheet with parchment paper. Spread the sugar in a shallow baking pan. Lightly beat the egg white in a cup with a fork. Brush each mint leaf on both sides with egg white (9) and dip in sugar. Place on the parchment paper and let dry overnight (10).

Decorate each ganache chocolate with a candied mint leaf and serve.

Note: If you cannot keep these ganaches in a cool room, store them in an airtight container in the refrigerator.

Makes about 4 dozen chocolates
Level: Intermediate
Prep: 30 min.
Set: at least 1 hr.
Dry: Overnight

Mint Ganache

1 cup (250 ml) heavy cream
30 mint leaves
14 oz. (400 g) bittersweet chocolate
   (60 to 70% cocoa)
3 tbsp. (1½ oz., 50 g) butter, diced

Candied Mint Leaves

¾ cup (5 oz., 150 g) sugar
1 egg white
48 medium mint leaves

1 Cut the mint leaves into the boiled cream and let infuse.

2 Strain the cream over the chopped chocolate.

3 Gently stir with a flexible spatula until the texture is smooth and shiny.

4 Stir in the diced butter.

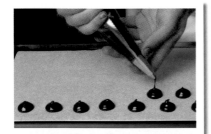

5 Pipe or spoon out small mounds of ganache onto a lined baking sheet.

6 This is what they should look like.

7 Carefully cover them with plastic wrap.

8 Lightly press each ball with the bottom of a small glass to flatten.

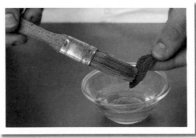

9 Carefully brush the mint leaves on both sides with egg white.

10 Dip the leaves in sugar and let set overnight.

Ganache au Citron Vert
Lime Ganache Squares

Measure and prep your ingredients and arrange them on the counter.

Lime Ganache
Finely chop the white chocolate. Place it in a medium bowl set over a saucepan filled with 1 inch (2.5 cm) of barely simmering water and let melt. Remove the bowl from the heat. Stir until smooth (1).

Finely grate the lime zest. Squeeze the juice.

Bring the cream to a boil in a small saucepan.

Add the lime zest to the melted chocolate (2).

Gradually pour the hot cream into the chocolate, stirring after each addition with a wooden spoon until smooth (3).

Add the lime juice (4). Stir until the ganache is perfectly smooth (5).

Line the baking pan with plastic wrap, leaving a generous overhang, and pour in the ganache (6).

Chill until firm, at least 1 hour.

Coating
Finely chop the white chocolate. Place it in a small bowl set over a saucepan filled with 1 inch (2.5 cm) of barely simmering water and let melt. Remove the bowl from the heat. Stir until smooth.

Transfer the ganache on the plastic wrap to a work surface. Pour the melted chocolate over the ganache (7) and spread it evenly with a thin spatula (8).

Let set slightly, about 2 minutes.

Carefully turn the ganache over and remove the plastic wrap. Sift the top with confectioners' sugar (9).

Cut the ganache into 1-inch (2.5 cm) squares (10). Serve chilled.

Note: Unless you can keep these chocolates in a cool room, store them in an airtight container in the refrigerator.

Level: Easy
Makes about 4 dozen 1-inch
(2.5 cm) chocolates
Prep: 20 min.
Chill: at least 1 hr.

Special equipment
An 8-inch (20 cm) square
baking pan

Lime Ganache

3½ oz. (100 g) white chocolate
1 lime
½ cup (100 ml) heavy cream

Coating

1½ oz. (50 g) white chocolate
⅓ cup (2 oz., 50 g) confectioners'
  sugar

1 Melt the white chocolate over hot water.

2 Add the finely grated lime zest and hot cream to the chocolate.

3 Stir gently with a wooden spoon.

4 Add the lime juice.

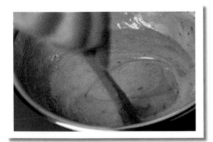

5 Stir until perfectly smooth.

6 Pour the ganache into a lined baking pan.

7 Transfer the firm ganache to a work surface and pour melted white chocolate over it.

8 Smooth the melted chocolate with a thin spatula.

9 Turn the ganache over and sift the other side with confectioners' sugar.

10 This is what the finished product looks like.

Coques de Chocolat, Caramel au Beurre Salé

Salted Caramel Chocolate Cups

Measure and prep your ingredients and arrange them on the counter (1).

Salted Caramel Filling

Pour the sugar into a small heavy saucepan. Melt it over medium heat, stirring with a wooden spoon.

Stir in the honey (2) and cook until the caramel reaches a light amber color (3). The best way to judge the color is to let the caramel run off the spoon.

Carefully pour the cream into the caramel in three batches, stirring with a wooden spoon after each addition, and cook until smooth and slightly thickened, about 2 minutes (4). The caramel will boil quickly after the first addition and may boil over!

Remove the pan from the heat and stir in the butter (5) until smooth.

Stir in the fleur de sel (6).

To check the caramel for doneness, drizzle a little on a plate (7): it should be pourable but not runny.

Scrape into a small bowl and let cool (8).

Makes 1 dozen small cups
Level: Intermediate
Prep: 30 min.

Special equipment
A 12-cup plastic egg carton
Chill and freeze: about 1 hr.

Salted Caramel Filling

½ cup (3½ oz., 100 g) sugar
1 tbsp. mild honey, such as acacia
⅓ cup (75 ml) heavy cream
5 tbsp. (3 oz., 80 g) butter, diced
2 pinches fleur de sel

Chocolate Cups

7 oz. (200 g) bittersweet chocolate
  (55% cocoa)

Garnish

Bittersweet chocolate (60 to 70%
  cocoa), for shaving

1 Have all your ingredients and utensils ready to go before cooking.

2 Melt the sugar in a heavy saucepan and add the honey.

3 Cook until it reaches a light amber color.

4 Pour the cream into the caramel in several additions. When it is all incorporated, let boil for 2 minutes.

5 Remove from the heat and stir in the butter.

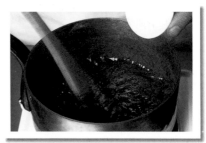

6 Stir in the fleur de sel.

7 Check the caramel for doneness by drizzling a little onto a plate.

8 Let the caramel cool in a bowl.

continued

Chocolate Cups
Melt the chocolate and temper it according to the instructions on page 362.

Brush the cups of the egg cartons with the tempered chocolate (9), making a fairly thin layer. Let the chocolate set and make another layer (10).
Chill for 10 minutes, then freeze for 30 minutes.

Carefully invert the chocolate shells onto a work surface (11), then turn right side up (12).
Beat the caramel to soften it and pour into the shells (13).

Garnish
Shave the chocolate with a knife or vegetable peeler over the shells (14).

9 Brush the cups of the egg carton with tempered chocolate to make a thin layer.

10 Brush a thicker layer over the first set layer.

11 Carefully invert the shells onto a work surface.

12 They should come out easily on their own.

13 Turn them right side up and fill with the caramel.

14 Decorate with chocolate shavings scraped with a small knife.

Rochers Praliné
Hazelnut-Praline Chocolate Clusters

Preheat the oven to 350° F (180° C).

Spread all the hazelnuts used in each part of the recipe on a baking sheet and bake for about 10 minutes, until lightly toasted.

Let cool slightly and rub off the skins with a kitchen towel.

Weigh out each quantity called for in the praline, garnish, and coating.

Chocolate-Hazelnut Praline

Split the vanilla bean lengthwise in half and scrape out the seeds.

Place half the sugar and the vanilla bean and seeds in a medium heavy saucepan (1). Melt the sugar over medium heat, stirring with a wooden spoon.

Pour in the remaining sugar and stir (2). Reduce the heat to low and cook, stirring, until the sugar changes from a light amber liquid-y paste to a fluid, medium amber caramel.

Remove the pan from the heat and carefully pick out the vanilla bean (3).

Add the hazelnuts and stir to coat them in the caramel (4).

Transfer the hazelnut praline to a silicone baking mat or piece of parchment paper (5) and let cool.

Break the hazelnut praline into large pieces and grind in a food processor until it forms a smooth paste, 5 to 10 minutes (6, 7, and 8).

Makes about 2½ dozen
Level: Easy
Prep: 40 min.
Cook: 10 min.
Chill: about 2 hr.

1 cup (5½ oz., 150 g) hazelnuts
1 vanilla bean
⅔ cup (4½ oz., 130 g) sugar
3 oz. (80 g) milk chocolate
1 oz. (20 g) bittersweet chocolate
(50 to 60% cocoa)

Garnish

⅔ cup (3 oz., 80 g) hazelnuts

Coating

14 oz. (400 g) bittersweet
chocolate (50 to 60% cocoa)
½ cup (2 oz., 50 g) hazelnuts
2 oz. (50 g) crushed hazelnut
praline (see Succès Praliné,
page 288)

1 Combine half the sugar with the vanilla bean and seeds in a heavy saucepan.

2 Melt over medium heat and stir in the remaining sugar.

3 When the sugar is a medium amber caramel, remove from the heat and carefully extract the vanilla bean.

4 Stir the hazelnuts into the caramel.

5 Pour the mixture onto a silicone baking mat or sheet of parchment paper.

6 Break the cooled caramel into pieces and place it in a food processor.

7 Grind for 5 to 10 minutes.

8 This is what the praline paste should look like.

continued

Meanwhile, finely chop the milk chocolate and bittersweet chocolate. Combine in a small bowl set over a saucepan filled with 1 inch (2.5 cm) of barely simmering water and let melt. Do not let the chocolate get too hot; it should be barely warm to the touch. Remove the bowl from the heat. Stir until smooth.

Transfer the praline paste to a medium bowl and stir in the melted chocolate (9).

Spoon the praline-chocolate mixture into a pastry bag and pipe it into trays of small hemispherical molds or ice cube trays (10). Or use a spoon.

Garnish

Place a hazelnut in each mold and gently press it with a toothpick (11).

Press a sheet of parchment paper directly on the surface of the mixture and chill until set, about 2 hours.

Coating

Melt the chocolate and temper it according to the instructions on page 362.

Finely chop the hazelnuts with a large knife or in the food processor. Stir into the tempered chocolate along with the crushed hazelnut praline (12).

Invert the chocolate clusters on a work surface. Stick flat sides of the clusters together, in pairs, to form a ball.

Place a sheet of parchment paper on the work surface. Dip each cluster into the chocolate-hazelnut coating with a fork (13), letting the excess chocolate drip back into the bowl, and transfer to the parchment paper to set (14 and 15).

Note: Rochers Praliné are even better the next day.

9 Stir the melted chocolate into the praline paste.

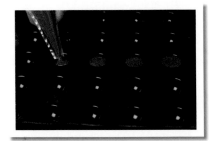

10 Fill the molds with the chocolate praline.

11 Place 1 hazelnut in the center of each filled mold and gently press it in with a toothpick.

12 Combine the melted chocolate, chopped hazelnuts, and crushed hazelnut praline to make the coating.

13 Turn the clusters out of the molds and stick pairs of them together. Coat with hazelnut chocolate.

14 Let the excess coating drip back into the bowl and transfer the chocolates to a sheet of parchment paper.

15 Let set.

Petits Pots de Chocolat à la Lavande

Little Lavender-Chocolate Pots

Measure and prep your ingredients and arrange them on the counter (1).

Bring the milk and cream to a boil in a medium saucepan over medium heat. Whisk in the lavender (2) and remove the pan from the heat. Let infuse for 5 minutes.

Meanwhile, finely chop the chocolate and place it in a medium bowl. Separate the eggs (3), reserving the whites for another recipe. Whisk the sugar into the egg yolks (4) just until the sugar dissolves (5).

Bring the milk back to a boil and whisk into the egg yolk–sugar mixture (6).

Serves 10
Level: Easy
Prep: 20 min.
Infuse: 5 min.
Chill: at least 3 hr.

1 cup (250 ml) milk
1 cup (250 ml) heavy cream
1 teaspoon lavender flowers, fresh
  or dried
6 oz. (180 g) bittersweet chocolate
  (70% cocoa)
4 eggs
¼ cup plus 2 tbsp. (3 oz., 80 g) sugar

1 Have all your ingredients and utensils ready to go before cooking.

2 Bring the milk and cream to a boil and add the lavender. Let infuse.

3 Separate the eggs.

4 Whisk the sugar into the egg yolks.

5 Whisk just until the sugar dissolves; do not let the mixture become pale.

6 Bring the milk to a boil again and whisk into the egg yolk–sugar mixture.

continued

Return this custard to the saucepan and cook over low heat, stirring with a wooden spoon, until the custard thickens slightly. It is ready when it coats a spoon; if you draw a finger across the back of the spoon, it should leave a clear trail (7).

Remove the pan from the heat.

Strain the custard through a fine sieve into a bowl (8).

Ladle it into the chopped chocolate in several batches, whisking after each addition until smooth (9, 10, 11, and 12).

When the chocolate cream is smooth and shiny (13), pour it into cups (14).

Chill until set, at least 3 hours.

7  Cook until a line drawn across the back of the spoon leaves a trail.

8  Strain the custard through a fine sieve.

9  Pour a small amount of the custard over the chopped chocolate.

10  Whisk the custard and chocolate together.

11  Pour in the remaining custard in several additions.

12  Continue to whisk, working from the center.

13 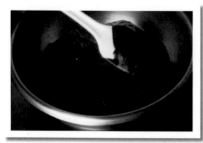 The ganache should be perfectly smooth.

14  Use a pitcher to fill the cups.

Samossas au Chocolat
Chocolate Samosas

Measure and prep your ingredients and arrange them on the counter (1).

Chocolate-Banana Filling
Combine the butter and sugar in a small bowl and beat until creamy (2).
Break 1 egg into the mixture (3) and stir in.
Combine the coconut with the flour and stir into the mixture (4) until smooth.
Break the second egg (5) into the mixture and beat until smooth (6).
Shave the chocolate with a knife or vegetable peeler into the filling (7).
Sift in the cocoa powder (8) and stir until smooth.

Makes 1 ½ dozen
Level: Intermediate
Prep: 25 min.
Bake: 10 min.

7 tbsp. (3½ oz., 100 g) butter, softened
½ cup (3½ oz., 100 g) sugar
2 eggs
1⅓ cups (3½ oz., 100 g) unsweetened shredded coconut
1 tbsp. all-purpose flour
1 oz. (30 g) bittersweet chocolate (50 to 60% cocoa)
3 tbsp. (1 oz., 20 g) unsweetened cocoa powder
2 bananas

3 tbsp. (50 g) butter
10 sheets brik pastry or 20 sheets thawed phyllo pastry
⅓ cup (2 oz., 50 g) confectioners' sugar

1 Have all your ingredients and utensils ready to go before cooking.

2 Beat the sugar into the softened butter.

3 Stir in the first egg.

4 Stir in the shredded coconut and flour.

5 Mix in the second egg.

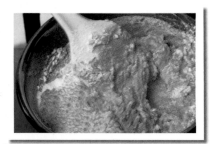

6 Continue to beat until the mixture is smooth.

7 Shave the chocolate into the filling.

8 Stir in the cocoa powder.

continued

Preheat the oven to 425° F (210° C).

Slice the banana.

Samosas

Melt the butter.

Remove the paper between the sheets of brick pastry and stack the sheets.

Cut the brick or phyllo sheets into 2½-inch (6 cm) strips (9). Trim any rounded edges.

Separate the strips and brush them, one by one, with melted butter (10). (You may need extra butter if using phyllo.)

Stack the strips so they do not dry out (11). Cover the phyllo sheets with a damp kitchen towel and work with 1 strip at a time.

Place a spoonful of chocolate filling at one short end of a strip, leaving a 1-inch (2.5 cm) border. Top the fillling with a banana slice (12).

Fold a corner over the filling to form a triangle, making sure the side of the triangle meets the edge of the strip. Continue folding the triangle along the length of the strip to form a triangular package (13, 14, and 15).

Brush the last fold with butter or filling to seal the package (16).

This will prevent the filling from oozing out (17).

Transfer the samosas to a nonstick baking sheet or a baking sheet lined with parchment paper.

Sift with confectioners' sugar (18).

Bake for 10 minutes, or until lightly browned, turning the samosas over halfway through baking.

Transfer the samosa to a rack and let cool.

9 Cut the pastry into 2½-inch (6 cm) strips.

10 Brush each strip with melted butter.

11 Stack the buttered strips to prevent them from drying out.

12 Place a pat of chocolate filling at one end of a strip and top it with a banana slice.

13 Fold the pastry over to make a triangle.

14 Continue folding neatly, turning the triangle along the strip of pastry.

15 Press down well at each corner.

16 Brush the last fold with a melted butter to seal the samosa.

17 Close it carefully so the filling does not ooze out.

18 Dust the samosas with confectioners' sugar.

Doigts de Fée
Chocolate-Dipped Coconut Meringues

Position racks in the upper and lower thirds of the oven. Preheat the oven to 200° F (90° C).

Coconut Meringue

Sift half the shredded coconut with the confectioners' sugar (1).

Whip the egg whites until foamy (2).

Gradually whip in the granulated sugar until the whites hold a soft peak. Whip until the meringue is firm, white, and shiny (3, 4, and 5).

Gently fold in the confectioners' sugar–coconut mixture (6) with a flexible spatula (7).

Makes about 2 dozen
Level: Easy
Prep: 30 min.
Bake: 3 hr.

Coconut Meringue

1 cup (3 oz., 80 g) unsweetened
  shredded coconut
¾ cup (3½ oz., 100 g) confectioners'
  sugar
4 egg whites
⅔ cup (4¼ oz., 120 g) granulated
  sugar

Coating

7 oz. (200 g) bittersweet chocolate
  (70% cocoa)

1 Sift half the shredded coconut with the confectioners' sugar.

2 Begin whipping the egg whites.

3 When the egg whites are foamy, add a little granulated sugar.

4 Gradually whip in the granulated sugar until firm and glossy.

5 This is the texture you are looking for.

6 Add the sifted dry ingredients.

7 Gently fold them in with a flexible spatula.

continued

Spoon the coconut meringue into a pastry bag fitted with a ⅓-inch (8 mm) plain tip (8).

Pipe a small dot of meringue in the corners of each of 2 baking sheets to keep the parchment paper in place during baking (9). Or use a spoon.

Line the baking sheets with parchment paper (10).

Pipe out little logs about 2½ inches (6 cm) long (11 and 12) on the prepared baking sheets.

Sprinkle with the remaining shredded coconut (13).

Bake for about 3 hours, until completely dry inside. Rotate the sheets halfway through baking.

Let cool on the baking sheet.

Coating

Melt the chocolate and temper it according to the instructions on page 362.

Dip half of each meringue into the tempered chocolate (14) and stick pairs of them together, with the chocolate at opposite ends.

Place on a sheet of parchment paper and let set completely before serving.

Store the meringues in an airtight container.

8 Spoon the coconut meringue into a pastry bag.

9 Dot a little meringue in the corners of each baking sheet.

10 Line the sheets with parchment paper.

11 Pipe the coconut meringue into thin logs.

12 This shows the shape of the meringues.

13 Sprinkle with the remaining shredded coconut.

14 Dip the cooled meringues halfway into the tempered chocolate.

Muffins au Chocolat
Double-Chocolate Cupcakes

Measure and prep your ingredients and arrange them on the counter (1).

Preheat the oven to 425° F (210° C). Butter the muffin cups and dust with flour.

Chocolate Cupcakes
Cut the banana lengthwise in half, then crosswise into half slices.

Finely chop the chocolate. Combine with the butter in a medium bowl set over a saucepan filled with 1 inch (2.5 cm) of barely simmering water, making sure that the bottom of the bowl does not touch the water. Let the chocolate melt (2). Remove the bowl from the heat. Stir until smooth (3).

Break the eggs into a medium bowl, add the sugar (4), and whip until pale and fluffy, about 5 minutes (5). It is easier to use an electric beater for this.

Gently whisk in the melted chocolate just until smooth (6).

Makes 1 dozen
Level: Easy
Prep: 20 min.
Bake: about 12 min.

Special equipment
A 12-cup muffin pan

½ banana
3½ oz. (100 g) bittersweet chocolate
    (50 to 60% cocoa)
7 tbsp. (4 oz., 110 g) butter, diced
4 eggs
¾ cup (5 oz., 150 g) sugar
½ cup (2 oz., 60 g) all-purpose flour
1 tbsp. unsweetened cocoa powder
12 raspberries

3½ oz. (100 g) bittersweet
    chocolate (60 to 70% cocoa)

1 Have all your ingredients and utensils ready to go before cooking.

2 Melt the chocolate and butter over a hot water bath.

3 Stir until completely melted and smooth.

4 Break the eggs into a medium bowl and add the sugar.

5 Whip until pale and fluffy.

6 Lightly whisk in the melted chocolate and butter.

continued

Sift the flour with the cocoa powder into the batter (7). Whisk just until smooth (8).
Spoon the batter into the muffin cups, filling them one-third full.
Add a raspberry to each one (9).

Spoon in more batter, filling the cups two-thirds full. Gently press a half banana slice into each cup (10).

Bake for about 12 minutes, until the cupcakes are rounded on top and the tip of a knife or a cake tester inserted in the center comes out clean.
Let cool for 5 minutes in the pan, then transfer the cupcakes to a rack and let cool completely.

Chocolate Coating
Finely chop the chocolate. Place in a small bowl set over a saucepan filled with 1 inch (2.5 cm) of barely simmering water and let melt. Remove the bowl from the heat. Stir until smooth.

Dip the base of each cupcake in the melted chocolate (11). Turn upside down and let the chocolate set before serving (12).

7 Sift the flour with the cocoa powder into the batter.

8 Lightly whisk just until the dry ingredients are incorporated.

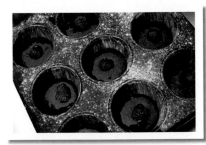

9 Spoon the batter into the muffin cups, filling them one-third full. Press in a raspberry.

10 Cover the raspberries with batter and insert a half banana slice.

11 Dip the base of the cooled cupcakes into melted chocolate.

12 Arrange the cupcakes melted chocolate-side up on a platter.

Diamants Chocolat-Framboise
Sparkly Chocolate-Raspberry Cookies

Preheat the oven to 350° F (180° C). Line a baking sheet with parchment paper.

Chocolate Cookies
Sift the flour onto a work surface. Add the butter, granulated sugar, cocoa powder, and cinnamon (1).
Rub the butter into the dry ingredients (2 and 3).
When the ingredients come together to form a smooth dough, gather it into a ball (4).

Spread the brown sugar in a shallow baking pan.
Cut the dough in half. Roll each half into an even log (5), both the same size.
Cut each log crosswise in half (6) and roll in the light brown sugar until well coated (7).
Transfer to a cutting board, cover with plastic wrap, and chill until firm, about 30 minutes.

Cut the logs into slices ½ inch (1 cm) thick with a sharp knife (8).
Transfer the slices to the prepared baking sheet, spacing slightly apart.
Bake for 15 to 20 minutes, until barely firm. The cookies will set when cool.
Transfer the cookies to a rack and let cool.

Raspberry-Chocolate Topping
Finely chop the chocolate. Place in a small bowl set over a saucepan filled with 1 inch (2.5 cm) of barely simmering water and let melt. Remove the bowl from the heat and stir until smooth.

Mound ½ tsp. of raspberry jam on each cookie (9). Stick a raspberry, cup side up, on each mound of jam. Using a parchment paper cone (see page 212) or a small spoon, fill the raspberries with melted chocolate (10).

Makes about 3 dozen
Level: Intermediate
Prep: 30 min.
Chill: 30 min.
Bake: 15 to 20 min. per sheet
of cookies

Chocolate Cookies

1⅔ cups (7 oz., 210 g) all-purpose
flour
1¼ sticks (5 oz., 150 g) butter, diced
⅓ cup (2½ oz., 75 g) granulated sugar
1 tbsp. unsweetened cocoa powder
1 tbsp. ground cinnamon
1 cup (7 oz., 200 g) light brown sugar

Raspberry-Chocolate Topping

2 oz. (60 g) bittersweet chocolate
(70% cocoa)
½ cup (7 oz., 200 g) raspberry jam
with seeds
½ pint raspberries

1 Sift the flour onto a work surface. Add the diced butter, sugar, cocoa powder, and cinnamon.

2 Begin rubbing the ingredients with your hands.

3 The butter should be completely incorporated into the dry ingredients.

4 Gather the dough into a smooth ball.

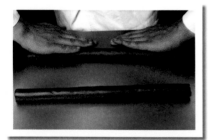

5 Cut the dough in half and roll out even logs. If necessary, lightly flour the work surface.

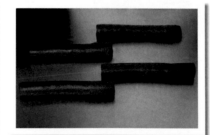

6 Cut the logs crosswise in half.

7 Spread the brown sugar in a baking pan, add the logs, and roll to coat.

8 Slice the logs crosswise about ½ inch (1 cm) thick.

9 Mound ½ tsp. raspberry jam on the cooled cookies.

10 Place a raspberry, cup side up, on each cookie and fill with melted chocolate.

Financiers Chocolat
Little Chocolate-Nut Cakes

Preheat the oven to 425° F (210° C). Butter the financier pans.

Chocolate-Almond Financiers

Place the butter in a small heavy saucepan. Cook over medium heat until it browns.

Strain through a small fine sieve (1) and let cool to lukewarm.

Finely chop the chocolate. Place in a medium bowl set over a saucepan filled with 1 inch (2.5 cm) of barely simmering water and let melt. Remove the bowl from the heat and stir until smooth.

Sift the confectioners' sugar with the ground almonds and flour into a bowl (2).

Pour in the egg whites and stir with a wooden spoon (3).

Pour in the warm melted butter (4) and the melted chocolate (5).

Stir until the batter is smooth (6).

Spoon the batter into the prepared pans (7). Tap the pans on a work surface to smooth the batter (8). Transfer to a baking sheet.

Nut Topping

Coarsely chop the hazelnuts.

Combine the four types of nuts in a bowl and sprinkle them over the financiers (9).

Lightly press them into the batter (10).

Bake for about 15 minutes, until the tip of a knife or a cake tester inserted into the center comes out clean. Let cool for 5 minutes in the pan, then transfer the cakes to a rack and let cool.

Notes: You can prepare the batter a day ahead, chill, and fill the molds just before baking.

Butter melted to a nut-brown color is called beurre noisette *(hazelnut butter) in French because it has the fragrance of hazelnuts.*

Makes about 1½ dozen
Level: Easy
Prep: 20 min.
Bake: 15 min.

Special equipment
20 financier pans or a 24-cup
mini muffin pan

Chocolate-Almond Financiers

1¼ sticks (5 oz., 150 g) butter
5½ oz. (160 g) bittersweet chocolate
    (60 to 70% cocoa)
¾ cup (3½ oz., 100 g) confectioners'
    sugar
1⅓ cups (4 oz., 120 g) ground almonds
¼ cup plus 2 tbsp. (2 oz., 50 g)
    all-purpose flour
5 egg whites

Nut Topping

½ cup (2 oz., 50 g) hazelnuts
⅓ cup (2 oz., 50 g) unsalted pistachios
¼ cup (2 oz., 50 g) pine nuts
⅓ cup (1 oz., 25 g) sliced
    blanched almonds

1 Cook the butter until it browns. Strain into a bowl and let cool slightly.

2 Sift the confectioners' sugar with the ground almonds and flour into a bowl.

3 Stir in the egg whites with a wooden spoon.

4 Stir in the browned butter.

5 Incorporate the melted bittersweet chocolate.

6 This is the texture you are looking for.

7 Spoon the batter into buttered financier pans.

8 Tap the pans on the work surface to smooth the batter.

9 Combine the four types of nuts and scatter them over the financiers.

10 Lightly press the nuts into the batter.

Madeleines Chocolat
Double-Chocolate Madeleines

Measure and prep your ingredients and arrange them on the counter (1).

Chocolate Madeleines
Place the butter in a small heavy saucepan. Cook over medium heat until it browns.
Strain through a small fine sieve (2) and let cool to lukewarm.

Chop the chocolate into small chips with a large knife.

Break the eggs into a medium bowl and add the vanilla extract (3). Whisk in the sugar (4) just until it dissolves.

Whisk in the honey until smooth (5).

Makes about 1½ dozen
small cakes
Level: Easy
Prep: 20 min.
Rest: 2 hr.
Bake: 12 min.

Special equipment
2 12-cup madeleine pans or
a 24-cup mini muffin pan

Chocolate Madeleines

1 stick plus 1 tbsp. (5 oz., 140 g)
butter
1½ oz. (40 g) bittersweet chocolate
(60 to 70% cocoa)
2 eggs
1 tsp. vanilla extract
¼ cup plus 2 tbsp. (3 oz., 90 g)
sugar
2 tbsp. mild honey, such as acacia
1 cup plus 1 tbsp. (5 oz., 140 g)
all-purpose flour
1 tsp. baking powder
3 tbsp. (¾ oz., 20 g) unsweetened
cocoa powder

Chocolate Coating

3½ oz. (100 g) bittersweet
chocolate (60 to 70% cocoa)

1 Have all your ingredients
and utensils ready to go
before cooking.

2 Cook the butter until it browns.
Strain it into a bowl and let
cool to lukewarm.

3 Break the eggs into a bowl
and add the vanilla extract.

4 Whisk the sugar into the eggs
until it dissolves.

5 Whisk in the honey.

continued

Sift the flour with the baking powder and cocoa powder into a medium bowl (6).

Add the dry ingredients to the egg mixture (7) and whisk until smooth (8).

Pour in the lukewarm melted butter (9). Stir in the homemade chocolate chips until evenly distributed (10).

Press a sheet of plastic wrap directly on the surface of the batter and let stand at room temperature for 2 hours.

Preheat the oven to 425° F (210° C). Generously butter the madeleine cups.

Spoon the batter into the cups (11).

Bake for about 12 minutes, until the characteristic little bump has formed and a cake tester inserted into the center comes out clean. Remove the madeleines from the pans, transfer to a rack, and let cool.

Chocolate Coating

Finely chop the chocolate. Place in a small bowl set over a saucepan filled with 1 inch (2.5 cm) of barely simmering water and let melt. Remove the bowl from the heat and stir until smooth.

Dip the scalloped bottoms of the madeleines in the melted chocolate (12).

Return to the madeleine pan, bottoms up, and let the chocolate set before serving.

6 Sift the flour with the baking powder and cocoa powder into a medium bowl.

7 Pour the sifted dry ingredients into the egg mixture.

8 Whisk until smooth.

9 Whisk in the lukewarm browned butter.

10 Incorporate the chocolate chips.

11 Fill the buttered molds.

12 Dip the bottoms of the cooled madeleines into melted chocolate.

Brownies Café-Marron
Coffee-Chestnut Brownie Bars

Measure and prep your ingredients and arrange them on the counter (1).

Preheat the oven to 350° F (180° C). Butter the baking pan and dust it with flour.
Coarsely chop the hazelnuts with a large knife or in the food processor.
Finely chop the chocolate (2). Place in a medium bowl set over a saucepan filled
with 1 inch (2.5 cm) of barely simmering water and let melt. Remove the bowl
from the heat and stir until smooth.

Beat the butter with a wooden spoon or flexible spatula in a medium bowl until
creamy.
Beat in the sugar until light and fluffy (3).

Makes about 2 dozen brownies
Level: Easy
Prep: 30 min.
Bake: 20 min.
Chill: 15 min.

Special equipment
An 11 by 7-inch (28 by 18 cm)
baking pan

½ cup (2 oz., 50 g) hazelnuts
(see *Notes*)
5 oz. (150 g) bittersweet chocolate
(50 to 60% cocoa)
7 tbsp. (3½ oz., 100 g) butter,
softened
½ cup (3½ oz., 100 g) sugar
2 eggs
⅓ cup (1½ oz., 40 g) all-purpose
flour
2 tbsp. (3 g) instant coffee powder

3½ oz. (100 g) bittersweet
chocolate (60 to 70% cocoa)
3 oz. (80 g) chestnut cream or
spread (see *Notes*)
1 tbsp. grapeseed oil

1 Have all your ingredients
and utensils ready to go
before cooking.

2 Finely chop the chocolate.

3 Using a flexible spatula, beat
the sugar with the butter.

4 Beat in the 2 eggs.

5 Sift in the flour and stir just
until combined.

6 Add the instant coffee.

7 Stir well to dissolve the coffee.

continued

Beat in the eggs until smooth (4).

Sift in the flour and stir just until smooth (5).

Stir in the instant coffee (6 and 7).

Add the melted chocolate to the batter. Stir it in until smooth (8 and 9).

Stir in the chopped hazelnuts until evenly distributed (10).

Pour the brownie batter into the prepared baking pan (11).

Bake for about 20 minutes, until a cake tester inserted in the center comes out with moist crumbs (12).

Let cool to lukewarm in the pan.

Chestnut-Chocolate Coating

Finely chop the chocolate. Place in a small bowl set over a saucepan filled with 1 inch (2.5 cm) of barely simmering water and let melt. Remove the bowl from the heat and stir until smooth.

Invert the pan of brownies onto a sheet of parchment paper. Turn right side up and spread the top with chestnut cream (13). Smooth with a thin spatula.

Stir the melted chocolate with the oil and spread over the chestnut cream (14). Smooth with a thin spatula (15).

Chill until set, about 15 minutes, before cutting into 1 by 3-inch (2.5 by 7.5-cm) rectangles (16).

Notes: If you like you can toast the hazelnuts for a deeper flavor. Spread them in a pie pan and bake in a 350° F (170° C) oven for about 10 minutes.

Crème de marrons, also known as chestnut spread, is made of chestnuts, sugar, and vanilla, and may also contain glucose and glacéed chestnuts.

8 Make sure the chocolate is completely melted before folding it into the batter.

9 Fold in the melted chocolate.

10 Stir in the chopped hazelnuts.

11 Fill the prepared pan with the batter.

12 The top should be a rich chocolate color.

13 Spread chestnut cream over the top.

14 Combine the melted chocolate with the oil and pour it over the chestnut cream.

15 Smooth the top with a thin spatula.

16 Cut into small rectangles.

Brioche Chocolat
Chocolate-Apple Brioche Bars

Measure and prep your ingredients and arrange them on the counter (1).

Chocolate Brioche Dough
Crumble the yeast into a large bowl. Pour in the milk and whisk to dissolve the yeast (2).

Add the flour, cocoa powder, sugar, eggs, and salt (3).

Beat with a wooden spoon (4) until the ingredients form a fairly thick, smooth dough (5).

Beat in the butter with a wooden spoon (6).

Cup your hand like a hook and knead the dough (7) until it is smooth and elastic, 5 to 10 minutes.

Scrape it into a large bowl and dust with flour (8).

Cover the bowl with plastic wrap and chill until doubled in volume, about 2 hours (9).

Makes about 2½ dozen
3 by 2-inch (7.5 by 5 cm) bars
Level: Intermediate
Prep: 40 min.
Chill: 2 hr.
Rise: 2 hr. 40 min.
Bake: 25 min.

Chocolate Brioche Dough

1 cake (.6-oz., 20 g) fresh yeast
2 tbsp. lukewarm milk
2½ cups (10½ oz., 300 g) all-purpose flour
¼ cup (1 oz., 30 g) unsweetened cocoa powder
¼ cup (2 oz., 50 g) sugar
3 eggs
2 pinches salt
1¾ sticks (7 oz., 200 g) butter, diced and softened

Apple Topping

4 Golden Delicious apples
3 tbsp. light brown sugar
1 tsp. ground cinnamon
5 tbsp. (3 oz., 80 g) butter, diced, plus more, if desired
3 tbsp. confectioners' sugar

1 Have all your ingredients and utensils ready to go before cooking.

2 Dissolve the yeast in the milk.

3 Add the flour, cocoa powder, sugar, salt, eggs, and salt to the dissolved yeast.

4 Beat with a wooden spoon.

5 The dough should be firm, elastic, and very smooth.

6 Beat in the softened butter.

7 Finish kneading by hand, cupping your hand like a hook.

8 Dust the dough with flour and chill for 2 hours.

9 The dough should double in volume.

continued

Line a baking sheet with parchment paper.

On a lightly floured work surface, flatten the brioche dough with your hand (10).

Roll it into a rectangle the same size as your baking sheet (11).

Check that the dough is uniformly thick (12).

Drape the dough over the rolling pin and transfer it the prepared baking sheet.

Make rows of indentations in the dough with your fingertips (13). This helps ensure that the texture of the cake is soft when baked.

Cover with a kitchen towel and let rise for 40 minutes.

Preheat the oven to 425° F (210° C).

Apple Topping

Cut the unpeeled apples into thin sticks and distribute them over the risen brioche (14).

Combine the brown sugar with the cinnamon.

Scatter the butter over the apples. Sprinkle with the cinnamon sugar (15).

Bake for 25 minutes, or until the apples are tender and lightly browned and the dough is soft and dry. Add a few additional tbsp. of butter to the top during baking, if desired.

Transfer the brioche to a rack and sift generously with confectioners' sugar (16).

Cut into bars and serve (17).

Note: You can also prepare this brioche dough in a stand mixer fitted with the dough hook.

10 Flatten the dough with your hand on a floured surface.

11 Roll out the dough into a rectangle with a rolling pin.

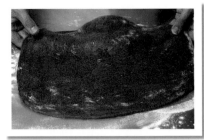

12 Check the thickness by feeling it on top and underneath.

13 Make small indentations with your fingers.

14 Cut the apple into thin sticks and distribute them on the risen brioche.

15 Dot knobs of butter over the apples and sprinkle with cinnamon sugar.

16 Dust with confectioners' sugar when it is baked.

17 Cut into small bars.

Fondant Chocolat-Gingembre
Molten Chocolate-Ginger Cups

Finely chop the chocolate. Place the chocolate and butter in a medium bowl set over a saucepan filled with 1 inch (2.5 cm) of barely simmering water, making sure that the bottom of the bowl does not touch the water. Let the chocolate melt (1). Remove the bowl from the heat and stir until smooth.

Break the eggs into a medium bowl and add the sugar (2).

Whisk well until the mixture is light and fluffy (3).

Whisk the melted chocolate and butter into the beaten eggs (4) until smooth.

Sift in the flour (5) and whisk it in gently (6).

The batter will be fairly liquid (7).

Butter 8 ovenproof demitasse cups.

Fill them halfway with the chocolate batter (8).

Add a piece of candied ginger to each cup (9).

Pour in the remaining batter to about ¼ inch (5 mm) below the rim (10).

Transfer the cups to a baking sheet and freeze until set, about 1 hr.

Preheat the oven to 400° F (200° C).

Bake for about 10 minutes, until the sides of the cups are firm but the centers are soft. Serve immediately.

Note: You can sift confectioners' sugar over the tops just before serving, if you like.

Serves 8
Level: Easy
Prep: 20 min.
Freeze: 1 hr.
Bake: 10 min.

Special equipment
8 ovenproof demitasse cups

3½ oz. (100 g) bittersweet chocolate (60 to 70% cocoa)
6 tbsp. (3 oz., 90 g) butter, diced and softened
3 eggs
¼ cup plus 2 tbsp. (3 oz., 80 g) sugar
⅓ cup (1½ oz., 40 g) all-purpose flour
8 pieces (2 oz., 50 g) candied ginger

1 Melt the chopped chocolate with the butter over a hot water bath.

2 Pour the sugar into a bowl with the eggs.

3 Whisk until light and fluffy.

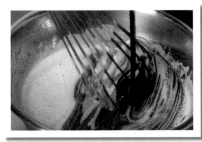

4 Whisk the melted chocolate and butter into the egg mixture.

5 Sift the flour into the batter.

6 Whisk in the flour.

7 This is what the batter should look like.

8 Fill the buttered cups halfway.

9 Place a piece of candied ginger in each cup.

10 Cover with the remaining batter.

Chocolate Desserts and Candies 445

LES GATEAUX

DE
L'A
VENT

Making Holiday Memories

When I was growing up, I loved lending a hand during the weeks before Christmas at our family bakery in Schirmeck, a small town in Alsace. I often found myself elbow deep in dough.

Every year my sister and I helped out, making the Advent cookies we were allowed to eat only on Christmas Eve. We competed to find the most original shape, mold, and ingredients that would best please our parents.

When I discovered a little moon-shaped cookie cutter buried beneath the stars, hearts, and Christmas trees, I thought I had found gold. I couldn't wait for Christmas dinner to taste our cookies, scented with vanilla and other spices, each of them different, each with its own story.

So today, in this chapter, I want to tell you the delicious story of our festive treats and share them with you, step by step.

Baking Cookies

Baking times are given mostly for single sheets of cookies. If you prefer, bake 2 sheets at once. Position racks in the upper and lower thirds of the oven. If you are not using convection heat, switch the baking sheets between racks halfway through and increase times by a few minutes.

Storing Cookies

Keep your cookies in a tin; that is, those that aren't eaten before you can put them away!

Ingredients

Citrus Fruits

Choose unsprayed or organic fruit when using the citrus zest (or peel). Wash them in warm water and dry them well before zesting.

Spices

Aniseed, cinnamon, and allspice or *quatre-épices*, a typical French four-spice blend of ground black pepper, nutmeg, ginger, and cloves, flavor cakes and cookies during the holidays. Store them in tins, away from light, to preserve their flavors and aromas.

Buy vanilla in whole beans. Make sure they are plump and fleshy. Keep them away from light in a glass jar or small tin.

Honey

The flavor that honey brings to recipes depends on its dominant source of nectar. Select the most appropriate type of honey for your recipe. The pronounced aromas of pine or rosemary honey are best for Pains d'Épices Moelleux (Gingerbread Muffins, page 474), while lavender honey — far subtler — is excellent for the Parfait Glacé au Miel (Frozen Honey Parfait, page 510).

Equipment

Use professional-quality cookie cutters for stunning festive cookies.

A pastry bag with assorted tips, a pastry brush, and a citrus zester will come in handy too.

Oranges et Citrons Confits
Candied Citrus Peel

Orange Peel

Bring a large saucepan of water to a boil.

Peel the oranges in wide strips with a sharp knife, removing all the white pith and a sliver of flesh.

Cut the peel with the flesh into ¼-inch-wide (6 mm) strips (1).

Add the orange peel to the boiling water, cook for 1 minute, and drain.

Repeat two more times to remove the bitter flavor. This is known as "blanching" the peel.

Combine the sugar and mineral water in a large saucepan. Bring to a boil over medium heat, stirring to dissolve the sugar. Add the orange peel and boil for 2 minutes. Stir in the honey.

Pour the contents of the saucepan into a canning jar. Let cool completely before sealing.

Store in the refrigerator.

Lemon Peel

Use the same procedure, but blanch the peel four times to remove the bitterness.

Sugar Coating

Drain the peel (2).

Transfer to a wire rack (3) and let dry for 1 hour.

Divide the coarse sugar between 2 shallow baking pans. In one pan, whisk the coarse sugar with the cinnamon.

In the second pan, whisk the coarse sugar with the vanilla sugar and coriander.

Add the orange peel to the cinnamon sugar and the lemon peel to the vanilla sugar and toss to coat (4).

Notes: You can store the orange or lemon peel in the syrup, omitting the sugar coating.

Or store the sugar-coated candied citrus in an airtight container for up to 2 months.

Level: Easy
Prep: 25 min.
Cook: 20 min.
Dry: 1 hr.

Orange Peel

5 oranges
1½ cups (10½ oz., 300 g) sugar
2 cups (500 ml) still mineral water
1 tbsp. mild honey or glucose syrup

Lemon Peel

5 lemons
1¼ cups (9 oz., 250 g) sugar
2 cups (500 ml) still mineral water
1 tbsp. mild honey or glucose syrup

Sugar Coating

1 cup (7 oz., 200 g) coarse sugar
1 tsp. ground cinnamon
1 tbsp. vanilla sugar
1 tsp. ground coriander

1 Cut the orange and lemon peel into strips.

2 Drain the candied, cooled peel.

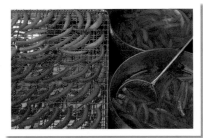

3 Place on a rack to dry.

4 Coat the peel in the spiced sugar mixtures.

Vin Chaud Mandarine
Mulled Tangerine Wine

Mulled Wine

Cut the lemon, orange, and tangerine into large pieces (1).

Combine the wine, sugar, spices, water, and fruit in a large saucepan.

Bring to a boil over medium heat and let simmer for 3 to 5 minutes (2).

Strain into a bowl (3).

Serve in glasses.

Note: The mulled wine can be refrigerated for up to 1 day and gently reheated.

If you like, garnish the glasses with strips of lemon or orange zest, star anise pods, or slices of lemon or orange.

Makes about 4 cups (1 liter)
Level: Easy
Prep: 10 min.

½ lemon
½ orange
1 tangerine
1 750-ml bottle full-bodied red wine
1 cup (7 oz., 190 g) sugar
1 stick cinnamon
2 star anise pods
2 whole cloves
1 pinch freshly grated nutmeg
¼ cup plus 2 tbsp. (100 ml) water

1 Cut the orange, lemon, and tangerine into large pieces.

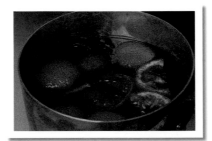

2 Bring all the ingredients to a boil and let simmer for 3 to 5 minutes.

3 Strain and serve.

Chocolat Chaud à la Cannelle Caramélisée

Hot Chocolate with Caramelized Cinnamon Sticks

Hot Chocolate

Finely chop the chocolate and place it in a medium bowl.

Bring the milk and cream to a boil in a medium saucepan over medium heat. Remove from the heat.

Combine the sugar, cinnamon sticks, and vanilla bean in a medium heavy saucepan. Melt the sugar over medium heat, stirring with a wooden spoon. Cook, stirring, until the sugar changes from a light amber liquid-y paste to a fluid, dark amber caramel (1). When the first plumes of smoke rise from the pan, remove it from the heat.

Carefully pour the hot milk mixture into the caramel in three batches (2), stirring with a wooden spoon after each addition until smooth.

Add the caramel cream to the chopped chocolate in three batches, whisking after each addition (3). This will make first a ganache (4) and then a hot chocolate drink (5).

Strain through a sieve to remove the spices (6).

Rim Sugar

Place the brown sugar in a small bowl. Dip the rims of the glasses in the hot chocolate and then into the brown sugar. Decorate the rims with the fruit.

Makes 2 cups (500 ml)
Level: Easy
Prep: 10 min.

Hot Chocolate

5 oz. (150 g) bittersweet chocolate
    (at least 60% cocoa)
1 cup (250 ml) milk
1 cup (250 ml) heavy cream
¼ cup (2 oz., 50 g) sugar
2 sticks cinnamon
1 vanilla bean, split lengthwise

Rim Sugar

¼ cup (2 oz., 50 g) light brown
    sugar
Small cubes of fresh or dried fruit,
    such as pear, pineapple, or apple

1 Cook the sugar with the spices in a heavy saucepan until it forms a caramel.

2 Carefully stir the hot milk mixture into the caramel in several additions.

3 Whisk the caramel cream into the chopped chocolate in three batches.

4 This shows the ganache consistency halfway through the mixing process.

5 This shows the final texture, once all the liquid is whisked into the chocolate.

6 Strain the hot chocolate.

Confiture de Noël
Christmas Jam

Measure and prep your ingredients and arrange them on the counter (1).

Coarsely chop the oranges and lemons with the skin (2) and place in a large heavy saucepan.

Split the vanilla bean lengthwise in half and scrape out the seeds. Add the vanilla bean and seeds to the pan.

Pour in the sugar (3), stir with a wooden spoon, and let macerate at room temperature for 1 hour (4).

Cook the fruit over low heat for about 1 hour.

Meanwhile, toast the pine nuts in a small dry skillet until lightly browned (5).

Check the jam for doneness: The fruit should be soft but not reduced to a puree (6).

Remove the vanilla bean.

Let cool slightly.

Process briefly with an immersion blender so the jam will be easier to serve and eat (7).

Stir in the cherries and toasted pine nuts (8).

Sterilize the canning jars in boiling water and dry them with a clean kitchen towel. Fill with hot jam (9). Seal the jars and turn them upside down.

Let cool overnight before serving.

Makes 2 14-oz. (400 g) jars
Level: Easy
Prep: 15 min.
Macerate: 1 hr.
Cook: 1 hr.

Special equipment
An immersion blender
2 14-oz. (400 g) canning jars

4 oranges (1 lb. 3 oz.; 550 g)
2 lemons (9 oz., 250 g)
1 vanilla bean
2⅓ cups (1 lb., 450 g) sugar
¼ cup (1½ oz., 35 g) pine nuts
3 oz. (80 g) pitted cherries, fresh or frozen

1 Have all your ingredients and utensils ready to go before cooking.

2 Coarsely chop the oranges and lemons.

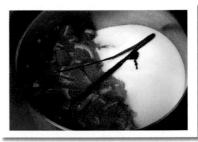

3 Place the citrus fruit, vanilla bean and seeds, and sugar in a large heavy saucepan.

4 Stir well and let macerate for 1 hour.

5 This is what the toasted pine nuts look like.

6 This shows the jam when it is cooked.

7 Briefly process the jam with an immersion blender.

8 Stir in the toasted pine nuts and cherries.

9 Fill the jam jars, seal, and turn them upside down.

Vanille Kipferl de Sébastien
Sébastien's Vanilla Kipferl

Preheat the oven to 350° F (170° C). Dust a baking sheet with flour.

Vanilla Cookies
Grind the sugar with the vanilla bean in a food processor (1) to make especially aromatic vanilla sugar.

Sift the vanilla sugar into a medium bowl (2).

Add the butter, flour, ground almonds, and vanilla extract (3).

Stir with a wooden spoon just until smooth (4).

Shape the dough into a ball (5).

Cut the ball into quarters.

On a lightly floured work surface, roll each quarter of dough into an even log (6).

Line up the logs and cut into 1-inch (2.5 cm) pieces (7).

Arrange them on the prepared baking sheet (8), spacing them slightly apart.

Bake for 15 to 20 minutes, until the cookies are firm but pale.

Transfer the cookies to a rack and let cool.

Sugar Coating
Whisk the confectioners' sugar with the vanilla sugar in a bowl or shallow baking pan.

Toss the cookies in the vanilla sugar to coat, patting off the excess (9).

Makes about 3 dozen cookies
Level: Easy
Prep: 15 min.
Bake: 15 to 20 min. per sheet of cookies

Vanilla Cookies

3 tbsp. (1½ oz., 35 g) sugar
1 vanilla bean, cut crosswise into thirds
1 stick (4 oz., 120 g) butter, diced and softened
1 cup plus 1 tbsp. (5 oz., 140 g) all-purpose flour
¾ cup (2 oz., 60 g) ground almonds
½ tsp. vanilla extract

Sugar Coating

¼ cup plus 2 tbsp. (2 oz., 60 g) confectioners' sugar
2 tbsp. vanilla sugar

1 Process the vanilla bean with the sugar.

2 Sift it into a medium bowl.

3 Add the softened butter, flour, ground almonds, and vanilla extract.

4 Beat with a wooden spoon until smooth.

5 Shape the dough into a ball and cut into quarters.

6 Roll the quarters into even logs.

7 Slice them into 1-inch (2 cm) pieces.

8 Place the cookies on the prepared baking sheet.

9 Toss the cooled cookies in the vanilla sugar.

Croissants et Boules de Noisettes
Hazelnut Crescents and Balls

Preheat the oven to 325° F (160° C). Butter a baking sheet and dust with flour.

Hazelnut Cookies
Spread the hazelnuts on another baking sheet and bake for about 10 minutes, until lightly toasted.

Leave the oven on.

Let the nuts cool slightly and rub off the skins with a kitchen towel.

Sift the flour with the salt, vanilla sugar, and cinnamon into a large bowl.

Makes about 6 ½ dozen cookies
Level: Easy
Prep: 35 min.
Bake: 10 to 12 min. per sheet
of cookies

1¼ cups (5 ½ oz., 150 g) hazelnuts
5 cups (1 lb. 5 oz., 600 g) all-purpose flour
3 pinches salt
1 tbsp. vanilla sugar
1 tsp. ground cinnamon
4 sticks (1 lb., 450 g) butter, diced and softened
1 whole egg
2 egg yolks
1⅓ cups (7 oz., 200 g) confectioners' sugar
½ orange
½ lemon

Chocolate-Hazelnut Balls

¼ cup (1 oz, 30 g) unsweetened cocoa powder
2 tbsp. milk, at room temperature

Cinnamon Sugar Coating

7 tbsp. (3½ oz., 100 g) butter
¼ cup (2 oz., 50 g) granulated sugar
2 tbsp. ground cinnamon
⅓ cup (2 oz., 50 g) confectioners' sugar

1 Beat the softened butter until creamy.

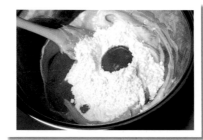

2 Incorporate the whole egg, egg yolks, and confectioners' sugar until fluffy and light.

3 Chop the toasted, skinned hazelnuts.

4 Add the chopped hazelnuts, sifted dry ingredients, and grated citrus zest to the egg-sugar mixture.

5 Stir just until combined.

6 Cut the dough in half. Mix the cocoa powder and milk into one half.

continued

Place the butter in a large bowl and beat until creamy. (1).

Beat in the whole egg, egg yolks, and confectioners' sugar (2) until light and fluffy.

Chop the cooled hazelnuts with a large knife (3) or in a food processor.

Add the chopped hazelnuts and sifted dry ingredients to the egg-sugar mixture.

Finely grate the orange and lemon zest into the mixture (4).

Stir just until combined (5).

Cut the dough in half, placing each half in a separate bowl.

Chocolate-Hazelnut Balls

Stir the cocoa powder and milk into one bowl (6).

Using about 1½ tbsp. (⅓ oz., 10 g) for each cookie, roll the plain dough into cylinders 3 in. (7.5 cm) long, tapering the ends (7). Place them on the prepared baking sheet.

Using about 1½ tbsp. (⅓ oz., 10 g) for each cookie, roll the chocolate dough into balls, place them on the prepared baking sheet, and flatten lightly (8).

Bake for 10 to 12 minutes, until firm but pale.

Transfer the cookies to a rack and let cool completely.

Cinnamon Sugar Coating

Melt the butter in a small saucepan. Whisk the granulated sugar with the cinnamon in a bowl or shallow baking pan. Sift the confectioners' sugar into another bowl.

Brush each crescent with butter and add to the cinnamon sugar, tossing to coat (9).

Brush the balls with butter, let the butter set, and toss them in the confectioners' sugar (10).

7 Shape the crescents.

8 Place the crescents and balls on the prepared baking sheet.

9 Brush the crescents with melted butter and toss them in the cinnamon sugar.

10 Brush the balls with melted butter, let set, and coat in confectioners' sugar.

Les Cannes de Saint Nicolas
Saint Nicholas' Walking Sticks

Line a baking sheet with parchment paper.

Beat the butter with the confectioners' sugar in a medium bowl with a wooden spoon until light and creamy (1).

Whisk in the milk and vanilla extract (2) until smooth (3).

Sift the flour.

Split the vanilla bean lengthwise in half and scrape out the seeds (4). (Keep the vanilla bean to use for another recipe.)

Add the vanilla seeds and flour to the dough and stir just until smooth (5).

Spoon the dough into the pastry bag (6) and pipe walking stick shapes on the prepared baking sheet (7).

Let them dry out at room temperature for about 30 minutes. This helps ensure that the edges made by the fluted tip do not disappear when the cookies bake.

Preheat the oven to 350° F (180° C).

Bake the cookies for 15 to 20 minutes, until firm and lightly browned.
Transfer the cookies to a rack and let cool.

Makes about 5 dozen cookies
Level: Easy
Prep: 25 min.
Dry: 30 min.
Bake: 15 to 20 min. per sheet of cookies

Special equipment
A piping bag fitted with a
½-inch (1 cm) fluted tip

2 sticks (8 oz., 250 g) butter, diced and softened
1 cup (5¼ oz., 150 g) confectioners' sugar
½ cup (120 ml) milk, at room temperature
1 tsp. vanilla extract
3 cups (13 oz., 375 g) all-purpose flour
½ vanilla bean

1 Beat the softened butter with the confectioners' sugar.

2 Whisk in the milk and vanilla extract.

3 Whisk until the mixture is smooth.

4 Split the vanilla bean and scrape out the seeds.

5 Stir in the vanilla seeds and flour.

6 Spoon the dough into a pastry bag.

7 Pipe walking stick shapes on a lined baking sheet.

Étoiles au Sucre
Cinnamon Sugar-Coated Stars

Cinnamon Cookies

Sift the flour with the salt, baking powder, cinnamon, and cocoa powder (1).

Place the butter in a medium bowl.

Pour the sugar into the butter and beat with a spatula until light and creamy (2).

Beat in the egg and milk until smooth.

Add the sifted dry ingredients (3) and stir just until smooth.

Flatten the dough into a disk, cover with plastic wrap, and chill for at least 2 hours.

Preheat the oven to 350° F (180° C). Line a baking sheet with parchment paper.

On a lightly floured work surface, roll out the dough into a sheet about ⅛ inch (2 to 3 mm) thick (4).

Stamp out stars with the cookie cutters (5).

To make hanging decorations, cut out a small hole near an edge in each cookie with the plain pastry tip.

Transfer the cookies to the prepared baking sheet, spacing them slightly apart.

Cinnamon Sugar Coating

Whisk the brown sugar with the cinnamon in a bowl or baking pan.

Lightly brush the cookies, top and bottom, with water (6).

Dredge them in the cinnamon sugar (7), patting off the excess.

Bake for 10 to 15 minutes, until firm.

Let cool on the baking sheet.

Note: These cookies keep in a tin for up to a week.

Makes about 3½ dozen cookies
Level: Easy
Prep: 40 min.
Chill: at least 2 hr.
Bake: 10 to 15 min. per sheet
of cookies

Special equipment
Star cookie cutters or other
holiday-shaped cookie cutters of
approximately the same size
A plain pastry tip or
plastic straw

Cinnamon Cookies

1⅔ cups (7 oz., 200 g) all-purpose
flour
1 pinch salt
½ tsp. baking powder
1 tsp. ground cinnamon
1 tsp. unsweetened cocoa powder
7 tbsp. (3½ oz., 100 g) butter, diced
and softened
½ cup (3½ oz., 100 g) sugar
1 egg
1 tbsp. milk

Cinnamon Sugar Coating

¾ cup (5 oz., 150 g) light brown
sugar
1 tsp. ground cinnamon
¼ cup plus 2 tbsp. (100 ml) water

1 Sift the flour with the salt, baking powder, cinnamon, and cocoa powder.

2 Beat the sugar into the softened butter until light and fluffy.

3 Stir in the egg and milk, followed by the sifted dry ingredients.

4 Roll out the dough into a sheet ⅛ inch (2 to 3 mm) thick.

5 Cut out the shapes.

6 Lightly brush the cookies with water on both sides.

7 Dredge them in the cinnamon sugar.

Petits Sablés d'Antan
Old-Fashioned Shortbread Cookies

Cookies

Measure and prep your ingredients and arrange them on the counter (1).

Grate the orange and lemon zest.

Combine the flour, sugar, ground almonds, cinnamon, baking powder, and ground aniseed on a work surface.

Add the butter and citrus zest to the dry ingredients (2).

Rub the butter into the dry ingredients with your fingertips until the mixture forms fine crumbs (3).

Make a well in the center and add the whole egg, egg yolk, orange flower water, and kirsch (4).

Knead just until the dough is smooth and shape into a ball (5).

Flatten the ball into a disk and, using the heel of your hand, scrape the dough on the work surface in a sliding motion (6). Press the dough into a disk and repeat.

Cover the dough with plastic wrap and chill for 2 hours.

Preheat the oven to 350° F (180° C). Butter a baking sheet and dust it with flour.

On a lightly floured work surface, roll out the dough into a sheet about ⅛ inch (3 to 4 mm) thick.

Stamp out assorted shapes with the cookie cutters (7). Transfer the cookies to the prepared baking sheet, spacing them slightly apart.

Egg Glaze

Lightly beat the egg yolk in a cup with a fork. Brush the tops of the cookies with the egg glaze (8).

Bake for 10 to 15 minutes, until firm (9). Transfer the cookies to a rack and let cool.

Makes about 4 dozen cookies
Level: Easy
Prep: 30 min.
Chill: 2 hr.
Bake: 15 min. per sheet
of cookies

Special equipment
Assorted holiday cookie cutters
of approximately the same size

Cookies

¼ lemon
¼ orange
2 cups (9 oz., 250 g) all-purpose
flour
⅔ cup (4 oz., 125 g) sugar
¾ cup (2¼ oz, 65 g) ground
almonds
1 tsp. ground cinnamon
1 pinch baking powder
1 pinch ground aniseed

1 stick (4 oz., 125 g) butter, diced
and softened
1 whole egg
1 egg yolk
1 tbsp. orange flower water
1 tsp. kirsch

Egg Glaze

1 egg yolk

1 Have all your ingredients and utensils ready to go before cooking.

2 Combine the flour, sugar, almonds, cinnamon, baking powder, aniseed, butter, and citrus zests on a work surface.

3 Rub in the butter with your fingertips.

4 Make a well in the center and add the whole egg, egg yolk, orange flower water, and kirsch.

5 Knead just until the dough is smooth and shape into a ball.

6 Scrape the dough in a sliding motion, using the heel of your hand.

7 Roll out the dough and cut out assorted shapes.

8 Brush the tops of the cookies with the egg glaze.

9 This is what the cookies will look like when baked.

Biscuits d'Anis
Green Anise Cookies

Break the eggs into a medium bowl, add the sugar (1), and whip at high speed with an electric mixer for 10 minutes.

Reduce the speed to medium and whip for 10 minutes (2).

Spread the green anise seeds on a work surface and remove any twigs (3).

Sift the flour into a bowl and add the anise seeds.

Gently fold the flour mixture into the whipped eggs with a flexible spatula (4).

Butter 2 baking sheets and dust them with flour (5).

Spoon the batter into the pastry bag and pipe 1½-inch (4 cm) mounds on the prepared baking sheets (6), spacing them slightly apart.

Let them dry in a warm place until a crust forms, about 4 hours.

Position racks in the upper and lower thirds of the oven. Preheat the oven to 350° F (180° C).

Bake for 6 to 8 minutes, until the tops are puffed but pale and the bottoms are lightly browned.

Let cool on the baking sheet. Store in an airtight container.

Makes about 8 dozen cookies
Level: Intermediate
Prep: 30 min.
Dry: about 4 hr.
Bake: 6 to 8 min. per 2 sheets
of cookies

Special equipment
A pastry bag fitted with a ⅓ to
½ inch (8 mm to 1 cm) plain tip

3 eggs
1¼ cups (9 oz., 250 g) sugar
½ oz. (15 g) green anise seeds
2 cups (9 oz., 250 g) all-purpose flour

1 Combine the eggs and sugar in the bowl of a mixer.

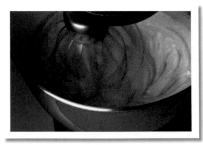

2 Whip for 10 minutes at high speed and then for 10 minutes at medium speed.

3 Sort through the anise seeds, removing any twigs.

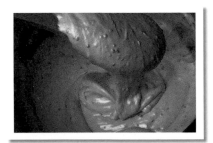

4 Fold the flour and anise seed mixture into the beaten eggs.

5 Butter the baking sheets and dust them with flour.

6 Pipe the batter in mounds on the baking sheets. Let stand until a dry crust forms.

Pains d'Épices Moelleux
Gingerbread Muffins

Preheat the oven to 350° F (170° C). Butter the muffin cups and dust them with flour.

Muffins

Bring the milk to a boil in a small saucepan. Add the star anise, remove from the heat, and let infuse for about 10 minutes (1).

Warm the honey in a small saucepan over low heat or briefly in the microwave oven.

Whisk both flours with the potato starch, baking powder, brown sugar, cinnamon, and allspice in a large mixing bowl (2).

Stir in the warm honey and orange marmalade with a wooden spoon (3).

Stir in the eggs, butter, and salt (4).

Strain the milk into the batter (5) and stir just until smooth.

Spoon the batter into the prepared muffin cups, filling them three-quarters full. Or pipe in the batter with a pastry bag fitted with a medium plain tip (6).

Bake for 25 to 30 minutes, until firm and a cake tester inserted into the center comes out clean.

Let the muffins cool in the pans for 5 minutes, then transfer to a rack to cool.

Glaze

Melt the apricot preserves and orange marmalade in a medium saucepan over medium heat, stirring occasionally. Brush over the tops of the gingerbread muffins (7).

Garnish

Decorate with the orange pieces.

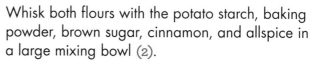

Makes about 1½ dozen
Level: Easy
Prep: 25 min.
Bake: 25 to 30 min.

Special equipment
2 12-cup muffin tins

Muffins

¼ cup plus 2 tbsp. (100 ml) milk
1 tbsp. star anise pods
⅔ cup (8 oz., 240 g) honey
2½ tbsp. (1 oz., 25 g) all-purpose flour
1½ cups (5 oz., 150 g) rye flour
2½ tbsp. (1 oz., 25 g) potato starch
1 tbsp. (⅓ oz., 11 g) baking powder
1 tbsp. (½ oz., 15 g) light brown sugar
1 tsp. ground cinnamon
½ tsp. ground allspice
¾ cup (8 oz., 240 g) orange marmalade
2 eggs
5 tbsp. (3 oz., 80 g) butter, softened
1 tsp. salt

Glaze

7 oz. (200 g) apricot preserves
3 tbsp. orange marmalade

Garnish

1 orange, thinly sliced and cut into 1-inch (2.5 cm) pieces

1 Let the hot milk infuse with the star anise.

2 Have all the other ingredients and utensils ready to go before cooking.

3 Stir the warmed honey and the marmalade into the dry ingredients.

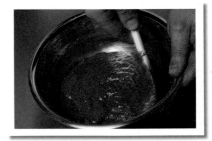

4 Beat in the eggs, softened butter, and salt.

5 Add the strained milk.

6 Fill the prepared muffin cups three-quarters full using a pastry bag, or spoon in the batter.

7 Brush the tops of the cooled muffins with the melted jam mixture.

Losanges Noix et Chocolat
Chocolate-Walnut Diamonds

Cookies

Grind the walnuts in a food processor to a fine powder.

Combine the ground walnuts, flour, baking powder, sugar, butter, cinnamon, and salt on a work surface (1).

Rub the butter into the dry ingredients with your fingertips until the mixture forms fine crumbs (2).

Make a well in the center and add the whole egg and egg yolk.

Finely grate the lemon zest into the well (3).

Knead just until the dough is smooth (4) and shape into a ball (5).

Flatten into a disk and cover with plastic wrap. Chill for 1 hour.

Position racks in the upper and lower thirds of the oven. Preheat the oven to 350° F (180° C). Line 2 baking sheets with parchment paper.

Egg Glaze

Lightly beat the egg yolk in a cup with a fork.

On a lightly floured work surface, roll out the dough into a sheet ⅛ inch (4 mm) thick.

Cut into 1¼-inch (3 cm) diamond shapes (6).

Place the cookies on the prepared baking sheets, spacing them ½ inch (1 cm) apart.

Brush the tops of the cookies with the egg glaze.

Bake for 10 to 15 minutes, until lightly browned.

Let the cookies cool on the baking sheet.

Coating

Finely chop the chocolate. Place in a medium bowl set over a saucepan filled with 1 inch (2.5 cm) of barely simmering water, making sure that the bottom of the bowl does not touch the water. Let the chocolate melt. Remove the bowl from the heat and stir until smooth.

Dip one half of each cookie in the chocolate.

Transfer to parchment paper and let the chocolate set slightly.

Place a walnut half on each cookie (7).

Let the chocolate set completely and serve.

Makes about 8 dozen cookies
Level: Easy
Prep: 25 min.
Chill: 1 hr.
Bake: 10 to 15 min. per 2 sheets
of cookies

Cookies

1 cup (4 oz., 125 g) chopped
  walnuts
3 cups (13 oz., 375 g) all-purpose
  flour
1 tsp. baking powder
⅔ cup (4 oz., 125 g) sugar
2 sticks (8 oz., 250 g) butter, diced
1 tsp. ground cinnamon
2 pinches salt
1 whole egg
1 egg yolk
1 lemon

Egg Glaze

1 egg yolk

Coating

7 oz. (200 g) bittersweet
  chocolate
⅓ cup (2 oz., 50 g) walnut halves

1 Combine the ground walnuts, flour, baking powder, sugar, butter, cinnamon, and salt.

2 Rub the butter into the dry ingredients with your fingertips.

3 Add the whole egg, egg yolk, and lemon zest.

4 Knead the dough with your hands.

5 Shape the dough into a ball.

6 Cut the rolled-out dough into diamond shapes.

7 Dip one half of each cooled cookie into the melted chocolate and decorate with a walnut half.

Macarons Croquants à la Noisette

Crunchy Hazelnut Macarons

Coarsely chop 1⅔ cups (10 oz., 300 g) of the hazelnuts with a large knife or in a food processor (1).

Whisk the sugar with the vanilla extract, cinnamon, and chopped hazelnuts in a medium bowl (2).

Add the egg whites, one at a time (3), whisking well after each addition.

Pour the batter into a medium heavy saucepan and cook over medium heat, stirring constantly with a wooden spoon, until the batter is hot to the touch and the temperature registers 149° F (65°C) on an instant-read thermometer.

Remove the pan from the heat and stir until cool (4).

Preheat the oven to 350° F (170° C). Butter a baking sheet and dust it with flour. Mark circles on the sheet with the cookie cutter, spacing them slightly apart, to use as guides

Drop the batter into 1-inch (3 cm) mounds on the prepared baking sheet (5).

Top each mound with a hazelnut (6).

Bake for about 10 minutes, until firm.

Let the macarons cool on the baking sheet. Remove them with a spatula (7) and store in an airtight container.

Makes about 3 dozen cookies
Level: Easy
Prep: 20 min.
Bake: 10 min. per sheet
of cookies

Special equipment
A 1-inch (3 cm) cookie cutter

2½ cups (12 oz., 350 g) hazelnuts
1½ cups (10½ oz., 300 g) sugar
1 tsp. vanilla extract
1 tsp. ground cinnamon
5 egg whites

1 Coarsely chop the hazelnuts.

2 Whisk the sugar with the vanilla extract, cinnamon, and chopped hazelnuts.

3 Add the egg whites, one at a time, whisking well after each addition.

4 Heat the batter over medium heat to 149° F (65°C), stirring, remove from the heat, and stir until cool.

5 Spoon 1-inch (3 cm) mounds onto the prepared baking sheet.

6 Top each mound with a whole hazelnut.

7 Remove the cooled macarons from the baking sheet using a spatula.

Le Petit Bonhomme de Neige
A Little Snowman

Knead the almond paste until smooth and pliable. If it is too dry, add a drop of water.

Knead a small piece of the almond paste with a drop of the red food coloring.

Knead a second small piece with a drop of the yellow food coloring.

Mix a little of the yellow and red food coloring. Knead a third small piece of the white almond paste with a drop of the orange food coloring.

Knead a fourth small piece of the white almond paste with enough of the cocoa powder to make a dark brown color.

Place the bittersweet chocolate and white chocolate in 2 small separate bowls. Set each over a saucepan filled with 1 inch (2.5 cm) of barely simmering water and let melt. Remove the bowls from the heat and stir until smooth. Let cool.

As you work, keep all unused almond paste covered with plastic wrap so it does not dry out.

The step-by-step instructions explain only how to make the snowman, not how to color the almond paste.

Makes 1 snowman
Level: Intermediate
Prep: 40 min., longer if working
with children

Special equipment
A parchment paper cone (see
page 212)
A fine paintbrush

8 oz. (250 g) white almond paste
Red food coloring
Yellow food coloring
¼ cup plus 3 tbsp. (1 ¾ oz., 50 g)
unsweetened cocoa powder
2 oz. (50 g) bittersweet chocolate,
finely chopped
2 oz. (50 g) white chocolate, finely
chopped
⅓ cup (2 oz., 50 g) confectioners'
sugar

1 Have all your ingredients and utensils ready to go before beginning.

2 Roll a small and a slightly larger ball from pieces of the white almond paste, one for the head and one for the body.

3 Place the head on the body.

4 Roll another piece of white almond paste into a log.

5 Cut one end to make the candle.

6 Roll the chocolate almond paste into a log.

continued

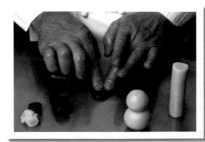

7 Flatten a small piece of chocolate paste to make a brim for the hat.

8 Take another piece of the chocolate log to make the top hat.

9 Lift the top hat off the counter with a small knife.

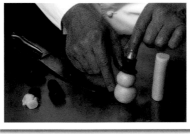

10 Place the hat on the snowman's head.

11 Using either a parchment paper cone or a spoon, drizzle a little of the white chocolate over the candle to imitate melted wax.

12 Shape a flame out of a piece of the orange almond paste and paint the tip with yellow food coloring.

13 Place the flame on top of the candle.

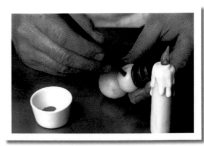

14 Make small indentations with the end of the brush for the snowman's eyes.

15 Shape a small carrot out of another piece of the orange almond paste. Stick it between the eyes to make a nose.

16 Roll out the red almond paste to make a scarf.

17 Cut out a neat strip.

18 Wrap the scarf around the snowman's neck.

19 Roll out a small square of chocolate almond paste. Make incisions halfway through it.

20 Roll the square around a toothpick to make a broom.

21 Insert the toothpick into the body of the snowman at the side.

22 Roll a small ball of chocolate almond paste and flatten it. Place it under the candle and there you have a candleholder.

23 Sift confectioners' sugar snow over the snowman.

Pumpernickel
Cinnamon-Almond Biscotti

Preheat the oven to 350° F (180° C). Butter a baking sheet and dust it with flour.

Combine the eggs with the sugar in a medium bowl (1) and whisk for 20 minutes (2). Or whip with an electric mixer at medium speed for 15 minutes. Whisk in the cinnamon (3).

Coarsely chop the whole almonds with a large knife (4) or in a food processor. Add them to the egg-sugar mixture.

Fold in the flour (5). The batter should be thick (6).

Spoon the batter into a pastry bag without a tip and pipe 2 loaves about 10 by 2 inches (25 by 5 cm) on the prepared baking sheet (7), spacing them well apart. Or divide the dough in half and shape each loaf on the baking sheet with wet hands.

Sprinkle the loaves with the sliced almonds (8) and tilt and tap the baking sheet to remove the excess (9).

Bake for about 30 minutes, until a cake tester inserted in the center comes out clean.

Leave the oven on.

Immediately transfer the loaves to a cutting board and slice them on the diagonal about ½ inch (1 cm) thick (10). Place the slices cut side down on the same baking sheet and bake for 7 to 10 minutes, until crisp but pale.

Let cool on the baking sheet.

Notes: You can replace the almonds with hazelnuts or walnuts.
Biscotti are excellent with tea or coffee.

Makes about 2½ dozen
Level: Easy
Prep: 30 min.
Bake: 40 min.

2 eggs
1¼ cups (9 oz., 250 g) sugar
1 tbsp. (8 g) ground cinnamon
1½ cups (9 oz., 250 g) whole almonds
2 cups plus 1 tbsp. (9 oz., 260 g) all-purpose flour
1⅓ cups (3½ oz., 100 g) sliced blanched almonds

1 Combine the eggs with the sugar.

2 Whisk for 20 minutes.

3 Whisk in the cinnamon.

4 Chop the whole almonds.

5 Add the chopped almonds and flour to the batter.

6 Fold in. The batter should be thick.

7 Pipe loaf shapes, spacing them well apart.

8 Scatter with sliced almonds.

9 Remove any extra sliced almonds.

10 Cut on the diagonal into slices as soon as you remove the loaves from the oven.

Baerewecke
Alsatian Dried-Fruit-and-Nut Loaf

Cut the pears, prunes, pineapple, and apples into ¼-inch-wide (6 mm) strips (1). Place in a large bowl and add the raisins.

Grind the almonds in a food processor to a fine powder.

Coarsely chop the walnuts with a large knife or in the food processor.

Pour the orange juice, red wine, and kirsch into a large saucepan and add the sugar, allspice, ground cinnamon, and cinnamon stick.

Bring to a simmer over medium heat, stirring, until the sugar dissolves. Pour it over the dried fruit (2).

Return the mixture to the saucepan and bring to a simmer. Remove from the heat and transfer to a large bowl.

Add the chopped walnuts (3). Stir them in and let macerate for 1 hour (4).

Pour the mixture into a colander and let drain for 10 minutes (5). Remove the cinnamon stick.

Preheat the oven to 300° F (150° C) using the conventional setting.

Return the drained fruit to the large bowl and stir in the ground almonds (6).

Cut a sheet of parchment paper into 5 12 by 8-inch (30 by 20 cm) rectangles. Dust the rectangles with flour.

Divide the dough into fifths and mound one-fifth slightly off center on each paper rectangle (7).

Fold the short end of the paper rectangle over the dough (8).

Snugly tuck the paper end under the dough with a spatula and tightly roll up each loaf (9).

Place the loaves on a baking sheet and bake for 50 minutes (10), until firm.

Transfer to a rack and let cool completely.

Wrap each loaf in foil and let stand at room temperature for 2 to 3 weeks for their flavors to develop fully.

Makes 5 small loaves
Level: Intermediate
Prep: 30 min.
Macerate: 1 hr.
Bake: 50 min.
Plan ahead: 2 to 3 weeks
(optional)

10 oz. (300 g) dried pear slices
10 oz. (300 g) pitted prunes
5 slices candied pineapple
3½ oz. (100 g) dried apple slices
⅔ cup (3½ oz., 100 g) golden
   raisins
½ cup (3½ oz., 100 g) almonds
1⅓ cups (5½ oz., 160 g) walnuts
1½ cups (350 ml) orange juice
1 cup (250 ml) red wine,
   traditionally Alsatian pinot noir
2 tbsp. (30 ml) kirsch
¼ cup plus 2 tbsp. (3 oz., 80 g)
   sugar
1 tsp. ground allspice
1 tsp. ground cinnamon
1 stick cinnamon

1 Cut the pears, prunes, pineapple, and apples into thin strips.

2 Heat the orange juice, wine, kirsch, sugar, and spices and pour over the dried fruit.

3 Stir in the walnuts.

4 Let macerate for 1 hour.

5 Let drain in a colander for 10 minutes.

6 Scrape the mixture into a bowl and stir in the ground almonds.

7 Divide the mixture equally on 5 floured paper rectangles.

8 Fold the short end of the paper rectangle over the dough.

9 Tuck the paper end under the dough with a spatula and tightly roll up.

10 Bake for 50 minutes and let cool.

Couronne de l'Avent
Candied-Fruit Christmas Wreath

Combine the butter, sugar, rum, and salt in a small saucepan. Grate in the orange and lemon zest (1). Cook over medium heat, stirring, until the sugar dissolves. Remove from the heat, let cool to lukewarm, and stir in the orange flower water.

Crumble the yeast into a large bowl. Pour in the water and whisk to dissolve the yeast. Add the flour and eggs and beat with a wooden spoon until the dough is crumbly (2).

Gradually pour the lukewarm syrup into the dough (3), beating well with a wooden spoon until all the liquid is absorbed (4).

Stir in the candied fruit until they are evenly distributed. Shape the dough into a ball.

Cover the bowl with a clean kitchen towel and let the dough rise (5) at room temperature for 1 hour.

Line a baking sheet with parchment paper.

On a lightly floured work surface, flatten the dough with the palms of your hands. Roll it into a log about 24 inches (60 cm) long (6).

Shape the log into a ring. To make it perfectly round, fit it inside an 8-inch (20 cm) pastry ring or tart pan (7); remove the ring, turn out the dough onto the prepared baking sheet, and join the 2 ends together (8).

Let rise at room temperature for 1 hour.

Preheat the oven to 350° F (180° C).

Egg Glaze
Lightly beat the egg with a fork. Brush the wreath with the egg glaze (9).

Dip the blades of a scissors in the egg glaze. Holding the scissors at a slight angle, snip regular incisions all round the top of the wreath (10).

Bake for 25 to 30 minutes, until nicely browned.

Transfer the bread to a rack and let cool.

Makes 1 bread
Level: Easy
Prep: 30 min.
Rise: 2 hr.
Bake: 25 to 30 min.

5 tbsp. (3 oz., 80 g) butter
¼ cup plus 2 tbsp. (3 oz., 80 g) sugar
3 tbsp. (40 ml) dark rum
1 tsp. salt
1 orange
1 lemon
3 tbsp. (40 ml) orange flower water
½ cake (.3 oz., 10 g) fresh yeast
1 tbsp. lukewarm water
3¼ cups (14 oz., 400 g) all-purpose flour
2 eggs
2½ oz. (70 g) diced candied fruit

Egg Glaze

1 egg

1 Make a syrup with the butter, sugar, rum, salt, and grated citrus zest.

2 Stir the flour and eggs into the yeast.

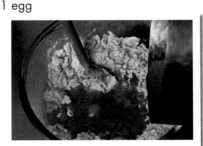

3 Stir the lukewarm syrup into the crumbly dough.

4 Beat until the dough is smooth.

5 Mix in the candied fruit. Shape into a ball and let rise.

6 Using the palms of your hands, roll out a long log.

7 You can use a pastry ring to help shape the wreath.

8 Join the ends neatly.

9 Brush the top with a lightly beaten egg.

10 Holding the scissors at slight angle, snip regular incisions around the top.

Pains d'Épice de Mon Enfance
My Childhood Gingerbread Cookies

Basic Dough

Measure and prep your ingredients and arrange them on the counter (1).

Warm the honey in a small saucepan over low heat.

Sift the all-purpose and whole wheat flours with the cinnamon into a medium bowl (2).

Add the warm honey (3) and stir with a wooden spoon until the dough is thick and smooth (4).

Cover the bowl with a kitchen towel and let stand at room temperature for 1 week.

Shape the dough into a ball and place it in the bowl of a stand mixer fitted with the paddle attachment.

Final Dough

Place the egg yolk on a work surface.

Pour the baking powder around it.

Smear the powder into the egg yolk with the flat side of a knife until smooth (5).

Add to the basic dough (6) with the cinnamon and allspice and knead at low speed (7) until the dough is perfectly smooth, about 5 minutes.

Shape the dough into ball, flatten it into a disk, and cover with plastic wrap. Chill for at least 30 minutes.

Preheat the oven to 350° F (170° C). Butter a baking sheet and dust it with flour.

Makes about 3 dozen
Level: Intermediate
Prep: 45 min.
Chill: 30 min.
Bake: 15 to 20 min.
Set: 1 hr.
Plan ahead: at least 1 week

Special equipment
Assorted holiday cookie cutters
of approximately the same size

Basic Dough

¾ cup (9 oz., 250 g) pine honey or other strong dark honey
1⅔ cups (7 oz., 200 g) all-purpose flour
⅓ cup (2 oz., 50 g) whole wheat flour
1 tbsp. ground cinnamon

Final Dough

1 egg yolk
1 tsp. baking powder (see *Note*)
1 pinch ground cinnamon
½ tsp. ground allspice
2 tbsp. milk

Royal Icing

1½ cups (7 oz., 200 g) confectioners' sugar
1 egg white
A few drops lemon juice or kirsch
A few drops food coloring (optional)
Multicolored sprinkles, nonpareils, colored sugars, edible pictures

1 Have all the ingredients and utensils ready to go for the basic dough.

2 Sift the flours with the cinnamon.

3 Combine the dry ingredients with the warm honey.

4 This shows the texture of the basic dough.

5 Pour the baking powder around the egg yolk and work it in with the flat side of a knife until smooth.

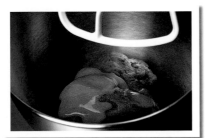

6 Add the mixture to the basic dough.

7 Knead the dough.

continued

Holiday Cakes, Cookies, and Other Treats   491

On a lightly floured work surface, roll out the dough about ⅛ inch (3 mm) thick. Roll the dough around the rolling pin and dust underneath with more flour (8). Unroll the dough.

Stamp out assorted shapes with the cookie cutters (9). Transfer them to the baking sheet, spacing them about 2 inches (5 cm) apart. Brush the cookies with milk.

Bake for 15 to 20 minutes, until barely firm and lightly browned. Let the cookies cool completely on the baking sheet.

Royal Icing

Measure and prep your ingredients and arrange them on the counter (10).

Stir the confectioners' sugar with the egg white in a medium bowl with a wooden spoon until evenly moistened. Add enough of the lemon juice (11) to make an icing that holds its shape but spreads smoothly (12). Or, if you prefer, use kirsch (13).

If you like, add a drop of food coloring to the royal icing.

Make sure the pastry brush is spotlessly clean and dry. Brush the gingerbread cookies with royal icing in a layer that is not too thick (14 and 15).

Decorate with multicolored sprinkles, nonpareils, colored sugars, or edible pictures (16).

Let the gingerbread cookies dry until the royal icing sets, about 1 hour.

Note: In Alsace, baker's ammonia and potash are the traditional leaveners in authentic gingerbread. If you would like to prepare the old-fashioned recipe, substitute ½ tsp. baker's ammonia and ½ tsp. potash for the 1 tsp. baking powder used here.

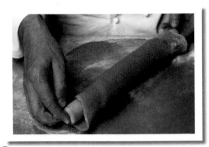

8 Roll the dough around the rolling pin.

9 On a lightly floured work surface, cut out shapes.

10 Have all the ingredients and utensils ready to make the royal icing.

11 Combine the confectioners' sugar with the egg white. Incorporate a few drops of lemon juice.

12 This shows the texture of the royal icing.

13 If you prefer, flavor the icing with a few drops of kirsch.

14 Brush the cookies with an even layer of royal icing.

15 Decorate some with edible pictures.

16 Scatter others with multicolored sprinkles or nonpareils.

Leckerlis
Gingerbread Cookies with Candied Citrus Peel

Basic Dough

Measure and prep your ingredients and arrange them on the counter (1).

Warm the honey in a small saucepan over low heat.

Sift the all-purpose and whole wheat flours with the cinnamon and allspice into a medium bowl. Add the warm honey (2) and stir with a wooden spoon until the dough is thick and smooth (3).

Cover the bowl with a kitchen towel and let stand at room temperature for 1 week.

Final Dough

Chop the hazelnuts into a coarse powder with a knife or in a food processor.

Finely dice the candied citrus peels.

Shape the dough into a ball and flatten it into a disk.

Slice the dough into strips (4), then crosswise into dice. Transfer to a medium bowl.

Place the egg yolk on a work surface.

Pour the baking powder around it (5).

Smear the powder into the egg yolk with the flat side of a knife until smooth (6).

If using traditional leaveners, smear the baker's ammonia into the egg yolk and dilute the potash in the kirsch (7).

Makes about 4 dozen
Level: Easy
Prep: 30 min.
Bake: 15 min.
Plan ahead: 1 week

Basic Dough

¾ cup (9 oz., 250 g) pine honey or other strong dark honey
1⅔ cups (7 oz., 200 g) all-purpose flour
⅓ cup (2 oz., 50 g) whole wheat flour
1 tsp. ground cinnamon
1 tsp. ground allspice

Final Dough

½ cup (2 oz., 50 g) hazelnuts
2 oz. (50 g) candied lemon peel (page 452)
2 oz. (50 g) candied orange peel (page 452)
1 tsp. baking powder (see *Notes*)
1 egg yolk
1 tbsp. kirsch

Icing

2 tbsp. (30 ml) kirsch
1½ cups (7 oz., 200 g) confectioners' sugar
2 tbsp. water

1 Have all the ingredients and utensils ready to go for the basic dough.

2 Pour the warm honey into the dry ingredients.

3 This shows the texture of the basic dough.

4 Shape the rested dough into a ball, flatten it, cut into strips and then into dice.

5 Pour the baking powder around the egg yolk on a work surface.

6 Work the powder into the egg yolk with the flat side of a knife until smooth.

7 If using potash, dissolve it in the kirsch.

continued

Holiday Cakes, Cookies, and Other Treats   495

Add the egg yolk–baking powder/baker's ammonia paste to the basic dough. Add the kirsch (with the potash, if using) (8). Add the hazelnut powder (9). Beat with a wooden spoon until smooth.

Beat in the diced candied citrus peels (10) until they are evenly distributed (11). Or use a stand mixer fitted with the paddle attachment.

Shape the dough into a ball, flatten it into a disk, and cover with plastic wrap. Chill for 10 minutes.

Preheat the oven to 350° F (170° C). Butter a baking sheet and dust it with flour.

On a lightly floured work surface, roll out the dough slightly less than ¼ inch (5 mm) thick. Drape it over the rolling pin and transfer to the prepared baking sheet (12).

Bake for about 15 minutes, until browned (13).

Icing
Combine the kirsch with the confectioners' sugar and water.

Brush the gingerbread with the icing while it's still warm (14). Immediately cut into small rectangles (15).

Let the cookies cool on the baking sheet for 5 minutes, then transfer to a rack to cool completely.

Notes: In Alsace, baker's ammonia and potash are the traditional leaveners in authentic gingerbread. If you would like to prepare the old-fashioned recipe, substitute ½ tsp. baker's ammonia and ½ tsp. potash for the 1 tsp. baking powder used here.

These cookies are even better the next day.

8 Add the leaveners to the diced dough.

9 Beat in the hazelnut powder.

10 When the dough is smooth, stir in the diced candied citrus peels.

11 Stir until evenly mixed in.

12 Transfer the dough to the prepared baking sheet.

13 This shows the gingerbread straight out of the oven.

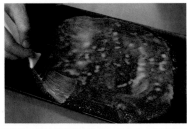

14 Brush the warm top with the icing.

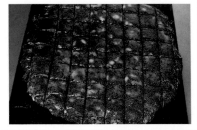

15 Cut into rectangles right after icing.

Bretzels Sucrés
Sweet Pretzels

Pretzels

Crumble the yeast into a large bowl. Pour in the milk and whisk to dissolve the yeast (1).

Add ½ cup plus 1 tbsp. (2½ oz., 70 g) of the flour and beat with a wooden spoon until the dough is elastic. Cover with the remaining flour (2).

Let rise in a warm place until it doubles in volume, about 30 minutes (3).

Add the eggs, granulated sugar, vanilla sugar, and salt (4).

Beat with a wooden spoon until the dough pulls away from the sides of the bowl (5).

Knead in the butter with your hands until the dough pulls away from the sides of the bowl (6).

Add the orange peel and orange flower water and knead until just combined (7).

Shape the dough into a ball (8), cover the bowl with plastic wrap, and chill for 3 hours.

Makes 3 pretzels
Level: Easy
Prep: 30 min.
Chill: 3 hr.
Rise: 1 hr. 10 min.
Bake: 35 min.

¾ cake (.45 oz., 15 g) fresh yeast
3 tbsp. lukewarm milk
2⅔ cups (11½ oz., 325 g) all-purpose flour
3 eggs
⅓ cup (2½ oz., 75 g) granulated sugar
1 tbsp. vanilla sugar
1 tsp. salt
1 stick (4 oz., 115 g) butter, diced and softened
3 oz. (80 g) candied orange peel (page 452), finely diced
1 tbsp. orange flower water

1 whole egg
1 egg yolk
1 tbsp. milk

⅓ cup (2½ oz., 70 g) sugar
⅓ cup (70 ml) water
2 tbsp. orange flower water

1 Dissolve the yeast in the lukewarm milk.

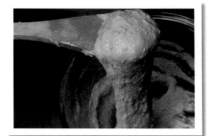

2 When the starter is elastic, cover it with the remaining flour.

3 The starter should double in volume.

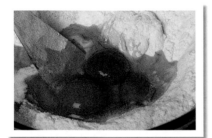

4 Add the eggs, granulated sugar, vanilla sugar, and salt.

5 Begin beating with a wooden spoon.

6 Add the butter and knead by hand, working until the dough pulls away from the sides of the bowl.

7 Stir in the diced orange peel and orange flower water.

8 Shape into a ball.

continued

Divide the dough into thirds, each about 9 oz. (270 g) (9).

On a lightly floured work surface, flatten one-third of the dough (10) and fold it over itself (11). Repeat with the remaining dough.

Roll and stretch one-third into a rope about 12 inches (30 cm) long (12 and 13).

Pick up the ends and make a horseshoe shape (14).

Holding the ends of the rope, cross them over each other once (15), then a second time, and fold back onto the bottom of the "U" to make a pretzel shape (16). Repeat with the remaining dough.

Line a baking sheet with parchment paper. Transfer the pretzels to the prepared baking sheet, cover them loosely with plastic wrap, and let rise in a warm place, about 77° F (25° C), until the dough springs back when touched, about 40 minutes.

Preheat the oven to 350° F (180° C).

Egg Glaze

Lightly beat the whole egg, egg yolk, and milk in a cup with a fork.

Brush the puffy pretzels with the egg glaze.

Bake for 10 minutes. Reduce the oven temperature to 340° F (170° C) and bake for 20 to 25 minutes, until golden. Keep an eye on them as they bake, particularly towards the end. If you see that they are coloring too much, cover them with foil.

Orange Flower Syrup

Combine the sugar and water in a small saucepan. Cook over medium heat, stirring, until the sugar dissolves. Remove from the heat, let cool, and stir in the orange flower water.

Brush the pretzels with the syrup while they are still warm.

Let cool slightly on the baking sheet, then transfer to a rack and let cool.

9 Divide the dough into thirds.

10 Flatten the dough slightly on a lightly floured surface.

11 Fold one-third over itself.

12 Shape it into a log.

13 Roll and stretch the log into a 12-inch (30 cm) rope.

14 Bend the rope to make a horseshoe shape.

15 Cross one end over the other.

16 Cross the ends again and fold back onto the bottom of the horseshoe.

La Maison en Pain d'Épice
Gingerbread House

Basic Dough

Measure and prep your ingredients and arrange them on the counter (1).

Warm the honey in a small saucepan over low heat.

Sift the all-purpose and whole wheat flours with the cinnamon into a medium bowl. Add the warm honey (2) and stir with a wooden spoon until the dough is thick and smooth (3).

Cover the bowl with a kitchen towel and let stand at room temperature for 1 week.

Shape the dough into a ball and place it in the bowl of a stand mixer fitted with the paddle attachment.

Final Dough

Place the egg yolk on a work surface.

Pour the baking powder around it (4).

Smear the powder into the egg yolk with the flat side of a knife until smooth.

Add to the basic dough (5) with the cinnamon and allspice and knead at low speed (6) until the dough is perfectly smooth, about 5 minutes.

Shape the dough into ball, flatten it into a disk, and cover with plastic wrap. Chill for at least 1 hour.

Preheat the oven to 350° F (170° C). Butter a baking sheet and dust it with flour.

On a lightly floured work surface, roll out the dough slightly less than ¼ inch (5 mm) thick. Drape it over the rolling pin and transfer to the prepared baking sheet (7).

Cut out cardboard shapes (8) and use them to help you cut out the slightly staggered triangles as shown (9). Space them about 2 inches (5 cm) apart. Brush with milk.

Bake for 15 to 20 minutes, until firm and lightly browned.

Makes 1 gingerbread house
Level: Intermediate
Prep: 45 min.
Chill: at least 1 hr.
Bake: 15 to 20 min.
Plan ahead: 1 week

Special equipment
Cardboard sheets

Basic Dough

¾ cup (9 oz., 250 g) pine honey or other strong dark honey
1⅔ cups (7 oz., 200 g) all-purpose flour
⅓ cup (2 oz., 50 g) whole wheat flour
1 tbsp. ground cinnamon

Final Dough

1 egg yolk
1 tsp. baking powder (see *Note*)
1 pinch ground cinnamon
½ tsp. ground allspice
2 tbsp. milk

Decoration

7 oz. (200 g) bittersweet chocolate
½ cup (2 oz., 60 g) hazelnuts
½ cup (2 oz., 60 g) almonds
A few slices candied orange peel (page 452)
7 oz. (200 g) white almond paste
3 tbsp. (¾ oz., 20 g) unsweetened cocoa powder
Confectioners' sugar, for dusting

1 Have all the ingredients and utensils ready to go for the basic dough.

2 Mix the warm honey into the dry ingredients.

3 The basic dough should look like this.

4 Pour the baking powder on the work surface around the egg yolk.

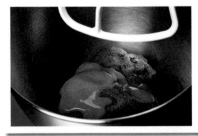

5 Combine the egg yolk with the baking powder and mix it into the basic dough.

6 Knead the dough until smooth.

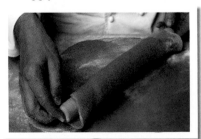

7 Drape the dough around the rolling pin and transfer it to the prepared baking sheet.

8 Cut out the shapes for the house.

9 Leave 2 inches (5 cm) between the shapes.

continued

Holiday Cakes, Cookies, and Other Treats   503

Transfer the triangles to a rack and let cool completely. Trim the edges of each piece neatly on a cutting board (10).

Decoration
Finely chop the chocolate. Place it in a medium bowl set over a saucepan filled with 1 inch (2.5 cm) of barely simmering water and let melt. Remove the bowl from the heat. Stir with a flexible spatula until smooth.
Let it cool, but if at any stage it sets too much to work with, reheat it slightly.

Paint the inside of the walls with chocolate (11). Stick the walls to one another to assemble the house (12, 13, and 14).

Cut out the doorway with a knife (15).

Decorate the roof with hazelnuts and almonds, using melted chocolate as glue. Decorate the doorway with slices of candied orange peel (16).

Knead the almond paste with enough of the cocoa powder to make a dark brown color. If it is too dry, add a drop of water.
Cut it into pieces and roll out thin logs (17) to the same length as the sides of the walls. Use melted chocolate to stick them to the edges of the walls (18).

Let the gingerbread house set, about 10 minutes.

Sift confectioners' sugar over the house to imitate snow (19).

Note: In Alsace, baker's ammonia and potash are the traditional leaveners in authentic gingerbread. If you would like to prepare the old-fashioned recipe, substitute ½ tsp. baker's ammonia and ½ tsp. potash for the 1 tsp. baking powder used here.

10 Trim the edges of the cooled pieces.

11 Paint the inside of the house with melted, cooled chocolate.

12 Paint the edges of the walls.

13 Assemble the four walls.

14 This is what the house looks like when the four walls are stuck together.

15 Cut out the doorway.

16 Decorate the roof with almonds and hazelnuts, and place orange peel around the doorway.

17 Shape chocolate almond paste into long, narrow logs.

18 Paint the edges of the walls with melted chocolate and stick on the almond paste shapes.

19 Let set for about 10 minutes and dust with confectioners' sugar.

Stollen

Buttery Dried-Fruit-and-Nut Loaf

Starter and Dough

Measure and prep your ingredients and arrange them on the counter (1).

Crumble the yeast into a large bowl. Pour in the milk and whisk to dissolve the yeast. Stir in 1⅔ cups (7 oz., 200 g) of the flour with a wooden spoon (2) until smooth (3).

Cover with a kitchen towel and let rise at room temperature until doubled in volume, about 1 hour (4 and 6).

Meanwhile, measure and prep the remaining dough ingredients and arrange them on the counter (5).

Finely grate the lemon zest.

Split the vanilla bean lengthwise in half and scrape out the seeds.

Dice the almond paste.

Add the remaining 1⅔ cups (7 oz., 200 g) flour, the lemon zest, vanilla seeds, almond paste, sugar, butter, cinnamon, salt and rum to the starter (7). Or combine the ingredients in the bowl of a stand mixer fitted with the hook attachment.

Knead the dough until the dough pulls away from the sides of the bowl, 4 to 5 minutes with the stand mixer, or longer by hand (8).

Shape the dough into a rounded loaf (9).

Makes 3 loaves
Level: Easy
Prep: 40 min.
Rise: 2 hr. 20 min.
Bake: 40 min.

1¼ cakes (.75 oz., 25 g) fresh yeast
⅔ cup (150 ml) lukewarm milk
3⅓ cups (14 oz., 400 g) all-purpose
  flour
1 lemon
1 vanilla bean
2 oz. (50 g) almond paste
2 tbsp. (1 oz., 25 g) sugar
1 stick plus 3 tbsp. (6 oz., 170 g)
  butter, diced and softened
2 pinches ground cinnamon
1 tsp. salt
1 tbsp. (20 ml) dark rum

½ cup (3 oz., 80 g) almonds
2 oz. (50 g) candied lemon peel
  (page 452)
1½ oz. (35 g) candied orange
  peel (page 452)
1⅓ cups (7 oz., 200 g) golden
  raisins
1⅓ cups (7 oz., 200 g) dried
  currants
3 tbsp. (50 g) butter
¼ cup (2 oz., 50 g) sugar
1 tsp. ground cinnamon

1 Have all your ingredients and utensils for the starter ready to go: yeast, milk, and flour.

2 Crumble the yeast into a bowl and add the milk and flour.

3 Mix until smooth.

4 Cover with a kitchen towel and let rise for 1 hour.

5 Have the ingredients and utensils for the dough ready to go.

6 The starter should double in volume.

7 Add the grated lemon zest, vanilla seeds, diced almond paste, flour, sugar, softened butter, cinnamon, salt, and rum.

8 Knead the ingredients, either by hand or in a stand mixer fitted with the dough hook.

9 Shape the dough into a rounded loaf shape.

continued

Cut off one-fifth of the dough, weighing 5 to 6 oz. (160 g) (10). Cover it with plastic wrap and chill.

Garnish and Finish

Coarsely chop the almonds and the candied citrus peel.

Mix the chopped almonds, citrus peel, raisins, and currants (11) into the remaining dough until they are evenly distributed (12).

Let the dough rise at room temperature for 30 minutes (13).

Punch it down and let rise again for 30 minutes.

On a lightly floured work surface (14), roll the chilled dough into a rectangle about ⅛ inch (4 mm) thick.

Divide the dough with the fruit and nuts into thirds, each 7 oz. (400 g) (15).

Shape them into 8-inch (20 cm) loaves.

Brush the rolled-out dough with water (16).

Cut it into rectangles large enough to wrap each of the 3 loaves. Roll up each loaf in a dough rectangle, tucking under the ends (17).

Preheat the oven to 350° F (180° C) Line a baking sheet with parchment paper or butter it and dust it with flour.

Slit the tops of the loaves with a knife, leaving about ¾ inch (2 cm) at each end (18).

Let rise until the dough springs back when touched, about 20 minutes.

Bake for about 40 minutes, until lightly browned (19).

Melt the butter in a small saucepan.

Mix the sugar and cinnamon in a small bowl.

Brush the loaves of stollen with the melted butter while they are still warm and sprinkle them generously with cinnamon sugar (20).

Transfer them to a rack and let cool before serving.

Note: Just before enclosing the loaves in the plain dough, you can insert a square of almond paste in the center.

10 Cut off one-fifth of the dough, 5 to 6 oz. (160 g).

11 Place the remaining dough in a bowl with the chopped almonds, candied citrus peel, raisins, and dried currants.

12 Knead in the ingredients.

13 This shows the risen dough.

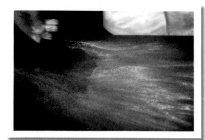

14 Dust the work surface with flour.

15 Roll out the chilled dough very thinly. Cut the dough with the fruit and nuts into thirds.

16 Shape each third into a 8-inch (20 cm) loaf. Brush the rolled-out dough with water.

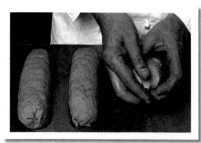

17 Wrap the loaves in the plain dough, tucking under the ends.

18 Slit the top of each stollen.

19 This shows the stollen straight out of the oven.

20 Brush them with melted butter and sprinkle with cinnamon sugar.

Parfait Glacé au Miel
Frozen Honey Parfait with Caramelized Pears

Measure and prep your ingredients and arrange them on the counter (1).

Frozen Honey Parfait
Pour the cream into a large bowl and chill.

Combine the egg yolks and honey in a medium bowl (2). Whisk (3) until the mixture is foamy and pale (4).

Whip the chilled cream until it holds a firm peak.

Gently fold it into the egg yolk–honey mixture (5) with a flexible spatula until smooth.

Fold in the kirsch (6).

Serves 4
Level: Easy
Prep: 40 min.
Freeze: 4 hr.

Special equipment
A 9 by 5-inch (24 by 13 cm)
loaf pan

Frozen Honey Parfait

1 cup (250 g) heavy cream
4 egg yolks
⅓ cup (4 oz., 120 g) lavender honey
1 tsp. kirsch

Caramelized Pears

2 firm, ripe pears
1 lemon, halved
1 tbsp. plus 2 tsp. (20 g) light brown
   sugar
2 tsp. (10 g) butter, diced

Finish

1 tbsp. mild honey, such as
   lavender
3 tangerines, peeled and
   separated into segments
Orange marmalade, for serving

1 Have all your ingredients and utensils ready to go.

2 Combine the egg yolks and honey in a medium bowl.

3 Whisk well.

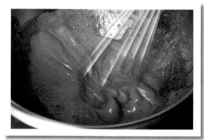

4 Whisk until the mixture is foamy and pale.

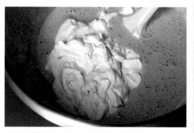

5 Gently fold the whipped cream in to the egg yolk–honey mixture.

6 When the mixture is smooth, fold in the kirsch.

continued

Line the loaf pan with parchment paper.

Pour the parfait mixture into the pan (7) and freeze until firm, at least 4 hours.

Caramelized Pears

Peel the pears with a vegetable peeler and squeeze some of the lemon juice on them to discourage browning (8).

Cut each pear lengthwise into eighths and remove the cores (9).

Place the pears in a medium skillet with the brown sugar and butter (10).

Cook over medium heat, stirring, until the pears are caramelized on all sides, about 5 minutes (11).

Finish

Invert the parfait onto a serving platter.

Drizzle honey over the top. Pass the caramelized pears, tangerine segments, and orange marmalade separately.

Note: The frozen parfait can be frozen overnight.

7 Pour the parfait mixture into the lined loaf pan.

8 Squeeze some of the lemon juice on the pears to keep them from browning.

9 Cut the pears lengthwise into eighths and remove the cores.

10 Place the pears, brown sugar, and butter in a medium skillet.

11 Cook over medium heat, stirring, until caramelized.

Tarte aux Poires
Pear Tart with Dried Fruits and Almonds

Tart Shell

On a lightly floured work surface, roll out the dough slightly less than ⅛ inch (2 mm) thick (1).

Prick it with a fork (2).

Line a baking sheet with parchment paper. Butter the pastry ring and place it on the prepared baking sheet.

Drape the dough over the rolling pin (3) and transfer it to the pastry ring (4).

Fit the dough into the pastry ring (5 and 6).

Trim the overhang so it is flush with the rim of the pan (7) and remove the excess dough (8).

Serves 6 to 8
Level: Intermediate
Prep: 30 min.
Bake: 30 min.

Special equipment
A 9-inch (24 cm) pastry ring or
a tart pan with
a removable bottom

Tart Shell

8 oz. (250 g) puff pastry dough
(see Chocolate Puff Pastry, page 78,
omitting the cocoa powder)

Almond Cream

1 tbsp. (20 g) butter
2 eggs
¼ cup (1 oz., 20 g) ground almonds
1 tsp. all-purpose flour
¼ cup plus 2 tbsp. (3 oz., 80 g) sugar
¼ cup plus 2 tbsp. (100 g) heavy
  cream
1 tbsp. dark rum

Fruit Filling

¼ cup (1 oz., 20 g) ground
  almonds
1½ tbsp. (1 oz., 20 g) light brown
  sugar
4 firm, ripe pears
1 lemon, halved
2 oranges
4 dried figs
5 pitted prunes
½ oz. (15 g) candied orange peel
  (page 452)
½ oz. (15 g) candied lemon peel
  (page 452)

1 Roll out the dough into a disk slightly less than ⅛ inch (2 mm).

2 Prick it with a fork.

3 Drape it on the rolling pin.

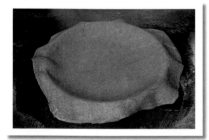

4 Transfer it to the buttered pastry ring.

5 Fit it into the ring.

6 Press the dough against the side of the ring.

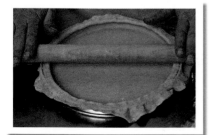

7 Roll the rolling pin over to remove the excess dough.

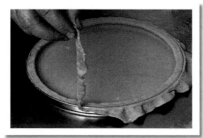

8 Trim the overhang so it is flush with the rim of the ring.

continued

Lightly press the edge of the dough up the side of the ring with your fingertips to make a raised border (9) and pinch to decorate (10).

Chill the tart shell for at least 10 minutes.

Position a rack in the lower third of the oven. Preheat the oven to 400° F (200° C).

Almond Cream

Melt the butter in a small saucepan and let cool to lukewarm.

Break the eggs into a medium bowl. Add the ground almonds, flour, lukewarm butter, sugar, cream, and rum. Whisk just until smooth.

Fruit Filling

Spread the ground almonds and brown sugar in the tart shell (11).

Peel the pears and squeeze some of the lemon juice on them to discourage browning.

Quarter the pears lengthwise, core them, and squeeze with more lemon juice.

Peel the oranges using a sharp knife and remove all the white pith. Cut between the membranes to release the segments. Drain on paper towels.

Cut the dried fruit into large pieces.

Arrange the pear quarters around the tart shell like a pinwheel. Fit the orange segments, candied orange and lemon peel, and pieces of dried fruit between the pear slices (12).

Pour in the almond cream, stopping ⅓ inch (8 mm) below the rim of the tart (13).

Bake for about 30 minutes, until the crust is golden and the pears are tender.

Note: Readymade all-butter puff pastry dough can replace the homemade.

9 Lightly press the edge of the dough up the side of the ring to make a raised border.

10 Pinch the edge of the dough evenly to make a decorative border.

11 Spread the brown sugar and ground almonds in the tart shell.

12 Arrange the pear quarters, orange segments, candied peel, and dried fruit.

13 Pour the almond cream into the tart.

Mont Blanc Griotte
Baked Meringue with Chestnut Cream and Cherries

Measure and prep your ingredients and arrange them on the counter (1).

Cherry Compote

Soak the gelatin sheets in cold water until softened, 5 to 10 minutes.

Split the vanilla bean lengthwise in half and scrape out the seeds.

Place the cherries in a medium saucepan, add the sugar and vanilla bean and seeds, and cook over medium heat until the juices have thickened, about 10 minutes.

Squeeze the gelatin dry and add to the hot cherries. Stir until dissolved.

Remove the vanilla bean, scrape the cherry compote into a bowl, and chill until set, about 2 hours.

Chestnut Cream

Beat the chestnut puree with the chestnut cream in a medium bowl until smooth. Stir in the cognac.

Meringue and Chantilly Cream

Pour the cream into a large bowl and chill.

Trim the meringues so they can be fit together into one long loaf (2).

Spread some of the chestnut cream on the flat end of each meringue to use as glue and stick together (3).

Spoon the cherry compote in a long strip on top of the meringue, being careful that it does not trickle down the sides (4).

Serves 6	Cherry Compote	Meringue and Chantilly Cream
Level: Intermediate	2 gelatin sheets (4 g)	1¼ cups (300 ml) heavy cream
Prep: 30 min.	1 vanilla bean	2 large baked meringues (see
Bake: 10 min.	7 oz. (200 g) pitted frozen cherries	Meringues Chantilly, page 98)
Chill: 2 hr.	¼ cup (2 oz., 50 g) sugar	¼ cup (2 oz., 50 g) sugar
Freeze: at least 30 min.		

Chestnut Cream

7 oz. (200 g) chestnut puree (see *Notes*)

7 oz. (200 g) chestnut cream or spread (see *Notes*)

1 tbsp. cognac

Chocolate Decoration

3½ oz. (100 g) bittersweet chocolate

⅓ cup (2 oz., 50 g) confectioners' sugar

1 Have all your ingredients and utensils ready to go before cooking.

2 Trim the meringues so they can be shaped into one long loaf.

3 Spread some of the chestnut cream on the flat end of each meringue to use as glue and stick together.

4 Carefully spoon the cherry compote in a strip on top of the meringue.

continued

Whip the chilled cream with the sugar until it holds a firm peak.

Spread this Chantilly cream over the meringue with a thin spatula, starting by covering the cherries (5).

Spread it all over the meringue and smooth to make a rounded shape.

Spoon the chestnut cream into a pastry bag fitted with a ⅛-inch (3 to 4 mm) plain tip. Or use a resealable sturdy plastic bag and snip off a corner.

Pipe the chestnut cream in looping spaghetti-like strands all over the top and sides of the meringue until it is completely covered and looks like an upside-down nest (6 and 7).

Decoration

Finely chop the chocolate. Place it in a small bowl set over a saucepan filled with 1 inch (2.5 cm) of barely simmering water and let melt. Remove the bowl from the heat. Stir until smooth.

Spoon it into a large resealable sturdy plastic bag (8). Lay it on a work surface and smooth the chocolate into a thin sheet with a metal spatula (9). Transfer to a shallow baking pan and freeze flat until firm, at least 30 minutes.

Sift the sides of the dessert with confectioners' sugar (10).

Cut open the plastic bag on one side and peel it to remove the sheet of chocolate. Break it into large pieces and arrange them on the Mont Blanc (11).

Notes: You can prepare this recipe with store-bought cherry preserves; just make sure it has whole fruit and is not too soft.

Baked meringues from a bakery can replace homemade.

Purée de marrons contains pureed chestnuts and water.

Crème de marrons, also known as chestnut spread, is made of chestnuts, sugar, and vanilla, and may also contain glucose and glacéed chestnuts.

If you like, reserve a few cherries from the compote before adding the gelatin and use to decorate the Mont Blanc.

5 Cover the cherry compote with whipped cream.

6 Pipe the chestnut cream all over the top and sides of the meringue.

7 Move the pastry bag around randomly to create spaghetti-like strands.

8 Spoon the melted chocolate into a sturdy plastic bag.

9 Lay the bag on a flat surface and smooth the chocolate with a spatula.

10 Sift the dessert with confectioners' sugar.

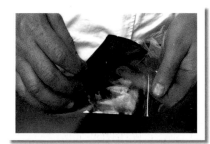

11 Remove the sheet of chocolate from the plastic bag and break it into decorative shards.

Bûche Mont d'Or
Passion Fruit–Fromage Blanc Yule Log

Preheat the oven to 350° F (180° C). Line a baking sheet with parchment paper.

Lemon Sponge Cake
Whip the egg whites until they hold a soft peak.
Finely grate in the lemon zest (1).
Add the sugar and whip until the egg whites are firm and glossy (2).
Add the egg yolks and whip until smooth, about 5 seconds.
Gradually sift the flour into the mixture (3) and gently fold in (4) with a flexible spatula.

Spread the batter on the prepared baking sheet (5) and smooth with a thin spatula (6).
Bake for 10 to 12 minutes, until lightly browned. Rotate the sheet halfway through baking.
Cover with a damp kitchen towel and let cool on the baking sheet so the cake remains soft and is easy to roll.

Fromage Blanc Mousse
Pour the cream into a large bowl and chill.
Soak the gelatin sheets in cold water until softened, 5 to 10 minutes.
Lightly whisk the fromage blanc and return it to the refrigerator.
Whisk the egg yolks with the sugar in a medium bowl (7) until pale and thick (8).

Serves 8 to 10
Level: Intermediate
Prep: 50 min.
Bake: 10 min.
Chill: about 1 hr. 30 min.

Lemon Sponge Cake

4 eggs, separated
1 lemon
½ cup (3½ oz., 100 g) sugar
¾ cup plus 2 tbsp. (3 oz., 100 g)
   all-purpose flour

Fromage Blanc Mousse

1¼ cups (300 ml) heavy cream
4 gelatin sheets (8 g)
1 cup (8 oz., 250 g) fromage blanc
   (see *Notes*) or mascarpone
2 egg yolks
⅓ cup (2½ oz., 75 g) sugar
1 tbsp. plus 1 tsp. passion fruit juice

Assemble

⅔ cup (150 ml) passion fruit juice
5 oz. (150 g) apricot preserves

Garnish

7 oz. (200 g) white chocolate

1 Whip the egg whites until they hold a soft peak.

2 Grate in the lemon zest, add the sugar, and whip until the whites are firm and glossy.

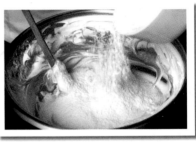

3 Briefly whip in the egg yolks, then gently fold in the sifted flour.

4 This shows the final texture of the batter.

5 Spread the batter on a lined baking sheet.

6 Smooth with a thin spatula, filling the corners of the sheet.

7 Whisk the egg yolks with the sugar in a medium bowl.

8 Continue until the mixture is light and creamy.

continued

Gently warm the passion fruit juice in a small saucepan over low heat.

Squeeze the gelatin dry and stir it into the warm juice (9) until completely dissolved.

Scrape into a large bowl.

Whip the chilled cream until it holds a firm peak.

Whisk the egg yolk–sugar mixture into the warm passion fruit juice (10).

Beat one-third of the whipped cream into the passion fruit mixture to lighten it.

Gently fold in the remaining whipped cream with a wooden spoon or flexible spatula, then the fromage blanc (11).

Assemble

Remove the kitchen towel from the sponge cake. Invert it on a sheet of parchment paper; carefully peel off the parchment paper from the cake.

Turn it onto another sheet so it is right side up, with a long side facing you.

Remove the parchment paper on top. Brush the cake with the passion fruit juice (12).

Spread a thick strip of the fromage blanc mousse across the upper third of the cake, leaving about 3 inches (7.5 cm) at the top (13).

Fold the top of the cake over the mousse and spoon a strip of apricot preserves next to the mousse (14).

Fold the top of the parchment paper over the cake, snugly tuck the paper under the cake with a sheet of cardboard or a spatula (15), and tightly roll up.

Wrap it in another sheet of parchment paper and chill for 15 minutes.

Chill the remaining mousse.

Carefully remove the parchment paper wrappers.

Spread the remaining mousse on the top and sides of the rolled cake. Smooth the mousse with a strip of parchment paper or a thin spatula (16).

Garnish

Shave the white chocolate with a serrated knife or vegetable peeler over the top of the cake (17).

Transfer to a serving plate and chill until firm, about 1 hour.

Notes: This rolled cake is a twist on the traditional French bûche de Noël, *a yule log.*

Fromage blanc is a tangy fresh cheese often served with fruit, a coulis (fruit sauce), or sugar for dessert.

Please note that the finished recipe contains raw egg.

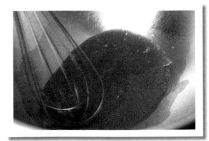

9 Whisk the softened gelatin into the warm passion fruit juice.

10 Whisk the egg yolk–sugar mixture into the juice.

11 Fold in the whipped cream and lightly whisked fromage blanc.

12 Brush the cooled sponge cake with passion fruit juice.

13 Spread a thick strip of the mousse across on the upper third of the cake. Begin rolling the sponge.

14 Spoon a strip of apricot preserves next to the mousse.

15 Fold the top of the parchment paper over the cake, snugly tuck the paper under the cake with a sheet of cardboard, and tightly roll up.

16 Remove the parchment paper and spread the remaining mousse over the cake. Smooth it with a strip of parchment paper.

17 Shave white chocolate over the top.

Christmas Pudding de Brian
Brian's Christmas Pudding

Pudding

Grind the bread in a food processor to make breadcrumbs.

Measure and prep the other ingredients and arrange them on the counter (1).

Finely dice the fat.

In a large bowl, combine the breadcrumbs, fat, sugar, currants, raisins, candied cherries, candied orange peel, spices, salt, and flour (2).

Beat with a wooden spoon until the ingredients are evenly distributed (3).

Beat in the eggs and whisky (4).

Line an 8-cup (2 liter) pudding mold or other heatproof bowl with plastic wrap, leaving a 2-inch (5 cm) overhang. Scrape in the pudding mixture (5).

Serves 8 to 10
Level: Easy
Prep: 20 min.
Cook: 10 hr.
Chill: up to 1 week
Reheat: 2 hr.

Pudding

8 slices (7 oz., 200 g) firm white bread, crusts removed
6 oz. (175 g) leaf fat or vegetable shortening
¾ cup plus 2 tbsp. (6 oz., 175 g) sugar
1½ cups (8 oz., 225 g) dried currants
⅔ cup (3½ oz., 100 g) golden raisins
8 oz. (225 g) candied cherries
4 oz. (110 g) candied orange peel (see page 452), finely diced
1 tsp. ground allspice
1 tsp. ground cinnamon
1 pinch freshly grated nutmeg
1 pinch salt
2 tbsp. all-purpose flour
3 eggs
¼ cup (60 ml) whisky

Whisky Butter

5 tbsp. (2½ oz., 75 g) butter, softened
Generous ½ cup (2¾ oz., 75 g) confectioners' sugar
¼ cup (60 ml) whisky

Finish

¼ cup (60 ml) whisky

1 Make the breadcrumbs and have all the other ingredients and utensils ready to go.

2 Combine the breadcrumbs, fat, sugar, currants, raisins, candied cherries, candied orange peel, spices, salt, and flour.

3 Beat until all the ingredients are evenly distributed.

4 Beat in the eggs and whisky.

5 Scrape the mixture into a lined bowl.

continued

Pack down the pudding mixture with the back of a spoon.

Press the plastic overhang onto the pudding (6) and wrap the mold completely in a kitchen towel (7).

Cover the pudding mold with a lid and place it on a rack in a large pot. Add enough water to the pot to come halfway up the sides of the mold. Cover the pot and cook the pudding over medium-low heat until a cake tester inserted into the center comes out clean, about 10 hours. Add more boiling water to the pot as necessary. Do not let the water in the pot come to a rolling boil; it should not bubble over into the pudding.

Carefully transfer the mold to a rack, remove the lid, and let cool. Chill for up to 1 week.

Whisky Butter

Whisk the butter in a small bowl until pale. Whisk in the confectioners' sugar. Gradually add the whisky (8 and 9). Or make the whisky butter in a food processor.

Finish

Cover the mold with a lid and place it on a rack in a large pot. Add enough water to the pot to come halfway up the sides of the mold. Cover the pot and cook the pudding over medium-low heat until heated through, about 2 hours. Or reheat the pudding in the microwave oven for 4 minutes at medium power.

Transfer the mold to a rack and let stand for 5 minutes. Remove the lid and towel, invert the pudding onto a serving platter, and remove the plastic.

Just before serving, heat the whisky in a small saucepan. Tilt the pan and carefully ignite the whisky with a match or lighter.

Pour the flaming whisky over the pudding (10).

Cut into slices and serve warm with the whisky butter.

6 Pack down the mixture with the back of a spoon. Cover with plastic wrap.

7 Enclose it in a kitchen towel.

8 Whisk the softened butter with the confectioners' sugar and add the whisky.

9 This is the texture of the whisky butter.

10 Pour the flaming whisky over the pudding.

Making Macarons

There are two schools when it comes to macarons, one based on French meringue, which beats uncooked sugar into egg whites, and another based on Italian meringue, which whips cooked sugar into the egg whites. In this book, I use mainly Italian meringue, but demonstrate both methods. Lesson 138 (page 538) explains how to use Italian Meringue, and Lesson 139 (page 544), French Meringue.

Whichever meringue is prepared is then folded into a paste of ground almonds, confectioners' sugar, and egg whites, then baked to make cookies.

Making Parisian Macarons

A Parisian macaron is one with a filling; basically, it's a kind of sandwich cookie. The recipes for filled macarons in this chapter all refer back to a string of steps in one of the two basic macaron recipes. These steps may vary according to whether an additional ingredient is incorporated, so read carefully!

The almond meringue in Parisian macarons is often tinted with food coloring to suggest the flavor of the filling. For instance, lemon macarons are tinted yellow. Then the macarons are baked and garnished with an array of creams, ganaches, and jams.

Coloring Macarons

Below are the main color mixes for tinting macarons.

Keep in mind that macarons tend to lighten in color as they bake. The amount of coloring you need depends on the concentration of the products you buy.

Macaron Flavor	Coloring
Strawberry/raspberry/rose/other red berries	Red (or pink) with a hint of cocoa powder to darken if necessary
Lemon	Yellow
Coffee/caramel/praline	Coffee extract with a hint of yellow color to lighten if necessary
Pistachio/lime/mint/olive oil	Green with a little yellow or blue to darken (for olive)
Mango/apricot/orange/passion fruit/orange blossom	Red and yellow
Violet/redcurrant/fig	Red with very little blue
Bittersweet or milk chocolate	Cocoa powder and a little red to reinforce the color
Licorice	Black

Baking Macarons

It is best to use convection heat, if possible, for faster and more even baking. Rotate the baking sheet halfway through to make sure the macarons are evenly colored.

Times are given for baking 1 sheet at a time in the center of the oven. If you prefer, bake 2 sheets at once, positioning racks in the upper and lower thirds of the oven. If you are not using convection heat, switch the baking sheets between racks halfway through and increase times by a few minutes.

Macaron Diameter	Baking Temperature	Baking Time
Petit four, less than 1½ inches (4 cm)	325° F (160° C)	8 to 10 minutes
Standard size, 1½ to 2 inches (4 to 5 cm)	340° F (170° C)	10 to 12 minutes
Individual, 2¼ to 3 inches (6 to 8 cm)	340 to 350° F (170 to 180° C)	12 to 15 minutes
Cake, more than 7 inches (18 cm)	340 to 350° F (170 to 180° C)	15 to 17 minutes

These baking times are given as guidelines, as ovens vary. If you can only set your oven to 350° F, watch carefully, as your macarons will cook more quickly. To test a macaron for doneness, peel it off the parchment paper. It is perfect when it barely sticks to the paper, though there may be traces of macaron on the paper.

Let the macarons cool completely on the baking sheet before filling.

Storing

Individual macarons develop their aroma and texture best when stored overnight in an airtight container in the refrigerator. The chilling time allows the slightly dry cookies to absorb moisture from the filling and the flavors to blend.

After that, continue to store them in the refrigerator in an airtight container, but for no longer than two or three days.

Individual macarons freeze remarkably well, in an airtight container, of course. Thaw them overnight in the refrigerator. After that, they keep for one to two days.

Ingredients

Almonds

Ground, blanched almonds are used to make macarons. Store-bought ground almonds are ideal for making macarons. For the most delicate macarons, I process ground almonds with confectioners' sugar in a food processor to get a finer texture. You can also use almond flour (finely ground blanched almonds) and whisk it with confectioners' sugar.

Once the package is opened, ground almonds should be stored in an airtight container.

Egg Whites

It is best to use egg whites from eggs that you have just separated. The whites achieve maximum volume in a clean, grease-free, perfectly dry bowl.

Sugar

Granulated sugar
Granulated sugar is used to transform the egg whites into meringue. It is finer than coarse sugar and dissolves better.

Confectioners' sugar
Confectioners' sugar comprises half the weight of the basic almond paste that's folded with meringue to make macarons. Always sift confectioners' sugar to remove lumps.

Tant Pour Tant

The almond paste into which the whipped egg whites are typically folded is made of equal weights of ground almonds and confectioners' sugar. In French, this is known as *tant pour tant*, literally, "so much for so much"—as much of one ingredient as the other. The exceptions here are chocolate, pistachio, and coconut macarons.

Equipment

The equipment varies slightly depending on the recipe you choose. Here is a basic list.

Baking Sheets

You'll need at least 2 baking sheets, preferably sturdy ones so they bake evenly and don't warp.

Electric Mixers

You can whip egg whites well using either a hand-held beater or a stand mixer. Both will save you a great deal of effort. If you use a hand-held mixer, make continuous circles in the mixing bowl as you work to make sure that the meringue is smooth.

Food Processor

I use a food processor to process ground almonds and confectioners' sugar to a fine powder. You can also buy almond flour and whisk it with confectioners' sugar instead.

Immersion Blender

This tool is useful for mixing small quantities until smooth without incorporating air bubbles.

Kitchen Scale

For best results, weigh all your ingredients, even the egg whites. A digital scale is the most precise.

Pastry Bag

A pastry bag is extremely practical when making macarons, as it lets you pipe even, round shapes. You should have two plain tips: one with a diameter of ⅓ to ½ inch (8 to 10 mm) to pipe the macaron cookies, and a smaller tip to pipe the filling.

To transfer batter and fillings to a pastry bag, first insert the tip. Place the bag, tip down, in a tall narrow container and fold the edge around the rim for stability. Spoon in enough batter to fill it halfway so you can manipulate it easily, and refill as needed. Twist the top of the bag to concentrate the batter or filling in the bottom of the bag and remove air pockets.

Thermometers

Use a candy thermometer with a range of 175 to 400° F (80 to 200° C). Do not use a chocolate thermometer: the typical range is more limited (from about 50 to 250° F, or 10 to 120° C) and it would soon be damaged. You can also use an instant-read thermometer.

Macarons à la Meringue Italienne

Italian Meringue Macarons

Preheat the oven to 340° F (170° C).

Combine the ground almonds and confectioners' sugar in a food processor (1).
Grind to a fine powder, about 30 seconds (2 and 3).
Sift through a medium sieve into a medium bowl (4).

Combine the water and granulated sugar in a medium heavy saucepan (5) and stir over medium heat until the sugar dissolves (6).

Makes about 6½ dozen cookies
Level: Intermediate
Prep: 30 min.
Bake: 10 to 12 min. per
baking sheet

Special equipment
A candy thermometer
A stand mixer
A pastry bag fitted with
a ⅓ to ½-inch (8 mm to 1 cm)
plain tip

2⅓ cups (7 oz., 200 g) ground
almonds
1½ cups (7 oz., 200 g)
confectioners' sugar
3½ tbsp. (50 ml) water
¾ cup plus 2 tbsp. (6 oz., 175 g)
granulated sugar
5½ oz. (150 g) egg whites (about 5)

1 Pour the ground almonds and confectioners' sugar into a food processor.

2 Process for 30 seconds to mix.

3 The result should be a fine powder.

4 Sift it into a bowl.

5 Pour the water and granulated sugar into a medium heavy saucepan.

6 Cook over medium heat, stirring, until the sugar dissolves.

continued

Bring to a boil, washing down the sides of the pan with a moistened pastry brush (7).

Dip the thermometer in the syrup, making sure it does not touch the bottom (8).

Cook the sugar, watching carefully, until it registers 244 to 246° F (118 to 119°C).

Meanwhile, weigh half the egg whites and place in the bowl of the stand mixer fitted with the whisk attachment (9).

Just before the sugar is ready, whisk the egg whites at medium speed until they hold a soft peak (10).

Carefully pour the sugar syrup down the side of the bowl into the whites (11) and whip until the Italian meringue cools to room temperature, about 10 minutes.

Pour the remaining egg whites into the almond–confectioners' sugar mixture (12).

Beat with a wooden spoon (13). The paste should be fairly thick (14).

The meringue should be shiny, thick (15), and hold a peak that bends over slightly when the whisk is lifted.

Check the temperature: It should feel slightly warm to your fingertip (16).

Add one-third of the meringue to the almond paste (17).

7 Wash down any crystals on the sides of the pan with a moistened pastry brush.

8 Dip the thermometer into the syrup, without touching the bottom. Cook to 244° to 246° F (118° to 119° C).

9 Meanwhile, pour half the egg whites into the bowl of the mixer.

10 Whip the egg whites at medium speed until they hold a soft peak.

11 When the syrup is ready, carefully pour it down the side of the bowl into the egg whites. Whip until the meringue cools down.

12 Pour the remaining egg whites into the almond–confectioners' sugar mixture.

13 Stir it with a wooden spoon.

14 The almond paste should be fairly thick.

15 This is what the meringue should look like: shiny, smooth, and thick.

16 The meringue should feel slightly warm to the finger.

17 Beat one-third of the meringue into the almond paste.

continued

Beat it in to lighten the paste (18). Gently fold in half of the remaining meringue with a flexible spatula (19), making sure to incorporate any paste on the bottom of the bowl.

Fold in the remaining meringue until the mixture is smooth and pourable (20).

Line 2 baking sheets with parchment paper.

Using a 1½-inch (4 cm) cookie cutter or glass as a template, draw circles on the paper, spacing them 1 inch (2.5 cm) apart, to use as guides (21). This will help you pipe macarons of the same size.

Cover with a second sheet of parchment paper (22) and attach with a paper clip.

Spoon the macaron batter into the pastry bag (23) and pipe 1½-inch (4 cm) flat mounds on the prepared baking sheets (24).

Tap the bottom of the baking sheets with the palm of your hand (25) to smooth the surface of the macarons (26).

Bake 1 sheet at a time for 10 to 12 minutes, or until just firm but pale. Rotate the sheet halfway through baking.

The macarons should have the characteristic "collar" all round the edge (27).

Let cool completely on the baking sheet before sandwiching pairs of them with filling.

18 The meringue lightens the texture of the almond paste.

19 Gently fold in the remaining meringue in 2 batches.

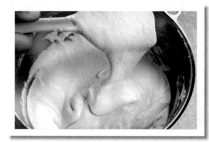

20 Continue until the batter is smooth and pourable.

21 Draw 1½-inch (4 cm) circles on a sheet of parchment paper.

22 Cover with another sheet of parchment paper.

23 Spoon the macaron batter into the pastry bag.

24 Pipe a flat mound within each circle.

25 Lightly tap the bottom of the baking sheet.

26 This smoothes the surface of the macarons.

27 The baked macarons should be pale and evenly colored, with a distinct "collar" around the base.

Macarons à la Meringue Française

French Meringue Macarons

Preheat the oven to 340° F (170° C).

Combine the ground almonds and confectioners' sugar in a food processor (1). Grind to a fine powder, about 30 seconds.

Sift through a medium sieve into a medium bowl.

Place the egg whites in the bowl of the stand mixer fitted with the whisk attachment and whip at medium speed until they hold a soft peak.

Add the granulated sugar (2) and whip until the French meringue is dense and very white, about 10 minutes (3).

Pour the almond–confectioners' sugar mixture into the meringue (4).

Gently fold in with a flexible spatula (5).

Stir quickly to deflate the meringue slightly. This helps break down the structure of the whipped egg whites and prevents them from cracking when they bake. The batter should be pourable but thick (6).

Line 2 baking sheets with parchment paper.

Using a 1½-inch (4 cm) cookie cutter or glass as a template, draw circles on the paper, spacing them 1 inch (2.5 cm) apart, to use as guides. This will help you pipe macarons of the same size.

Cover with a second sheet of parchment paper and attach with a paper clip.

Spoon the macaron batter into the pastry bag and pipe 1½-inch (4 cm) flat mounds on the prepared baking sheets (7).

Tap the bottom of the baking sheets with the palm of your hand to smooth the surface of the macarons.

Bake 1 sheet at a time for 10 to 12 minutes, or until just firm but pale. Rotate the sheet halfway through baking. The macarons should have the characteristic "collar" all round the edge.

Let cool completely on the baking sheet before sandwiching pairs of them with filling.

Note: If your macarons crack on the surface, remember to stir the meringue more to deflate it in step 6 on your next try.

Makes about 6½ dozen cookies
Level: Intermediate
Prep: 30 min.
Bake: 10 to 12 min. per
baking sheet

Special equipment
A stand mixer
A pastry bag fitted with a ⅓ to
½-inch (8 mm to 1 cm) plain tip

1½ cups (4½ oz, 125 g) ground
  almonds
1⅓ cups (8 oz., 225 g) confectioners'
  sugar
3½ oz. (100 g) egg whites (about 3½)
2 tbsp. (1 oz., 25 g) granulated sugar

1 Pour the ground almonds and confectioners' sugar into a food processor.

2 When the egg whites hold a soft peak, pour in the sugar and whip for 10 minutes.

3 The meringue should be dense and white.

4 Pour the almond–confectioners' sugar mixture into the meringue.

5 Fold in the dry ingredients.

6 Continue stirring to deflate the mixture slightly. It should be smooth and pourable.

7 Pipe flat mounds of batter on the prepared baking sheet.

Macarons à la Framboise
Raspberry Macarons

Raspberry Jam

Place the raspberries in a medium heavy saucepan with the jam sugar (1) and cook over medium heat (2) until softened.

Stir with a flexible spatula to crush them (3).

If you prefer smooth jam, remove the pan from the heat and process the raspberries and sugar with an immersion blender (4 and 5).

Return the pan to medium heat and strain in the lemon juice (6).

Bring to a boil and cook for 2 to 3 minutes (7). To test for doneness, spoon a little jam on a cold plate (8). It should set and thicken fairly quickly.

Let cool to lukewarm and scrape into a bowl. Chill until set.

Preheat the oven to 340° F (170° C). Line 2 baking sheets with parchment paper.

Macarons

Follow steps 1 to 16 of the Italian Meringue Macarons (page 538).

Gradually beat a few drops of the food coloring into the meringue (9). The quantity needed depends on its concentration.

Makes about 3 dozen
Level: Advanced
Prep: 50 min.
Bake: 10 to 12 min. per
baking sheet
Chill: at least 1 hr.

Special equipment
A pastry bag fitted with a ⅓ to
½-inch (8 mm to 1 cm) plain tip

Raspberry Jam

12 oz. (350 g) fresh or frozen
raspberries
1 cup (7 oz., 200 g) jam sugar
(see Note)
1 tbsp. (15 ml) lemon juice

Macarons

2⅓ cups (7 oz., 200 g) ground
almonds
1½ cups (7 oz., 200 g)
confectioners' sugar

3½ tbsp. (50 ml) water
1 cup (7 oz., 200 g) granulated
sugar
5½ oz. (150 g) egg whites (about 5)
Red food coloring
A few pinches unsweetened cocoa
powder (optional)

1 Pour the raspberries and jam sugar into a medium heavy saucepan.

2 Soften the raspberries over medium heat.

3 Crush the fruit with a flexible spatula.

4 Process with an immersion blender for a smooth jam.

5 The mixture should be as smooth as a puree.

6 Strain in the lemon juice.

7 Reduce over medium heat.

8 To check for doneness, pour a little on a cold plate; it should set quickly.

9 Add the food coloring to the meringue.

continued

For raspberry macarons the result should be bright pink (10). If it is too pale, add the cocoa powder.

Beat one-third of the meringue into the almond paste to lighten it (11).

Gently fold in the remaining meringue in 2 batches with a flexible spatula. (12).

Spoon the macaron batter into the pastry bag and pipe 1½-inch (4 cm) flat mounds on the prepared baking sheets.

Tap the bottom of the baking sheets with the palm of your hand to smooth the surface of the macarons.

Bake 1 sheet at a time for 10 to 12 minutes, or until just firm with a light gloss. Rotate the sheet halfway through baking.

Let cool completely on the baking sheet.

Make a small indentation in the flat side of a macaron with your thumb (13). Repeat with the remaining macarons.

Alternate rows of macarons, facing up and down (14).

Spoon the jam into the pastry bag and pipe mounds onto the indented sides of half the macarons (15).

Sandwich with a plain macaron and lightly press so the filling spreads to the edge (16).

Chill until set, at least 1 hour.

Note: Jam sugar contains pectin for setting jams and jellies. Alternatively, use granulated sugar and cook for about 15 minutes in step 7. Prepared raspberry jam can replace the filling.

10 The meringue with the food coloring should be bright pink.

11 Beat one-third of the meringue into the almond paste to lighten it.

12 Fold in the remaining meringue.

13 Turn over each cooled macaron and make a small indentation in the flat side.

14 Alternate rows of macarons, facing up and down.

15 Pipe raspberry jam onto the indented sides of half the macarons.

16 Lightly press to close so that the filling spreads to the edge.

Macarons au Citron Jaune et Basilic

Lemon-Basil Macarons

Lemon-Basil Filling

Soak the gelatin sheet in a medium bowl of cold water until softened, 5 to 10 minutes.

Place the butter in a medium bowl.

Combine the eggs (1) and sugar in a medium heavy saucepan (2) and whisk lightly (3).

Whisk in the lemon juice (4) and cook, stirring constantly, over medium heat (5).

Tear the basil leaves into the pan (6).

Cook the mixture, stirring constantly, just until it comes to a boil and thickens like pastry cream. Remove the pan from the heat.

Squeeze the gelatin dry, add to the lemon cream, and stir until dissolved (7).

Strain the lemon cream into the butter (8).

Process with an immersion blender until smooth and shiny, about 1 minute (9).

Makes about 3 dozen
Level: Advanced
Prep: 1 hr.
Bake: 10 to 12 min. per baking sheet
Chill: at least 3 hr.

Special equipment
A pastry bag fitted with a ⅓ to ½-inch (8 mm to 1 cm) plain tip

Lemon-Basil Filling

½ gelatin sheet (1 g)
1 ½ sticks (6 oz., 175 g) butter, diced
2 eggs
¾ cup (5 oz., 135 g) sugar
½ cup (130 ml) lemon juice (from about 2½ lemons)
10 medium basil leaves
¼ cup plus 2 tbsp. (1 oz., 30 g) ground almonds

Macarons

2⅓ cups (7 oz, 200 g) ground almonds
1½ cups (7 oz., 200 g) confectioners' sugar
3½ tbsp. (50 ml) water
1 cup (7 oz., 200 g) granulated sugar
5½ oz. (150 g) egg whites (about 5)
Yellow food coloring

1 Pour the eggs into a heavy saucepan.

2 Add the sugar.

3 Whisk the eggs with the sugar.

4 Whisk in the lemon juice.

5 Continue to whisk over medium heat.

6 Tear the basil leaves into the pan and cook just until the cream comes to a boil and thickens.

7 Whisk in the softened gelatin.

8 Strain the cream into the diced butter.

9 Process the cream with an immersion blender for 1 minute.

continued

Stir the ground almonds into the cream with a flexible spatula (10).
Press a piece of plastic wrap directly on the surface and chill completely, at least 2 hours.

Preheat the oven to 340° F (170° C). Line 2 baking sheets with parchment paper.

Macarons

Follow steps 1 to 16 of the Italian Meringue Macarons (page 538).
Gradually beat a few drops of the yellow food coloring into the meringue (11 and 12). The quantity needed depends on its concentration. For lemon macarons, the result should be bright yellow.

Beat one-third of the meringue into the almond paste to lighten it.
Gently fold in the remaining meringue in 2 batches with a flexible spatula (13).

Spoon the macaron batter into the pastry bag and pipe 1½-inch (4 cm) flat mounds on the prepared baking sheets (14).
Tap the bottom of the baking sheets with the palm of your hand to smooth the surface of the macarons.
Bake 1 sheet at a time for 10 to 12 minutes, or until just firm with a light gloss. Rotate the sheet halfway through baking.
Let cool completely on the baking sheet.

Make a small indentation in the flat side of a macaron with your thumb (15).
Repeat with the remaining macarons.
Alternate rows of macarons, facing up and down (16).
Spoon the filling into the piping bag and pipe mounds onto the indented sides of half the macarons (17).
Sandwich with a plain macaron (18) and lightly press so the filling spreads to the edge (19 and 20).
Chill to develop the flavors and texture, at least 1 hour.

Notes: This filling is best refrigerated overnight so it has time to firm up for easy piping.
You can also prepare the recipe without basil.

10 Stir in the ground almonds.

11 Add the yellow food coloring to the meringue.

12 This shows the desired color.

13 Fold the cooled meringue into the almond paste until smooth.

14 Pipe flattened mounds on the prepared baking sheets.

15 Make a small indentation in the flat side of each macaron with your thumb.

16 Alternate rows of macarons, facing up and down.

17 Pipe the filling onto the indented sides of half the macarons.

18 Top with a plain macaron.

19 Lightly press to close.

20 The filling should spread evenly to the edge.

Macarons au Chocolat
Chocolate Macarons

Chocolate Ganache

Combine the cream with the sugar in a medium heavy saucepan (1). Bring to a boil over low heat.

Finely chop the chocolate and place it in a bowl.

Pour half of the hot cream into the chopped chocolate (2). Let the chocolate melt for a few minutes.

Begin stirring with a flexible spatula at the center of the bowl (3) to incorporate the cream. Add the remaining cream and stir (4 and 5) until the ganache is smooth and shiny (6).

Stir in the butter (7) until smooth (8).

Press a piece of plastic wrap directly on the surface and let stand at room temperature.

Makes about 3 dozen
Level: Advanced
Prep: 50 min.
Bake: 10 to 12 min. per
baking sheet
Chill: at least 1 hr.

Special equipment
A pastry bag fitted with a ⅓ to
½-inch (8 mm to 1 cm) plain tip

Chocolate Ganache

¾ cup (200 g) heavy cream
1 tbsp. sugar
8 oz. (250 g) bittersweet chocolate
(at least 60% cocoa)
3 tbsp. (40 g) butter, diced

Macarons

2 cups plus 1 tbsp. (6½ oz.,
185 g) ground almonds
1½ cups (6½ oz., 185 g)
confectioners' sugar
¼ cup (1 oz, 30 g) unsweetened
cocoa powder
3½ tbsp. (50 ml) water
1 cup (7 oz., 200 g) granulated
sugar
5½ oz. (150 g) egg whites
(about 5)
Red food coloring

1 Bring the cream to a boil with the sugar.

2 Pour half of the hot cream into the chopped chocolate.

3 To incorporate the cream, begin stirring at the center and work outwards.

4 The texture should be shiny.

5 Pour in the remaining cream.

6 Incorporate the cream using the same stirring method, from the center outwards.

7 Add the diced butter.

8 Mix until smooth.

continued

Lesson 142

Preheat the oven to 340° F (170° C). Line 2 baking sheets with parchment paper.

Macarons
Combine the ground almonds, confectioners' sugar, and cocoa powder in a food processor (9).
Grind to a fine powder, about 30 seconds.
Sift through a medium sieve into a medium bowl.

Follow steps 5 to 11 of the Italian Meringue Macarons (page 538).
Gradually beat a few drops of the food coloring into the meringue (10). The quantity needed depends on its concentration. For chocolate macarons, the result should be light pink (11) — enough to heighten the color.

Stir the remaining egg whites into the almond-cocoa mixture with a wooden spoon (12) to make a fairly thick paste (13).
Beat one-third of the meringue into the almond paste to lighten it (14).
Gently fold in the remaining meringue in 2 batches with a flexible spatula (15).

Spoon the macaron batter into the pastry bag and pipe 1½-inch (4 cm) flat mounds on the prepared baking sheets (16).
Tap the bottom of the baking sheets with the palm of your hand to smooth the surface of the macarons.
Bake 1 sheet at a time for 10 to 12 minutes, or until just firm with a light gloss. Rotate the sheet halfway through baking.
Let cool completely on the baking sheet.

Make a small indentation in the flat side of a macaron with your thumb (17).
Repeat with the remaining macarons.
Alternate rows of macarons, facing up and down.
Spoon the ganache into the piping bag and pipe mounds onto the indented sides of half the macarons.
Sandwich with a plain macaron and lightly press (18) so the filling spreads to the edge (19).
Chill until set, at least 1 hour.

9 Grind the almonds, confectioners' sugar, and cocoa powder in a food processor to a fine powder.

10 Add a few drops of red food coloring to the meringue.

11 This shows the correct color.

12 Stir the egg whites into the dry ingredients.

13 This makes a chocolate-almond paste.

14 Fold the meringue into the chocolate–almond paste in batches.

15 This shows the chocolate macaron batter.

16 Pipe flat mounds on the prepared baking sheets.

17 Turn over the cooled macarons and make small indentations on the flat side.

18 Lightly press to close.

19 The filling should spread evenly to the edge.

Macarons au Café
Coffee Macarons

Coffee Filling

Whisk the butter in a medium bowl until creamy (1 and 2).

Sift the confectioners' sugar into the butter (3).

Whisk until pale and soft (4).

Whisk in the ground almonds (5) until the butter is light and airy (6).

Add the dissolved coffee to the butter mixture (7). Whisk again (8).

The butter should be smooth, and the coffee flavor should be strong (9).

Cover the bowl with plastic wrap and let stand at room temperature.

Makes about 3 dozen
Level: Advanced
Prep: 1 hr.
Bake: 10 to 12 min. per
baking sheet
Chill: at least 1 hr.

Special equipment
A pastry bag fitted with a ⅓ to ½-inch (8 mm to 1 cm) plain tip

2 sticks (9 oz., 250 g) butter, diced and softened
1¼ cups (6 oz., 160 g) confectioners' sugar
2 cups (6 oz., 170 g) ground almonds
⅓ cup (20 g) instant coffee dissolved in 1 tbsp. hot water

2⅓ cups (7 oz., 200 g) ground almonds
1½ cups (7 oz., 200 g) confectioners' sugar
3½ tbsp. (50 ml) water
1 cup (7 oz., 200 g) granulated sugar
5½ oz. (150 g) egg whites (about 5)
Liquid coffee extract

1 Whisk the butter until creamy.

2 It should be very soft and light.

3 Sift in the confectioners' sugar.

4 Whisk until pale.

5 Incorporate the ground almonds.

6 Whisk them in until fluffy.

7 Add the dissolved coffee to the butter.

8 Whisk to incorporate the coffee.

9 This shows the texture of the coffee cream.

continued

Preheat the oven to 340° F (170° C). Line 2 baking sheets with parchment paper.

Macarons

Follow steps 1 to 14 of the Italian Meringue Macarons (page 538).

Gradually beat a few drops of the coffee extract into the meringue (10) to color it (11). The quantity needed depends on its concentration. For coffee macarons, the result should be brown (12).

Beat one-third of the meringue into the almond paste to lighten it.
Gently fold in the remaining meringue in 2 batches with a flexible spatula (13).

Spoon the macaron batter into the pastry bag and pipe 1½-inch (4 cm) flat mounds on the prepared baking sheets (14).
Tap the bottom of the baking sheets with the palm of your hand to smooth the surface of the macarons.
Bake 1 sheet at a time for 10 to 12 minutes, or until just firm with a light gloss. Rotate the sheet halfway through baking.
Let cool completely on the baking sheet.

Make a small indentation in the flat side of a macaron with your thumb (15).
Repeat with the remaining macarons.
Alternate rows of macarons, facing up and down (16).

Whisk the coffee filling briefly. Spoon it into the pastry bag and pipe mounds onto the indented sides of half the macarons (17).
Sandwich with a plain macaron (18) and lightly press so the filling spreads to the edge (19).
Chill until set, at least 1 hour.

10 Color the meringue with coffee extract.

11 Whip until well colored.

12 This shows the color of the meringue.

13 Fold the meringue into the almond paste in several additions. The batter should be smooth and pourable.

14 Pipe slightly flattened mounds onto the prepared baking sheets.

15 Make a small indentation in the flat side of each macaron with your thumb.

16 Alternate rows of macarons, facing up and down.

17 Pipe the filling onto the indented sides of half the macarons.

18 Top with a plain macaron.

19 The filling should spread evenly to the edge.

Macarons à la Pistache
Pistachio Macarons

Pistachio Filling

Whisk the butter in a medium bowl until soft and creamy (1).

Sift the confectioners' sugar into the butter (2) and whisk until pale and fluffy (3).

Whisk in, one at a time, the ground almonds (4), pistachios (5), and pistachio paste (6).

Whisk well until the mixture is smooth and light (7).

Cover the bowl with plastic wrap and let stand at room temperature.

Makes about 3 dozen
Level: Advanced
Prep: 1 hr.
Bake: 10 to 12 min. per baking sheet
Chill: at least 1 hr.

Special equipment
A pastry bag fitted with a ⅓ to ½-inch (8 mm to 1 cm) plain tip

Pistachio Filling

1¾ sticks (7 oz., 200 g) butter, diced and softened
1 cup (4½ oz., 130 g) confectioners' sugar
¾ cup plus 2 tbsp. (3 oz., 80 g) ground almonds
⅓ cup (2 oz., 50 g) unsalted pistachios, finely chopped
1½ oz. (40 g) pistachio paste (see *Note*)

Macarons

1½ cups (4½ oz., 130 g) ground almonds
1½ cups (7 oz., 200 g) confectioners' sugar
½ cup (2½ oz., 65 g) unsalted pistachios
5½ oz. (150 g) egg whites (about 5)
3½ tbsp. (50 ml) water
1 cup (7 oz., 200 g) granulated sugar
Green food coloring
Yellow food coloring

1 Whip the butter until soft and smooth.

2 Sift in the confectioners' sugar.

3 Whisk briskly until pale.

4 Whisk in the ground almonds.

5 Whisk in the finely chopped pistachios.

6 Whisk in the pistachio paste.

7 Whisk until light and fluffy.

continued

Preheat the oven to 340° F (170° C). Line 2 baking sheets with parchment paper.

Macarons
Combine the ground almonds, confectioners' sugar, and pistachios in a food processor (8). Grind to a coarse powder, about 30 seconds. There should be some small pieces of pistachio.
Transfer to a medium bowl (9).
Stir in half the egg whites (10) to make almond-pistachio paste (11).

Follow steps 5 to 11 of the Italian Meringue Macarons (page 538).
Gradually beat a few drops of the green food coloring into the meringue, then the yellow food coloring (12), to tone down a too-bright green. The quantity needed depends on its concentration. For pistachio macarons, the result should be light green (13).

Beat one-third of the meringue into the almond paste to lighten it (14).
Gently fold in the remaining meringue in 2 batches with a flexible spatula (15).

Spoon the macaron batter into the pastry bag and pipe 1½-inch (4 cm) flat mounds on the prepared baking sheets (16).
Tap the bottom of the baking sheets with the palm of your hand to smooth the surface of the macarons.
Bake 1 sheet at a time for 10 to 12 minutes, or until just firm with a light gloss. Rotate the sheet halfway through baking.
Let cool completely on the baking sheet.

Make a small indentation in the flat side of a macaron with your thumb (17).
Repeat with the remaining macarons.
Alternate rows of macarons, facing up and down.
Lightly whip the pistachio filling. Spoon it into the pastry bag and pipe mounds onto the indented sides of half the macarons (18).
Sandwich with a plain macaron and lightly press so the filling spreads to the edge (19).
Chill until set, at least 1 hour.

Note: To make pistachio paste, place 7 oz. (200 g) unsalted pistachios in a food processor. Add ⅓ cup (80 ml) almond syrup and process until a paste forms, 4 to 5 minutes.
Alternatively, you can use readymade pistachio paste.

8 Process the ground almonds with the confectioners' sugar and pistachios until coarsely ground.

9 Transfer the ground ingredients to a medium bowl.

10 Add half of the egg whites.

11 Stir to make almond–pistachio paste.

12 Color the meringue with the green and yellow food colorings.

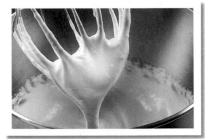

13 This is the color you are looking for.

14 Beat one-third of the meringue into the almond-pistachio paste.

15 Fold in the remaining meringue until the batter is smooth.

16 Pipe flat mounds on the prepared baking sheets.

17 Make a small indentation in the center of the flat side of each macaron with your thumb.

18 Pipe pistachio cream onto the indented sides of half the macarons.

19 Lightly press to close; the filling should spread evenly to the edge.

Macarons à la Noix de Coco
Coconut Macarons

Coconut Ganache

Finely chop the milk chocolate and place it in a medium bowl.

Split the vanilla bean lengthwise in half and scrape out the seeds.

Bring the cream and vanilla bean and seeds to a boil in a medium heavy saucepan over medium heat.

Pour one-third of the hot cream into the chopped chocolate (1).

Let the chocolate melt for 30 seconds (2).

Begin stirring with a flexible spatula at the center of the bowl (3) to incorporate the cream. Add another third of the cream (4) and stir (5).

Add the remaining cream (6) and stir until the ganache is smooth and shiny.

Pour in the coconut (7) and stir until incorporated (8).

Cover the bowl with plastic wrap and let stand at room temperature.

Makes about 3 dozen
Level: Advanced
Prep: 1 hr.
Bake: 10 to 12 min. per
baking sheet
Chill: at least 1 hr.

Special equipment
A pastry bag fitted with a ⅓ to
½-inch (8 mm to 1 cm) plain tip

Coconut Ganache

6½ oz. (180 g) milk chocolate
½ vanilla bean
1¼ cups (300 ml) heavy cream
1¾ cups (4½ oz., 130 g)
unsweetened shredded coconut

Macarons

3½ tbsp. (50 ml) water
1 cup (7 oz., 200 g) granulated
sugar
3 egg whites
1¾ cups plus 1 tbsp. (5½ oz.,
160 g) ground almonds
1¼ cups (5½ oz., 160 g)
confectioners' sugar
1 cup (3 oz., 80 g) unsweetened
shredded coconut
3 tbsp. (40 ml) grapeseed oil

1 Pour one-third of the hot vanilla cream into the chocolate.

2 Let the chocolate melt for 30 seconds.

3 Stir gently, starting from the center of the bowl.

4 Pour in the second third of the cream.

5 Stir gently, starting from the center.

6 Stir in the remaining cream until smooth.

7 Add the shredded coconut.

8 Stir in carefully.

continued

Preheat the oven to 340° F (170° C). Line 2 baking sheets with parchment paper.

Macarons

Follow steps 5 to 11 of the Italian Meringue Macarons (page 538), using the water, sugar, and 2 egg whites.

Combine the ground almonds, confectioners' sugar, and coconut in a medium bowl (9).

Stir in the remaining egg white and the oil (10) to make a fairly dry almond-coconut paste.

The Italian meringue used to make coconut macarons is a little lighter than that of the other recipes (11).

Beat one-third of the meringue into the almond-coconut paste to lighten it (12).

Gently fold in the remaining meringue in 2 batches with a flexible spatula (13).

Spoon the macaron batter into the pastry bag and pipe 1½-inch (4 cm) flat mounds on the prepared baking sheets (14).

Tap the bottom of the baking sheets with the palm of your hand to smooth the surface of the macarons.

Bake 1 sheet at a time for 10 to 12 minutes, or until just firm with a light gloss. Rotate the sheet halfway through baking.

Let cool completely on the baking sheet.

Make a small indentation in the flat side of a macaron with your thumb (15).

Repeat with the remaining macarons.

Alternate rows of macarons, facing up and down.

Lightly whip the coconut ganache. Spoon it into the pastry bag and pipe mounds onto the indented sides of half the macarons (16).

Sandwich with a plain macaron and lightly press (17) so the filling spreads to the edge (18).

Chill until set, at least 1 hour.

9 Combine the ground almonds, confectioners' sugar, and shredded coconut.

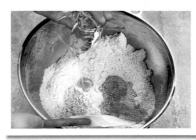

10 Add the remaining egg white and the oil to the dry ingredients.

11 The Italian meringue is lighter than that of the other recipes.

12 Beat one-third of the meringue into the almond-coconut paste.

13 Fold in the remaining meringue in 2 batches until smooth.

14 Pipe 1½-inch (4 cm) flat mounds on the prepared baking sheets.

15 Make a small indentation in the flat side of each macaron with your thumb.

16 Pipe the ganache onto the indented sides of half the macarons.

17 Lightly press to close.

18 The filling should spread evenly to the edge.

Macarons au Caramel Beurre Salé

Macarons with Salted Caramel

Salted Caramel Filling

Pour one-third of the sugar into a medium heavy saucepan (1). Melt it over medium heat, stirring with a spatula or wooden spoon. Pour in the second third of the sugar (2) and cook, stirring, until melted. Stir in the remaining sugar until completely melted (3).

Reduce the heat to low and cook, stirring, until the sugar changes from a light amber liquidy paste to a fluid, medium amber caramel (4). The best way to judge the color is to let the caramel run off the spoon.

Slowly pour in a little cream, stirring (5). Be careful not to burn yourself: the mixture can boil up quickly.

Gradually stir in the remaining cream. Check the temperature: the thermometer should register 226° F (108° C) (6).

Immediately remove from the heat and stir in the butter to stop the cooking (7 and 8).

Makes about 3 dozen
Level: Advanced
Prep: 1 hr.
Bake: 10 to 12 min. per
baking sheet
Chill: at least 1 hr.

Special equipment
A candy thermometer
A pastry bag fitted with a ⅓ to
½-inch (8 mm to 1 cm) plain tip

Salted Caramel Filling

1½ cups (10 oz., 280 g) sugar
½ cup (130 ml) heavy cream
1¾ sticks (7 oz., 200 g) salted
butter, diced and chilled

Macarons

2⅓ cups (7 oz., 200 g) ground
almonds
1½ cups (7 oz., 200 g)
confectioners' sugar
3½ tbsp. (50 ml) water
1 cup (7 oz., 200 g) granulated
sugar
5½ oz. (150 g) egg whites
(about 5)
Liquid coffee extract
Yellow food coloring

1 Cook one-third of the sugar in a medium heavy saucepan over medium heat until melted.

2 Add another third of the sugar to the melted sugar and cook, stirring, until melted.

3 Repeat with the remaining sugar, stirring carefully with a spatula.

4 Cook until the caramel reaches a medium amber color.

5 Over low heat, incorporate the cream in several additions.

6 The thermometer should register 226° F (108° C).

7 Remove from the heat and add the diced butter to stop the cooking.

8 The butter melts in the hot caramel.

continued

Process the caramel with an immersion blender (9) until perfectly smooth (10). Or use a spatula or wooden spoon, but it will take longer.

Pour the caramel into a bowl, cover with plastic wrap, and chill until thickened.

Preheat the oven to 340° F (170° C). Line 2 baking sheets with parchment paper.

Macarons

Follow steps 1 to 16 of the Italian Meringue Macarons (page 538).

Gradually beat a few drops of coffee extract into the meringue (11), then a little yellow food coloring (12). The quantity needed depends on its concentration. The addition of yellow changes the coffee color to caramel and makes the mixture paler (13).

Beat one-third of the meringue into the almond paste to lighten it.

Gently fold in the remaining meringue in 2 batches with a flexible spatula (14).

Spoon the macaron batter into the pastry bag and pipe 1½-inch (4 cm) flat mounds on the prepared baking sheets (15).

Tap the bottom of the baking sheets with the palm of your hand to smooth the surface of the macarons.

Bake 1 sheet at a time for 10 to 12 minutes, or until just firm with a light gloss. Rotate the sheet halfway through baking.

Let cool completely on the baking sheet.

Make a small indentation in the flat side of a macaron with your thumb (16).

Repeat with the remaining macarons.

Alternate rows of macarons, facing up and down.

Spoon the filling into the pastry bag and pipe mounds onto the indented sides of half the macarons (17).

Sandwich with a plain macaron and lightly press (18) so the filling spreads to the edge (19).

Chill until set, at least 1 hour.

9 Process with an immersion blender to incorporate the butter.

10 This is what the hot salted caramel looks like.

11 Add the coffee extract to the meringue.

12 Add a few drops of yellow food coloring and whip.

13 This shows the desired color of the meringue.

14 Fold the meringue into the almond paste in three batches.

15 Pipe slightly flattened mounds on the prepared baking sheets.

16 Make a small indentation in the flat side of each macaron with your thumb.

17 Pipe the filling onto the indented sides of half the macarons.

18 Lightly press to close.

19 The filling should spread evenly to the edge.

Macarons à la Fraise
Strawberry Macarons

Strawberry Ganache

Finely chop the white chocolate and place in a medium bowl.

Hull and halve the strawberries and place them in a medium heavy saucepan with the sugar. Crush them with a small spatula (1).

Using an immersion blender, process the strawberries until smooth (2). Cook over medium heat until warm.

Strain the puree, pressing down with the spatula, into the white chocolate (3 and 4) and let the white chocolate melt (5).

Stir with the spatula until smooth (6). If the chocolate is not completely melted, heat the mixture over a saucepan filled with 1 inch (2.5 cm) of barely simmering water until the consistency is right.

Cover the bowl with plastic wrap and chill for at least 3 hours. This ganache takes a considerable time to set, but the result is delicious.

Makes about 3 dozen
Level: Advanced
Prep: 50 min.
Bake: 10 to 12 min. per
baking sheet
Chill: at least 4 hr.

Special equipment
A pastry bag fitted with a ⅓ to
½-inch (8 mm to 1 cm) plain tip

10½ oz. (300 g) white chocolate
10 oz. (300 g) strawberries
2½ tbsp. (1 oz., 30 g) sugar

2⅓ cups (7 oz., 200 g) ground
  almonds
1½ cups (7 oz., 200 g)
  confectioners' sugar
3½ tbsp. (50 ml) water
1 cup (7 oz., 200 g) granulated
  sugar
5½ oz. (150 g) egg whites
  (about 5)
Red food coloring

1 Heat the hulled, halved strawberries with the sugar, crushing them with a spatula.

2 Process with an immersion blender until smooth.

3 Strain the pureed strawberries into the white chocolate.

4 Press down hard with the spatula to recover as much pulp as possible.

5 Let the warmed fruit puree melt the white chocolate.

6 Stir carefully with a spatula until perfectly smooth.

continued

Preheat the oven to 340° F (170° C). Line 2 baking sheets with parchment paper.

Macarons

Follow steps 1 to 16 of the Italian Meringue Macarons (page 538).

Gradually beat a few drops of the red food coloring into the meringue (7). The quantity needed depends on its concentration. The result should be strawberry red (8).

Beat one-third of the meringue into the almond paste to lighten it (9).

Gently fold in the remaining meringue in 2 batches with a flexible spatula (10).

Spoon the macaron batter into the pastry bag and pipe 1½-inch (4 cm) flat mounds on the prepared baking sheets.

Tap the bottom of the baking sheets with the palm of your hand to smooth the surface of the macarons.

Bake 1 sheet at a time for 10 to 12 minutes, or until just firm with a light gloss. Rotate the sheet halfway through baking.

Let cool completely on the baking sheet.

Make a small indentation in the flat side of a macaron with your thumb (11).

Repeat with the remaining macarons.

Alternate rows of macarons, facing up and down (12).

Spoon the ganache into the pastry bag and pipe onto the indented sides of half the macarons.

Sandwich with a plain macaron and lightly press (13) so the filling spreads to the edge (14).

Chill until set, at least 1 hour.

7 Add the red food coloring to the meringue.

8 The result should be strawberry red.

9 Beat one-third of the meringue into the almond paste.

10 Gently fold in the remaining meringue in 2 batches.

11 Make a small indentation in the flat side of each macaron with your thumb.

12 Alternate rows of macarons, facing up and down.

13 Lightly press to close the macaron.

14 The filling should spread evenly to the edge.

15 Sandwiched macarons and unfilled cookies waiting to be garnished.

Macarons au Caramel à la Banane

Banana-Caramel Macarons

Banana-Caramel Filling

Blend the bananas, lemon juice, and rum in a food processor until smooth. Or use an immersion blender.

Finely chop the white chocolate and place it in a medium bowl.

Melt the sugar in a medium heavy saucepan, stirring, over medium heat (1).

Cook, stirring, until it turns into a dark amber caramel (2).

Remove the pan from the heat and carefully pour in the cream (3) to stop the cooking.

Add the banana mixture (4) and stir it in (5).

Stir in the butter until smooth (6).

Pour the hot banana-caramel mixture into the white chocolate (7).

Stir to combine (8), then process with an immersion blender until perfectly smooth (9).

Cover with plastic wrap and chill until set.

Makes about 3 dozen
Prep: 50 min.
Bake: 10 to 12 min. per
baking sheet
Chill: at least 1 hr.

Special equipment
A pastry bag fitted with a ⅓ to
½-inch (8 mm to 1 cm) plain tip

Banana-Caramel Filling

1¾ medium (7 oz., 200 g) peeled
    bananas
2 tbsp. lemon juice
1 tbsp. dark rum
10 oz. (280 g) white chocolate
¼ cup plus 2 tbsp. (3 oz., 80 g)
    sugar
3½ tbsp. (50 ml) heavy cream
3 tbsp. (40 g) butter, diced

Macarons

2⅓ cups (7 oz., 200 g) ground
    almonds
1½ cups (7 oz., 200 g)
    confectioners' sugar
3½ tbsp. (50 ml) water
1 cup (7 oz., 200 g) granulated
    sugar
5½ oz. (150 g) egg whites
    (about 5)
Yellow food coloring
Red food coloring, if needed
6 tbsp. (1½ oz, 40 g)
    unsweetened cocoa powder

1 Melt the sugar in a medium heavy saucepan over medium heat.

2 Cook, stirring, until it forms a dark amber caramel.

3 Gradually pour in the cream to stop the cooking.

4 Add the banana mixture to the caramel.

5 Stir well.

6 Stir in the diced butter.

7 Pour the hot caramel over the chopped white chocolate.

8 Stir gently.

9 Process with an immersion blender until perfectly smooth.

continued

Preheat the oven to 340° F (170° C). Line 2 baking sheets with parchment paper.

Macarons

Follow steps 1 to 16 of the Italian Meringue Macarons (page 538).

Beat a few drops of yellow food coloring into the meringue and, if necessary, a drop of red (10). The quantity needed depends on its concentration. The result should be a slightly orange-tinted yellow (not lemon yellow, but banana yellow) (11).

Beat one-third of the meringue into the almond paste to lighten it (12).
Gently fold in the remaining meringue in 2 batches with a flexible spatula (13).

Spoon the macaron batter into the pastry bag and pipe 1½-inch (4 cm) flat mounds on the prepared baking sheets (14).
Tap the bottom of the baking sheets with the palm of your hand to smooth the surface of the macarons.
Sprinkle a little cocoa powder over the macarons to imitate banana skins (15).
Bake 1 sheet at a time for 10 to 12 minutes, or until just firm with a light gloss. Rotate the sheet halfway through baking.
Let cool completely on the baking sheet.

Make a small indentation in the flat side of a macaron with your thumb (16). Repeat with the remaining macarons.
Alternate rows of macarons, facing up and down.
Spoon the filling into the pastry bag and pipe mounds onto the indented sides of half the macarons (17 and 18).
Sandwich with a plain macaron and lightly press (19) so the filling spreads to the edge (20).
Chill until set, at least 1 hour.

10 Add yellow food coloring and a little of the red, if needed, to the meringue.

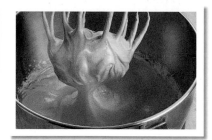

11 This is the color you are looking for.

12 Beat one-third of the meringue into the almond paste.

13 Gently fold in the remaining meringue in 2 batches.

14 Pipe 1½-inch (4 cm) flat mounds on lined baking sheets.

15 Using your fingertips, sprinkle a little cocoa powder over the macarons.

16 Make a small indentation in the flat side of each macaron with your thumb.

17 Begin piping banana-caramel filling onto the indented sides of the macarons.

18 Pipe until half the macarons are covered.

19 Lightly press to close.

20 The filling should spread evenly to the edge.

Macarons à la Rose

Rose-Flavored Macarons

Rose Buttercream

Place the whole eggs, egg yolk, and sugar in a medium bowl (1). Set over a saucepan filled with 1 inch (2.5 cm) of barely simmering water and whip with a hand-held electric mixer (2) until pale and the texture is that of a light mousse (3).

When the mixture is hot to the touch, remove the bowl from the heat and continue whipping until lukewarm (4).

Add the butter in several additions (5). Continue whipping until the cream is smooth (6).

Stir in the rosewater and rose syrup and taste for flavoring.

Cover the bowl with plastic wrap and chill.

Makes about 3 dozen
Level: Advanced
Prep: 50 min.
Bake: 10 to 12 min. per
baking sheet
Chill: at least 1 hr.

Special equipment
A pastry bag fitted with a ⅓ to
½-inch (8 mm to 1 cm) plain tip

2 whole eggs
1 egg yolk
¼ cup plus 2 tbsp. (3 oz., 80 g)
sugar
2 sticks (8 oz., 230 g) butter, diced
and softened
2 tsp. (10 ml) rosewater
About 2 tsp. (10 ml) rose syrup

2⅓ cups (7 oz., 200 g) ground
almonds
1½ cups (7 oz., 200 g)
confectioners' sugar
3½ tbsp. (50 ml) water
1 cup (7 oz., 200 g) granulated
sugar
5½ oz. (150 g) egg whites
(about 5)
Red food coloring

1 Place the whole eggs, egg yolk, and sugar in a bowl.

2 Set the bowl over a hot water bath and whip with an electric beater.

3 The mixture should become pale and light.

4 When the mixture is hot to the touch, remove the bowl from the heat and whip until lukewarm.

5 Add the softened butter.

6 Whip until the cream is smooth.

continued

Preheat the oven to 340° F (170° C). Line 2 baking sheets with parchment paper.

Macarons

Follow steps 1 to 16 of Italian Meringue Macarons (page 538).

Beat the red food coloring into the meringue (7). The quantity needed depends on its concentration. For rose-flavored macarons, the result should be light pink (8).

Beat one-third of the meringue into the almond paste (9) to lighten it (10).
Gently fold in the remaining meringue in 2 batches with a flexible spatula (11).

Spoon the macaron batter into the pastry bag and pipe 1½-inch (4 cm) heart shapes on the prepared baking sheets (12): Pipe a drop in one direction, and right next to it, a drop in the other direction.

Tap the bottom of the baking sheets with the palm of your hand to smooth the surface of the macarons.
Bake 1 sheet at a time for 10 to 12 minutes, or until just firm with a light gloss. Rotate the sheet halfway through baking.
Let cool completely on the baking sheet.

Make a small indentation in the flat side of a macaron with your thumb (13).
Repeat with the remaining macarons.
Alternate rows of macarons, facing up and down.
Whip the buttercream until light and airy. Spoon it into the pastry bag and pipe mounds onto the indented sides of half the macarons (14).
Sandwich with a plain macaron and lightly press (15) so the filling spreads to the edge (16).
Chill until set, at least 30 minutes.

Note: If you like, place half a fresh raspberry in the center of each macaron.

7 Tint the Italian meringue with a few drops of red food coloring.

8 This is the shade of pink you are looking for.

9 Beat one-third of the meringue into the almond paste.

10 This lightens the paste.

11 Gently fold in the remaining meringue in 2 batches.

12 Pipe small heart shapes on the prepared baking sheets.

13 Make a small indentation in the flat side of each macaron with your thumb.

14 Pipe the buttercream filling onto the indented sides of half the macarons.

15 Lightly press to close.

16 The filling should spread evenly to the edge.

Macarons Pamplemousse-Fraise-Vanille

Strawberry-Grapefruit Macarons with Vanilla Pastry Cream

Pastry Cream

Split the vanilla bean lengthwise in half and scrape out the seeds.

Bring the milk and vanilla bean and seeds to a boil in a medium heavy saucepan over medium heat (1).

Remove from the heat and let infuse for 10 minutes.

Meanwhile, combine the egg yolks and sugar in a medium bowl (2).

Whisk just until the sugar dissolves; do not let the mixture become pale. Whisk in the cornstarch and flour (3).

Whisk the milk into the egg-sugar mixture (4).

Strain the mixture into the saucepan and cook over medium heat, whisking constantly.

Let the cream simmer for 30 seconds to thicken (5). Remove it from the heat.

Whisk in the butter until smooth (6).

Scrape the pastry cream into a shallow bowl, press a piece of plastic wrap directly on the surface, and chill completely, at least 2 hours.

Preheat the oven to 340° F (170° C). Line 2 baking sheets with parchment paper.

Macarons

Follow steps 1 to 16 of the Italian Meringue Macarons (page 538).

Beat a few drops of the red food coloring into the meringue (7). The quantity needed depends on its concentration. For strawberry-grapefruit macarons, the result should be a definite pink color (8).

Makes about 1½ dozen
large macarons
Level: Advanced
Prep: 50 min.
Bake: 12 to 15 min. per
baking sheet
Chill: at least 3 hr.

Special equipment
A pastry bag fitted with a ⅓ to
½-inch (8 mm to 1 cm) plain tip

Pastry Cream

1 vanilla bean
2 cups (500 ml) milk
6 egg yolks
⅔ cup (4½ oz., 125 g) sugar
⅓ cup (1¾ oz., 50 g) cornstarch
1 tbsp. (10 g) all-purpose flour
3 tbsp. (50 g) butter, diced

Macarons

2⅓ cups (7 oz., 200 g) ground
almonds
1½ cups (7 oz., 200 g)
confectioners' sugar

3½ tbsp. (50 ml) water
1 cup (7 oz., 200 g) granulated
sugar
5½ oz. (150 g) egg whites
(about 5)
Red food coloring

Garnish

2 pink grapefruits
1 lb. (500 g) strawberries
1 tbsp. (15 ml) orange flower
water
Confectioners' sugar, for sifting

1 Heat the milk with the vanilla bean and seeds over medium heat.

2 Whisk the egg yolks and sugar until the sugar dissolves.

3 Whisk in the cornstarch and flour.

4 Whisk the hot milk into the egg mixture.

5 Return the mixture to medium heat, whisking until thickened. Let simmer for 30 seconds.

6 Remove from the heat and incorporate the butter.

7 Add red food coloring to the meringue.

8 This shows the color of the meringue.

9 Beat one-third of the meringue into the almond paste.
continued

Beat one-third of the meringue into the almond paste to lighten it (9).

Gently fold in the remaining meringue in 2 batches with a flexible spatula until smooth (10).

Spoon the macaron batter into the pastry bag and pipe 2¼-inch (6 cm) flat mounds on a prepared baking sheet (11). Tap the bottom of the sheet lightly with the palm of your hand to smooth surface of the macarons (12).

On another prepared baking sheet, pipe rings of the same diameter to form the tops of the macarons (13).

Bake for 12 to 15 minutes, or until just firm with a light gloss. Rotate the sheet halfway through baking.

Let cool completely on the baking sheet.

Garnish

Peel the grapefruits using a sharp knife and remove all the white pith. Cut between the membranes to release the segments. Cut them in half crosswise and drain on paper towels.

Hull the strawberries and cut half of them lengthwise in half.

Turn the whole macarons bottoms up and alternate rows of them and macaron rings.

Whisk the pastry cream until light and smooth. Spoon it into the pastry bag and pipe small mounds onto the whole macarons (14).

Alternate pieces of strawberry and grapefruit around the pastry cream (15).

Lightly brush the fruit with orange flower water (16).

Pipe a thin layer of pastry cream to cover the fruit (17).

Sift confectioners' sugar (18) over the tops and sandwich with a macaron ring. Place a whole strawberry in the center (19).

Chill until firm, at least 1 hour.

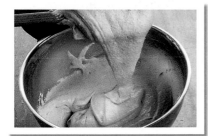

10 Fold in the remaining meringue in 2 batches. The batter should be smooth.

11 Pipe 20 2¼-inch (6 cm) flat mounds on a prepared baking sheet.

12 Tap the bottom of the baking sheet lightly with your hand to smooth the macarons.

13 Pipe 20 2¼-inch (6 cm) rings.

14 Pipe a small mound of pastry cream onto the flat side of each whole macaron.

15 Arrange the fruit around the cream.

16 Brush the fruit lightly with orange flower water.

17 Pipe a round of pastry cream over the fruit.

18 Sift lightly with confectioners' sugar.

19 Top with a macaron ring and place a strawberry in the center.

Macarons Passion-Chocolat
Passion Fruit-Chocolate Macarons

Crush the crêpes dentelles (1) with your fingertips (2).

Preheat the oven to 340° F (170° C). Line 2 baking sheets with parchment paper.

Macarons
Follow steps 1 to 6 of the French Meringue Macarons (page 544).

Beat a few drops of the coffee extract into the meringue (7). The quantity needed depends on its concentration. The result should be pale brown (8).

Makes 1½ dozen large
macarons
Level: Advanced
Prep: 40 min.
Bake: 12 to 15 min. per
baking sheet
Chill: at least 1 hr.

Special equipment
A pastry bag fitted with a ⅓ to
½-inch (8 mm to 1 cm) plain tip

Macarons

1½ cups (4 ½ oz, 125 g) ground
almonds
1⅓ cups (8 oz., 225 g)
confectioners' sugar
3½ oz. (100 g) egg whites
(about 3½)
2 tbsp. (1 oz., 25 g) granulated
sugar
Liquid coffee extract

Decoration

6 crêpes dentelles (see Note)
½ cup (2 oz., 50 g) unsweetened
cocoa powder

Passion Fruit Chocolate Filling

⅔ cup (150 ml) passion fruit juice
2 tbsp. (1 oz., 25 g) sugar
12 oz. (340 g) milk chocolate
4 tbsp. (60 g) butter, diced

Assemble

3½ tbsp. (50 ml) passion fruit juice

1 These are Breton crêpes dentelles.

2 Crush them with your fingertips.

3 Add the sugar to the egg whites when they form soft peaks.

4 Sift the confectioners' sugar into a bowl.

5 Add the ground almonds.

6 Whisk to combine the confectioners' sugar with the ground almonds.

7 Add the coffee extract to the meringue.

8 The meringue should be pale brown.

continued

Pour the almond–confectioners' sugar mixture into the meringue (9) and gently fold in with a flexible spatula (10). Stir quickly to deflate the meringue slightly.

Spoon the macaron batter into the pastry bag and pipe 2½-inch (6 cm) rounds on the prepared baking sheets. Tap the bottom of the baking sheets with the palm of your hand to smooth the macarons.

Decoration
Sprinkle the crushed crêpes dentelles over the tops (11) and sift with cocoa powder (12).
Bake for 12 to 15 minutes, or until just firm with a light gloss. Rotate the sheet halfway through baking.
Let cool completely on the baking sheet.

Passion Fruit–Chocolate Filling
Bring the passion fruit juice and sugar to a boil in a medium saucepan over medium heat (13).
Finely chop the chocolate and place it in a medium bowl. Set over a saucepan filled with 1 inch (2.5 cm) of barely simmering water, making sure that the bottom of the bowl does not touch the water. Let the chocolate melt. Remove the bowl from the heat and stir until smooth.
Pour the hot syrup into the melted chocolate (14) and stir until smooth and shiny.
Add the butter (15) and stir until the texture is smooth (16).
Chill until lightly set, about 30 minutes.

Assemble
Lightly brush the flat sides of the macarons with passion fruit juice (17). Spoon the filling into the pastry bag and pipe a spiral onto the flat sides of half the macarons (18), leaving a border.
Sandwich with a plain macaron (19).
Chill until set, at least 1 hour.

Note: Crêpes dentelles are a crisp, buttery Breton specialty. You can also use finely crushed ice cream cones.

9 Add the almond–confectioners' sugar mixture to the meringue.

10 Fold in with a flexible spatula. The batter should be smooth and semi-liquid.

11 Sprinkle the macarons with crushed crêpes dentelles.

12 Sift the tops lightly with cocoa powder.

13 Bring the passion fruit juice and sugar to a boil.

14 Pour the hot liquid over the melted chocolate and stir until smooth.

15 Add the diced butter.

16 The filling should be perfectly smooth.

17 Lightly brush the flat sides of the macarons with passion fruit juice.

18 Pipe a spiral of filling onto the flat sides of half the macarons.

19 Top with a plain macaron.

Macarons au Citron et Framboises

Lemon-Raspberry Macarons

Lemon Curd

Soak the gelatin sheet in a medium bowl of cold water until softened, 5 to 10 minutes.

Combine the lemon juice, sugar, and eggs in a medium heavy saucepan. Heat over medium heat, whisking constantly. Bring the mixture to a simmer, whisking.

Place the butter in a medium bowl. Squeeze the gelatin dry and add to the butter.

Pour the hot lemon mixture into the butter. Process with an immersion blender until smooth, about 2 minutes. Or use a whisk.

Chill until set, about 2 hours.

Raspberry Jam

Melt the raspberry jam in a medium heavy saucepan over medium heat, stirring occasionally. Add the liqueur, lemon juice, and, if desired, the aniseed and stir until smooth. Chill.

Preheat the oven to 340° F (170° C). Line 2 baking sheets with parchment paper.

Macarons

Follow steps 1 to 16 of the Italian Meringue Macarons (page 538).

Gradually beat a few drops of the yellow food coloring into the meringue (1). The quantity needed depends on its concentration. For lemon macarons, the result should be bright yellow (2), smooth, and shiny (3).

Beat one-third of the meringue into the almond paste to lighten it (4).

Gently fold in the remaining meringue in 2 batches with a flexible spatula (5).

Makes about 1½ dozen
large macarons
Level: Advanced
Prep: 1 hr.
Bake: 12 to 15 min. per
baking sheet
Chill: at least 3 hr.

Special equipment
A pastry bag fitted with a ⅓ to
½-inch (8 mm to 1 cm) plain tip
A toothbrush
A pair of gloves

Lemon Curd

1 gelatin sheet (2 g)
½ cup (130 ml) lemon juice
(from about 2½ lemons)
¾ cup (5 oz., 135 g) granulated
sugar
3 eggs
1½ sticks (6 oz., 175 g) butter, diced

Raspberry Jam

½ cup (125 ml) raspberry jam
2 tbsp. anise-flavored liqueur, such
as pastis or ouzo
1 tbsp. lemon juice
1 pinch aniseed (optional)

Macarons

2⅓ cups (7 oz., 200 g) ground
almonds
1½ cups (7 oz., 200 g)
confectioners' sugar
3½ tbsp. (50 ml) water
1 cup (7 oz., 200 g) granulated
sugar
5½ oz. (150 g) egg whites
(about 5)
Yellow food coloring
Red food coloring

Garnish

8 oz. (250 g) raspberries

1 Add the yellow food coloring to the cooled meringue.

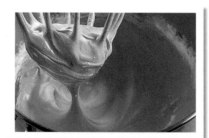

2 The meringue should be bright yellow.

3 This shows the texture of the meringue.

4 Beat one-third of the meringue into the almond paste.

5 Gently fold in the remaining meringue in 2 batches until smooth and pourable.

continued

Spoon the macaron batter into the pastry bag and pipe 2¼-inch (6 cm) flat mounds on the prepared baking sheets (6).

Tap the bottom of the baking sheets with the palm of your hand to smooth the surface of the macarons.

Dip the tips of the toothbrush bristles into the red coloring (7).

Hold the toothbrush above the macarons and spatter red dots over the tops (8 and 9).

Bake 1 sheet at a time for 10 to 12 minutes, or until just firm with a light gloss. Rotate the sheet halfway through baking.

Let cool completely on the baking sheet.

Using a teaspoon, spread a thin layer of raspberry jam on the flat sides of half the macarons (10).

Garnish

Place 5 raspberries around the edge of each macaron, spacing them evenly (11).

Spoon the lemon curd into the pastry bag and pipe the curd between each raspberry (12) and in the center of the raspberries (13).

Sandwich with a plain macaron (14).

Chill until set, at least 1 hour.

Note: The lemon curd is best made a day ahead so it can firm up for easy piping.

6 Pipe 2½-inch (6 cm) diameter balls on the prepared baking sheets.

7 Dip the tips of the toothbrush bristles in the red coloring.

8 Lightly splatter it over the macarons.

9 This shows the dotted effect.

10 Spread a thin layer of raspberry jam on the flat sides of half the macarons.

11 Arrange 5 raspberries around the macarons, spacing them evenly.

12 Pipe small dollops of lemon cream between the raspberries.

13 Pipe a dollop of lemon cream in the center.

14 Sandwich with a plain macaron.

Amaretti à l'Orange
Orange-Flavored Amaretti

Line 2 baking sheets with parchment paper.

Orange-Almond Paste
Combine the ground almonds, sugar, and candied orange peel in a food processor (1).
Add the egg whites (2) and process until perfectly smooth, about 2 minutes (3 and 4).

Meringue
Whip the egg whites until they hold a soft peak. Gradually add the sugar (5) and whip until the meringue is firm and dense (6).

Makes about 2½ dozen
sandwich cookies
Level: Easy
Prep: 20 min.
Dry: Overnight plus 1 hr.
Bake: 8 to 10 min. per
baking sheet

Special equipment
A pastry bag fitted with a ⅓ to
½-inch (8 mm to 1 cm) plain tip

Orange-Almond Paste

1⅔ cups (5 oz., 140 g) ground
almonds
¾ cup plus 2 tbsp. (6 oz., 175 g)
sugar
2 oz. (50 g) candied orange peel
(see page 452)
2 egg whites

Meringue

2 egg whites
¼ cup (2 oz., 50 g) sugar

Finish

Confectioners' sugar, for sifting

1 Combine the ground almonds, sugar, and candied orange peel in a food processor.

2 Add the egg whites.

3 Process for 2 minutes.

4 The orange-almond paste will be perfectly smooth.

5 Whip the egg whites until they hold a soft peak. Gradually add the sugar.

6 Whip until the meringue is firm and dense.

continued

Beat one-third of the meringue into the orange-almond paste (7) to lighten it. The batter will be dense (8).

Gently fold in the remaining meringue in 2 batches with a flexible spatula.

Spoon the batter into the pastry bag and pipe ½-inch (1 cm) mounds onto the prepared baking sheets (9).

Generously sift confectioners' sugar over the tops (10).

Let the amaretti dry out, uncovered, overnight.

Preheat the oven to 350° F (180° C).

Pinch the tops of the amaretti with your fingers (11 and 12).

Bake for about 10 minutes, or until lightly colored.

Carefully pour ¾ cup (200 ml) water under the parchment paper (13). This makes it easier to peel the amaretti off the paper and then stick pairs of them together.

Let the amaretti cool on the baking sheet. Gently peel them off the paper and sandwich pairs of them, flat ends together (14).

Let dry out, at least 1 hour.

7 Add the meringue to the orange-almond paste.

8 Fold in with a flexible spatula until the macaron batter is perfectly smooth.

9 Pipe small mounds on lined baking sheets.

10 Generously sift the tops with confectioners' sugar and let dry out overnight.

11 Pinch the amaretti with your fingertips to shape them.

12 They should look like this.

13 Carefully pour water under the parchment paper.

14 Sandwich the cooled cookies together.

Macarons à l'Ancienne
Old-Fashioned Macarons

Preheat the oven to 325° F (160° C). Line 2 baking sheets with parchment paper.

Pour the ground almonds into a medium bowl and add the granulated sugar (1), honey (2), almond extract, and egg whites (3).

Beat with a flexible spatula (4) to make a thick paste (5).

Place the bowl over a saucepan filled with 1 inch (2.5 cm) of barely simmering water and beat (6) until the paste softens and is slightly hot to the touch (7).

Remove the bowl from the heat. Scoop out 2 tbsp. of the paste and reserve.

Makes about 2½ dozen
Level: Intermediate
Prep: 25 min.
Bake: 20 min. per
baking sheet

Special equipment
A pastry bag fitted with a ⅓ to
½-inch (8 mm to 1 cm) plain tip

2⅓ cups (7 oz., 200 g) ground
almonds
1½ cups (10½ oz., 300 g)
granulated sugar
2 tsp. (15 g) honey
A few drops bitter almond extract
(see *Note*)
4 egg whites
Confectioners' sugar, for sifting

1 Combine the ground almonds
and sugar in a bowl.

2 Add the honey.

3 Stir in a little bitter almond
extract and the egg whites.

4 Mix with a flexible spatula.

5 The ingredients form a thick,
smooth paste.

6 Heat the paste over a hot
water bath.

7 When the paste is slightly hot to
the touch it will soften slightly.

continued

Spoon the macaron batter into the pastry bag and pipe 1-inch (2.5 cm) flat mounds on the prepared baking sheets (8).

Dampen a few paper towels and lightly press them on the macarons to moisten them (9).

Remove the paper towels and sift confectioners' sugar over the tops (10).

The mounds will be smooth and shiny before baking (11).

Bake for about 20 minutes, or until lightly browned (12).

Carefully pour ¾ cup (200 ml) water under the parchment paper (13).

Sift confectioners's sugar over the macarons (14).

Let cool completely on the baking sheets.

Transfer them to a cool, dry baking sheet and turn them upside down (15).

Using a small knife (16), spread small mounds of the reserved almond paste on the flat sides of half the macarons (17).

Sandwich with a plain macaron (18 and 19).

Note: Be careful to add the extract sparingly, because the taste is very strong.

8 Pipe flat mounds on lined baking sheets.

9 Lightly press moistened paper towels on the macarons.

10 Sift confectioners' sugar over the tops.

11 This is what they look like before baking.

12 This is they look like when baked.

13 Carefully pour ¾ cup (200 ml) water under the parchment paper.

14 Lightly sift with confectioners' sugar.

15 Transfer the macarons to a cool, dry baking sheet and turn them upside down.

16 Take a little of the reserved almond paste with the tip of a knife.

17 Spread small mounds on the flat sides of half the macarons.

18 Sandwich with a plain macaron.

19 Enclose the filling completely.

Macaron à la Mangue
Mango-Caramel Macaron Cake

Macarons

Preheat the oven to 340° F (170° C). Line 2 baking sheets with parchment paper. Using a plate or lid as a template, draw 2 7- to 8-inch (18 to 20 cm) circles on each prepared baking sheet, spacing them slightly apart.

Follow steps 1 to 16 of the Italian Meringue Macarons (page 538).

Beat a few drops of the two colorings into the meringue (1). The quantity needed depends on its concentration. For mango macarons, the result should be bright orange (2).

Beat one-third of the meringue into the almond paste to lighten it (3).

Gently fold in the remaining meringue in 2 batches with a flexible spatula (4).

Spoon the macaron batter into the pastry bag and pipe 2 disks on each prepared baking sheet, working in a spiral from the center out (5).

Bake 1 sheet at a time for 15 to 20 minutes, or until just firm with a light gloss. Rotate the sheet halfway through baking.

Let cool completely on the baking sheet.

Mango Filling

Peel, pit, and cut the mango into ½ inch (1 cm) dice.

Warm the honey in a medium skillet over medium heat.

Add the diced mango and lemon juice (6) and cook, stirring occasionally, until the mango is coated all over in the honey, about 2 minutes.

Transfer to a bowl and chill.

Makes 2 7- to 8-inch
(18 to 20 cm) cakes
Level: Advanced
Prep: 1 hr.
Bake: 15 to 17 min. per
baking sheet
Chill: at least 1 hr.

Special equipment
A pastry bag fitted with a
½-inch (1 cm) plain tip

Macarons

2⅓ cups (7 oz., 200 g) ground
almonds
1½ cups (7 oz., 200 g)
confectioners' sugar
3½ tbsp. (50 ml) water
¾ cup plus 2 tbsp. (6 oz., 175 g)
granulated sugar
5½ oz. (150 g) egg whites (about 5)
Yellow food coloring
Red food coloring

Mango Filling

1 ripe mango
1 tbsp. mild honey
Juice of ½ lemon

Salted Caramel Cream

¾ cup (5 oz., 140 g) sugar
¼ cup (65 ml) heavy cream
7 tbsp. (3½ oz., 100 g) salted
butter, diced and chilled
1¼ cups (8 oz., 250 g) plain
buttercream (page 583) omitting
the rosewater and rose syrup
2 cups (8 oz., 250 g) pastry
cream (page 586)

1 Tint the meringue with the yellow and red colorings.

2 The result should be bright orange.

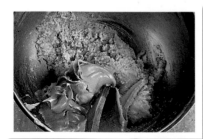

3 Beat one-third of the meringue into the almond paste to lighten it.

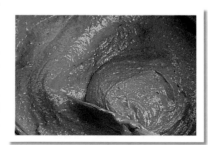

4 Gently fold in the remaining meringue in 2 batches with a flexible spatula.

continued

Salted Caramel Cream

Pour half of the sugar into a medium heavy saucepan. Melt it over medium heat, stirring with a spatula or wooden spoon. Stir in the remaining sugar until completely melted. Reduce the heat to low and cook, stirring, until the sugar changes from a light amber liquidy paste to a fluid, medium amber caramel. The best way to judge the color is to let the caramel run off the spoon.

Slowly pour in a little cream, stirring. Be careful not to burn yourself: the mixture can boil up quickly.

Gradually stir in the remaining cream. Check the temperature: the thermometer should register 226° F (108° C).

Immediately remove from the heat and stir in the butter to stop the cooking.

Process the caramel with an immersion blender until perfectly smooth. Or use a spatula or wooden spoon, but it will take longer.

Pour the caramel into a bowl, cover with plastic wrap, and chill until thickened.

Whip the buttercream at medium speed until very light, about 10 minutes.

Whisk the pastry cream until it is perfectly smooth. Add to the buttercream and whip at low speed until smooth, about 1 minute.

Add a little more than half of the caramel and whip until smooth. Reserve the remaining caramel for garnish.

Spoon the caramel cream into the pastry bag and pipe a thick ring next to the edge on the flat side of 1 macaron (7).

Pipe a thin spiral of caramel cream in the center (8).

Arrange the diced mango in the center with a spoon (9).

Drizzle the reserved caramel in zigzags on top, using a parchment paper cone (see page 212) or a spoon (10).

Pipe a spiral of caramel cream in a thin layer over the caramel stripes (11).

Sandwich with a plain macaron (12). Repeat to make a second macaron cake. Chill until set, at least 1 hour.

Notes: Do not tap the bottom of the baking sheets as you would for the smaller macarons.

If you like, garnish the cake with sliced seasonal fruit.

5 Pipe 2 7- to 8-inch (18 to 20 cm) spirals on each prepared baking sheet.

6 Cook the diced mango with the honey and lemon juice.

7 Pipe a thick ring of caramel cream around the edges of 2 macarons.

8 Pipe more caramel cream into the center of the macarons.

9 Arrange the diced mango over the cream in the center.

10 Drizzle zigzags of caramel to accentuate the flavor of the caramel cream.

11 Cover with a thin layer of caramel filling.

12 Sandwich with a plain macaron.

Macaron Pistache-Framboise
Pistachio-Raspberry Macaron Cake

Macarons

Preheat the oven to 340° F (170° C). Line 2 baking sheets with parchment paper. Using a plate or lid as a template, draw 2 7- to 8-inch (18 to 20 cm) circles on each prepared baking sheet, spacing them slightly apart.

Combine the ground almonds, confectioners' sugar, and 2½ oz. (65 g) of the pistachios in a food processor. Grind to a coarse powder, about 30 seconds. There should be some small pieces of pistachio.

Transfer to a medium bowl. Stir in half the egg whites to make almond-pistachio paste.

Follow steps 5 to 11 of the Italian Meringue Macarons (page 538) but cook the sugar syrup, watching carefully, until it reaches 250° F (121° C).

Gradually beat a few drops of the green food coloring into the meringue, then the yellow food coloring (1), to tone down a too-bright green. The quantity needed depends on its concentration. For these pistachio macarons, the result should be pronounced green (2).

Beat one-third of the meringue into the almond-pistachio paste to lighten it (3).

Gently fold in the remaining meringue in 2 batches with a flexible spatula. The batter will be thick (4).

Spoon the macaron batter into the pastry bag and pipe 2 disks on each prepared baking sheet, working in a spiral from the center out (5).

Coarsely chop the remaining pistachios. Lightly sprinkle the tops of the macarons with pistachios (6).

Bake 1 sheet at a time for 15 to 20 minutes, or until just firm with a light gloss. Rotate the sheet halfway through baking.

Let cool completely on the baking sheet.

Makes 2 7- to 8-inch
(18 to 20 cm) cakes
Level: Advanced
Prep: 1 hr.
Bake: 15 to 17 min. per
baking sheet
Chill: at least 1 hr.

Special equipment
A pastry bag fitted with a
½-inch (1 cm) plain tip

Macarons

1½ cups (5 oz., 130 g) ground
almonds
1½ cups (7 oz., 200 g)
confectioners' sugar
4½ oz. (115 g) unsalted pistachios
5½ oz. (150 g) egg whites (about 5)
3½ tbsp. (50 ml) water
1 cup (7 oz., 200 g) granulated
sugar
Green food coloring
Yellow food coloring

Pistachio Cream

2 whole eggs
1 egg yolk
¼ cup plus 2 tbsp. (3 oz., 80 g)
sugar
2 sticks (8 oz., 230 g) butter,
diced and softened
6 oz. (170 g) pastry cream
(see page 586)
1 oz. (30 g) pistachio paste
(see Note)

Raspberry Filling

¼ cup (50 g) raspberry jam with
seeds
1 lb. 5 oz. (600 g) raspberries

1 Tint the Italian meringue, cooked to 250° F (121° C), with green and yellow food coloring.

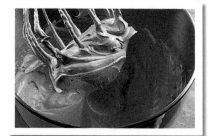

2 The meringue should be a pronounced green.

3 Beat one-third of the meringue into the almond-pistachio paste.

4 Gently fold in the remaining meringue in 2 batches with a flexible spatula. The batter should be thick.

5 Pipe 4 spiral disks within the circles drawn on the parchment paper.

6 Lightly sprinkle them with chopped pistachios.

continued

Pistachio Cream

Place the whole eggs, egg yolk, and sugar in a medium bowl. Set over a saucepan filled with 1 inch (2.5 cm) of barely simmering water and whip with a hand-held electric mixer until pale and the texture is that of a light mousse.

When the mixture is hot to the touch, remove the bowl from the heat and continue whipping until lukewarm.

Add the butter in several batches, whipping after each addition until smooth.

Cover the bowl with plastic wrap and let stand at room temperature.

Whisk the pastry cream until it is perfectly smooth. Add to the pistachio buttercream and whip at low speed until smooth, about 1 minute (7 and 8).

Add the pistachio paste (9) and whip until smooth (10).

Raspberry Filling

Using a parchment paper cone (see page 212) or a spoon, drizzle raspberry jam around the edge on the flat side of 1 macaron (11).

Arrange raspberries on the ring of jam so they are touching (12).

Pipe a thin spiral of pistachio cream inside the raspberries (13).

Cover the cream with rings of raspberries (14).

Pipe a spiral of pistachio cream over the raspberries (15) and sandwich with a plain macaron (16).

Repeat to make a second macaron cake.

Chill for at least 1 hour, or until set.

Notes: This macaron recipe differs slightly from the rest. It contains more than the usual amount of confectioners' sugar, and the sugar syrup for the Italian meringue should cook to 250° F (121° C).

Do not tap the bottom of the baking sheets as you would for the smaller macarons.

You can replace the pistachio cream with the recipe for pistachio filling on page 562. It is not quite as light but is easier to prepare.

To make your own pistachio paste, see page 564.

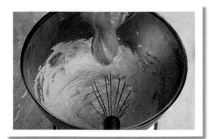

7 Add the pastry cream to the buttercream.

8 Whip until smooth.

9 Incorporate the pistachio paste.

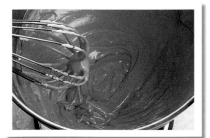

10 The cream should be perfectly smooth.

11 Draw a thin line of cooled raspberry jam around the rims of 2 macarons.

12 Place raspberries all around the rim.

13 Pipe a thin layer of pistachio cream within the raspberries.

14 Cover the cream with raspberries.

15 Cover the raspberries with a thin layer of pistachio cream.

16 Sandwich with a macaron.

Pyramide de Macarons
Macaron Pyramid

Finely chop the chocolate. Place in a medium bowl set over a saucepan filled with 1 inch (2.5 cm) of barely simmering water, making sure that the bottom of the bowl does not touch the water. Let the chocolate melt. Remove the bowl from the heat and stir until smooth.

Turn the glass bowl upside down on a work surface and brush it all over with melted chocolate (1), making a fine, even layer (2). Let set slightly.

Brush a little chocolate on one side of each macaron (3) and stick it to the bowl, starting at the bottom (4).

Alternate the colors and arrange the macarons so they are touching.

When you have finished the bottom layer, work upwards (5), alternating colors in diagonal lines (6).

At the top of the bowl, stick the macarons on their sides (7).

Let the chocolate set completely. Chill the pyramid or let stand on the serving table until served.

Notes: The quantity of macarons depends on the size of the bowl and the macarons.

Whatever shape of bowl you choose as a base, make sure it is dry and clean.

Serves 12 to 16
Level: Easy
Prep: 20 min.
Chill: 20 min.

Special equipment
A glass bowl to use as a base

8 oz. (250 g) bittersweet chocolate
40 to 50 assorted macarons,
   preferably 2 colors

1 Brush the bowl with melted chocolate.

2 Make sure that the layer of chocolate is even and let it set slightly.

3 Brush a little chocolate on one side of each macaron.

4 Immediately stick it to the bottom of the base. Alternate the colors.

5 Repeat for the upper rows.

6 Alternate the colors in diagonal lines.

7 To increase the height, stick the last macarons to the top on their sides.

LE BRIOCHES ET

S VIENNOISERIES

Making Brioches and Breakfast Pastries

These are the stages in making yeasted pastries.

Mixing

Mix the basic ingredients, including the yeast, following the directions given.

First Rise

Let the dough rise at room temperature, 68° to 86° F (20° to 30° C), for 1 to 2 hours, or chill it in the refrigerator for 12 hours, until doubled in volume.

Punching Down

On a lightly floured work surface, flatten the dough with your hands to remove the air pockets that have formed during the first rise.

Chilling

Chill the dough until firm before proceeding. These doughs are all rich in butter, which warms and softens rapidly. You may need to chill a dough more than once while working with it.

Shaping

Follow the recipe to make the shapes and fillings. You may need to flatten the dough if it has risen in the refrigerator.

Second Rise

Let the shaped pastries rise at room temperature, covered or not with plastic wrap, depending on the humidity, until doubled in volume. Allow at least 1 hour 30 minutes. The temperature range of the room should be 72 to 86° F (22 to 30° C); 77° F (25° C) is the ideal temperature.

Glazing

When the pastries have doubled in volume, they require brushing, usually with egg glaze, sometimes with milk.

Baking

Use convection heat, if possible, which produces the most even results. Have the oven preheated and bake the pastries as soon as they have doubled in bulk and have been glazed. Rotate the baking sheets halfway through so the pastries color evenly. Always check on their progress, whatever the time specified; ovens vary slightly and yours may cook slightly faster or slower than the average.

Make Ahead

The shaped pastries can be covered with plastic wrap and refrigerated overnight; they will rise in the refrigerator (second rise) so they will be ready for glazing and baking.

They can also be frozen before baking, but be careful: freezing tends to "kill" yeast, so do not keep raw leavened pastry in the freezer for more than four or five days.

Storing

Baked brioches and breakfast pastries keep for two days, but after more than 24 hours they no longer taste very good. It really is best to eat them soon after they are baked! If you wish to serve them the following day, reheat them in a 325° F (160° C) oven for 5 minutes. Loaves and cooked brioches can be frozen for 1 to 2 weeks immediately after baking and cooling.

The Five Basic Leavened Pastry Recipes

Pâte à Croissant (Croissant Pastry)

This is a yeasted puff pastry, comprising two main components: a sweet, yeast dough and butter. Preparing the dough involves the same rolling and folding as for puff pastry but there are fewer folds.

Pâte à Danish (Danish Pastry)

This is a folded brioche pastry. The dough is softer than croissant dough and when baked is slightly less crisp. It stays soft longer than brioche dough after baking and freezes well unbaked.

Pain au Lait (Milk Bread)

This pastry is similar to brioche but not as rich. Although it is easier to prepare, it is harder to work with, so make sure to chill it for at least 2 hours before rolling it out. You can even place it briefly in the freezer if your kitchen is warm. Recipes that call for brioche dough can be prepared with milk bread dough, and vice versa.

Pâte à Brioche (Brioche Pastry)

Brioche dough is rich because of the large amount of butter it contains, which also is what makes it melt in your mouth.

Pâte à Kouglof (Kouglof Pastry)

This type of brioche dough uses a starter. Kouglof pastry is easy to make: just put all the ingredients in the bowl of a stand mixer, switch it on, and it's practically done. It is just as delicious sweet as it is savory (with cheese, for instance, or sautéed cubes of bacon).

Variations

Note that the prep times given for the recipe variations do not include the time it takes to make the basic recipe.

Ingredients

Flour

All-purpose flour, a mix of soft (low-gluten) and hard (high-gluten) flours, is appropriate for all brioche and breakfast pastries.

Sugar

Use granulated sugar. In these recipes, confectioners' sugar is appropriate only for decoration.

Butter

Don't substitute margarine for butter. Buy the butter with the highest butterfat content, if indicated, or the one that feels firmest in its wrapping, an indication of a high butterfat content. And always use unsalted butter.

Yeast

Fresh yeast is simple to use but has a short shelf life. Store it in a small airtight container in the refrigerator for no more than one week.

One package or 2¼ teaspoons of active dry yeast can be substituted for each .6-ounce cake of fresh yeast. Add the dry yeast to the lukewarm liquid in the recipe and let stand until foamy, about 5 minutes, before proceeding with the recipe.

Equipment

Baking Pans

Yeasted doughs adapt easily to all sorts of shapes, so use different types of molds and pans: cake pans, tart pans, kouglof molds, etc.

Baking Sheets

If you have several baking sheets, it's easier to make large quantities.

Cookie Cutters

Have several sizes of cookie cutters on hand to help make neat shapes.

Marble Board

A marble work surface helps keep butter-rich doughs cool and firm. You can also cool your work surface with ice packs.

Pastry Brush

All the doughs require glazing, best done with a pastry brush.

Rolling Pin

A medium-sized rolling pin is indispensable.

Ruler

A ruler is handy to measure the thickness of the dough and to check the other dimensions given in the recipes.

Stand Mixer

Even if all the recipes can easily be prepared using your hands, a stand mixer will make the work easier.

Croissants au Beurre
Buttery Croissants

Croissant Pastry

Place the flour, sugar, powdered milk, salt, and softened butter in the bowl of a stand mixer fitted with a dough hook. Crumble in the yeast, making sure it does not touch the salt (1).

Knead at medium speed, gradually pouring in the water (2), until smooth (3), about 6 minutes. The dough should pull away from the sides of the bowl (4). Or knead by hand.

On a lightly floured work surface, flatten the dough into a rectangle (5). Cover with plastic wrap (6) and chill until firm, at least 2 hours.

Ten minutes before you begin working again, place the chilled butter in the freezer.

On a lightly floured work surface, roll out the chilled dough into a rectangle ¼ inch (6 mm) thick (7).

Dust the chilled butter with flour. Roll out the butter into a rectangle half the size of the dough (8). (If the butter is soft, roll it out on a sheet of lightly dusted parchment paper.)

Arrange the dough with a short side facing you. Place the butter on the bottom half of the dough (9).

Makes about 1½ dozen pastries;
2 lb. 4 oz. (1 kg) dough
Level: Advanced
Prep: 40 min.
Chill: 4 hr.
Rise: 2 hr.
Bake: 12 to 15 min. per sheet

Croissant Pastry

4 cups (1 lb. 2 oz., 500 g)
all-purpose flour
⅓ cup (2 oz., 60 g) sugar
1 tbsp. plus 1 tsp. (10 g) powdered
milk
2 tsp. (12 g) salt
7 tbsp. (3½ oz., 100 g) butter,
softened
1¼ cakes (.75 oz., 25 g) fresh yeast
Scant cup (230 ml) cold water
2 sticks (8 oz., 250 g) butter, chilled

Egg Glaze

1 whole egg
1 egg yolk

1 Place the flour, sugar, powdered milk, salt, softened butter, and crumbled yeast in the bowl of a stand mixer.

2 Gradually add the water.

3 Knead at medium speed until the dough is smooth and elastic, about 6 minutes.

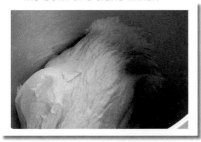

4 The dough should pull away from the sides of the bowl.

5 Flatten it into a rectangle.

6 Cover with plastic wrap.

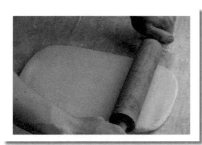

7 Roll the chilled dough into a rectangle ¼ inch (6 mm) thick.

8 Roll the butter into a rectangle half the size of the dough.

9 Arrange the butter on the bottom half of the dough.

continued

Fold the top half of the dough over the butter (10) to enclose it completely (11).

Rotate the dough clockwise a quarter-turn (90°) so that an open edge is facing you. Roll out the dough lengthwise (12) into a rectangle ¼ inch (6 mm) thick.

Fold up the bottom third of the dough so it covers one-third of the dough (13). Fold down the top third to meet the edge (14 and 15).

Fold the entire dough in half (16) to make a "double turn." Press down lightly so it is smooth and even (17).

This makes 4 layers of dough (18).

Cover with plastic wrap and chill for 1 hour.

On a lightly floured surface, arrange the dough with an open side facing you and the closed side to your right.

Roll out again into a rectangle about ¼ inch (6 mm) thick (19).

10 Fold over the top half of the dough.

11 The butter should be enclosed.

12 Rotate the dough clockwise 90° (a quarter turn) and roll it out into a rectangle ¼ inch (6 mm) thick.

13 Fold up the bottom third of the dough.

14 Fold down the top third to touch the bottom third.

15 The edges should meet.

16 Fold the dough in half.

17 Smooth it with your hands.

18 The dough has 4 layers.

19 Arrange the dough with an open edge facing you and roll out into a rectangle ¼ inch (6 mm) thick.

continued

Fold the dough in thirds, like a letter (20 and 21). There are now 3 layers of dough (22).
Cover with plastic wrap and chill for 1 hour.

Arrange the dough on the floured work surface with an open edge facing you (23).
Roll out the dough into a 20-inch (50 cm) square ⅛ inch (3 to 4 mm) thick (24).
Cut the dough in half (25) to make 2 large rectangles. Drape 1 rectangle over a rolling pin and transfer to a baking sheet. Cover with plastic wrap and chill.
Using a pastry cutter or sharp knife, cut the other rectangle into isosceles triangles with a 2-inch (5 cm) base (26). Transfer the triangles to a baking sheet, cover with plastic wrap, and chill. Repeat with the second rectangle.

Roll up the croissants, starting at the base (27). Push gently from the corners (28), rolling toward the tip. Tuck the tips underneath the croissants (29).

Line 2 baking sheets with parchment paper.
Arrange the croissants on the prepared baking sheets, spacing well apart, with the tips of the triangles tucked underneath so they do not unroll during baking.
Let rise in a warm place, no hotter than 86° F (30° C), until doubled in volume (30), about 2 hours.

Preheat the oven to 350 to 375° F (180 to 190° C).

Egg Glaze
Lightly beat the whole egg and yolk in a cup with a fork.
Lightly brush the puffy croissants with the egg glaze (31).
Bake 1 sheet at a time for 12 to 15 minutes, or until golden brown.
Transfer the croissants to a rack and let cool.

Notes: Croissants may seem hard to make, but when you've tried this recipe, you'll see that it is simple and delicious.
Once the croissants are rolled, in steps 27 to 29, they can be frozen raw.
Double the quantities so you can also make the croissant variations on the following pages.

20 Fold up the bottom third.

21 Fold the top third over it, like a letter, to make 3 layers.

22 This is what it looks like.

23 Arrange the dough with an open edge facing you.

24 Roll into a square ⅛ inch (4 mm) thick.

25 Cut the square into 2 rectangles.

26 Cut triangles with 2-inch (5 cm) bases and chill.

27 Roll up the croissants from the base.

28 Lightly push from the tips at the base.

29 Tuck the tips underneath the croissants.

30 The croissants should double in volume.

31 Lightly brush the tops with the egg glaze.

Croissants aux Amandes
Almond Croissants

Almond Croissants
Follow steps 1 to 26 of the Buttery Croissants (page 624).
Chill the triangles for 10 minutes.

Beat the ground almonds with the confectioners' sugar, almond extract, egg yolk, and milk until smooth.

Arrange 5 triangles on the work surface and place about 1 tsp. of the almond paste at the base of each, leaving a ½-inch (1 cm) border (1).

Fold in the 2 corners of the base (2), lightly press to seal (3 and 4), and gently roll up the triangles (5, 6, and 7).

Repeat with the remaining triangles.

Line 2 baking sheets with parchment paper.

Arrange the croissants on the prepared baking sheets, spacing well apart, with the tips of the triangles tucked underneath (8) so they do not unroll during baking.

Let rise in a warm place, no hotter than 86° F (30° C), until doubled in volume, about 2 hours.

Preheat the oven to 350° F (180° C).

Orange Flower Syrup
Combine the sugar and water in a small saucepan. Cook over medium heat, stirring, until the sugar dissolves. Remove from the heat, let cool, and stir in the orange flower water.

Egg Glaze
Lightly beat the egg and egg yolk in a cup with a fork.

Lightly brush the puffy croissants with the egg glaze and sprinkle with sliced almonds (9).

Bake 1 sheet at a time for 12 to 15 minutes, or until golden brown.

Brush the almond croissants with the syrup while they are still warm (10).

Transfer to a rack and let cool.

Makes about 1½ dozen pastries
Level: Advanced
Prep: 10 min.
Chill: 10 min.
Rise: 2 hr.
Bake: 12 to 15 min. per sheet

1 recipe Buttery Croissants
(page 624)
1¾ cups (5 oz., 150 g) ground
almonds
½ cup (2¾ oz., 75 g) confectioners'
sugar
5 drops bitter almond extract
1 egg yolk
2 tbsp. milk
⅔ cup (2 oz., 50 g) sliced almonds

Orange Flower Syrup

¼ cup (2 oz., 50 g) sugar
3½ tbsp. (50 ml) water
1 tbsp. orange flower water

Egg Glaze

1 whole egg
1 egg yolk

1 Place about 1 tsp. of the almond paste at the base of each triangle, leaving a ½-inch (1 cm) border.

2 Fold in the 2 corners to make a collar shape.

3 Lightly press the dough to seal.

4 The almond paste should be completely enclosed.

5 Gently roll the croissants from the base.

6 Keep rolling.

7 Continue to the tip.

8 The tips should be tucked underneath the croissants.

9 Brush the puffy croissants with egg glaze and sprinkle with sliced almonds.

10 Brush the hot croissants with syrup.

Carrés à l'Ananas
Pineapple Croissants

Pineapple Croissants

Follow steps 1 to 23 of the Buttery Croissants (page 624). Cover with plastic wrap and chill for 1 hour.

Line a baking sheet with parchment paper.

On a lightly floured work surface, roll out the dough into an 11 by 6-inch (28 by 14 cm) rectangle ⅛ inch (4 mm) thick (1).

Cut into 3-inch (7 cm) squares (2) and transfer them to the prepared baking sheet.

Let rise in a warm place, no hotter than 86° F (30° C), until doubled in volume, about 2 hours.

Preheat the oven to 350° F (180° C).

Peel the pineapple, cut it lengthwise into quarters, and remove the core. Slice the quarters crosswise into ⅛-inch-thick (3 mm) pieces.

Melt the brown sugar in a skillet over medium heat. Add the butter and pineapple (3) and cook, stirring occasionally, until the pineapple is coated with the caramel, 2 to 3 minutes. Let stand at room temperature.

Beat the pastry cream with a spatula to loosen it and stir in three-quarters of the shredded coconut (4).

Sugar Syrup

Combine the sugar and water in a small saucepan. Cook over medium heat, stirring, until the sugar dissolves. Remove from the heat and let cool.

Egg Glaze

Lightly beat the whole egg and egg yolk in a cup with a fork. Brush the puffy squares with the egg glaze (5).

Pipe or spoon out the coconut pastry cream in the center of each square (6). Arrange 3 pieces of pineapple on top of the pastry cream (7 and 8).

Bake for 12 to 15 minutes, or until golden brown.

Brush the pineapple croissants with the syrup while they are still warm (9).

Sprinkle the edges with the remaining coconut (10).

Transfer to a rack and let cool.

Makes about 10 pastries
Level: Intermediate
Prep: 20 min.
Chill: 1 hr.
Rise: 2 hr.
Bake: 12 to 15 min.

½ recipe Buttery Croissants
    (page 624)
½ pineapple (see *Note*)
2½ tsp. (10 g) light brown sugar
2 tsp. (10 g) butter
¾ cup (9 oz., 250 g) pastry cream
    (page 672)
½ cup (1½ oz., 40 g) unsweetened
    shredded coconut

Sugar Syrup and Egg Glaze

¼ cup (2 oz., 50 g) sugar
3½ tbsp. (50 ml) water
1 whole egg
1 egg yolk

1 Roll out the chilled dough into an 11 by 6-inch (28 by 14 cm) rectangle about ⅛ inch (4 mm) thick.

2 Cut the dough into 3-inch (7 cm) squares.

3 Cook the pineapple pieces with the caramelized brown sugar and butter, coating them well.

4 Mix three-quarters of the coconut into the pastry cream.

5 Brush the puffy squares with egg glaze.

6 Pipe pastry cream into the center of each square.

7 Arrange 3 pieces of pineapple on the pastry cream.

8 This is what they look like.

9 Lightly brush the baked squares with syrup.

10 Sprinkle the edges with shredded coconut.

Pains au Chocolat
Chocolate Croissants

Chocolate Croissants

Follow steps 1 to 23 of the Buttery Croissants (page 624). Cover with plastic wrap and chill for 1 hour.

On a lightly floured work surface, roll out the dough into a 13 by 10-inch (33 by 25 cm) rectangle ⅛ inch (4 mm) thick (1).

Cut the rectangle in half lengthwise (2) to make two 13 by 5-inch (33 by 12 cm) rectangles. The dough will shrink very slightly.

Cut each rectangle crosswise into 5 by 3-inch (12 by 8 cm) rectangles. You can use a chocolate stick as a guide (3).

Line a baking sheet with parchment paper.

Place a chocolate stick on a short end of each rectangle, leaving a ¾-inch (1.5 cm) border (4). Fold the border over it (5), place a second chocolate stick at the fold (6), and roll the dough over it (7).

Roll the dough again to shape the chocolate croissants (8).

Arrange the croissants on the prepared baking sheet, spacing well apart, with the edges of the rolls tucked underneath (9) so they do not unroll during baking.

Cover loosely with plastic wrap and let rise in a warm place, no hotter than 86° F (30° C), until doubled in volume, about 2 hours.

Preheat the oven to 375° F (190° C).

Egg Glaze

Lightly beat the egg and salt in a cup with a fork.

Lightly brush the puffy croissants with the egg glaze (10).

Bake for 12 to 15 minutes, or until golden brown.

Transfer the croissants to a rack and let cool.

Notes: To make 16 pastries, use the entire Buttery Croissants recipe.

The chocolate sticks can be replaced with 3 oz. (90 g) chopped bittersweet chocolate (55% cocoa).

Makes 8 pastries
Level: Advanced
Prep: 20 min.
Chill: 1 hr.
Rise: 2 hr.
Bake: 12 to 15 min.

½ recipe Buttery Croissants
(page 624)
16 semisweet pain au chocolat sticks
(see *Notes*)

1 egg
1 pinch salt

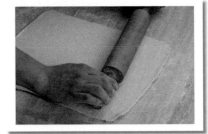

1 Roll out the chilled dough into a 13 by 10-inch (33 by 25 cm) rectangle ⅛ inch (4 mm) thick.

2 Cut the dough lengthwise in half into 2 13 by 5-inch (33 by 12 cm) rectangles.

3 Cut each rectangle crosswise into 5 by 3-inch (12 by 8 cm) rectangles.

4 Place a chocolate stick on a short end of each rectangle, leaving a ¾-inch (1.5 cm) border.

5 Fold the dough over the chocolate stick.

6 Place a second chocolate stick at the fold.

7 Roll the dough without crushing it.

8 Continue to roll.

9 Make sure that the fold is underneath the finished chocolate croissant.

10 Brush with egg glaze.

Lunettes à la Vanille
Vanilla Croissants

Vanilla Croissants

Follow steps 1 to 23 of the Buttery Croissants (page 624). Cover the dough with plastic wrap and chill for 1 hour.

On a lightly floured work surface, roll out the dough into a rectangle ⅛ inch (4 mm) thick (1).

Using a pastry cutter or sharp knife, cut the rectangle lengthwise into ¾-inch (1.5 cm) strips (2).

Transfer the strips to a baking sheet, cover with plastic wrap, and chill. Work with 1 strip at a time, leaving the rest refrigerated.

Line 2 baking sheets with parchment paper.

Holding both ends of a strip, twist it from end to end (3).

Pinch the 2 ends together (4) and fold back onto the bottom of the "U" to look like spectacles (5). Make sure the pastry is tightly twisted (6).

Place on the prepared baking sheets. Repeat with the remaining strips.

Cover loosely with plastic wrap and let rise in a warm place, no hotter than 86° F (30° C), until doubled in volume (7), about 2 hours.

Preheat the oven to 350° F (180° C).

Egg Glaze

Lightly beat the whole egg and egg yolk in a cup with a fork.

Light brush the puffy pastries with the egg glaze (8).

Spoon or pipe the pastry cream into the holes of the pastries (9).

Bake 1 sheet at a time for 12 to 15 minutes, or until golden brown.

Kirsch Syrup

Combine the confectioners' sugar with the kirsch in a small bowl.

Brush the hot pastries with a thin layer of the kirsch syrup while they are still hot (10).

Transfer to a rack and let cool.

Note: Replace the kirsch with water if you are preparing these pastries for children.

Makes about 15 pastries
Level: Advanced
Prep: 25 min.
Chill: 1 hr.
Rise: 2 hr.
Bake: 12 to 15 min. per sheet

Vanilla Croissants

½ recipe Buttery Croissants
    (page 624)
⅔ cup (7 oz., 200 g) pastry cream
    (page 672)

Egg Glaze

1 whole egg
1 egg yolk

Kirsch Syrup

¾ cup (3½ oz., 100 g)
    confectioners' sugar
2 tbsp. (25 ml) kirsch

1 Roll out the chilled dough into a rectangle ⅛ inch (4 mm) thick.

2 Cut the rectangle lengthwise into ¾-inch (1.5 cm) strips.

3 Twist the strips one at a time, leaving the rest chilled.

4 Pinch the ends together.

5 Fold them back onto the bottom of the "U" to look like spectacles.

6 This is the shape they should have.

7 This shows the pastry when it has risen.

8 Brush with the egg glaze.

9 Fill the holes with pastry cream.

10 Brush the hot pastries with the kirsch syrup.

Danish Pomme-Framboise
Apple-Raspberry Danish

Danish Pastry
Place the flour, sugar, salt, and powdered milk in a large bowl. Crumble in the yeast (1), making sure it does not touch the salt. Add the egg and water.

Knead with your hands (2) until the dough is firm.

Add the softened butter (3) and knead until it is incorporated (4).

The dough should be smooth and elastic (5).

Shape it into a ball, cover with plastic wrap, and chill until firm, at least 2 hours.

Almond Paste
Combine the ground almonds and confectioners' sugar in a medium bowl. Add the milk and egg yolks (6) and beat with a wooden spoon to make a firm paste (7).

Ten minutes before you begin working again, place the chilled butter in the freezer.

On a lightly floured work surface, roll out the dough into a rectangle ¼ inch (6 mm) thick (8).

Dust the chilled butter with flour. Roll out the butter into a rectangle half the size of the dough (9). (If the butter is soft, roll it out on a sheet of lightly dusted parchment paper.)

Makes about 1 ½ dozen pastries;
2 lb. (950 g) dough
Level: Intermediate
Prep: 40 min.
Chill: 4 hr.
Rise: 2 hr.
Bake: 12 to 15 min. per sheet

Danish Pastry

3 cups (13 oz., 375 g) all-purpose flour
2 tbsp. (1 oz., 25 g) sugar
2 tsp. (5 g) salt
2 tbsp. (½ oz, 15 g) powdered milk
1 ¼ cakes (.75 oz., 25 g) fresh yeast
1 jumbo egg
½ cup (115 ml) water
3 tbsp. (40 g) butter, softened
2 sticks (9 oz., 250 g) butter, chilled

Almond Paste

1 ¾ cups (5 oz., 150 g) ground almonds
Generous ½ cup (2¾ oz., 75 g) confectioners' sugar
2 tbsp. milk
2 egg yolks

Apple-Raspberry Filling

5 Golden Delicious apples
2 tbsp. sugar
2 tbsp. (30 g) butter
20 raspberries
2 tbsp. water

Sugar Syrup and Egg Glaze

¼ cup (2 oz., 50 g) sugar
3 ½ tbsp. (50 ml) water
1 whole egg
1 egg yolk

1 Place the flour, sugar, salt, powdered milk, and crumbled yeast in a large bowl.

2 Knead the ingredients by hand.

3 When the dough is smooth, add the softened butter.

4 Keep kneading.

5 The dough should be smooth and elastic.

6 Combine the ground almonds and confectioners' sugar in a bowl. Add the 2 egg yolks and milk.

7 Stir with a wooden spoon until a paste forms.

8 Roll out the dough into a rectangle.

9 Roll out the chilled butter until it is half the size of the dough.

continued

Arrange the dough with a short side facing you. Place the butter on the bottom half of the dough (10) and press it in. Fold the top half of the dough over the butter (11 and 12) to enclose it completely (13).

Rotate the dough clockwise 90° (a quarter-turn) so that an open edge is facing you. Roll out the dough lengthwise ¼ inch (7 mm) thick (14).

Fold up the bottom third of the dough so it covers one-third of the dough (15). Fold down the top third to meet the edge (16).

Fold the entire dough in half (17) to make a "double turn." This makes 4 layers of dough.

Cover with plastic wrap and chill for 1 hour.

On a lightly floured surface, arrange the dough with an open side facing you and the closed side to your right.

Roll out again into a rectangle about ¼ inch (7 mm) thick (18).

Fold the dough in thirds, like a letter (19 and 20). There are now 3 layers of dough.

Cover with plastic wrap and chill for 1 hour.

Cut the dough in half so it is easier to work with. Cover one half with plastic wrap and chill. Roll out the other half into a 12 by 7-inch (32 by 16 cm) rectangle ⅛ inch (4 mm) thick (21).

10 Arrange the butter on the bottom half of the dough and press it with your fingertips.

11 Fold the top half of the dough.

12 Fold it over the butter.

13 The butter should be completely enclosed.

14 Rotate the dough clockwise 90° (a quarter-turn) and roll it out into a rectangle ¼ inch (7 mm) thick.

15 Fold up the bottom third of the dough.

16 Fold down the top third down to meet the bottom third.

17 Fold the rectangle in half to make 4 layers.

18 Arrange the dough with an open side facing you and roll it out again ¼ inch (7 mm).

19 Fold up the bottom third.

20 Fold the top third over it, like a litter, to make 3 layers.

21 Cut the dough in half and roll out each piece into to a 12 by 7-inch (32 by 16 cm) rectangle ⅛ inch (4 mm) thick.

continued

Cut the rectangle lengthwise in half (22) to make 2 3-inch (8 cm) bands.
Using a pastry wheel or sharp knife, cut each into 3-inch (8 cm) squares (23).
Repeat with the remaining dough.

Place about 1 tsp. of the almond paste in the center of each square (24).
Fold each corner into the center (25, 26, and 27), pressing lightly with your fingertips. You should have squares with slightly open corners (28).

Line 2 baking sheets with parchment paper.
Arrange the pastries on the prepared baking sheets, spacing well apart.
Let rise in a warm place, no hotter than 86° F (30° C), until doubled in volume, about 2 hours.

Preheat the oven to 350° F (180° C).

Apple-Raspberry Filling
Peel and core the apples and cut them into large dice.
Melt the sugar in a large skillet over medium heat and cook, stirring, until it turns a medium amber color. Stir in the butter to stop the cooking.
Add the apples, raspberries, and water to the skillet (29) and cook over low heat, stirring occasionally, until the apples are red, 3 to 5 minutes (30).
Transfer to a shallow bowl and reserve at room temperature.

Sugar Syrup
Combine the sugar and water in a small saucepan. Cook over medium heat, stirring, until the sugar dissolves. Remove from the heat and let cool.

Egg Glaze
Lightly beat the whole egg and egg yolk in a cup with a fork.
Lightly brush the puffy pastries with the glaze (31).
Press a piece of apple in the center of each pastry (32).
Bake 1 sheet at a time for 12 to 15 minutes, or until golden brown.
Brush the pastries with the sugar syrup while they are still warm (33).
Transfer to a rack and let cool.

Notes: You can prepare the Danish pastries through step 28 and freeze them raw. Let them thaw in the refrigerator overnight, then proceed with the recipe. Dried fruit, peaches, or another fruit can be swapped for the apples.

22 Cut the rectangles in half.

23 Cut the 2 bands into 3-inch (8 cm) squares.

24 Place about 1 tsp. of almond paste in the center of each square.

25 Fold one corner into the center.

26 Fold the opposite corner into the center.

27 Press the third corner into the center.

28 This makes small, open-cornered squares.

29 Melt the sugar to a caramel, add the butter, and cook the diced apple and the raspberries.

30 Cook over low heat until the apples are tender, 3 to 5 minutes.

31 Lightly brush the puffy Danish pastries with egg glaze.

32 Place a piece of apple in the center of each Danish pastry.

33 As soon as the pastries come out of the oven, brush them with syrup.

Escargots aux Raisins et Noix
Raisin-Walnut Swirls

Raisin-Walnut Danish Pastry

Follow steps 1 to 20 of the Danish pastry (page 638), omitting steps 6 and 7. Chill the dough for 1 hour.

On a floured work surface, roll out the dough (1) into a rectangle ⅛ inch (4 mm) thick (2).

Whisk the pastry cream to loosen it. Spoon the pastry cream over the dough (3), then spread it evenly with a thin spatula (4), leaving a ¾-inch (1.5 cm) border on a long side (5).

Combine the dark and golden raisins with the walnuts and sprinkle them over the pastry cream (6).

Lightly press in the mixture with a rolling pin (7).

Lightly brush the border with water (8).

Makes about 1 dozen pastries
Level: Intermediate
Prep: 25 min.
Chill: 1 hr. 30 min.
Rise: 2 hr.
Bake: 12 to 15 min. per sheet

½ recipe Danish pastry (page 638)
⅔ cup (7 oz., 200 g) pastry cream (page 672)
⅓ cup (2 oz., 50 g) dark raisins
⅓ cup (2 oz., 50 g) golden raisins
2 oz. (50 g) chopped walnuts

Orange Flower Syrup

¼ cup (2 oz., 50 g) sugar
3½ tbsp. (50 ml) water
1 tbsp. orange flower water

Egg Glaze

1 whole egg
1 egg yolk

1 On a lightly floured surface, roll out the chilled Danish pastry dough.

2 Roll it into a rectangle ⅛ inch (4 mm) thick.

3 Spoon the pastry cream over the dough.

4 Spread it out in a layer with a thin spatula.

5 Leave a ¾-inch (1.5 cm) border on a long side.

6 Sprinkle with the raisins and chopped walnuts.

7 Lightly press them in with a rolling pin.

8 Moisten the border with a pastry brush dipped in water.

continued

Fold over ½ inch (1 cm) of the long side opposite the border (9 and 10).
Roll up the dough (11) as tightly as possible (12), working toward the border.
Press along the border to seal the dough (13).
Transfer to a baking sheet, cover with plastic wrap, and freeze until firm, about 30 minutes.

Line 2 baking sheets with parchment paper.
Using a bread knife (14), slice the roll ¾ inch (2 cm) thick (15).
Transfer the slices to the prepared baking sheets, spacing well apart.
Cover loosely with plastic wrap and let rise in a warm place, no hotter than 86° F (30° C), until doubled in volume, about 2 hours.

Preheat the oven to 350° F (180° C).

Orange Flower Syrup
Combine the sugar and water in a small saucepan. Cook over medium heat, stirring, until the sugar dissolves. Remove from the heat, let cool, and stir in the orange flower water.

Egg Glaze
Lightly beat the whole egg and yolk in a cup with a fork.

The pastries may unroll as they rise (16). Tuck the end of the dough underneath (17).
Lightly brush with the egg glaze (18).
Bake 1 sheet at a time for 12 to 15 minutes, or until golden brown.
Brush the pastries with the syrup while they are still warm (19).
Transfer to a rack and let cool.

Notes: You can prepare the pastries through step 15 and freeze them. Let them thaw them in the refrigerator overnight, then proceed with the recipe.

9 Begin folding a long side.

10 This will form the center of the roll.

11 Roll up the dough evenly toward yourself.

12 Roll as tightly as possible.

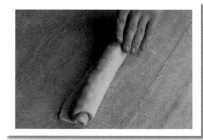

13 Press the moistened border to the pastry to seal the roll.

14 Cut slices with a bread knife.

15 Cut ¾ inch (2 cm) thick.

16 The buns might unroll as they rise.

17 Tuck the end of the dough under the pastry to reattach it.

18 Lightly brush with the egg glaze.

19 Brush the buns with syrup as soon as you remove them from the oven.

Pains au Lait
Milk Buns

Milk Buns

Crumble the yeast into a large bowl. Pour in the milk (1) and stir to dissolve the yeast.

Add the flour, sugar, and salt (2) and then the egg (3).

Stir with a wooden spoon (4) until a firm dough forms (5 and 6), 1 to 2 minutes.

Add the butter (7) and knead until smooth (8).

Knead or stir well with a wooden spoon until the dough pulls away from the sides of the bowl (9), 5 to 6 minutes.

Makes about 1½ dozen buns;
1 lb. (500 g) dough
Level: Easy
Prep: 30 min.
Rise: 3 hr.
Chill: 2 hr.
Bake: 8 to 10 min. per sheet

Milk Buns

½ cake (.3 oz., 10 g) fresh yeast
½ cup (115 ml) lukewarm milk
2 cups (9 oz., 250 g) all-purpose flour
2½ tbsp. (1 oz., 30 g) sugar
1 tsp. salt
1 egg
1 stick (4 oz., 115 g) butter, diced and softened

Sesame Glaze

1 whole egg
1 egg yolk
1 pinch salt
2 tbsp. (¾ oz., 20 g) sesame seeds

1 With a wooden spoon, dissolve the yeast in the milk.

2 Pour in the flour, sugar, and salt.

3 Add the egg.

4 Mix it in with the wooden spoon.

5 Continue until the dough is firm and smooth.

6 This is what it should look like.

7 Add the diced butter to the dough.

8 Knead it in with your hands.

9 Knead well until the dough pulls away from the sides of the bowl.

continued

The dough should be smooth and elastic (10).

Let the dough rise in the bowl (11) in a warm place until doubled in volume, about 1 hour. The ideal temperature is 77° F (25° C).

On a lightly floured work surface (12), flatten the dough into a rectangle with the palms of your hands (13).

Cover it with plastic wrap and chill until firm, about 2 hours.

Line 2 baking sheets with parchment paper.

On a lightly floured work surface, roll out the dough into a rectangle ½ inch (1 cm) thick (14).

Using a 2½-inch (6 cm) cookie cutter or a glass, stamp out rounds of dough (15).

Transfer the rounds to the prepared baking sheets (16).

Cover loosely with plastic wrap and let rise at room temperature until doubled in volume, about 2 hours.

Preheat the oven to 350° F (180° C).

Sesame Glaze

Lightly beat the whole egg, egg yolk, and salt in a cup with a fork.

Brush the puffy buns with the egg glaze (17) and sprinkle them with sesame seeds (18 and 19).

Bake 1 sheet at a time for 8 to 10 minutes, or until golden brown.

Transfer to a rack and let cool.

Notes: Serve the buns plain or, if you like, slice them in half when cool, spread with a little berry jam, and fill with raspberries and sliced strawberries. Pass a bowl of sweetened whipped cream separately.

These buns also make excellent hamburger rolls.

You can make the buns in larger sizes and use them for sandwiches. If you choose this option, roll out the dough in step 14 about 1 inch (2.5 cm) thick.

The dough can also be prepared in a stand mixer fitted with the dough hook. Follow the same steps.

Shape any leftover dough into a round loaf of milk bread. Let it rise for 2 hours and bake at 350° F (180° C) for 10 to 15 minutes.

10 The dough should be smooth and elastic.

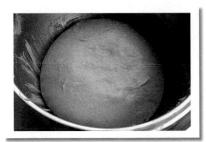

11 Let it rise in a warm place until it doubles in volume, about 1 hour.

12 Transfer the risen dough to a lightly floured work surface.

13 Flatten it into a rectangle.

14 Lightly dust the work surface again and roll out the dough ½ inch (1 cm) thick.

15 Stamp out 2 ½-inch (6 cm) rounds.

16 Transfer the rounds to a lined baking sheet and let rise for 2 hours.

17 Brush the tops with the beaten egg.

18 Sprinkle with sesame seeds.

19 This is a bun ready for baking.

Pains au Lait Navettes
Sweet Dinner Rolls

Follow steps 1 to 11 of the Milk Buns (page 648). Let the dough rise in the bowl in a warm place until doubled in volume, about 1 hour. The ideal temperature is 77° F (25° C).

On a lightly floured work surface, flatten the dough into a rectangle with the palms of your hands.
Cover it with plastic wrap and chill until firm, about 2 hours.

Cut the dough into 8 equal rectangles each about 1 oz. (30 g) (1).
Transfer to a baking sheet and chill for 10 minutes.

Remove the dough rectangles from the refrigerator one at a time to shape.
Place a small mound of flour on the work surface.
Using one hand, flatten the rectangle in the flour (2).
Fold 1 long side into the center (3), then the other side (4).
Fold the dough lengthwise in half to make a smooth log shape (5).
Return the shaped dough to the refrigerator and repeat with the remaining dough.

Line a baking sheet with parchment paper.
On a lightly floured work surface, roll a piece of shaped dough with your fingertips (6) until it is 3 to 4 inches (8 to 10 cm) long (7).
Arrange the roll on the prepared baking sheet with the fold on the bottom. Repeat with the remaining dough, spacing the rolls well apart.

Cover loosely with plastic wrap and let rise in a warm place, no hotter than 86° F (30° C), until doubled in volume, about 2 hours.

Preheat the oven to 350° F (180° C).

Lightly beat the whole egg and egg yolk in a cup with a fork.
Lightly brush the puffy rolls with the egg glaze (8).
If you wish to decorate the rolls, dip the blades of a scissors in cold water (9).
Holding the scissors at a slight angle, snip regular incisions in the tops (10).
Bake for 8 minutes, or until golden brown.
Transfer the rolls to a rack and let cool. Serve plain or filled.

Note: You can use half the recipe for Milk Buns (page 648), as indicated, but it is more practical to make the full quantity and save the remaining dough for another recipe.

Makes about 10 rolls
Level: Easy
Prep: 20 min.
Rise: 3 hr.
Chill: about 2 hr.
Bake: 8 min.

½ recipe Milk Buns (page 648)
1 whole egg
1 egg yolk

1 Cut the dough into 8 rectangles, each about 1 oz. (30 g).

2 Remove the pieces of dough one at a time from the refrigerator to flatten them in the flour.

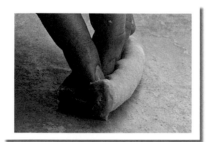

3 Fold one long side into the center.

4 Fold the other long side into the center.

5 Fold the dough lengthwise in half to make a smooth log shape.

6 Roll the first shaped piece of dough with your fingertips.

7 The log should be 3 to 4 inches (8 to 10 cm) long.

8 Lightly brush the puffy bread rolls with beaten egg.

9 Dip the tips of a pair of scissors in cold water.

10 Snip the tops to decorate.

Kouglof Sucré aux Raisins
Almond-Raisin Coffee Cake

Rum Raisins
Soak the raisins in the rum in a small bowl (1) at room temperature until plump; drain.

Kouglof Pastry
Crumble the yeast into the bowl of a stand mixer fitted with a dough hook. Pour in the water (2) and whisk to dissolve the yeast.

Add ½ cup (2 oz., 50 g) of the flour (3) and whisk until a firm ball of dough forms (4).

Cover this starter with the remaining flour (5) and let rise in a warm place until the starter has risen underneath the flour, about 30 minutes (see *Notes*).

Garnish
Butter the molds (6). Sprinkle the almonds in the indentations at the bottom (7).

Tap out any excess.

When the starter is ready, there will be cracks in the flour above it (8).

Add the egg, milk, sugar, salt, and butter to the bowl (9).

Makes 2 5-inch (12 cm) kouglofs;
1 lb. 5 oz. (600 g) dough
Level: Intermediate
Prep: 30 min.
Rise: about 4½ hr.
Bake: 20 to 25 min.

Special equipment
2 5-inch (12 cm) kouglof molds
or fluted Bundt pans

Rum Raisins

⅓ cup (2 oz., 50 g) raisins
1 tbsp. dark rum

Kouglof Pastry

½ cake (.3 oz., 10 g) fresh yeast
2 tbsp. plus 1 tsp. (35 ml) lukewarm
  water
2¼ cups (10 oz., 275 g) all-purpose
  flour
1 egg
½ cup (125 ml) lukewarm milk
3 ½ tbsp. (1 ½ oz., 40 g) sugar
1 tsp. salt
4 tbsp. (2 oz., 65 g) butter, softened

Garnish

⅔ cup (2 oz., 50 g) sliced blanched
  almonds
⅓ cup (2 oz., 50 g) confectioners'
  sugar

1 Soak the raisins in the rum.

2 Crumble the yeast into the bowl of a stand mixer and whisk in the water.

3 Stir in the flour.

4 The ingredients should come together to form a firm ball of dough.

5 Cover the starter with the remaining flour.

6 Brush the molds with melted butter.

7 Sprinkle the almonds into the bottom of the molds and tap out any excess.

8 When the starter has risen sufficiently, the flour above it will show cracks.

9 Add the egg, milk, sugar, salt, and softened butter.

continued

Knead the dough at low speed for 7 to 8 minutes. Increase the speed to high and knead until the dough is smooth and elastic and pulls away from the sides of the bowl, 2 to 3 minutes (10).

Add the drained raisins (11) and knead them briefly into the dough until evenly distributed. Or knead by hand.

The dough should be soft, elastic, and not at all sticky (12).

Let rise in a warm place until doubled in volume, about 2 hours (13).

On a lightly floured work surface (14), cut the dough in half.

Working with your fingertips, shape each half into a ball (15). Work as quickly and as lightly as possible.

Place the dough in the prepared molds (16), pressing them in lightly (17).

Let rise in a warm place until doubled in volume, about 2 hours.

Preheat the oven to 340° F (170° C).

When the dough completely fills the pans (18), bake for 20 to 25 minutes, or until golden brown and a cake tester comes out clean.

Invert the cakes onto racks and let cool completely. Sift the confectioners' sugar over the tops.

Notes: Bakers in Alsace often cover the starter with additional flour before letting it rise instead of using plastic wrap. The extra flour is later beaten into the starter to make the dough.

You can brush the cakes with melted butter while they are still warm from the oven and sprinkle them with cinnamon sugar.

This Alsatian specialty is traditionally made using a turbanlike, hand-painted earthenware mold; a Bundt pan works just as well.

10 Knead the dough at low speed for 7 to 8 minutes, then at high speed for 2 to 3 minutes, or until it pulls away from the sides of the bowl.

11 Add the drained raisins.

12 Knead them in briefly until the dough looks like this.

13 The dough should double in volume.

14 On a lightly floured work surface, cut the dough in half.

15 Working as quickly and lightly as possible, shape each half into a ball.

16 Place the balls in the molds.

17 Press down lightly.

18 The dough should amply fill the molds before baking.

Brioches à Tête
Parisian Brioches

Brioche Pastry

Place the flour, sugar, and salt in the bowl of a stand mixer fitted with the dough hook. Crumble in the yeast, making sure it does not touch the salt (1).

Add the eggs (2) and knead at low speed until a dense dough forms, 2 to 3 minutes.

Add the butter (3) and incorporate at medium speed (4).

Continue kneading until the dough is elastic (5) and pulls away from the sides of the bowl, 5 to 10 minutes. Or knead by hand.

Stop when you can hold the dough in your hand and it keeps its shape (6).

Cover the bowl with a clean kitchen towel and let rise at room temperature until doubled in volume, about 1 hour.

On a lightly floured work surface, shape the dough into a loaf (7).

Cover with plastic wrap and chill until firm and cold, about 2 hours.

Cut the dough into 20 to 30 pieces (8), each about 2 oz. (30 to 40 g).

Transfer to a baking sheet and chill for 10 minutes.

Makes about 2 dozen
individual brioches;
1 lb. 5 oz. (600 g) dough
Level: Advanced
Prep: 35 min.
Rise: 3 hr.
Chill: 2 hr.
Bake: 10 to 12 min. per sheet

Special equipment
24 individual brioche molds

Brioche Pastry

2 cups (9 oz., 250 g) all-purpose
    flour
2½ tbsp. (1 oz., 30 g) sugar
1 tsp. salt
½ cake (.3 oz., 10 g) fresh yeast
3 eggs
1 stick plus 3 tbsp. (6 oz., 165 g)
    butter, diced and softened

Egg Glaze

2 egg yolks

1 Place the flour, sugar, and salt in the bowl of a stand mixer. Crumble in the yeast, making sure it does not touch the salt.

2 Knead in the eggs at low speed.

3 Add the softened butter to the dense dough.

4 Knead at medium speed.

5 The dough should be smooth and elastic.

6 The dough keeps its shape when you hold it in your hand.

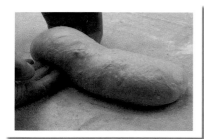

7 On a lightly floured surface, roll the dough to a long loaf.

8 Cut it into 20 to 30 pieces. Dust with flour on both sides.

continued

Remove the pieces of dough from the refrigerator one at a time to shape.

Dust a piece of dough on both sides with flour. Flatten it with the palm of your hand (9).

Cup your hand and roll the dough on the work surface into a ball (10).

Return the shaped dough to the refrigerator and repeat with the remaining dough.

Butter the molds and place on baking sheets.

On a lightly floured work surface, roll each ball into a small log (11).

Place the edge of your hand one-third of the way along the log (12) and gently roll the log back and forth to shape the "head" (13).

Place each brioche in a prepared mold, pinching it around the "head" (14).

Repeat with the remaining dough.

With a flour-dipped finger, press into the space between the "head" and the "body" (15). Your finger should touch the bottom of the mold. Work your finger around the "head" (16) to separate it completely from the "body" (17).

Let rise until doubled in volume, about 2 hours (18).

Preheat the oven to 350° F (180° C).

Egg Glaze
Lightly beat the egg yolks in a cup with a fork.

Brush the tops of the puffy brioches with the egg glaze (19).

Bake 1 sheet at a time for 10 to 12 minutes, or until golden brown.

Let the brioches cool slightly in the molds. Transfer to racks and let cool completely.

9 Flatten each piece with the palm of your hand.

10 Cup your hand and roll the dough into a ball.

11 Roll the ball into a log.

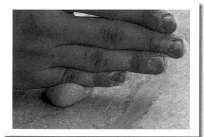

12 Place the edge of your hand one-third of the way along the log and make back-and-forth movements.

13 This shapes the "body" and the "head."

14 Pinch the head as you place each piece of dough in a buttered mold.

15 Dip your finger in flour and crook it to separate the head from the body.

16 Reach down to the bottom of the mold as you move your finger around the head.

17 This is what the Parisian brioche should look like.

18 This shows the brioches when they have risen.

19 Lightly brush with egg glaze.

Brioches Nid d'Abeille
Honey-Almond Brioches

Honey-Almond Brioches
Follow steps 1 to 7 of the Parisian Brioches (page 658). Cover with plastic wrap and chill until firm, about 2 hours. If the weather is hot, place it in the freezer for 10 minutes.

Line a baking sheet with parchment paper.

On a lightly floured work surface, roll out the dough into a 17-inch (44 cm) square about ¼ inch (6 mm) thick (1). To make this easier, roll it out on a sheet of floured parchment paper.

To make 2 large brioches, cut out 8-inch (22 cm) rounds, using a tart ring or a plate as a guide (2).

To make individual brioches, stamp out 3-inch (8 cm) rounds, using a cookie cutter or a glass as a guide (3).

Transfer the rounds of dough to the prepared baking sheet. Cover loosely with plastic wrap and let rise at room temperature until doubled in volume, about 2 hours.

Heat the honey and sugar in a medium heavy saucepan over medium heat. Grate in the orange zest (4). Stir in the butter (5) and let boil for 10 seconds (6). Add the almonds and stir to coat (7).

Remove from the heat and let cool.

Preheat the oven to 350° F (180° C).

Egg Glaze
Lightly beat the whole egg and egg yolk in a cup with a fork.

Brush the puffy brioches with the egg glaze (8).

Place the honey-almond mixture on the brioches, using a spoon for the small ones (9) or a thin spatula for the large ones, leaving a ½-inch (1 cm) border (10).

Bake the small brioches for 10 minutes and the large brioches for 15 minutes, or until golden on the sides and underneath.

Transfer to a rack and let cool.

Note: To measure honey easily, lightly brush the measuring spoon or cup with neutral oil; the honey will slip right out.

Makes 2 8-inch (22 cm) brioches
or 12 small brioches
Level: Advanced
Prep: 15 min.
Chill: 2 hr.
Rise: 2 hr.
Bake: 10 to 15 min.

Honey-Almond Brioches

1 recipe Parisian Brioches
(page 658)
⅓ cup (3½ oz., 100 g) honey
(see *Note*)
½ cup (3½ oz., 100 g) sugar
1 orange
7 tbsp. (3½ oz., 100 g) butter
1⅓ cups (4 oz., 100 g) sliced
blanched almonds

Egg Glaze

1 whole egg
1 egg yolk

1 Roll out the chilled brioche dough into a to 17-inch (44 cm) square about ¼ inch (6 mm) thick.

2 Cut out 2 8-inch (22 cm) rounds of dough to make large brioches.

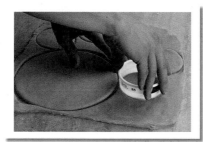

3 Or stamp out 12 3-inch (8 cm) rounds to make small brioches.

4 Heat the honey and sugar with the orange zest over medium heat.

5 Stir in the butter.

6 Let boil for 10 seconds.

7 Add the sliced almonds and stir to coat.

8 Brush the rounds of puffy dough with the egg glaze.

9 Place the honey-almond mixture in the center.

10 Leave a ½-inch (1 cm) border.

Triangles aux Fruits Secs
Nut-Filled Brioche Triangles

Nut Triangles

Follow steps 1 to 11 of the Milk Buns (page 648). Cover the bowl with a clean kitchen towel and let rise at room temperature until doubled in volume, about 1 hour.

On a lightly floured work surface, flatten the dough into a rectangle.

Cover with plastic wrap and chill until firm, at least 1 hour.

Coarsely chop the nuts and combine them in a small bowl.

Whisk the pastry cream to loosen it. This makes it easier to spread.

Line a baking sheet with parchment paper.

On a lightly floured work surface or floured sheet of parchment paper, roll out the dough into a large rectangle about ⅛ inch (4 mm) thick (1).

Fold it lengthwise in half to make a visible crease (2), then unfold it. Spoon the pastry cream over one half of the dough (3) and spread it evenly from crease to edge with a thin spatula (4).

Sprinkle the nuts (5) evenly over the pastry cream.

Fold over the plain dough to cover the pastry cream (6). Smooth the top with your hand to eliminate any air pockets (7).

Transfer the filled rectangle to the prepared baking sheet (8).

Cover loosely with plastic wrap and let rise at room temperature for 2 hours 30 minutes.

Preheat the oven to 350° F (180° C).

Egg Glaze

Lightly beat the egg and egg yolk in a cup with a fork.

Brush the puffy dough with the egg glaze (9).

Bake for 12 to 15 minutes, or until golden brown on the top and bottom.

Transfer to a rack and let cool.

Place on a cutting board and cut into squares, then triangles (10).

Makes about 1 dozen pastries
Level: Intermediate
Prep: 25 min.
Rise: 2 hr. 30 min.
Chill: 1 hr.
Bake: 12 to 15 min.

Nut Triangles

1 recipe Milk Buns (page 648)
⅓ cup (2 oz., 60 g) hazelnuts
⅓ cup (2 oz., 60 g) almonds
⅓ cup (2 oz., 60 g) walnuts or pecans
⅔ cup (7 oz., 200 g) pastry cream (page 672), chilled

Egg Glaze

1 whole egg
1 egg yolk

1 Roll out the dough into a rectangle about ⅛ inch (4 mm) thick.

2 Fold it lengthwise in half to make a visible crease in the center.

3 Unfold and spoon the pastry cream on one half.

4 Spread it with a thin spatula.

5 Sprinkle evenly with the nuts.

6 Fold over so that one side meets the other.

7 Pat out any air pockets.

8 Transfer the rectangle to a prepared baking sheet.

9 Brush the risen dough with the egg glaze.

10 Cut the baked pastry lengthwise in half, then into squares, and last, into triangles.

Rectangles Briochés au Sucre
Sugar Brioche Squares

Sugar Brioches

Follow steps 1 to 6 of the Parisian Brioches (page 658). Cover the bowl with a clean kitchen towel and let rise at room temperature until doubled in volume, about 1 hour.

On a lightly floured work surface, flatten the dough into a rectangle. Cover with plastic wrap and chill until firm, at least 1 hour.

Line a baking sheet with parchment paper.

On a lightly floured work surface, roll out the dough into a rectangle about ⅛ inch (4 mm) thick (1). Cut crosswise into 2 ¾-inch (7 cm) bands (2). Trim the edges (3) and cut the bands crosswise into rectangles 2 inches (5 cm) wide (4).

Use the first rectangle you cut as a template for the others (5).

Place the rectangles of dough on the prepared baking sheet, spacing them well apart (6).

Cover loosely with plastic wrap and let rise at room temperature until doubled in volume (7), about 2 hours 30 minutes.

Preheat the oven to 350° F (180° C).

Egg Glaze

Lightly beat the egg and egg yolk with a fork.

Brush the puffy brioches with the egg glaze (8) and sprinkle with the pearl sugar (9).

Bake for 10 to 12 minutes, or until puffed and golden.

Transfer to a rack, let cool to lukewarm, and serve.

Note: If you don't have pearl sugar, substitute coarse sugar or light brown sugar.

Makes about 1½ dozen pastries
Level: Advanced
Prep: 20 min.
Chill: at least 1 hr.
Rise: about 3 hr. 30 min.
Bake: 10 to 12 min.

Sugar Brioches

1 recipe Parisian Brioches
  (page 658)
5 oz. (150 g) pearl sugar (see *Note*)

Egg Glaze

1 whole egg
1 egg yolk

1 Roll out the dough into a rectangle about ⅛ inch (4 mm) thick.

2 Cut into 2¾ inch (7 cm) bands.

3 Trim the edges.

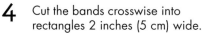

4 Cut the bands crosswise into rectangles 2 inches (5 cm) wide.

5 Use the first rectangle as a template for cutting the others.

6 Transfer to a prepared baking sheet, spacing them well apart.

7 This shows the rectangles when they have risen.

8 Brush them with egg glaze.

9 Sprinkle with pearl sugar.

Brioches Tressées
Braided Brioches

Braided Brioches
Follow steps 1 to 7 of the Parisian Brioches (page 658).

On a lightly floured work surface, flatten the dough with the palms of your hands into a rectangle. Cut it into 6 equal 3½-oz. (100 g) rectangles.

You will need 3 rectangles to make each braided loaf (1). Transfer the remaining dough to a plate and chill while making the first loaf.

Line a baking sheet with parchment paper.

On a lightly floured work surface, roll a rectangle of dough with both hands into a rope 10 inches (25 cm) long (2 and 3). Repeat with the 2 other pieces.

Place the 3 strands of dough side by side. Spread the 2 outer strands to make a fan shape (4).

Place the strand on the right between the 2 strands on the left (5).

Place the strand on the left between the 2 on the right (6) and repeat by placing the strand on the right between the 2 on the left. Continue until the loaf is half braided (7).

Pinch the tips together (8).

Makes 2 loaves
Level: Advanced
Prep: 15 min.
Rise: 2 to 3 hr.
Bake: 12 to 15 min.

1 recipe Parisian Brioches
(page 658)

2 egg yolks
1 pinch salt

1 Cut the brioche dough into 6 rectangles, each about 3½ oz. (100 g).

2 On a lightly floured surface, roll each rectangle into a rope.

3 Continue rolling to a length of 10 inches (25 cm).

4 Arrange 3 pieces side by side and turn the 2 outer strands outwards to make a fan shape.

5 Place the strand on the right between the 2 on the left.

6 Place the strand on the left between the 2 on the right.

7 Continue until half the loaf is braided.

8 Pinch the ends together to join them.

continued

Take the braided half in your hand and pivot it around so that the 3 unbraided strands are facing you (9 and 10).

Continue by placing the strand on the right over the 2 strands on the left (11), and the strand on the left over the strands on the right (12). Continue until you reach the end and pinch the tips together (13).

Transfer the braided loaf to the prepared baking sheet (14).

Repeat with the 3 remaining pieces of dough to make the second loaf.

Cover loosely with plastic wrap and let rise in a warm place until doubled in volume, 2 to 3 hours.

You can also make 1 long braid and shape it into a wreath (15).

Preheat the oven to 350° F (180° C).

Egg Glaze

Lightly beat the 2 egg yolks and salt in a cup with a fork.

Brush the puffy brioches with the egg glaze (16) and bake for 12 to 15 minutes, or until lightly browned.

Transfer to a rack and let cool.

9 Take the braided half in your hand.

10 Pivot it so that the unbraided side is facing you.

11 Continue braiding: place the strand on the right between the 2 on the left.

12 Place the strand on the left between the 2 on the right.

13 When you reach the end, pinch the 3 strands together.

14 Transfer to a lined baking sheet.

15 You can also make a longer braid and shape it to make a wreath.

16 When the loaves have doubled in volume, brush them with the egg glaze.

Brioches Suisses
Pastry Cream–Filled Brioches

Chocolate Chip Brioches

Follow steps 1 to 6 of the Parisian Brioches (page 658).

Cover the bowl with a clean kitchen towel and let the dough rise for 1 hour.

Flatten the dough into a rectangle.

Cover in plastic wrap and chill for 40 minutes, then freeze for 20 minutes. Or, if you have the time, chill it in the refrigerator until firm, about 2 hours.

Pastry Cream

Split the vanilla bean lengthwise in half and scrape out the seeds.

Combine the milk, butter, and vanilla bean and seeds in a medium heavy saucepan. Bring to a boil over medium heat.

Whisk the egg yolks with the sugar in a medium bowl until the sugar dissolves. Whisk in the cornstarch and flour.

Strain the hot milk into the egg-sugar mixture, whisking constantly (1).

Return the mixture to the saucepan (2) and cook, stirring or whisking constantly, until the cream thickens (3).

Remove the pan from the heat and scrape the pastry cream into a shallow bowl. Press a piece of plastic wrap directly on the surface and chill completely.

On a lightly floured cold work surface or a floured sheet of parchment paper, roll out the dough into a rectangle about ⅛ inch (4 to 5 mm) thick (4).

Cover with plastic wrap and freeze until cold, a few minutes.

Whisk the pastry cream to loosen it.

On a lightly floured surface, fold the dough lengthwise in half to make a visible crease, then unfold it. Spread the pastry cream with a thin spatula (5) over half of the rectangle (6). The layer of cream should be no thicker than about ⅛ inch (4 to 5 mm).

Makes 8 to 10 individual pastries
Level: Advanced
Prep: 25 min.
Rise: 2 hr. 30 min.
Chill: 1 to 2 hr.
Bake: 10 to 12 min.

1 recipe Parisian Brioches
   (page 658)
⅔ cup (4 oz., 120 g) chocolate chips

½ vanilla bean
1 cup (250 ml) milk
1 tsp. butter
2 egg yolks
¼ cup (2 oz., 50 g) sugar
2 tbsp. (20 g) cornstarch
1 tbsp. all-purpose flour

¼ cup (2 oz., 50 g) sugar
3½ tbsp. (50 ml) water
1 tbsp. orange flower water

1 whole egg
1 egg yolk

1 Whisk the hot milk with the butter and vanilla into the egg-sugar mixture.

2 Return this mixture to the saucepan over medium heat.

3 Stir constantly until thickened.

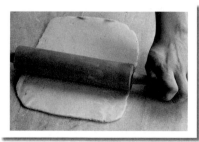

4 Roll out the dough into a rectangle ⅛ inch (4 to 5 mm) thick.

5 Spread the whipped pastry cream.

6 Cover one half of the dough.

continued

Line a baking sheet with parchment paper.

Sprinkle the chocolate chips over the cream (7), making sure that they are evenly distributed (8).

Lightly press them in with a rolling pin (9).

Fold the plain dough over the dough with the cream (10) and press lightly with your hands to remove any air pockets (11).

Smooth the pastry with a rolling pin (12).

With a sharp knife, cut the dough into rectangles 1¼ to 1½ inches (3 to 4 cm) wide (13).

Place the pastries on the prepared baking sheet, spacing well apart (14).

Cover loosely with plastic wrap and let rise at room temperature for 2 hours 30 minutes.

Orange Flower Syrup
Combine the sugar and water in a small saucepan. Cook over medium heat, stirring, until the sugar dissolves. Remove from the heat, let cool, and stir in the orange flower water.

Preheat the oven to 350° F (180° C).

Egg Glaze
Lightly beat the egg and egg yolk in a cup with a fork.

Brush the puffy brioches with the egg glaze (15).

Bake for 10 to 12 minutes, or until golden brown.

While the brioches are still warm, brush them with the orange flower syrup (16).

Transfer to a rack and let cool slightly.

Notes: If you don't have a marble board, chill your work surface with an ice pack.
The syrup adds a delicate flavor to the brioches but isn't required.
You can replace the chocolate chips with chopped chocolate or diced candied orange peel (page 452).

7 Sprinkle the pastry cream with chocolate chips.

8 The chocolate chips should be evenly distributed.

9 Press them in lightly with a rolling pin.

10 Fold the plain dough over the chocolate chip cream.

11 Press out any air pockets with your hands.

12 Flatten with a rolling pin to make a well-shaped rectangle.

13 Cut rectangles 1¼ to 1½ inches (3 to 4 cm) wide.

14 Let them rise on a prepared baking sheet.

15 Brush with the egg glaze.

16 Brush the hot Swiss Brioches with syrup.

Brioche aux Noix de Pécan et à la Cannelle

Pecan-Cinnamon Brioche Loaf

Pecan-Cinnamon Brioche

Follow steps 1 to 6 of the Parisian Brioches (page 658). As soon as the dough has been kneaded and is elastic and smooth, add the cinnamon and pecans (1).

Knead in with your hands until evenly distributed (2).

Cover with a clean kitchen towel and let rise at room temperature until doubled in volume, about 1 hour.

Butter the loaf pan.

On a lightly floured work surface, flatten the dough into a rectangle (3 and 4).

Cut it into 4 equal pieces (5).

Roll each piece into a ball in your hands (6).

Place the 4 balls side by side in the prepared loaf pan (7).

Cover with plastic wrap and let rise for 3 hours at room temperature, until doubled in volume.

Preheat the oven to 340° F (170° C).

Egg Glaze

Lightly beat the egg and salt in a cup with a fork.

Brush the puffy brioche with the egg glaze (8).

Dip the blades of a scissors in cold water (9) and snip the top of each ball (10), dipping the scissors in water each time so that the dough does not stick to the blades.

Bake the loaf for about 20 minutes, or until golden brown.

Let cool slightly in the pan, then transfer to a rack and let cool completely.

Note: You can also omit the cinnamon or substitute other nuts.

Makes 1 9-inch (28 cm) loaf
Level: Advanced
Prep: 20 min.
Rise: 4 hr.
Bake: about 20 min.

Special equipment
A 9 by 4½-inch (28 cm) loaf pan

Pecan-Cinnamon Brioche

1 recipe Parisian Brioches (page 658)
¼ cup (1 oz., 30 g) ground cinnamon
3½ oz. (100 g) pecans, coarsely chopped

Egg Glaze

1 egg
1 pinch salt

1 Add the cinnamon and pecans to the smooth, elastic dough.

2 Knead them in by hand.

3 Flatten the dough to remove the air pockets.

4 Shape into a rectangle. Be careful not to overwork the dough.

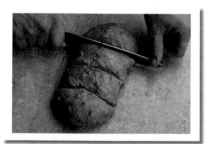

5 Cut it into 4 equal pieces.

6 Roll each piece into a ball between your hands.

7 Place the balls in the buttered loaf pan.

8 Brush the risen dough with the egg glaze.

9 Dip the tips of a pair of scissors in cold water.

10 Make an incision in the center of each ball, dipping the scissors in water each time.

Brioche Cœur Streusel
Heart-Shaped Streusel Brioche

Coconut-Blueberry Brioche
Follow steps 1 to 7 of the Parisian Brioches (page 658). On a lightly floured work surface, flatten the dough into a square. Cover with plastic wrap and chill until firm, about 2 hours.

Line a baking sheet with parchment paper.
On a lightly floured work surface, roll out the dough about ¼ inch (6 mm) thick (1).
Stamp out a heart or round shape (2) or use a sharp knife to cut the shape.
Remove the excess dough (3) and reserve for another use.
Transfer the heart to the prepared baking sheet. Cover with plastic wrap and let rise at room temperature until doubled in volume, about 2 hours.

Peel, quarter, and core the pears. Cut them into ½-inch (1 cm) dice. Squeeze some of the lemon juice on them to keep them from browning.

Place the sugar in a medium skillet and cook over medium heat (4), stirring with a wooden spoon, until it caramelizes.

Add the butter, diced pear (5), and cinnamon (6). Reduce the heat to low and cook, stirring occasionally, until the pear is coated in the caramel, about 5 minutes.

Makes 1 9-inch (24 cm) heart
or round cake
Level: Advanced
Prep: 20 min.
Chill: 2 hr.
Rise: about 2 hr.
Bake: about 15 min.

Special equipment
A 9-inch (24 cm) heart
or round cake ring

Cinnamon-Blueberry Brioche

1 recipe Parisian Brioches
(page 658)
3 firm, ripe pears, such as Comice
½ lemon
1½ tbsp. (⅔ oz., 20 g) light brown
sugar
1 tsp. butter
1 tsp. ground cinnamon
20 blueberries, fresh or frozen

Coconut Streusel

3 tbsp. (2 oz., 50 g) butter
¼ cup (2 oz., 50 g) sugar
⅔ cup (2 oz., 50 g) unsweetened
shredded coconut
½ cup (2 oz., 50 g) all-purpose flour
1 pinch salt

Egg Glaze

1 egg

Decoration

Confectioners' sugar, for sifting

1 Roll out the dough about ¼ inch (6 mm) thick.

2 Stamp or cut out a heart.

3 Remove the excess dough.

4 Cook the light brown sugar until it forms a caramel.

5 Add the diced pears and butter.

6 Sprinkle with cinnamon and cook over low heat for 5 minutes.

continued

Preheat the oven to 340° C (170° C).

Coconut Streusel
Place the butter, sugar, coconut, flour, and salt in a medium bowl (7).
Squeeze the ingredients together with your hands, then knead when they begin to come together. Using your fingertips, crumble the dough into small clumps. You can also do this on a work surface (8).

Egg Glaze
Lightly beat the egg in a cup with a fork.

Brush the puffy dough with the egg glaze (9).
Press the blueberries evenly into the dough (10).
Spoon the pear mixture over the top, leaving a ½-inch (1 cm) border (11).
Sprinkle the coconut streusel on top (12) and bake for about 15 minutes, or until the brioche is puffed and golden brown.

Transfer the brioche to a rack and let cool. Sift the confectioners' sugar over the top and serve.

Note: You can also make this recipe in a round or square shape, without cutting it out.

7 Place the streusel ingredients in a medium bowl: butter, sugar, coconut, flour, and salt.

8 Rub together with your fingertips until large crumbs form.

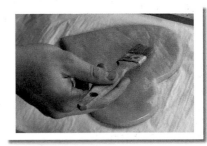

9 Brush the risen brioche with the beaten egg.

10 Press the blueberries into the dough, distributing them evenly.

11 Spoon the caramelized pears over the top of the brioche.

12 Sprinkle with the streusel.

Pognes aux Pralines Roses
Pink Almond Praline Brioches

Pink Almond Praline Buns

Coarsely chop the praline with a large knife or in a food processor (1).

Follow steps 1 to 7 of the Parisian Brioches (page 658).

On a lightly floured work surface, flatten the dough into a rectangle (2).

Sprinkle it with the chopped pralines (3). Fold the dough lengthwise in half to enclose the pralines (4).

Knead until they are evenly distributed (5) and shape the dough into a ball.

Cut into 8 equal pieces, each about 3½ oz. (100 g) (6). Transfer to a baking sheet and chill for 10 minutes.

Makes 8 large brioches
Level: Advanced
Prep: 20 min.
Chill: 2 hr.
Rise: at least 2 hr. 30 min.
Bake: 15 min.

3½ oz. (100 g) pink almond praline
   (pralines roses) or Jordan almonds
1 recipe Parisian Brioches
   (page 658)

1 whole egg
1 egg yolk
Pink almond praline (pralines roses),
   Jordan almonds, or chopped or
   sliced almonds (optional)

1 Coarsely chop the pink pralines.

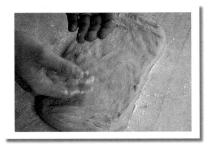

2 Flatten the dough into a rectangle on the floured work surface.

3 Sprinkle a strip of pink pralines down the center.

4 Fold the dough lengthwise in half.

5 Knead well to distribute the pink pralines evenly.

6 Cut the dough into 8 equal portions.

7 On a lightly floured work surface, work with one piece at a time.

continued

Line a baking sheet with parchment paper.

Remove the pieces of dough from the refrigerator one at a time to shape.

On a lightly floured work surface (7), flatten a piece of dough with the palm of your hand (8).

Cup your hand (9) and roll the dough on the work surface into a ball (10, 11, and 12).

Transfer the shaped dough to the prepared baking sheet (13 and 14) and repeat with the remaining dough.

Cover lightly with plastic wrap and let rise at room temperature until doubled in volume, at least 2 hours 30 minutes.

Preheat the oven to 350° F (180° C).

Egg Glaze
Lightly beat the whole egg and egg yolk in a cup with a fork.
Brush each brioche with the egg glaze (15 and 16).

There are various ways to finish these buns: press a pink praline or Jordan almond into the center of each brioche (17), sprinkle with chopped or sliced almonds (18), or simply leave them plain (19).

Bake for about 15 minutes, or until golden brown.

Transfer to a rack and let cool.

Notes: You can make small buns by cutting the dough into 10 or even 16 pieces.
You can also prepare this recipe using a loaf pan or other mold.
Plain pognes, *dating back to the Middle Ages, are a specialty of the Drôme region in southeastern France. When they are made with chocolate-coated nuts, they are known as Saint-Génix.*

8 Flatten each piece of dough with the palm of your hand.

9 Begin shaping the dough on the work surface.

10 Cup your hand and roll.

11 Make small circular movements on the work surface until the dough is smooth.

12 They should be shaped like balls.

13 Carefully pick them up.

14 Transfer to the prepared baking sheet.

15 Brush the balls with egg glaze.

16 Apply the egg glaze lightly.

17 To garnish, insert a whole praline in the center.

18 Or sprinkle with chopped almonds.

19 You can also leave them plain.

Bugnes
Angel Wing Fritters

Follow steps 1 to 7 of the Parisian Brioches (page 658), using half the butter.

On a lightly floured work surface, flatten the dough into a rectangle. Cover with plastic wrap and chill until firm, about 2 hours.

Line a baking sheet with parchment paper.

Lightly flour the work surface and dust the dough with flour (1).

Roll out the dough into a rectangle about ⅛ inch (3 mm) thick (2 and 3).

Using a sharp knife, cut diagonal strips (4) about 2 ½ inches (6 cm) wide. Cut them into diamond shapes with 1½-inch (4 cm) sides (5).

Make a 1-inch (2 cm) lengthwise slit in the center of each diamond (6).

Holding a diamond shape in your hand (7), push one tip through the slit (8). Pull on it gently to thread it through (9).

Makes about 2½ dozen fritters
Level: Intermediate
Prep: 25 min.
Chill: about 2 hr.
Rise: 1 hr. 30 min.
Cook: about 5 min. per batch

Special equipment
A deep-fry thermometer

1 recipe Parisian Brioches (page 658), omitting half the butter
1 cup (7 oz., 200 g) sugar
1 tbsp. ground cinnamon
4 cups (1 liter) grapeseed or other neutral oil
¼ cup plus 2 tbsp. (100 ml) orange flower water

1 Place the well-chilled brioche dough on a floured surface and dust with flour.

2 Roll it out to a rectangle about ⅛ inch (3 mm) thick.

3 Shape it into a neat rectangle.

4 Cut strips on the diagonal.

5 Cut them into diamond shapes, 2½ by 1½ inches (6 by 4 cm).

6 Make a 1-inch (2 cm) lengthwise slit in the center of each diamond.

7 Take a diamond shape in your hand.

8 Push one tip through the slit.

9 Pull gently to thread it through.

continued

Transfer the angel wing to the prepared baking sheet (10) and repeat with the remaining dough.

Let rise, uncovered, for 1 hour 30 minutes at room temperature.

Combine the sugar with the cinnamon in a large shallow bowl.

Heat the oil to 350° F (180° C) in a large saucepan or a deep fryer. Line a baking sheet with paper towels.

Working in small batches, carefully add the angel wings to the oil (11), dropping them in close to the hot oil so it doesn't splash. Do not crowd the pan. Fry on one side until golden brown (12), then turn over with a slotted spoon (13) and fry until golden brown all over, 3 to 5 minutes total (14).

Transfer them to the prepared baking sheet to drain (15).

Drizzle the warm fritters with orange flower water (16) and roll in the cinnamon sugar (17) until well coated (18).

Serve quickly!

Note: The recipe for these fritters is centuries old. Bugnes are now considered a specialty of Lyon, but versions of them are available in pastry shops all over France the week before Lent.

10 Let the angel wings rise at room temperature for 1 hour 30 minutes.

11 Heat the oil to 350° F (180° C) and carefully add the angel wings to the oil.

12 Try them in batches until golden brown on one side.

13 Turn them with a slotted spoon to fry the other side.

14 Continue frying until uniformly browned.

15 Drain on paper towels.

16 Drizzle the warm fritters with orange flower water.

17 Roll in cinnamon sugar.

18 Coat them well.

Scones aux Figues et Griottes
Fig and Cherry Scones

Fig and Cherry Scones

Finely dice the dried figs and cherries.

Sift the flour with the baking powder into a large bowl (1 and 2).

Add the sugar (3) and the butter (4).

Rub the butter into the dry ingredients with your hands (5) as if you were making a crumble (6).

Add the egg and milk (7) and stir with a wooden spoon (8). Add the fruit (9).

Makes about 1 ½ dozen scones
Level: Easy
Prep: 20 min.
Freeze: 10 min.
Bake: 10 to 15 min.

3 oz. (80 g) dried figs
2 oz. (60 g) frozen pitted cherries
3¼ cups (14 oz., 400 g) all-purpose flour
2 tbsp. plus ½ tsp. (25 g) baking powder
¼ cup plus 2 tbsp. (3 oz., 80 g) sugar
4 tbsp. (2 oz., 55 g) butter, softened
1 egg
⅔ cup (150 ml) milk

2 egg yolks

1 Combine the flour and baking powder in a sieve.

2 Shake into a large bowl.

3 Add the sugar.

4 Add the butter.

5 Rub the ingredients with your hands.

6 Incorporate the butter into the dry ingredients until large crumbs form.

7 Add the egg and milk.

8 Beat in with a wooden spoon.

9 Incorporate the fruit.

continued

Stir until the dough is firm (10).

On a lightly floured work surface (11), shape the dough into a rectangle (12). Freeze until slightly firm, about 10 minutes.

Preheat the oven to 425° F (210° C). Line a baking sheet with parchment paper.

On a lightly floured sheet of parchment paper, roll out the dough into a 10 by 8-inch (25 by 20 cm) rectangle about ¾ inch (2 cm) thick (13).

Cut the rectangle into strips 1½ to 2 inches (4 to 5 cm) wide (14 and 15). Cut into 1½ to 2-inch (4 to 5 cm) squares (16).

Transfer the scones to the prepared baking sheet, spacing them slightly apart (17).

Egg Glaze

Lightly beat the egg yolks in a cup with a fork.

Brush the tops of the scones with the egg glaze (18).

Bake for about 10 minutes, or until golden brown and soft but not raw in the middle.

Transfer to a rack, let cool slightly, and serve.

Notes: Make these scones with any dried fruit of your choice, like prunes and raisins, or even diced fresh fruit.

The dough can be prepared through step 17 and frozen. Thaw in the refrigerator overnight before baking.

10 Continue stirring until the fruit is mixed in and the dough is firm.

11 Place the dough on a floured work surface.

12 Shape it into a rectangle.

13 Roll out the dough on a lightly floured sheet of parchment paper.

14 Use a sharp knife to cut the scones.

15 Cut the rectangle into strips 1½ to 2 inches (4 to 5 cm) wide.

16 Then cut it into squares.

17 Place the scones on a lined baking sheet.

18 Brush the tops with the egg glaze.

Pain de Mie à l'Orange et au Chocolat

Orange-Chocolate Loaf

Place the flour, sugar, and salt in the bowl of a stand mixer fitted with the dough hook. Crumble in the yeast, making sure it does not touch the salt (1).

In a small bowl, dissolve the powdered milk in the water. Pour it into the bowl of the mixer (2).

Knead at low speed until smooth, about 3 minutes (3).

Finely dice the candied orange peel (4).

Add the butter (5). Increase the speed to medium and knead until the butter is incorporated, 2 to 3 minutes. Or knead by hand.

Add the chocolate chips (6) and the diced candied orange peel (7). Knead in by hand (8) until evenly distributed. The dough should be firm and elastic.

Makes 1 9-inch (25 cm) loaf;
1 lb. 5 oz. (600 g) dough
Level: Easy
Prep: 20 min.
Rise: 3 hr.
Bake: 20 to 30 min.

Special equipment
A 9-inch (25 cm) loaf pan

3 cups (13 oz., 375 g) all-purpose flour
1 tbsp. (15 g) sugar
2 tsp. salt
¾ cake (½ oz., 15 g) fresh yeast
2 tbsp. plus 2 tsp. (20 g) powdered milk
¾ cup (200 ml) lukewarm water
2 oz. (60 g) candied orange peel (page 452)
3 tbsp. (1½ oz., 50 g) butter, softened
½ cup (2½ oz., 70 g) chocolate chips

1 Place the dry ingredients in the bowl of a mixer, making sure that the yeast does not touch the salt.

2 Dissolve the powdered milk in the water and add to the dry ingredients.

3 Knead at low speed for 3 minutes.

4 Finely dice the candied orange peel.

5 Knead the butter into the dough until fully incorporated.

6 Add the chocolate chips.

7 Add the diced candied orange peel.

8 Incorporate with your hands.

continued

Return the dough to the bowl of the mixer and let rise in a warm place until doubled in volume, about 1 hour 30 minutes.

On a lightly floured work surface, flatten the dough into a rectangle.
Fold one long side into the center (10 and 11).
Fold in the other long side (12), pressing down hard with your fingertips.
Fold the dough lengthwise in half into a log shape (13).
Brush the pan with melted butter (14).
Place the dough in the pan with the fold at the bottom (15).
Press the dough into the pan (16).
Let rise in a warm place until doubled in volume, about 1 hour 30 minutes (17).

Preheat the oven to 250° F (180° C).
Bake the loaf for 20 to 30 minutes, or until the crust is golden. Rap the bottom: it should sound hollow.
Transfer the loaf to a rack and let cool.

9 Let the dough rise in a warm place until doubled in volume, about 1 hour 30 minutes.

10 Place the dough on a floured work surface.

11 Flatten the dough into a rectangle and fold one long side into the center.

12 Fold the other long side into the center, pressing down hard to seal.

13 Fold the dough lengthwise in half to make a smooth log shape.

14 Butter the loaf pan.

15 Place the dough, fold down, in the pan.

16 Press it into the pan.

17 The loaf should double in volume.

STE N 1 GNAR

Making Petit Fours

Baking

Use convection heat except for choux pastry, which bakes better with conventional heat.

Party Planning

For a cocktail party, plan on 4 savory bites and 4 petits fours per person.

For a dinner of finger food, prepare 4 to 8 savory pieces and 3 to 4 petits fours per person.

Many of the recipes in this chapter build on basic recipes like pastry crusts and glazes. It's a good idea to make them ahead in the quantities you'll need. Note that the prep times for the basic recipes are not included in the compound recipes.

Serving

Remove the petits fours from the refrigerator about 10 minutes before serving to bring to room temperature.

Storing

Most of the small pastries here can be refrigerated for up to 2 days or frozen for up to 1 month. The exceptions are petit fours made with choux pastry, which are best assembled at the last minute.

Equipment

Molds and Pans

Silicone molds and pans are particularly well adapted for the recipes in this chapter. Molds with small cavities are invaluable for getting glazes smooth and even. Some of the small cakes and the marshmallows are best assembled in cake rings, preferably stainless steel, but you can also make cardboard frames yourself.

To clean silicone kitchenware, simply soak it in soapy water. When needed, use a soft sponge. Do not dry with a kitchen towel, as this will create static. Just shake out the molds. Or place them in a 200° F (100° C) oven for 2 minutes to dry and sterilize them.

Store silicone molds upside down. It is fine to pile them up, but do not place anything heavy on them, or they will lose their shape. Roll silicone mats; never fold them.

Place small molds on a baking sheet for stability before filling them. This makes it easier to transfer them to the oven, refrigerator, or freezer.

Soft and silicone molds are suitable for all types of ovens, even for the microwave. Just be careful not to leave them near an open flame or too close to the side of the oven, and don't use them under the broiler.

You can freeze the pastries in the flexible molds, which withstand temperatures down to −40° F (−40° C). You can also use them to freeze ice cream and sorbet.

To remove a filling from a mold, invert a plate on top and turn it upside down. If you are using a flexible mold, you may need to peel the sides away from the cake. Always turn out your cakes before cutting them. Never cut pastries in flexible or silicone molds, as this will damage them.

Offset Spatula

An offset spatula is more practical than a plain spatula for smoothing surfaces and layers.

Glaçage Fruits
Fruit Glaze

Soak the gelatin sheets in a medium bowl of cold water until softened, 5 to 10 minutes.

Combine the sugar and water in a small heavy saucepan (1).

Using a vegetable peeler, remove the colored zest from the orange and lemon, leaving the white pith. Add the citrus zest to the pan (2 and 3).

Split the vanilla bean lengthwise in half and scrape out the seeds. Add the vanilla bean and seeds to the pan (4).

Bring to a boil and cook over medium heat, stirring, until the sugar dissolves. Remove from the heat.

Squeeze the softened gelatin dry and add to the pan (5). Gently whisk to dissolve (6).

Strain the sugar syrup through a fine sieve into a bowl (7).

Let cool slightly (8). It should not set completely if you are planning to use it immediately.

Note: The glaze can be refrigerated for several days or frozen for up to 4 weeks. Gently warm the glaze over a hot water bath when needed to coat your petit fours.

Glazes about 3 dozen petit fours
Level: Easy
Prep: 10 min.

5 gelatin sheets (10 g)
1 cup (7 oz., 200 g) sugar
⅔ cup (150 ml) still mineral water
¼ orange
¼ lemon
½ vanilla bean

1 Combine the sugar and water in a small heavy saucepan.

2 Add the orange zest.

3 Add the lemon zest.

4 Add the vanilla bean and seeds and bring to a boil.

5 Add the softened, drained gelatin sheets.

6 Gently whisk in the gelatin until dissolved.

7 Strain the mixture through a fine sieve into a bowl.

8 Let cool slightly.

Glaçage Blanc Opaque
White Glaze

Makes 1 lb. 2 oz.
(520 g) glaze
Level: Easy
Prep: 10 min.

Special equipment
A candy thermometer

⅓ cup (2½ oz., 60 g) apricot preserves
3½ gelatin sheets (7 g)
Scant ½ cup (100 ml) heavy cream
⅓ cup (1½ oz, 40 g) powdered milk
1 cup (7 oz., 200 g) sugar
¼ cup (60 ml) water
3½ tbsp. (2½ oz., 75 g) honey or glucose syrup
Food coloring (optional)

Melt the apricot preserves in a small heavy saucepan over medium heat, stirring occasionally. Strain through a sieve into a small bowl. You should have about ¼ cup (2 oz., 50 g).

Soak the gelatin sheets in a medium bowl of cold water until softened, 5 to 10 minutes.

Heat the cream with the powdered milk in a small bowl set over a small saucepan filled with 1 inch (2.5 cm) of barely simmering water.

Cook the sugar, water, and honey in a medium heavy saucepan over medium heat, stirring with a wooden spoon, until the sugar dissolves.

Dip the candy thermometer in the syrup, making sure it does not touch the bottom.

Cook the sugar, watching carefully, until it registers 230° F (110° C). Remove the pan from the heat.

Add the cream-milk mixture to the sugar syrup. Squeeze the gelatin sheets dry and stir them in until dissolved.

Stir in the apricot preserves.

If you are adding food coloring, stir in a few drops, depending on its concentration.

Let cool slightly. It should not set completely if you are planning to use it immediately.

Notes: The glaze can be refrigerated for several days or frozen for up to 4 weeks. Gently warm the glaze over a hot water bath when needed to coat your petit fours.

Use this recipe to glaze Raspberry Cream Tartlets (page 726).

Glaçage au Cacao
Chocolate Glaze

Glazes about 2½
dozen petit fours
Level: Easy
Prep: 10 min.

4 gelatin sheets (8 g)
¾ cup (5 oz., 145 g) sugar
½ cup (120 ml) water
7 tbsp. (2 oz., 50 g) unsweetened cocoa powder
¼ cup plus 2 tbsp. (100 ml) heavy cream
1 drop red food coloring

Soak the gelatin sheets in a medium bowl of cold water until softened, 5 to 10 minutes.

Combine the sugar, water, cocoa, and cream in a medium heavy saucepan. Bring to a boil over medium heat, stirring gently to avoid creating bubbles, until the sugar dissolves. Remove from the heat.

Squeeze the softened gelatin dry and add to the pan with the food coloring. Stir until the gelatin dissolves.

Strain through a fine sieve into a shallow bowl.

Let cool slightly. It should not set completely if you are planning to use it immediately.

Notes: You can add a few ice cubes to the cold water when softening gelatin. You want the gelatin to become pliable but not dissolve.

The glaze can be refrigerated in an airtight container for up to 1 week. Gently warm the glaze over a hot water bath when needed to coat your petit fours.

Fonds de Tartelettes en Pâte Sablée

Crumbly Sweet Tartlet Shells

Place the flour, baking powder, sugar, and orange zest on a work surface (1).

Add the butter (2). Using your fingertips, rub the butter into the dry ingredients (3).

Continue rubbing until the mixture forms coarse crumbs (4).

Make a well in the center and add the egg yolk and water (5).

Lightly knead (6) just until the dough is smooth and forms a ball (7). Do not overwork it.

Cut the dough in half. Flatten into 2 disks, cover with wrap plastic wrap (8), and chill for 1 hour.

Makes about 2 dozen mini tartlet shells; 10 oz. (300 g) dough
Level: Basic
Prep: 10 min.
Chill: 1 hr.
Bake: about 10 to 12 min.

Special equipment
24 mini tartlets molds or
2 12-cup mini muffin pans

1 cup plus 2 tbsp. (5 oz., 150 g) all-purpose flour
1 pinch baking powder
⅓ cup (2½ oz., 75 g) sugar
Finely grated zest of ¼ orange
5 tbsp. (2½ oz., 75 g) butter, softened
1 egg yolk
1 tbsp. cold water

1 Place the flour, baking powder, sugar, and orange zest in a mound on the work surface.

2 Add the butter.

3 Rub the butter into the dry ingredients with your fingertips.

4 Continue until large crumbs form.

5 Place the egg yolk and water in a well.

6 Knead the ingredients together without overworking the dough.

7 Smooth it with your fingertips.

8 Cover with plastic wrap. Note the date if you're freezing it.

continued

Preheat the oven to 350° F (180° C). If you are using tartlet molds, place them on a baking sheet.

On a lightly floured work surface, roll out the dough slightly less than ⅛ inch (2 mm) thick (9).
Drape over the rolling pin and transfer to a baking sheet. Chill for 5 minutes.

Prick the dough with a fork (10).
Using a 2½-inch (6 cm) cookie cutter or glass, stamp out rounds (11).
Line the tartlet molds or pans with the rounds (12).
Bake for 10 to 12 minutes, or until firm and lightly browned.
Let cool slightly in the pans, then transfer to racks and let cool completely.

Notes: The unbaked tartlet shells can be refrigerated for up to 2 days or frozen for up to 3 months. If you freeze the dough, don't forget to write the date! Thaw overnight in the refrigerator.

9 Roll out the dough to less than ⅛ inch (2 mm) thick.

10 Prick with a fork.

11 Cut out rounds.

12 Line the pans with the rounds of dough.

Tartelettes à la Frangipane
Almond Cream Tartlets

Preheat the oven to 350° F (180° C).

Measure and prep your ingredients and arrange them on the counter (1).

Follow steps 1 to 12 of the Crumbly Sweet Tartlet Shells (page 708) and chill.

Whisk the butter in a medium bowl until creamy (2).

Add the eggs (3) and half the sugar (4) and whisk well (5).

Lightly whisk in the remaining sugar, the rum, and ground almonds (6). Do not let the mixture become too pale (7).

Spoon the almond cream into a pastry bag and pipe mounds of cream into the unbaked tartlet shells (8). Or use a spoon.

Bake for 12 to 15 minutes, or until puffed and lightly browned on top (9).

Let cool slightly in the pans, then transfer to racks and let cool completely.

The filling will deflate a little.

Notes: It's best to have the butter and eggs at room temperature so they combine easily.

The almond cream can be frozen in an airtight container for up to 1 month.

You can add fruit garnishes to these tartlets and brush them with one of the glazes for a professional finish.

Makes about 2 dozen
mini tartlets
Level: Intermediate
Prep: 10 min.
Bake: 12 to 15 min.

1 recipe Crumbly Sweet Tartlet Shells (page 708)
1 stick (4 oz., 120 g) butter, softened
2 eggs
⅔ cup (4 oz., 120 g) sugar
1 tbsp. dark rum
1⅓ cups (4 oz, 120 g) ground almonds

1 Have all your ingredients and utensils ready to go before cooking.

2 Whisk the butter until creamy.

3 Add the eggs.

4 Add half the sugar.

5 Whisk in the sugar.

6 Gently whisk in the remaining sugar, the rum, and ground almonds.

7 This shows the texture of the almond cream.

8 Pipe mounds of almond cream into the unbaked tartlet shells.

9 This is what they look like when baked.

Pâte Sablée Très Friable
Delicate Sweet Pastry

Place the butter in a medium bowl and beat with a wooden spoon until creamy. Add the confectioners' sugar and salt (1).

Whisk until smooth (2). Add the flour (3) and whisk until the ingredients come together to form a dough (4). Or use a flexible spatula.

Place the dough between 2 sheets of parchment paper. Flatten into a rectangle with a rolling pin (5).

Roll out to a sheet about ⅛ inch (3 mm) thick (6), avoiding any creases in the parchment paper.

Transfer, still covered and flat, to a baking sheet and freeze until firm, 3 to 5 minutes.

Peel off the top sheet of parchment paper (7). Lightly flour the dough, turn it over onto a clean sheet of parchment paper, and lightly flour the second side.

Using a 2½-inch (6 cm) cookie cutter or a glass, stamp out rounds or follow the instructions of the individual recipe.

Notes: This recipe contains a large quantity of butter, which gives the dough an excellent taste but makes it tricky to handle. Make sure that the dough is very cold, even slightly frozen, following step 6 so you can work with it easily. It can only be baked flat, not shaped.

Makes about 2 dozen mini
tartlets; 8 oz. (250 g) dough
Level: Basic
Prep: 10 min.

1 stick (4 oz., 125 g) butter, softened
⅓ cup (1 ½ oz., 45 g) confectioners' sugar
¼ tsp. (1 g) salt
1 cup (4 oz., 115 g) all-purpose flour

1 Whisk the confectioners' sugar and salt into the creamed butter.

2 Whisk well until smooth.

3 Add the flour.

4 Continue whisking until the ingredients form a dough.

5 Roll out the dough between 2 sheets of parchment paper.

6 It should be about ⅛ inch (3 mm) thick.

7 Peel off the top sheet of parchment paper.

Guimauves à la Fleur d'Oranger
Orange Flower Water Marshmallows

Soak the gelatin sheets in a large bowl of cold water until softened, 5 to 10 minutes.

Combine the granulated sugar, water, and glucose syrup in a medium heavy saucepan (1).

Cook over medium heat, stirring with a wooden spoon, until the sugar dissolves.

Dip the candy thermometer in the syrup, making sure it does not touch the bottom.

Cook the sugar, watching carefully, until it registers 266° F (130° C). Remove the pan from the heat.

Gently warm the orange flower water in a small bowl very briefly in the microwave oven.

Squeeze the gelatin sheets dry. Add to the orange flower water and stir to dissolve.

Meanwhile, whip the egg whites in the bowl of a standing mixer fitted with the whisk attachment at medium speed until they hold a soft peak.

Carefully pour the hot sugar syrup down the side of the bowl into the whites (2), then add the orange flower gelatin and food coloring (3 and 4) and whip until the mixture cools to room temperature, about 10 minutes (5).

Sift the confectioners' sugar with the potato starch.

Line the baking pan with parchment paper and sprinkle with half of the sugar-starch mixture (6).

Scrape the marshmallow mixture into the pan (7) and sprinkle with the remaining sugar-starch mixture (8).

Cover with a sheet of parchment paper (9) and spread in an even layer with an offset spatula or rolling pin (10).

Let stand until set, about 2 hours.

Cut into squares with a lightly oiled knife and serve.

Makes 1 13 by 9-inch
(30 by 24 cm) pan
Level: Intermediate
Prep: 15 min.
Set: 2 hr.

Special equipment
A candy thermometer
A stand mixer
A 13 by 9-inch (30 by 24 cm)
baking pan

11 gelatin sheets (22 g)
2⅓ cups (1 lb., 440 g) granulated
sugar
¼ cup plus 2 tbsp. (100 ml) water
2½ tbsp. (1½ oz, 45 g) glucose
syrup or light corn syrup
2 tbsp. (30 ml) orange flower water
2 egg whites
A few drops red food coloring
¾ cup (3½ oz., 100 g) confectioners'
sugar
⅔ cup (3½ oz., 100 g) potato starch

1 Stir the sugar, water, and glucose syrup in a medium saucepan.

2 Carefully pour the hot syrup down the side of the bowl into the whipped egg whites.

3 Pour in the orange flower gelatin.

4 Add the red food coloring.

5 Whip until the mixture is smooth and creamy.

6 Sprinkle the parchment paper with half of the confectioners' sugar–potato starch mixture.

7 Scrape the marshmallow mixture onto the sheet.

8 Sprinkle it with the remaining confectioners' sugar–potato starch mixture.

9 Cover the marshmallow with another sheet of parchment paper.

10 Roll it out 1 inch (2 cm) thick.

Guimauves à la Framboise
Raspberry Marshmallows

Soak the gelatin sheets in a large bowl of cold water until softened, 5 to 10 minutes.

Combine 10 oz. (300 g) of the raspberry puree and 1 scant cup (6 oz., 175 g) of the sugar in a medium heavy saucepan (1).

Cook over medium heat, stirring with a wooden spoon, until the sugar dissolves.

Dip the candy thermometer in the syrup, making sure it does not touch the bottom.

Cook the mixture, watching carefully, until it registers 221° F (105° C). Remove the pan from the heat.

Squeeze the softened gelatin sheets dry. Add to the raspberry-sugar mixture and stir to dissolve (2).

Add the remaining raspberry puree and sugar to the saucepan (3) and stir in with a flexible spatula (4).

Scrape the mixture into a large bowl. Whip at medium speed until the mixture cools to room temperature, about 10 minutes. As the mixture cools, it becomes foamy and the color changes to light pink (5).

Lightly oil 2 sheets of parchment paper (6) and place the rulers on one of the sheets to contain the mixture. Or line the baking pan with an oiled sheet of parchment paper.

Scrape the marshmallow mixture between the rulers or into the pan (7).

Cover with the second sheet of parchment paper, oiled side down (8).

Spread the marshmallow mixture in an even layer about 1 inch (2 cm) thick with a rolling pin or offset spatula (9 and 10).

Let stand under the parchment paper (this prevents a crust from forming) at room temperature until set, about 2 hours.

Cut into squares with a lightly oiled knife and serve.

Note: Dust the top of the marshmallow mixture with unsweetened cocoa powder before cutting, if desired.

Makes 1 13 by 9-inch
(30 by 24 cm) pan
Level: Intermediate
Prep: 15 min.
Set: 2 hr.

Special equipment
A candy thermometer
2 four-sided rulers or
a 13 by 9-inch (30 by 24 cm)
baking pan

14 gelatin sheets (28 g)
13 oz. (370 g) strained raspberry
   puree
1⅔ cups (11½ oz., 325 g) sugar

1 Combine 10 oz. (300 g) raspberry puree with 1 scant cup (6 oz., 175 g) sugar over medium heat.

2 Stir in the softened gelatin sheets.

3 Add the remaining raspberry puree and sugar.

4 Mix until thoroughly combined.

5 Whip at medium speed. The mixture will become paler in color.

6 Lightly oil 2 sheets of parchment paper.

7 Scrape the marshmallow mixture onto a prepared sheet.

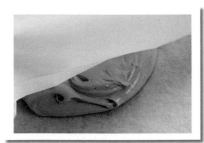

8 Cover with the second sheet, oiled side down.

9 Keep the mixture in place between 2 four-sided rulers.

10 Smooth it with a rolling pin.

Raisins dans leur Coque Caramel
Caramel Grapes

Combine the sugar and water in a medium heavy saucepan (1).

Add the lemon juice (2).

Cook over medium heat, stirring with a wooden spoon, until the sugar dissolves.

Dip the candy thermometer in the syrup, making sure it does not touch the bottom.

Cook the sugar, watching carefully, until it registers 300° F (150° C) (3). Remove the pan from the heat.

Let the syrup stand at room temperature until it turns a light amber color, a few minutes.

Place the pan over high heat and cook without stirring (otherwise the caramel would crystallize) until melted. Remove from the heat.

Meanwhile, have ready a nonstick baking sheet or a silicone baking mat, or line a baking sheet with parchment paper.

Cut each grape off the stem, selecting grapes of the same size and leaving a small piece of stem as a handle (4).

Holding the stem with the tweezers, dip each grape briefly in the caramel (5). Immediately transfer it to the prepared baking sheet (6).

Notes: You can also use firm strawberries, but they will keep for only a few hours.

Your grapes will keep better if you replace ¼ cup (2 oz., 50 g) of the sugar with 2 ½ tbsp. (1 ¾ oz., 50 g) glucose syrup.

Makes about 2½ dozen grapes
Level: Easy
Prep: 15 min.
Cook: 10 min.

Special equipment
A candy thermometer
A pair of tweezers

1¼ cups (9 oz., 250 g) sugar
Scant ½ cup (100 ml) water
A few drops lemon juice
1 large bunch green grapes

1 Combine the sugar and water in a medium saucepan.

2 Add a few drops of lemon juice.

3 Cook to 300° F (150° C) on a candy thermometer.

4 Cut the grapes, leaving enough of the stem to grip with a pair of tweezers.

5 Dip the grapes, one by one, into the caramel.

6 Let them set on a nonstick baking sheet.

Tartelettes à l'Ananas
Pineapple Tartlets

Follow steps 1 to 8 of the Almond Cream Tartlets (page 712) and chill.

Preheat the oven to 350° F (180° C).

Sprinkle the coconut on the unbaked tartlets (1).
Bake for 12 to 15 minutes, or until puffed and lightly browned on top.
Sprinkle the rum over the tartlets while they are still warm (2).
Let cool slightly in the pans, then transfer to racks and let cool completely.

Cut the pineapple crosswise into slices about ¼ inch (5 mm) thick (3).

Trim the edges with a cookie cutter (4) or use a small plate and a knife. Remove the core with a small cookie cutter, metal pastry tip, or apple corer (5).
Stack the slices and cut them into thin sticks (6). Pat dry with paper towels.

Mound the pineapple on each tartlet (7).
Using a citrus zester, remove the colored zest from the lime in fine julienne strips, leaving the white pith. Or use a vegetable peeler and cut the zest into julienne strips with a knife.
Arrange 3 julienned lime strips on the pineapple (8).
Finely dice the strawberries and arrange 3 pieces on each tartlet.
Chill for 30 minutes.
Brush the tartlets with the glaze (9) and chill until serving.

Note: Select a firm pineapple that isn't too juicy so it won't make the tartlets soggy.

Makes about 2 dozen
mini tartlets
Level: Intermediate
Prep: 45 min.
Bake: 12 to 15 min.
Chill: 30 min.

1 recipe Almond Cream Tartlets (page 712)
⅔ cup (2 oz., 50 g) unsweetened shredded
  coconut
Dark rum, for sprinkling
1 firm pineapple
1 lime
5 strawberries, hulled
1 recipe Fruit Glaze (page 704), warmed

1 Sprinkle the unbaked filled tartlets with shredded coconut.

2 Drizzle a little rum over the baked tartlets.

3 Thinly slice the pineapple.

4 Remove the peel with a cookie cutter.

5 Cut out the core.

6 Cut the sliced pineapple into thin sticks.

7 Mound the pineapple on the almond cream.

8 Decorate with julienned lime zest.

9 Top with finely diced strawberry and brush with glaze.

Tartelettes aux Fruits
Mixed Fruit Tartlets

Follow steps 1 to 8 of the Almond Cream Tartlets (page 712) (1) and chill.

Preheat the oven to 350° F (180° C).

Place 1 cherry on each of one-third of the tartlets (2).

Peel, quarter, and core the pear. Cut into large dice (3) and arrange 1 piece on each of another third of the tartlets (4).

Pat the apricots dry with paper towels. Place 1 apricot half, rounded side down, on each of the remaining tartlets (5).

Finely chop the pistachios and use them to decorate the cherry tartlets (6).

Scatter the almonds over the apricots (7).

Sprinkle the center of each tartlet with vanilla sugar (8).

Finely dice the butter. Dot the top of each apricot tartlet with the butter (9).

Bake for 12 to 15 minutes, or until the fruits are softened and the shells are lightly browned.

Let cool slightly in the pans, then transfer to racks and let cool completely.

Notes: You want the cherries to be frozen when you use them or they will make the tartlets soggy.

For variety, sift confectioners' sugar over some of the baked tartlets once they have cooled completely.

Makes about 2 dozen
mini tartlets
Level: Intermediate
Prep: 1 hr.
Bake: 12 to 15 min.

1 recipe Almond Cream Tartlets (page 712)
3½ oz. (100 g) frozen pitted cherries (see *Notes*)
1 firm, ripe Bartlett pear
5 oz. (150 g) drained canned apricot halves
2½ oz. (50 g) unsalted pistachios
⅔ cup (2½ oz., 50 g) sliced blanched almonds
Vanilla sugar, for sprinkling
2 tbsp. (1 oz., 25 g) butter

1 Make the Almond Cream Tartlets (page 712).

2 Garnish one-third of the tartlets with frozen cherries.

3 Peel, quarter, and core the pear and cut into large dice.

4 Place the pear pieces on one-third of the tartlets.

5 Arrange the apricots, rounded sides down, on the remaining tartlets.

6 Decorate the cherry tartlets with chopped pistachios.

7 Scatter sliced almonds on the apricot tartlets.

8 Sprinkle the centers of all the tartlets with vanilla sugar.

9 Dot the apricots with butter.

Tartelettes à la Framboise
Raspberry Cream Tartlets

Raspberry Creams

Soak the gelatin sheets in a medium bowl of cold water until softened, 5 to 10 minutes.

Combine the raspberry puree and sugar in a medium heavy saucepan (1).

Whisk in the egg yolks and whole egg (2).

Cook over low heat, whisking constantly, until the mixture comes to a boil (3). Remove from the heat.

Squeeze the softened gelatin dry. Add it to the pan and whisk until dissolved.

Whisk in the butter until smooth (4).

Strain the raspberry cream through a fine sieve into a medium bowl (5).

Process the mixture with an immersion blender (6) until very smooth, about 1 minute.

Pour the cream into trays of small hemispherical molds or ice cube trays (7). If you are using flexible molds, place them on a baking sheet.

Freeze until set, about 1 hour.

Makes about 2 dozen mini tartlets
Level: Intermediate
Prep: 15 min.
Freeze: 1 hr.
Bake: 12 to 15 min.

Raspberry Creams

2 gelatin sheets (4 g)
7 oz. (200 g) strained raspberry puree
⅓ cup (2 oz., 60 g) sugar
3 egg yolks
1 whole egg
5 tbsp. (2½ oz., 75 g) butter, diced and softened

Raspberry Tartlets

1 recipe Almond Cream Tartlets (page 712)
4 oz. (125 g) fresh raspberries
A few drops pink food coloring
1 recipe White Glaze (page 706), warmed
Candied Rose Petals (page 190), frozen, for garnishing

1 Combine the raspberry puree and sugar in a medium saucepan over low heat.

2 Add the egg yolks and whole egg to the pan.

3 Whisk constantly until the mixture comes to a boil.

4 Remove from the heat and stir in the softened gelatin and butter.

5 Press the mixture through a sieve.

6 Process with an immersion blender until silky smooth.

7 Pour the raspberry cream into the molds.

continued

Raspberry Tartlets

Follow steps 1 to 8 of the Almond Cream Tartlets (page 712) and chill.

Preheat the oven to 350° F (180° C).

Place 1 raspberry on each unbaked tartlet (8).
Bake for 12 to 15 minutes, or until puffed and lightly browned on top.
Let cool slightly in the pans, then transfer to racks and let cool completely.

Add the food coloring to the glaze and stir until smooth.
Turn the raspberry creams out of the molds and transfer to a rack, rounded sides up (9).
Set the rack over a baking sheet or parchment paper and carefully spoon the glaze over them (10) to coat (11).
Dip a thin spatula in water and use to place each raspberry cream on a tartlet (12). Dip the spatula in water each time so the cream does not stick.

Garnish with Candied Rose Petals, either whole or in bits.
Chill until serving.

8 Top the unbaked tartlets with a raspberry.

9 Turn the frozen raspberry creams out of their molds.

10 Transfer to a rack set over a baking sheet or parchment paper to catch the glaze.

11 Spoon the glaze over the molded creams.

12 Carefully place them on the baked tartlets.

Tartelettes au Citron Vert
Lemon-Lime Tartlets

Lemon-Lime Cream

Soak the gelatin sheets in a medium bowl of cold water until softened, 5 to 10 minutes.

Combine the lemon juice, lime juice, and sugar in a medium heavy saucepan. Whisk in the egg yolks and whole egg.

Cook over low heat, whisking constantly (1), until the mixture comes to a boil. Remove from the heat.

Squeeze the softened gelatin dry. Add it to the pan and whisk until dissolved.

Whisk in the butter (2) until smooth (3).

Strain the lemon-lime cream through a fine sieve into a medium bowl.

Process the mixture with an immersion blender (4) until very smooth, about 1 minute.

Scrape the cream into a shallow bowl, press a piece of plastic wrap directly on the surface, and chill completely, at least 2 hours.

Lemon-Lime Tartlets

Follow steps 1 to 12 of the Crumbly Sweet Tartlet Shells (page 708).

Preheat the oven to 350° F (180° C). If you are using tartlet molds, place them on a baking sheet.

Bake for 10 to 12 minutes, or until firm and lightly browned.

Let cool slightly in the pans, then transfer to racks and let cool completely.

Transfer the cooled tartlet shells to a baking sheet. Spoon the lemon-lime cream into a pastry bag and pipe

Makes about 2 dozen
mini tartlets
Level: Intermediate
Prep: 45 min.
Chill: 2 hr.
Bake: 10 to 12 min.
Freeze: 1 hr.

Lemon-Lime Cream

Lemon-Lime Cream

1½ gelatin sheets (3 g)
⅔ cup (150 ml) lemon juice
3½ tbsp. (50 ml) lime juice
⅓ cup (2 oz., 60 g) sugar
3 egg yolks
1 egg
5 tbsp. (2½ oz., 75 g) butter, diced
and softened

Lemon-Lime Tartlets

1 recipe Crumbly Sweet Tartlet
Shells (page 708)
2 drops green food coloring, or
1 drop yellow and 1 drop blue
food coloring
1 recipe Fruit Glaze (page 704),
warmed
Finely grated zest of 1 lime

1 Combine the lemon and lime juices with the sugar in a medium saucepan over low heat.

2 Whisk in the butter.

3 Whisk until smooth.

4 Process with an immersion blender until silky smooth.

5 Pipe mounds of cream into the baked tartlet shells.

mounds of cream into the shells (5). Or use a spoon. Freeze until set, about 1 hour.

Transfer the tartlets to a rack set over a baking sheet or parchment paper.
Add the food coloring to the glaze and stir until smooth. Carefully spoon it over the frozen tartlets.
Sprinkle with a little finely grated lime zest. Chill until serving.

Tartelettes au Caramel et aux Fruits Secs

Caramel-Nut Tartlets

Follow steps 1 to 12 of the Crumbly Sweet Tartlet Shells (page 708).

Preheat the oven to 350° F (180° C). If you are using tartlet molds, place them on a baking sheet.

Bake for 10 to 12 minutes, or until firm and lightly browned. Leave the oven on. Let cool slightly in the pans, then transfer to racks and let cool completely.

Coarsely chop the nuts with a large knife (1) or in a food processor.

Spread the chopped nuts on a baking sheet and bake for about 10 minutes, or until lightly toasted.

Bring the cream to a boil in a small heavy saucepan. Remove from the heat and let cool to lukewarm.

Place the sugar in a small heavy saucepan. Melt it over medium heat, stirring with a wooden spoon. Reduce the heat to low and cook, stirring, until the sugar changes from a light amber liquidy paste to a fluid, medium amber caramel (2).

Stir in the lukewarm cream with a wooden spoon (3). Be careful: the mixture may boil up quickly!

Remove from the heat and stir in the honey. Stir in the butter until the mixture is smooth (4).

Stir in the chopped nuts until coated in the caramel (5 and 6).

Spoon the praline into the baked tartlet shells (7 and 8) and let cool to room temperature.

Chill until serving.

Makes about 2 dozen
mini tartlets
Level: Intermediate
Prep: 45 min.
Bake: 10 to 12 min.

1 recipe Crumbly Sweet Tartlet Shells (page 708)
½ cup (2½ oz., 75 g) blanched almonds
3 tbsp. (¾ oz., 20 g) pine nuts
3 tbsp. (¾ oz., 20 g) unsalted pistachios
3 tbsp. (¾ oz., 20 g) hazelnuts
3½ tbsp. (50 ml) heavy cream
½ cup plus 2 tbsp. (5½ oz., 160 g) sugar
3 tbsp. (2 oz., 60 g) pine honey or other strong dark honey
2 tbsp. (1½ oz., 35 g) butter, diced and softened

1 Coarsely chop all the nuts together.

2 Cook the sugar, stirring with a wooden spoon, until it turns a medium caramel color.

3 Carefully stir in the lukewarm cream; it will sputter.

4 Stir in the pine honey and butter until smooth.

5 Add the chopped nuts to the caramel.

6 Stir until the nuts are coated in the caramel.

7 Spoon the praline into the baked tartlet shells.

8 They should be generously filled.

Tartelettes à l'Orange
Orange-Almond Tartlets

Poached Orange Slices

Cut the oranges into very thin slices, slightly less than ⅛ inch (2 mm) thick (1).

Combine the sugar and water in a large saucepan (2). Cook over medium heat, stirring, until the sugar dissolves. Remove the pan from the heat, add the orange slices, and let cool to room temperature (3). Chill overnight if desired.

Orange-Almond Tartlets

Follow steps 1 to 8 of the Almond Cream Tartlets (page 712) and chill.

Preheat the oven to 350° F (180° C).

Finely chop the chocolate and sprinkle over the tartlets (4).

Bake for 12 to 15 minutes, or until puffed and lightly browned on top.

Sprinkle the orange liqueur over the tartlets while they are still warm.

Let cool slightly in the pans, then transfer to racks and let cool completely.

Drain the orange slices and reserve 3 or 4 slices for garnishing. Finely chop the remaining oranges (5).

Mound the chopped orange on each tartlet (6 and 7). Freeze the tartlets for 15 minutes.

Brush the tartlets with the glaze (8) and chill until serving.

Cut the reserved orange slices into triangles. Garnish each tartlet with an orange triangle.

Notes: A mandoline makes cutting the oranges into even slices easy. The flavor of the poached oranges develops overnight. You can use tangerines instead of oranges.

Makes about 2 dozen
mini tartlets
Level: Intermediate
Prep: 45 min.
Chill: 15 min.
Bake: 12 to 15 min.
Plan ahead: 1 day (optional)

3 oranges
¾ cup (5 oz., 150 g) sugar
1¼ cups (300 ml) water

1 recipe Almond Cream Tartlets (page 712)
2 oz. (50 g) bittersweet chocolate
Orange liqueur, such as Cointreau or
  Grand Marnier, for sprinkling
1 recipe Fruit Glaze (page 704), warmed

1 Finely slice the oranges with a sharp knife.

2 Combine the sugar and water in a large saucepan and bring to a boil.

3 Let the oranges soak in the hot syrup.

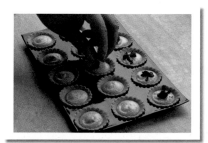

4 Sprinkle the unbaked filled tartlets with the chopped chocolate.

5 Reserve 3 oranges slices and finely chop the rest.

6 Spoon the chopped orange on the baked tartlets.

7 Make a mound of the chopped orange.

8 Brush each tartlet with fruit glaze.

Tartelettes Chocolat-Café
Coffee-Chocolate Tartlets

Follow steps 1 to 12 of the Crumbly Sweet Tartlet Shells (page 708).

Preheat the oven to 350° F (180° C). If you are using tartlet molds, place them on a baking sheet.

Bake for 10 to 12 minutes, or until firm and lightly browned.

Let cool slightly in the pans, then transfer to racks and let cool completely.

Finely chop the chocolate and place in a medium bowl.

Bring the cream and water to a boil in a small heavy saucepan. Stir in the instant coffee (1).

Pour half of the coffee cream into the chocolate (2) and let melt.

Stir (3), then pour in the remaining coffee cream (4).

Stir in the butter (5) until this ganache is smooth (6). Or use an immersion blender.

Spoon the ganache into a pastry bag and pipe mounds into the cooled shells (7). Or use a spoon.

Chill the tartlets until the ganache sets, about 20 minutes.

Let the remaining ganache stand at room temperature.

If the remaining ganache is too firm, warm it over a hot water bath. Whisk to loosen it. Spoon into the pastry bag fitted with a small fluted tip and pipe a small rosette on each tartlet.

Makes about 2 dozen
mini tartlets
Level: Intermediate
Prep: 25 min.
Bake: 10 to 12 min.
Chill: 20 min.

Special equipment
A pastry bag fitted with a small
fluted tip

1 recipe Crumbly Sweet Tartlet Shells
(page 708)
7 oz. (200 g) bittersweet chocolate
(70% cocoa)
¾ cup (200 ml) heavy cream
1 tbsp. water
1 tsp. instant coffee powder
2 tbsp. (1 oz., 30 g) butter, diced and
softened

1 Add the instant coffee to the hot cream and water.

2 Pour half of the hot coffee cream into the chopped chocolate.

3 When the chocolate has begun to melt, stir gently.

4 Pour in the remaining coffee cream.

5 Add the diced butter.

6 Stir gently, without incorporating bubbles, until perfectly smooth.

7 Pipe the ganache into the baked tartlet shells.

Mini Tartes Tatins
Caramelized Apple Tartlets

Follow steps 1 to 7 of the Delicate Sweet Pastry (page 714).

Preheat the oven to 350° F (180° C).

Lightly flour the dough, turn it over onto a clean sheet of parchment paper, and lightly flour the second side.

Using a 2½-inch (6 cm) cookie cutter or a glass, stamp out rounds. Remove the excess dough. Slide the rounds on the parchment paper onto a baking sheet.

Bake for 10 to 12 minutes, or until firm and lightly browned. Leave the oven on.

Let cool on the baking sheet.

Peel and finely dice the apples (1).

Spread the apples in an even layer in a shallow baking dish.

Place the sugar in a medium heavy saucepan. Melt it over medium heat, stirring with a wooden spoon (2). Reduce the heat to low and cook, stirring, until the sugar changes from a light amber liquidy paste to a fluid, light amber caramel (3). The best way to judge the color is to let the caramel run off the spoon.

Stir in the warm water (4), then 2 tbsp. (25 g) of the butter (5).

Makes about 2 dozen
mini tartlets
Level: Intermediate
Prep: 30 min.
Bake: about 45 min.
Freeze: 1 hr.

1 recipe Delicate Sweet Pastry (page 714)
1 lb. (500 g) Golden Delicious or other baking apples
5 oz. (150 g) Granny Smith or other tangy apples
1 cup (7 oz., 200 g) sugar
3½ tbsp. (50 ml) warm water
4 tbsp. (2 oz., 55 g) butter
1 recipe Fruit Glaze (page 704), warmed

1 Peel and dice the apples.

2 Melt the sugar over high heat.

3 Let it cook until it forms a light brown caramel.

4 Stir in the warm water with a wooden spoon.

5 Then stir in the butter.

continued

Pour the caramel over the diced apples (6). Cover with foil (7).

Bake for 30 minutes, or until the apples are tender.

Remove the foil and bake for about 5 minutes, or until the liquid has evaporated (8).

Let the caramelized apples cool.

Spoon the apples into small hemispherical molds or ice cube trays (9). If you are using flexible molds, place them on a baking sheet.

Freeze until set, about 1 hour.

Melt the remaining butter in a small saucepan and let it cool to lukewarm.

Brush the pastry with the melted butter (10).

Turn the caramelized apple mounds out of the molds and transfer to a rack, rounded sides up.

Set the rack over a baking sheet or parchment paper and carefully brush the apple mounds with the glaze (11).

Using a small knife or thin spatula, carefully place each apple mound on a pastry round (12).

Chill until serving.

Note: Warm liquids are more easily incorporated into hot caramel than cold.

6 Pour the caramel over the diced apples.

7 Cover with foil.

8 This is what the baked caramelized apples look like.

9 Press them into the molds.

10 Brush the baked pastry rounds with warm melted butter.

11 Brush the apple mounds with glaze.

12 Carefully place the apple mounds on the pastry rounds.

Sablés Caraïbes
Chocolate Mousse Tartlets

Delicate Chocolate Sweet Pastry

Follow steps 1 to 7 of the Delicate Sweet Pastry (page 714), incorporating the cocoa powder with the flour in step 3.

Preheat the oven to 350° F (180° C). Using a 2½-inch (6 cm) cookie cutter or a glass, stamp out rounds. Remove the excess dough. Slide the rounds on the parchment paper onto a baking sheet.
Bake for 10 to 12 minutes, or until firm. Let cool on the baking sheet.

Chocolate Mousse

Warm the chocolate in a small heavy saucepan with the butter over low heat to 104° F (40° C). Remove from the heat.

Whip the egg whites with the sugar in a medium bowl until firm (1).

Grate in the lemon zest (2) and gently fold in with a flexible spatula.

Add the egg yolks (3) and gently fold in (4) until smooth.

Slowly pour in the melted chocolate and butter (5), turning the bowl with one hand as you move the spatula from the center (6) with the other hand, until smooth.

Spoon the mousse into a pastry bag and pipe it into small hemispherical molds or ice cube trays (7). Or use a spoon.
Lightly tap to smooth the surface of the mousses. Freeze until firm, at least 2 hours.

Decoration

Turn out the mousses and transfer to a rack, rounded sides up (8).

Set the rack over a baking sheet or parchment paper and carefully spoon the glaze over the mounds (9).

Place each mousse on a pastry round.

Grate the chocolate. Sprinkle it around the edges of the tarts. Chill.

Note: Please note that the finished recipe contains raw egg.

Makes about 2 dozen
mini tartlets
Level: Intermediate
Prep: 30 min.
Bake: about 10 min.
Freeze: at least 2 hr.

Delicate Chocolate Sweet Pastry

1 recipe Delicate Sweet Pastry
(page 714)
1½ tbsp. (⅓ oz., 10 g) unsweetened
cocoa powder

Chocolate Mousse

3½ oz. (100 g) bittersweet chocolate
(66% cocoa), finely chopped
1 tbsp. (20 g) butter
3 egg whites
¼ cup (2 oz., 50 g) sugar
1 lemon
2 egg yolks

Decoration

1 recipe Chocolate Glaze
(page 707), warmed
Bittersweet chocolate, for grating

1 Whip the egg whites with the sugar until they hold a firm peak.

2 Grate in the lemon zest.

3 Add the egg yolks.

4 Gently fold them in.

5 Slowly pour in the melted chocolate and butter.

6 Fold in, being careful not to deflate the whipped egg whites. This is what the mousse should look like.

7 Pipe the chocolate mousse into the molds.

8 Turn out the frozen mousses and transfer to a rack.

9 Spoon over the chocolate glaze.

Forêts-Noires
Black Forest Sandwich Cookies

Chocolate Cookies
Follow steps 1 to 7 of the Delicate Sweet Pastry (page 714), incorporating the cocoa powder with the flour in step 3.

Preheat the oven to 350° F (180° C).

Using a 2½-inch (6 cm) cookie cutter or a glass, stamp out rounds. Remove the excess dough. Slide the rounds on the parchment paper onto a baking sheet.
Bake for 10 to 12 minutes, until firm. Let cool on the baking sheet.

Milk Chocolate Mousse
Whip the cream in a medium bowl until it holds a firm peak; chill.

Finely chop the chocolate. Place in a medium bowl set over a saucepan filled with 1 inch (2.5 cm) of barely simmering water and let melt. Remove the bowl from the heat.

Bring the milk to a boil in a small heavy saucepan over medium heat.
Combine the sugar and egg yolk in a small bowl (1) and whisk just until the sugar dissolves (2).
Whisk a little hot milk into the sugar-egg mixture (3) and then return it to the saucepan. Cook over low heat, stirring constantly with a wooden spoon, until the custard thickens slightly and registers 180° F (82° C) on an instant-read thermometer (4). It is ready when it coats a spoon; if you draw a finger across the back of the spoon, it should leave a clear trail. Remove the pan from the heat and let cool slightly to 122° F (50° C).

Makes about 1 dozen cookies
Level: Intermediate
Prep: 30 min.
Bake: about 10 min.
Chill: 30 min.

Special equipment
A thermometer

1 recipe Delicate Sweet Pastry
(page 714)
1½ tbsp. (⅓ oz.,10 g) unsweetened
cocoa powder

1 cup (225 ml) heavy cream
10 oz. (275 g) milk chocolate
(40% cocoa)
½ cup (120 ml) milk
1 tbsp. (10 g) sugar
1 egg yolk

5 oz. (150 g) cherries, pitted

1 Combine the sugar and egg yolk.

2 Whisk just until the sugar dissolves.

3 Gradually whisk a little hot milk into the egg mixture.

4 Cook the custard to 180° F (82° C), then let cool to 122° F (50° C).

5 Pour the custard over the partially melted chocolate.

6 Stir to finish melting the chocolate.

continued

Lesson 198

Gradually pour the custard into the melted chocolate (5). Stir with a flexible spatula until completely melted (6) and check the temperature. It should register 104 to 113° F (40 to 45° C).

Gently fold half of the whipped cream into the chocolate custard (7). Fold in the remaining cream (8) until smooth (9).
Chill for about 30 minutes, or until slightly firm.

Spoon the mousse into a pastry bag fitted with a small plain tip and pipe dollops on half the chocolate cookies. Or use a spoon.

Garnish
Arrange 3 cherries around the edge of each mousse-topped cookie (10).
Pipe another small mound of mousse in the center (11).
Sandwich with a plain chocolate cookie (12 and 13).
Pipe a small mound of chocolate mousse on top and garnish with a cherry.

7 Add half the whipped cream to the chocolate mixture.

8 Gently fold it in.

9 This is what the chocolate cream looks like when all the whipped cream is folded in.

10 Pipe small mounds of chocolate cream on half of the chocolate cookies and place 3 cherries around the edge.

11 Add another mound of chocolate cream.

12 Sandwich with a plain chocolate cookie.

13 These cookies await their final garnish.

Moelleux Pistache
Melt-in-the-Mouth Pistachio Cakes

Preheat the oven to 350° F (180° C). Butter the muffin pan.

Combine the ground almonds and confectioners' sugar in a food processor (1).
Melt the butter over low heat and let cool to lukewarm (2).
Add the pistachio paste to the food processor (3), then the eggs, one by one (4), processing after each addition until smooth.
Pour in the melted butter (5) and process until incorporated, just a few seconds.

Spoon the batter into a pastry bag fitted with a medium plain tip and fill the molds three-quarters full (6). Or use a spoon.

Lightly press a raspberry into each mold (7).
Coarsely chop the pistachios with a large knife or in the food processor (8).
Scatter them over the small cakes (9).
Bake for 12 to 15 minutes, or until golden and a cake tester comes out clean.

Notes: You can swap black grapes or cherries for the raspberries.

Instead of pistachio paste, try chocolate-hazelnut spread, peanut butter, or chestnut paste. In this case, don't garnish the cakes with pistachios.

Makes about 1½ dozen mini cakes
Level: Easy
Prep: 20 min.
Bake: 12 to 15 min.

Special equipment
A 24-cup mini muffin pan

2 cups (6 oz., 165 g) ground almonds
¾ cup plus 2 tbsp. (4 oz., 125 g)
  confectioners' sugar
1 stick (4 oz., 125 g) butter
1 tbsp. (1 oz., 20 g) pistachio paste
  (see *Notes*, page 564)
4 eggs
4 oz. (125 g) raspberries
⅔ cup (3½ oz., 100 g) unsalted pistachios

1 Combine the ground almonds and confectioners' sugar in a food processor.

2 Melt the butter over low heat and let cool to lukewarm.

3 Add the pistachio paste to the ingredients in the food processor.

4 Blend in the eggs, one by one.

5 Lastly, incorporate the melted butter.

6 Fill the molds three-quarters full.

7 Lightly press a raspberry into each mold.

8 Coarsely chop the pistachios.

9 Sprinkle the chopped pistachios over the cakes.

Choux Tricotés
Choux Puffs with Knitted Jackets

Coating

Whisk the butter in a medium bowl until creamy (1).

Add the brown sugar (2) and whisk until smooth.

Whisk in the flour (3) just until combined (4).

Divide the paste into 3 or 4 equal parts, depending on the number of colors you plan to make, and place in separate small bowls (5).

Stir a little food coloring into each bowl of paste until smooth (6).

Between 2 sheets of parchment paper, roll out each paste slightly less than ⅛ inch (2 to 3 mm) thick (7 and 8). Stack the sheets of colored paste in the parchment paper on a baking sheet and freeze flat.

Choux Pastry

Preheat the oven to 400° F (200°C), using conventional heat. Lightly butter a baking sheet and dust it with flour. Mark circles on the sheet with a plain 1-inch (2.5 cm) cookie cutter, spacing them slightly apart, to use as guides.

Makes about 3 dozen
Level: Advanced
Prep: 45 min.
Bake: 20 to 25 min.

3 tbsp. (50 g) butter, softened
⅓ cup (2 oz., 60 g) light brown sugar
½ cup (2 oz., 60 g) all-purpose flour
A selection of food colorings

1 cup plus 2 tbsp. (5 oz., 150 g)
  all-purpose flour
⅔ cup (150 ml) milk
⅓ cup (100 ml) water
½ tsp. salt
1 tbsp. sugar
5 tbsp. (3 oz., 80 g) butter, softened
5 eggs

1 Whisk the butter until it is creamy.

2 Add the light brown sugar.

3 Then add the flour.

4 Whisk until combined.

5 Divide the paste among 3 or 4 bowls to color them separately.

6 Stir in the coloring until smooth.

7 Roll each colored paste between 2 sheets of parchment paper.

8 The paste is ready to be placed in the freezer.

continued

Sift the flour into a medium bowl.

Combine the milk, water, salt, sugar, and butter in a medium saucepan. Bring to a simmer over medium heat (9).

When the butter melts, remove the pan from the heat. Add the flour and beat well with a wooden spoon until the dough pulls away from the side of the pan.

Return the saucepan to medium heat and beat to dry out the dough, about 1 minute.

Scrape the dough into a large bowl.

Break 4 of the eggs into the bowl, one by one (10, 11, and 12), beating with a wooden spoon after each addition until smooth.

Lightly beat the remaining egg in a cup with a fork. Beat as much as needed into the bowl to make a dough that is very shiny and just falls from the spoon.

Spoon the dough into a pastry bag fitted with a plain tip and pipe 1-inch (2 cm) mounds on the prepared baking sheet, spacing 1 inch (2 cm) apart (13). Or use a spoon.

Peel the top sheet off the colored paste and cut out 1-inch (2 cm) squares (14), one for each of the choux puffs.

Carefully place a colored square on each choux puff (15).

Bake for 20 to 25 minutes, or until puffed and browned.

Notes: Do not use convection heat; the conventional setting is better for baking choux pastry.

It is important not to open the oven door or the choux puffs will deflate.

Fill the choux puffs with the cream of your choice, such as pastry cream (page 755). Pipe the cream into the choux puffs through a small hole in the base.

Choux pastry does not freeze well.

9 Heat the milk, water, salt, sugar, and butter in a saucepan.

10 When you have beaten in the flour, add an egg.

11 When the first egg is incorporated, beat in a second egg.

12 Beat in the third and fourth eggs, and use the indications given on the facing page to decide whether to add the fifth.

13 Pipe small mounds of the dough on the prepared baking sheet.

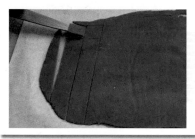

14 Cut out squares of colored paste.

15 Fit them over the choux puffs.

Choux Fondants
Choux with Fondant Icing

Pastry Cream

Combine half of the sugar and the cornstarch in a medium bowl. Add the egg yolks (1) and whisk just until the dry ingredients dissolve (2). The mixture should not become pale.

Combine the milk with the remaining sugar in a medium heavy saucepan and bring to a boil. Whisk the hot milk into the egg-sugar mixture (3). Return the mixture to the pan and cook over medium heat, whisking constantly (4).

As soon as the pastry cream begins to thicken, remove it from the heat and whisk in the butter.

Line a baking sheet with plastic wrap. Spread the pastry cream on the baking sheet (5). Cover it with plastic wrap, pressing out all the air (6). This prevents a skin from forming. Chill completely.

Makes about 3 dozen
Level: Intermediate
Prep: 1 hr.
Bake: 20 to 25 min.

Special equipment
A pastry bag
A medium plain tip

Pastry Cream

⅔ cup (4 oz., 120 g) sugar
⅓ cup (2 oz., 50 g) cornstarch
6 egg yolks (4 oz., 120 g)
2 cups (500 ml) milk
3 tbsp. (2 oz., 50 g) butter
4 flavorings such as vanilla extract, rose water, almond extract, and orange liqueur

Choux Pastry

1 cup plus 2 tbsp. (5 oz., 150 g) all-purpose flour
⅔ cup (150 ml) milk

⅓ cup (100 ml) water
½ tsp. salt
1 tbsp. sugar
5 tbsp. (3 oz., 80 g) butter, softened
1 cup plus 2 tbsp. (5 oz., 150 g) all-purpose flour, sifted
5 eggs

Fondant Glaze

8 oz. (250 g) white fondant icing
3½ tbsp. (50 ml) water
A selection of food colorings

1 Combine the sugar and cornstarch and add the egg yolks.

2 Whisk just until the dry ingredients dissolve.

3 Whisk the hot milk into the egg mixture.

4 Return to the saucepan and cook, stirring constantly, until the pastry cream thickens.

5 Pour the pastry cream onto a lined baking sheet.

6 Cover in plastic wrap, pressing out all the air.

continued

Choux Pastry

Preheat the oven to 400° F (200° C), using conventional heat. Lightly butter a baking sheet and dust it with flour.

Combine the milk, water, salt, sugar, and butter in a medium saucepan. Bring to a simmer over medium heat.

When the butter melts, remove the pan from the heat. Add the flour and beat well with a wooden spoon until the dough pulls away from the side of the pan.

Return the saucepan to medium heat and beat to dry out the dough, about 1 minute. Scrape the dough into a large bowl.

Break 4 of the eggs into the bowl, one by one, beating with a wooden spoon after each addition until smooth. Lightly beat the remaining egg in a cup with a fork. Beat as much as needed into the bowl to make a dough that is very shiny and just falls from the spoon.

Spoon the dough into a pastry bag fitted with a plain tip and pipe 1-inch (2 cm) mounds on the prepared baking sheet, spacing 1 inch (2 cm) apart. Or use a spoon.

Bake for 20 to 25 minutes, or until puffed and browned.

Divide the pastry cream among 4 shallow bowls and add a different flavoring to each one. Whip each pastry cream until smooth and spoon it into the pastry bag. Make a small hole in the base of the choux puffs and pipe in the pastry cream.

Fondant Glaze

Melt the fondant icing in the water in a small heavy saucepan over low heat, stirring with a wooden spoon (7).

Cook until it registers 95° F (35°C) on an instant-read thermometer (8).

Divide among 4 small heatproof bowls, add a different food coloring to each (9), and stir with a wooden spoon until smooth (10).

Dip each choux puff into the fondant (11), making sure the top is evenly coated (12).

Let the glaze set and serve.

You can also pour the fondant icing into small hemispherical molds or ice cube trays (13 and 14) and place the filled choux puffs in the cavities.

Notes: You can combine food colorings to make different colored glazes.
Suggest the flavor of the filling with an appropriate garnish.

7 Heat the fondant icing with the water.

8 The icing should reach 95° F (35° C).

9 Add the food coloring.

10 Mix it in well.

11 Dip the tops of the choux puffs in the fondant icing.

12 Spread it evenly.

13 Or you can spoon fondant icing into small cups.

14 Insert the choux puff to coat it.

Financiers à la Fraise
Little Almond Cakes with Strawberries

Preheat the oven to 350° F (180° C). Butter the pans and, if using individual pans, set on a baking sheet.

Melt the butter in a small heavy saucepan (1). Cook over medium heat until it browns and smells nutty.

Strain through a small fine sieve (2) and let cool to lukewarm.

Combine the ground almonds and hazelnuts, confectioners' sugar, and flour in a medium bowl (3).

Split the vanilla bean lengthwise and scrape out the seeds (4). Add the seeds to the almond mixture (5). Pour in the egg whites (6) and apricot puree and stir with a wooden spoon until combined.

Pour in the lukewarm browned butter (7) and stir gently until the batter is smooth (8).

Spoon the batter into the prepared pans.

Quarter the strawberries lengthwise and place a piece in each pan (9).

Bake for 12 to 15 minutes, or until golden and the tip of a knife or a cake tester inserted into the center comes out clean.

Sprinkle the financiers with vanilla sugar while they are still warm. Let cool for 5 minutes in the pan, then transfer the cakes to a rack and let cool.

Makes about 1½ dozen cakes	1¼ sticks (5 oz., 150 g) butter
Level: Easy	¾ cup plus 1 tbsp. (2½ oz., 70 g) ground almonds
Prep: 15 min.	⅓ cup (1 oz., 30 g) ground hazelnuts
Bake: 12 to 15 min.	1⅓ cups (6 oz., 170 g) confectioners' sugar
	¼ cup plus 2 tbsp. (2 oz., 50 g) all-purpose flour
Special equipment	1 vanilla bean
20 financier pans or a 24-cup	5 egg whites
mini muffin pan	2 tbsp. (1 oz., 20 g) apricot puree or applesauce
	5 large strawberries
	Vanilla sugar, for sprinkling

1 Melt the butter over medium heat until it browns and smells of hazelnuts.

2 Strain the browned butter.

3 Combine the dry ingredients in a medium bowl.

4 Split the vanilla bean lengthwise and scrape out the seeds.

5 Mix the vanilla seeds into the dry ingredients.

6 Stir the egg whites into the dry ingredients.

7 Pour in the lukewarm browned butter.

8 Stir until smooth and thick.

9 Fill the molds with the batter and top with a strawberry quarter.

Roulés aux Figues
Fig Swirls

Follow steps 1 to 8 of the Crumbly Sweet Tartlet Shells (page 708), substituting the lemon zest for the orange zest and making only 1 disk.

Place the figs in a food processor (1) and finely chop. Pour in the cream in several batches (2), processing after each addition, until perfectly smooth.

On a lightly floured work surface, flatten the dough with a rolling pin (3) so that it spreads more easily and tears less.

Roll out the dough into a rectangle about ⅛ inch (4 mm) thick (4) and 8 to 9 inches (22 cm) long.

Dust the dough lightly with flour, drape it over the rolling pin (5), and unroll on a sheet of parchment paper (6).

Trim the edges (7) so you have a neat rectangle.

Makes about 2 dozen cookies
Level: Intermediate
Prep: 30 min.
Chill: at least 1 hr.
Bake: 10 min.

1 recipe Crumbly Sweet Tartlet Shells
(page 708)
Finely grated zest of ½ lemon
7 oz. (200 g) dried figs, trimmed
½ cup (120 ml) heavy cream

1 Finely chop the figs in a food processor.

2 Gradually add the cream and process until smooth.

3 Flatten the chilled dough with a rolling pin.

4 Roll out the dough into a rectangle about ⅛ inch (4 mm) thick.

5 Roll it around the rolling pin.

6 Transfer it to a sheet of parchment paper.

7 Trim the edges to shape a neat rectangle.

continued

Cover with another sheet of parchment paper, slide onto a baking sheet, and freeze flat until firm, a few minutes.

Remove the top sheet of parchment paper. Spread the fig cream evenly over the dough with a thin spatula (8).

Arrange the dough with a long side facing you. Using the edge of the parchment paper as a guide, begin rolling up the dough tightly (9 and 10).

Snugly tuck the paper end under the dough with a spatula to keep the roll tight (11). Chill until firm, at least 1 hour.

Preheat the oven to 350° F (180° C). Line a baking sheet with parchment paper or a silicone baking mat.

Cut into ¼ inch (6 mm) slices (12) and transfer them to the prepared baking sheet (13).

Bake for about 10 minutes, or until lightly browned.

8 Spread the fig cream over the dough.

9 Begin rolling up the dough.

10 Make sure that it is very tightly rolled when you start.

11 Use the spatula to tuck in the parchment paper.

12 Cut the roll into ¼-inch (6 mm) slices.

13 Place the slices on the prepared baking sheet.

Cannelés aux Poires
Crisp Custard Cakes with Pear Brandy

Bring the milk to a boil in a small heavy saucepan.

Split the vanilla bean lengthwise and scrape out the seeds (1).

Remove the pan from the heat, add the vanilla bean and seeds, and let infuse for 5 minutes.

Place a medium bowl over a saucepan filled with 1 inch (2.5 cm) barely simmering water. Add the butter (2) and whisk until very creamy.

Remove the bowl from the heat and whisk in the sugar (3), egg yolk, whole egg, and brandy (4), then whisk in the flour and salt (5). Whisk gently to avoid creating bubbles.

Remove the vanilla bean from the milk and pour the milk into the batter (6), whisking very gently (7).

Chill for at least 12 hours or overnight.

Preheat the oven to 425° F (220° C). Butter the molds.

Fill the pans two-thirds full and bake for 30 to 35 minutes, or until a rich brown shell forms.

Immediately transfer the cakes to racks and let cool. Serve at room temperature.

Makes about 2 dozen mini cakes
Level: Easy
Prep: 15 min.
Chill: 12 hr. or overnight
Bake: 30 to 35 min.

Special equipment
A cannelé pan with small cups
or a 24-cup mini muffin pan

1 cup (250 ml) milk
½ vanilla bean
2 tbsp. (25 g) butter, softened
½ cup plus 2 tbsp. (3½ oz., 100 g)
   sugar
1 egg yolk
1 whole egg
1½ tbsp. (25 ml) Poire Williams or
   other pear brandy
½ cup (2 oz., 60 g) all-purpose flour
Pinch salt

1 Scrape the seeds out of the split vanilla bean.

2 Whip the softened butter over a hot water bath.

3 Whisk in the sugar.

4 Whisk in the egg yolk, whole egg, and brandy.

5 Gently whisk in the flour and salt.

6 Pour in the hot milk.

7 Stir it in carefully.

Cheesecakes Carrés
Cheesecake Squares

Preheat the oven to 350° F (180° C). Line a baking sheet with parchment paper or a silicone baking mat.

Crust
Place all the ingredients in a food processor (1) and process until a smooth dough forms (2).

Place the cake ring on the prepared baking sheet. Spread the dough in the ring (3) and smooth with an offset spatula (4).

Makes about 2 dozen
small squares
Prep: 1 hr.
Bake: 30 min.

Special equipment
A 9 by 6-inch (23 by 16 cm)
cake ring
An offset spatula

continued

Crust

3½ oz. (100 g) salted crackers,
such as Tuc by LU
5 tbsp. (2½ oz., 75 g) butter,
softened
¼ cup (2 oz., 50 g) sugar
2½ tbsp. (25 g) all-purpose flour
1 tsp. water

Filling

11 oz. (320 g) cream cheese,
diced and softened
1 stick plus 3 tbsp. (5½ oz., 160 g)
butter, diced and softened
¾ cup plus 1 tbsp. (5½ oz., 160 g)
sugar
4 eggs

Topping

4 cubes Kiri cheese or 3 oz. (80 g)
cream cheese, diced and
softened
1 tbsp. granulated sugar
1 vanilla bean
⅔ cup (150 ml) heavy cream
2½ tbsp. (1 oz., 20 g)
confectioners' sugar
4 oz. (125 g) drained canned
cherries

1 Combine all the ingredients for the crust in a food processor.

2 Process until they form a smooth dough.

3 Spread the dough in the prepared cake ring.

4 Smooth it with an offset spatula.

Filling

Place the cream cheese and butter in a medium bowl (5). Add the sugar and eggs (6) and whisk well until smooth (7).

Pour the filling into the ring (8) and smooth the top. Bake for 30 minutes, or until set and lightly browned (9).

Let cool completely.

Topping

Beat the cheese with the granulated sugar in a medium bowl until smooth (10).

Split the vanilla bean lengthwise in half and scrape out the seeds.

Whip the cream with the confectioners' sugar and vanilla seeds in a medium bowl until it holds a firm peak.

Add one-third of the whipped cream to the cheese and beat to lighten the mixture.

Gently fold the remaining whipped cream into the cheese (11), taking care not to deflate the mixture (12). Work from the bottom of the bowl to the top.

Spread the topping over the cheesecake and smooth with a metal spatula (13).

Carefully remove the frame. Cut the cheesecake into small squares and garnish each with a cherry.

5 Beat the softened cream cheese with the butter.

6 Whisk in the sugar and eggs.

7 The mixture should be perfectly smooth.

8 Pour the cream cheese mixture into the ring.

9 This is what it looks like when baked.

10 Beat the Kiri cheese with the granulated sugar.

11 Add the sweetened vanilla whipped cream.

12 Fold it in carefully so the mixture does not deflate.

13 Spread the topping evenly over the cheesecake.

Congolais
Coconut Macaroons

Preheat the oven to 425° F (220° C). Line a baking sheet with parchment paper or a silicone baking mat.

Combine the shredded coconut and sugar in a medium bowl (1). Pour in the egg whites (2). Add the applesauce (3).

First beat with a flexible spatula (4), then knead the mixture with your hands (5).

Set the bowl over a saucepan filled with 1 inch (2.5 cm) of barely simmering water. Cook, stirring constantly, until the mixture comes together, about 10 minutes.

Remove the bowl from the heat. Spoon the batter into a pastry bag and pipe small mounds on the prepared baking sheet (6).

Let the macaroons cool.

Lightly wet your hands and roll them into smooth balls (7), then form tall rounded pyramid shapes (8).

Bake for 6 to 7 minutes, rotating the sheet after 3 minutes so they are evenly colored, until lightly browned.

Note: You may need to try a few brands of shredded coconut for this recipe. They don't all work successfully: sometimes the mixture does not come together as it's gently cooked.

Makes about 2 dozen macaroons
Level: Easy
Prep: 10 min.
Bake: 6 to 7 min.

1⅓ cups (3½ oz., 100 g) unsweetened shredded coconut
½ cup (3 oz., 90 g) sugar
3 tbsp. (1½ oz., 40 g) egg whites (about 1½)
2 tsp. (10 g) applesauce

1 Combine the shredded coconut and sugar in a medium bowl.

2 Pour in the egg white.

3 Add the applesauce.

4 Beat the ingredients with a flexible spatula.

5 Knead the mixture with your hands before gently heating it.

6 Pipe out small mounds on the prepared baking sheet.

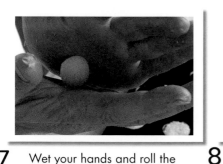

7 Wet your hands and roll the mounds into balls.

8 Then lengthen one side until it has a tip.

Mont Blancs
Chestnut Cream–Chantilly Tartlets

Follow steps 1 to 7 of the Delicate Sweet Pastry (page 714).

Preheat the oven to 350° F (180° C).

Lightly flour the dough, turn it over onto a clean sheet of parchment paper, and lightly flour the second side.

Using a 2 ½-inch (6 cm) cookie cutter or a glass, stamp out rounds. Remove the excess dough. Slide the rounds on the parchment paper onto a baking sheet.

Bake for 10 to 12 minutes, until firm and lightly browned.

Let cool on the baking sheet (1).

Whip the butter at medium speed in a medium bowl (2) until light and airy.

Add the chestnut cream in batches, whipping until smooth after each addition (3 and 4).

Whip the heavy cream in a medium bowl at low speed and then increase the speed, stopping when it holds tightly between the branches of the whisk and has doubled in volume.

Brush the pastry rounds with the melted butter.

Spoon the whipped cream into a pastry bag fitted with a medium plain tip and pipe pointy mounds on the pastry rounds (5). Or use a spoon.

Stir the rum into the chestnut cream (6).

Spoon the chestnut cream into the pastry bag.

Place the cream-filled pastries on a slightly raised base and pipe looping spaghetti-like strands to cover them (7).

Sift the confectioners' sugar into a small bowl. Dip a 3-inch (7.5 cm) cookie cutter or glass into the confectioners' sugar so it doesn't stick to the chestnut cream and carefully trim the strands (8).

Makes about 2 dozen mini tartlets
Level: Intermediate
Prep: 45 min.
Bake: 10 to 12 min.

Special equipment
A pastry bag
fitted with a very fine plain tip

1 recipe Delicate Sweet Pastry (page 714)
3 tbsp. (40 g) butter, softened
5 oz. (150 g) chestnut cream, at room temperature
¾ cup (200 ml) heavy cream, chilled
Melted lukewarm butter
1 tsp. dark rum
Confectioners' sugar, for sifting

1 Let the pastry rounds cool on the baking sheet.

2 Whip the butter until very light.

3 Add some of the chestnut cream.

4 Whip the chestnut cream into the butter in several batches.

5 Pipe a mound of whipped cream on each pastry round.

6 Stir the rum into the chestnut cream.

7 Pipe spaghetti-like strands over the whipped cream.

8 Trim each tartlet with a cookie cutter dipped in confectioners' sugar.

APPENDICES

F

J

K

N

O

Q

R

CONVERSION CHART

All conversions are approximate.

Liquid Conversions

U.S.	Metric
1 tsp.	5 ml
1 tbsp.	15 ml
2 tbsp.	30 ml
3 tbsp.	45 ml
¼ cup	60 ml
⅓ cup	75 ml
⅓ cup + 1 tbsp.	90 ml
⅓ cup + 2 tbsp.	100 ml
½ cup	120 ml
⅔ cup	150 ml
¾ cup	180 ml
¾ cup + 2 tbsp.	200 ml
1 cup	240 ml
1 cup + 2 tbsp.	275 ml
1¼ cups	300 ml
1⅓ cups	325 ml
1½ cups	350 ml
1⅔ cups	375 ml
1¾ cups	400 ml
1¾ cups + 2 tbsp.	450 ml
2 cups (1 pint)	475 ml
2½ cups	600 ml
3 cups	720 ml
4 cups (1 quart)	945 ml

(1,000 ml = 1 liter)

Weight Conversions

U.S./U.K.	Metric
½ oz.	14 g
1 oz.	28 g
1½ oz.	43 g
2 oz.	57 g
2½ oz.	71 g
3 oz.	85 g
3½ oz.	100 g
4 oz.	113 g
5 oz.	142 g
6 oz.	170 g
7 oz.	200 g
8 oz.	227 g
9 oz.	255 g
10 oz.	284 g
11 oz.	312 g
12 oz.	340 g
13 oz.	368 g
14 oz.	400 g
15 oz.	425 g
1 lb.	454 g

Oven Temperatures

°F	Gas Mark	°C
250	½	120
275	1	140
300	2	150
325	3	165
350	4	180
375	5	190
400	6	200
425	7	220
450	8	230
475	9	240
500	10	260
550	Broil	290

United States

Amazon
800-201-7575
amazon.com
Baking equipment, couverture chocolate, condiments, flavorings, oils, preserves, spices.

Arrowhead Mills
The Hain-Celestial Group, Inc.,
4600 Sleepytime Dr.
Boulder, CO 80301
800-434-4246
arrowheadmills.com
Organic and specialty flours, beans, grains, seeds.

Bob's Red Mill
13521 SE Pheasant Ct.
Milwaukie, OR 97222
800-349-2173
bobsredmill.com
Organic and whole-grain flours and meals, oats, grains, beans, seeds, cereals, potato starch.

Bridge Kitchenware
17 Waverly Pl.
Madison, NJ 07940
973-377-3900
bridgekitchenware.com
Baking equipment, utensils.

Broadway Panhandler
65 E. 8th St.
New York, NY 10003
866-266-5927
broadwaypanhandler.com
Baking equipment, utensils.

Cayuga Organics
18 Banks Rd.
Brooktondale, NY 14817
607-793-0085
cporganics.com/store
Organic flours, grains, beans.

Chocosphere
P.O. Box 2237
Tualatin, OR 97062
877-992-4626
chocosphere.com
Couverture chocolate.

Culinary Cookware
Matfer Bourgeat USA
16150 Lindbergh St.
Van Nuys, CA 91406
800-305-5415
culinarycookware.com
French baking equipment.

Dakota Prairie Organic Flour Co.
500 North Street West
Harvey, ND 58341
701-324-4330
dakota-prairie.com
Organic and specialty flours.

Dean and Deluca
4115 E. Harry
Wichita, KS 67218
800-221-7714
deananddeluca.com
Baking equipment, utensils, condiments, dairy products, spices, flavorings, sweeteners.

L'Epicerie
106 Ferris St.
Brooklyn, NY 11231
866-350-7575
lepicerie.com
French pastry flours, couverture chocolate, flavorings, fruit purees, gelatin sheets, sweeteners.

The Frenchy Bee
15520 Woodinville Redmond Rd. NE, Suite D400
Woodinville, WA 98072
866-379-9975
thefrenchybee.com
French gourmet groceries, condiments, flavorings, preserves, spices, sweeteners.

iGourmet
507 Delaware Ave.
West Pittston, PA 18643
877-446-8763
igourmet.com
Dairy products, condiments, flavorings, nuts, preserves, spices, sweeteners.

J. B. Prince Company, Inc.
36 E. 31st St., 11th Floor
New York, N.Y. 10016
800-473-0577
jbprince.com
Baking equipment, utensils, baking and chocolate molds.

Kalustyan's
123 Lexington Ave.
New York, NY 10016
800-352-3451
kalustyans.com
Spices, condiments, flavorings, gelatin sheets, preserves.

King Arthur Flour
135 US Route 5 South
Norwich, VT 05055
800-827-6836
kingarthurflour.com
Specialized flours, baking equipment, flavorings, spices, sweeteners.

Lehman's
P.O. Box 270
Kidron, OH 44636
888-438-5346
lehmans.com
Baking equipment, utensils, canning jars and equipment.

Murray's Cheese
254 Bleecker St.
New York, NY 10014
888-692-4339
murrayscheese.com
Dairy products, condiments, spices.

N.Y. Cake & Baking Dist.
56 W. 22nd St.
New York, NY 10010
800-942-2539
nycake.com
Baking equipment, utensils, couverture chocolate, decorating supplies, flavorings, sweeteners.

Penzey's Spices
12001-W. Capitol Dr.
Wauwatosa, WI 53222
800-741-7787
penzeys.com
Spices, herbs, seasonings, flavorings.

The Spice House
1031 North Old World Third St.
Milwaukee, WI 53203
847-328-3711
thespicehouse.com
Spices, herbs, seasonings, flavorings.

Sur La Table
P.O. Box 840
Brownsburg, IN 46112
800-243-0852
surlatable.com
Baking equipment, utensils, condiments,
couverture chocolate, flavorings,
sweeteners.

Tenda-Bake
Midstate Mills, Inc.
11 N. Brady Ave.
Newton, NC 28012
800-222-1032
midstatemills.3dcartstores.com
Bulk specialty flour and cornmeal.

Vanilla, Saffron Imports
949 Valencia St.
San Francisco, CA 94110
415-648-8990
saffron.com
Spices, flavorings.

Williams-Sonoma
3250 Van Ness Ave.
San Francisco, CA 94109
877-812-6235
williamssonoma.com
Baking equipment, utensils, condiments,
flavorings, sweeteners.

Wilton Industries
2240 W. 75th St.
Woodbridge, IL 60517
800-794-5866
wilton.com
Baking equipment, utensils, cake
decorating supplies.

Cooking Schools

Le Cordon Bleu
Various locations across the United States
800-736-6126
chefs.edu

Culinary Institute of America
1946 Campus Dr.
Hyde Park, NY 12538

2555 Main St.
St. Helena, CA 94574

312 Pearl Pkwy.
Building 2, Suite 2102
San Antonio, TX 78215

800-285-4627
ciachef.edu

French Culinary Institute
462 Broadway
New York, NY 10013
888-324-2433

700 West Hamilton Ave.
Campbell, CA 95008
866-318-2433

frenchculinary.com

The French Pastry School
226 West Jackson Blvd.
Chicago, IL 60606
312-726-2419
frenchpastryschool.com

Institute of Culinary Education
50 W. 23rd St.
New York, NY 10010
888-354-2433
iceculinary.com

France

Tableware Shops

Atelier N'omades Authentics
21 ave Daumesnil, 12th Arrond., Paris
01-43-46-26-26

Azag
9 rue François-Miron, 4th Arrond., Paris
01-48-04-08-18
azag.fr

Bernardaud
11 rue Royale, 8th Arrond., Paris
01-40-98-00-43
bernardaud.fr

Casa
92 rue Saint-Lazare, 9th Arrond., Paris
01-49-70-01-90
casashops.com/fr

The Conran Shop
117 rue du Bac, 7th Arrond., Paris
01-42-84-10-01
conran.com

Côté Maison
Bercy Village
44 cour Saint-Emilion, 12th Arrond.,
Paris
01-43-44-12-12

Deshoulières
101 rue du Bac, 7th Arrond., Paris
01-53-63-01-71
deshoulieres.com

Fous de Dînettes
49 rue de Cambronne, 15th Arrond.,
Paris
01-44-49-96-22
fousdedinettes.fr

Garnier Thiebaut
79 bd Raspail, 6th Arrond., Paris
01-45-49-06 19
garnier-thiebaut.fr

Geneviève Lethu
95 rue de Rennes, 6th Arrond., Paris
01-45-44-40-35
genevievelethu.com

Le Grand Comptoir
116 rue du Bac, 7th Arrond., Paris
01-40-49-00-95

Haviland
6 rue Royale, 8th Arrond., Paris
01-40-06-91-08
haviland.fr/boutique.php

Honoré
121 rue Sainte, Marseille
04-91-54-98-63
honore-france.com

Kitchen Bazaar
Galerie des Trois Quartiers
23 bd de la Madeleine,
1st Arrond., Paris
01-42-60-50-30
kitchenbazaar.fr

Ledéan & Pauvert
83 rue des Sorins, Montreuil
06-10-07-68-26
ledean-pauvert.com

Maison de Famille
10 place de la Madeleine,
8th Arrond., Paris
01-53-45-82-00
maisondefamille.fr/mdf

Maisons du Monde
32 rue du Faubourg-Saint-Antoine,
12th Arrond., Paris
01-53-33-83-07
maisonsdumonde.com

Natalia Franquet
12 rue de la Brasserie, Nantes
02-40-69-48-60

21 Porcelaine Raynaud
8 bis rue Boissy-d'Anglas,
8th Arrond., Paris
01-40-17-01-00
raynaud.fr

Le Printemps
64 bd Haussmann, 9th Arrond.,
Paris
01-42-82-50-00
printemps.com

Résonances
Bercy Village
3 cour Saint-Emilion, 12th Arrond.,
Paris
01-44-73-82-82
resonances.fr

Revol Porcelaine
3 rue Hector-Revol, Saint-Uze
04-75-03-99-99
revol-porcelaine.fr

Sentou
29 rue François-Miron,
4th Arrond., Paris
01-45-49-00-05
sentou.fr

Siècle
24 rue du Bac, 7th Arrond., Paris
01-47-03-48-03

La Vaissellerie
80 bd Haussmann, 8th Arrond.,
Paris
01-45-22-32-47
lavaissellerie.fr

Kitchen Equipment

Brehmer
27 rue des Tuilleries,
Souffelweyersheim
03-88-18-18-22

Mora
13 rue Montmartre, 1st Arrond.,
Paris
01-45-08-19-24
mora.fr

Cake Decorating Supplies

Artgato
5 ave Docteur Arnold-Netter,
12th Arrond., Paris
01-44-73-93-13
argato.com

PCB Création
7 rue de Suède, Benfeld
03-88-58-73 33
pcb-creation.fr

Specialty Food Shops

G. Detou
5 rue Tiquetonne. 2nd Arrond.,
Paris
01-42-36-54-67

La Grande Épicerie de Paris
38 rue de Sèvres, 7th Arrond.,
Paris
01-44-39-81-00

Izrael, l'Épicerie du Monde
30 rue François Miron,
4th Arrond., Paris
01-42-72-66-23

Christophe Felder's Cooking Schools

L'École de Christophe Felder
Classes for the general public and
professionals
christophe-felder.com
christophefelder@wanadoo.fr

**Atelier Chocolat—La Pâtisserie de
Christophe Felder**
Jardin d'Acclimatation
Bois de Boulogne, 16th Arrond.,
Paris
01-40-67-99-05
contact@christophe-felder.com

Studio Christophe Felder
2–4 rue de la Râpe, Strasbourg
06 18 82 60 19
contact@christophe-felder.com

How to Use This Book

Before You Begin

Read through the recipe from beginning to end, noting if you need to plan ahead. Some recipes involve an overnight rest for one of their components; others may require some chilling or freezing; still others may need longer for flavors to develop.

Check that you have all the ingredients and equipment and buy whatever you need.

All professional chefs practice *mise en place* (putting everything in its place): measuring all the ingredients and ensuring that all utensils are at hand. If you do this in your home kitchen, you will not have to dig out that little sifter when your hands are sticky and your whipped egg whites have reached just the right consistency. *Mise en place* is an essential stage in successful baking.

All the recipes have been categorized by the level of baking skill required. "Easy" recipes are perfectly manageable by novice bakers, but of course experienced bakers can make them too. "Intermediate" recipes require some degree of skill, but after making a few easy recipes, they should be within the reach of beginners, and of course advanced bakers won't need to think twice about making them. "Advanced" recipes require practice and experience, but other bakers can quickly acquire the skills and confidence to make them.

You'll see that certain lessons include the word "Basic." This means that, sometimes as part of a more complex recipe, you'll find the method for one of the many elements of French pastry making—various pastry doughs, pastry cream, buttercream, and more.

Why Precision Is Important

No pastry chef would think of working without an accurate scale. Kitchen scales are found in most French homes, and professionals work with scientific precision when weighing their ingredients. All metric measurements have been converted to cups and spoons (and sticks for solid butter), as well as to Imperial measurements. This inevitably involves some rounding up or down to avoid awkward amounts. For optimal results, invest in a digital scale, preferably one that gives both metric and Imperial read-outs, though you should use one system only for any given recipe. There's a good chance that you will be won over! But if you use cups and spoons, remember that they must all be level.

You will notice that conversions from some metric amounts may vary. For example, 250 g of flour is converted to 9 oz, because accuracy is important in this case. When precision is less important, say for 250 g of strawberries, we have converted this weight to a standard 8 oz.

Equipment

Special equipment for particular recipes is only listed when there is something in particular that readers may have to purchase, such as a candy thermometer, kitchen torch, or a cake ring of particular dimensions.

Convection or Conventional Heat?

All the recipes in this book were tested using convection heat, with the exception of choux pastry, which is best baked using conventional heat. If you have a conventional oven, increase the temperature by 25° F (15 to 20° C) and bake for approximately the same length of time, or use the same temperature but increase the length of time. Since all ovens have their quirks, nothing replaces keeping a careful eye on your cake as it bakes and following indications for doneness.

Ingredients

Throughout the book, keep in mind that:

Apricot preserves are smooth—without pieces.

Butter is unsalted, unless otherwise specified.

Chocolate is often listed with cocoa percentages. If you can't find a chocolate with the exact percentage, use one as close as possible. Because cocoa butter acts as a "hardener," its percentage affects the texture of your cake or dessert. The percentage also affects the amount of cream required, so don't try to substitute milk chocolate for bittersweet, for example.

Eggs are large, unless otherwise specified.

Milk is whole, which retains and imparts flavors far better than reduced-fat milk.

Nuts are whole, shelled, and unpeeled.

Salt is fine table salt.

Sugar is granulated unless otherwise specified.

Vanilla extract is pure vanilla extract.

—*Carmella Abramowitz Moreau*

Acknowledgments

My sweet, sincere thanks to:

Hervé de La Martinière;

Florence Lécuyer, always brimming with ideas;

Laure Aline, for her delicacy, diplomacy, and conscientiousness;

Brian Joyeux, for his energy and efficient help;

Ollivier Christien, so passionate about food;

Alain Gelberger and Catherine Bouillot, for their refined work in tandem;

Carmen Barea, for going through the lessons;

Benjamin, for his patience and talent;

Sylvie Kempler, for her wise advice and straightforwardness;

Françoise Vauzeilles, for her ideas;

Sandrine Giacobetti and Jean Claude Amiel, for their outstanding talent;

My family;

Edith Beckers.

This book is adapted from the nine books in the collection *Les Leçons de pâtisserie de Christophe Felder.*

First editions:

Les Gâteaux de l'Avent de Christophe, © 2005 Éditions Minerva, Geneva, Switzerland

Les Chocolats et petites bouchées de Christophe, © 2005 Éditions Minerva, Geneva, Switzerland

Les Pâtes et les tartes de Christophe, © 2006 Éditions Minerva, Geneva, Switzerland

Les Crèmes de Christophe, © 2006 Éditions Minerva, Geneva, Switzerland

La Décoration en pâtisserie de Christophe, © 2006 Éditions Minerva, Geneva, Switzerland

Les Macarons de Christophe, © 2007 Éditions Minerva, Geneva, Switzerland

Les Brioches et viennoiseries de Christophe, © 2007 Éditions Minerva, Geneva, Switzerland

Les Gâteaux classiques de Christophe, © 2008 Éditions Minerva, Geneva, Switzerland

Les Mignardises de Christophe, © 2010 Éditions Minerva, Geneva, Switzerland